THE POST-WAR NOVELLA
IN GERMAN-LANGUAGE LITERATURE

AMS STUDIES IN GERMAN LITERATURE AND CULTURE

ISSN 1045-6023

edited by Peter M. Daly

No. 5. Bruce Plouffe, *The Post-War Novella in German-Language Literature: An Analysis*

THE POST-WAR NOVELLA
IN GERMAN-LANGUAGE LITERATURE
An Analysis

by

Bruce Plouffe

AMS Press, Inc.
New York

Library of Congress Cataloging-in-Publication Data

Plouffe, Bruce.
  The post-war novella in German language literature: an
  analysis / Bruce Plouffe
      p.   cm. – (AMS studies in German literature and
      culture; no. 5 – ISSN 1045-6023)
      Includes bibliographical references and index.
      ISBN 0-404-64055-9
      1. German fiction – 20th century – History and
      criticism. 2. Short stories, German – History and
      criticism. I. Title. II. Series.
  PT772.P53   1998
  833'.91409 – dc20   96-41619
                                                            CIP

All AMS Books are printed on acid-free paper that meets the guidelines for performance and durability of the Committee on Production Guidelines for Book Longevity of the Council on Library Resources.

AMS Press, Inc.
56 East 13th Street
New York, NY 10003-4686 U.S.A.

MANUFACTURED IN THE UNITED STATES OF AMERICA

Table of Contents

Acknowledgements

I would like to thank Peter M. Daly for his encouragement and support throughout the process of writing this manuscript. I am also grateful to my colleagues Klaus Burmeister, Elisabeth Kim and Gerhard Steckhan for their translation expertise and for proofreading the final draft. Finally, I would like to thank Bev Weston for her secretarial support and her ability to make computers do what she wants them to do.

Partial funding for this project was provided by the University of Regina President's SSHRCC General Research Grant.

Preface

Bruce Plouffe presents us here with a sophisticated and challenging study of an important corpus of shorter fiction written in the German language since 1945. The texts examined include representative works by Rolf Hochhuth, Friedrich Dürrenmatt and Martin Walser.

The study has two centres of interest, one generic and the other interpretative. Plouffe considers the generic possibilities of the *Novelle* and its related form in Anglo-Saxon fiction, the short story. The interpretational approach to the underlying themes of the uncertainty of existence and the ambiguity of language derives in large measure from the writings of Freud and Lacan.

This book is important not only because the authors discussed - Hochhuth, Dürrenmatt and Walser - are significant writers, but also because Plouffe brings to bear on these *Novellen* several different but complementary approaches, literary and poetological, sociological and psychological. Aspects of genre theory, especially theoretical questions about the *Novelle* and short story, shed welcome light on issues of production and reception. His discussion of the generic and narratological affiliations of these works is, however, not another example of intellectual acrobatics or insider trading in jargon. Plouffe uses these literary discourses to shed interpretive light on the literature itself.

Equally illuminating is his application to these expressions of post-war German culture of notions of metaphor, metonymy, allegory, myth, archetype and intertextuality. The *Novellen* are shown to be significant fiction, which can be read in different ways and at different levels. Since they bespeak an experience of life which is as complex as it is fragile, the analytical insights prove to be particularly valuable. One need be neither an ardent adherent of Freud or Lacan to recognize the applicability of some of their more fertile ideas to this literature.

Peter M. Daly, McGill University

Introduction

The generic label *Novelle* on the title page of a work by a contemporary German-language author is an anomaly. In general, current practice seems to favour the use of the term *Erzählung* for shorter prose fiction. It could be speculated that a Martin Walser or a Friedrich Dürrenmatt chooses or endorses the choice of an historical, or as some would have it, of a "reactionary" genre label in order to suggest a classical lineage, provoking some, encouraging others, but ultimately drawing in readers from across the political spectrum. An equally facile observation would be that this is merely a reactivation of an "in-between" label for a volume too thin to be a novel, more substantial than a short story, in short, of a conventional classification device for those who prefer to have things neatly categorized. Of course, the texts analyzed in this monograph can be read and discussed on a number of different levels. For many readers, the fact that they are the work of such high-profile authors as Dürrenmatt, Hochhuth and Walser is enough to guarantee their acquisition and basic reception. They are, with the possible exception of Hochhuth's *Atlantik-Novelle*, accessible and entertaining: plot-lines and characters are representational in design, and there is an apparent focus on the lurid and the grotesque. This has lead some to conclude that the overriding features of these texts are their sensationalism and ease of consumption, and that their authors have become epigones and purveyors of pulp fiction.

However, careful scrutiny uncovers complex and dynamic structures that are consciously imbedded, both diachronically and synchronically, within the continuum of the genre of prose narrative. The texts have been written both within and against the tradition of the novella, and within the trajectory of contemporary literary theory. The extensive close readings of this study, not done in critical writing to date, will follow this conceptual framework.

In the first chapter entitled *Contemporary Poetics*, more recent investigations into the nature of prose narrative and its interpretation are outlined. This is a crucial step, since all of the texts in question thematize topics central to contemporary literary theory, whose terms of reference cannot be assumed to be common currency. The first question to be addressed is the concept of genre itself. Gérard Genette and Jean-Marie Schaeffer are cited in their description of the concept as one which places itself within the flux of a nexus of dialectical transtextual relationships:

texts are not concrete objects to be measured and dissected with any finality, rather they are open-ended acts of communication whose configuration changes with each new interpretation. Thomas Winner's reflections on the work of Mikhail Bakhtin support this view. Bakhtin understands genre as a type of creative memory, as a framework of expectations for encoding and decoding texts. In the same train of thought, he draws the analogy between genre and grammar, the latter being a set of evolving guidelines for generating intelligible discourse, which, once produced, is always at variance with and, when most imaginative and economical, will subvert the rules of its production. Modern novelistic prose demonstrates the same dynamic on the level of culture and ideology; it is, as Bakhtin describes it, the discourse of actual speaking persons with a sense that they are individual subjects not subsumed by the culture and ideology within which they exist. The result is the collision and hybridization of discourses which Bakhtin calls "heteroglossia."

Narrowing the focus from the broader parameters of genre to those of interpreting individual texts, Jonathan Culler's discussion of the theories of Genette and Roland Barthes make clear that artistic prose has both an external, empirical referent and its own internal, self-referential principles for communicating meaning. Roman Jakobsen is the first to delineate the fundamental structure at the core of this secondary modelling system as one of metaphor versus metonymy, of the subordination of the syntagmatic (metonymic) to the paradigmatic (metaphoric) axis in poetic discourse. By this he means that metaphor juxtaposes and connects paradigms contrary to conventional logic or established knowledge, and that these new connections add to, change and become a part of the established inventory. Metonymy, even though it is a rhetorical figure of non-logical deletion, makes use of established, contingent associations. It is, as he sees it, the mode of referential discourse, whereas metaphor is the defining feature of poetic discourse. Paul Ricoeur, Paul de Man and Jacques Lacan revise this distinction to one of superimposed axes rather than opposing functions. The imagination, the new connections of metaphor would not be possible without the binding, connecting, structure of metonymy. Jacques Lacan, perhaps illustrating metaphor at work, correlates the paradigms of metaphor and metonymy to the "Imaginary" and the "Symbolic" structures of the psyche. By the "Imaginary," he understands the pre-conscious wholeness, the undifferentiated state of integration in which infants have no sense of "self" and "other" (cf. the metaphoric formula A is B). The acquisition of language ruptures this unity, in that it is an imposed system of signs or symbols based on differentiation and absence. Words stand in for objects and concepts that are not present; they are representations of things that are not there, and the connotations which surround their denotative function vary from individual to individual, distancing them even further from any certifiable sense of truth or objectivity. The pronoun "I" enables the individual to perceive that there is such a thing as an individual, but it is simply a sign whose true referent can only be circumscribed with other signs. Further definition happens along a constraining, metonymic chain, more signs that are contingent upon and associated with other signs according to the conventions and rules language. For this reason Lacan reverses Saussure's s/S, meaning (signified) over word-sound and/or transcription (signifier), to S/s, signifier over signified, to indicate the primacy of signifiers. The inversion might be described as a reversal of Descartes's *cogito, ergo sum* to "I am in language; therefore I think, where I am not." This is the provenance of the current literary-theoretical terms "aphanisis (becoming invisible) of the subject" and "*mise en abyme* (placed in the [bottomless] abyss [of language])."[1] Thus a human life-span is in essence an ongoing mediation between the incipiently discordant Symbolic and Imaginary modes, between cultural, ideological, societal imperatives and the primordial instincts to reappropriate the undifferentiated wholeness or nothingness of the place of origin. Freud presented this "reappropriation" in his work "*Beyond the Pleasure Principle*" as an oxymoron. It is a manifestation of *Eros*, the life instinct, the aspiration to be in union with "the other," and it is *Thanatos,* the death instinct, the predisposition of every organism to revert to the original state of non-differentiation, to return to death. That is the dilemma of conscious perception's creation of meaning in both referential and artistic discourse; it is always a fictional, allegorical construct delimited and undermined by the very structures that make it possible.

The second chapter of this book entitled *Theory of the Novella* presents an overview of novella- and of short story theory in both the German and American traditions. The fundamental significance accorded to metaphor and metonymy by Jakobsen, Ricoeur, de Man and Lacan make it possible to describe the subjectivity and open-endedness, the depiction of new and perplexing experiences or even the "shocking nature"

---

[1] As J. Hillis Miller describes it, this term designates the relationship of meaning as a constant displacement from one figurative sign to another. "The name for this displacement is allegory. Story-telling, the putting into language of man's 'experience' of his life, is in its writing or reading a hiatus in that experience. Narrative is the allegorizing along a temporal line of this perpetual displacement from immediacy." J. Hillis Miller, "Ariadne's Thread: Repetition and the Narrative Line," *Critical Inquiry* 3 (1976): p. 72.

of the novella and short story, so often mentioned in theory, as properties of form and structure not specific to a particular plot or topic. Novella and short story tend to valorize the metaphoric paradigm over the metonymic, contingent sequence; while not exclusive to shorter artistic prose, this characteristic is certainly facilitated by a shorter text's gap-filled, elliptical relationship to an empirical referent, and complements the principles of concision, economy and efficiency traditionally posited as the global defining features of the type.

Within the German tradition, Hans-Jörg Neuschäfer develops a line of argument and reaches conclusions similar to Bakhtin's. He determines that from its beginnings in the late Middle Ages and Renaissance, novelistic prose has always been iconoclastic, innovative and protean. Similarly, E. K. Bennett describes the novella as a type of text that is always at the outermost limits of its boundaries. As does Neuschäfer, Roger Paulin and Walter Silz write of an inherent tension between the individual and institutions, with particular emphasis on the subjectivity and frailty of perception and judgement when confronted with the incongruities of lived experience; Martin Swales speaks of the "hermeneutic challenge" at the heart of all nineteenth-century novella-writing. Rolf Schröder, discussing the novella of the Biedermeier period, describes its overall thematic concern as overcoming dogmatic rigorism through humanist values. He takes up a position with Friedrich Sengle, stating that the novel and the novella do not constitute fundamentally different forms, and that the nineteenth century saw a preponderance of the novella in German-speaking regions. It is also a time in which much of the theory of the novella begins to emerge.

Of particular significance are the definitions proposed by Friedrich Schlegel, by his brother August Wilhelm, and by Goethe. Common to all of these is the observation that a novella describes an unprecedented, out-of-the-ordinary event while maintaing a "real," factual profile. This view is shared by Ludwig Tieck, who further defines A. W. Schlegel's terms *Wendepunkt* (turning point) as *Mittelpunkt* (central point). The terms *Silhouette* and *Falke* are delineated by Paul Heyse; more significantly, he hypothesizes that all narrative prose uses greater or lesser amounts of the same components: the proportions and the effects vary, but they are not an indication of artistic merit or aesthetic achievement. Heyse also describes the best examples of prose fiction as ones that question conventional wisdom and an entrenched morality. Finally, Theodor Storm describes the novella as "the epic sister of the drama," both forms being intensely focused and highly crafted.

Twentieth-century theorists in the German tradition attempt to refine and differentiate these concepts with varying degrees of success.

One monograph which provides excellent critical commentary is Hermann Malmede's *Wege zur Novelle* (Approaches to the Novella). Malmede attempts to formulate an abstract concept on the basis of formal and structural attributes culled from the established (nineteenth and twentieth-century) canon of theory. He argues that the thematic particulars of any given text or group of texts cannot be an indicator of genre, since a genre concept can only describe a range of possibilities of abstract formal characteristics. There is, as he states, no reason why a given theme can be accommodated by only one particular text type. However, there are several shortcomings in his deliberations. One is the failure to realize that the recognition of a single chain of motifs - an attribute at the centre of his definition - is not an unmediated process of registering what is "plainly" there, and he makes no distinction between the self-referential modelling systems of artistic texts and the referential discourse of empirical experience. Secondly, there is no attempt made to compare or contrast the novella with other types of narrative prose, or to define what fictional narrative is. Finally, Malmede's inventory of artistic texts is very much limited to an historical, pre-twentieth-century canon, consisting of novellas that tend to be of a more representational, compact and abreviated design. Nevertheless, his definition, derived from other theorists, does distill a compendium of formal characteristics attendant to the attributes of concision, efficiency and economy of means, and he does attempt to define the relationship between a vertical (paradigmatic), and a horizontal (syntagmatic) axis. Judith Leibowitz' monograph *Narrative Purpose in the Novella* investigates works that are less compact, more complex and more stratified. She, like Malmede, describes a profile of formal and structural attributes associated with concision; unlike Malmede, she recognizes that any perception of the contours of plot rests on a hypothetical premise of a text's thematic constellation, and she can therefore extend the list of formal, structural properties to include the concept of a theme-complex of restricted dimensions. Moreover, she contends that the foreground sequences of motifs or images, that is, the metonymic axis, also has a cyclical, parallel and repetitive structure effected by the thematic paradigms of the metaphoric axis. This dialectic has a paradoxical, aesthetic effect: it is both "microcosmic," that is, delimited and self-contained, and it is "macrocosmic," or plurivocal and monumental in scope.

 While American theorists are fewer in number, less prolific and not as prone to classify and categorize, their treatment of the short story bears a strong resemblance to the work of their German counterparts on the *Novelle*. A case in point is Norman Friedman, whose criteria run a close parallel to Malmede's definition. Valerie Shaw and Nadine

Gordimer speak of the short story as an experimental and innovative text type, particularly suited to demonstrating the fragility and illusory nature of human perception; this echoes Martin Swales' "hermeneutic challenge," or E. K. Bennett's characterization of the *Novelle* as a form whose best examples extend the limits of its boundaries. Richard Kostelanetz defines the short story as a form in which metaphor can best transcend reportage, and David Lodge uses excerpts from both novels and short stories to show how narrative prose realizes its metaphoric potential through a subtle displacement or disarrangement of its metonymic underpinnings.

The dialectic of metaphor and metonymy serves as a pivotal conceptual model for a plurality of dynamic systems, from the specifics of the secondary modelling systems of artistic texts and the primary modelling system of language, to the extensive context of cognition and of the psychic apparatus. It is therefore a model which names, elucidates and places within a human context the otherwise abstruse and rarified aesthetic principles and formal strategies of artistic texts. This framework, outlined in the first and second chapters, bears a direct relationship to the texts under discussion.

For example, Hochhuth's *Atlantik-Novelle* contains a metafictional reference to the theory of the genre of the *Novelle*, specifically to Goethe's criterion of the unprecedented event (*unerhörte Begebenheit),* yet its narrative structure is a diffuse and self-abrogating admixture of incompatibles, and it is anything but concise, compact or economically proportioned. Hochhuth seems to have begun with all of the traditional formal attributes of the genre and written a text that negates them all. Each novella in the following pairs of texts contains the seminal theme that any narrative is the product of the "dramaturgy of a subject," (an individual's singular, perceptual construct of reality) not at one with itself; in Dürrenmatt's novella *The Assignment,* the conversation between the main character F. and her mentor D. clearly establishes the *mise en abyme* of the subject. She summarizes his thesis about

> ... man's not ever being identical with himself because he was always an other, thrown into time, ... which, however, would mean that there was no self, or rather, only a countless chain of selves emerging from the future, flashing into the present, and sinking back into the past, so that what one commonly called one's self was merely a collective term for all the selves gathered up in the past, a great heap of selves perpetually growing under the constant rain of selves drifting down through the present

from the future, an accumulation of shreds of experience
and memory, comparable to a mound of leaves that grows
higher and higher under a steady drift of other falling
leaves, while the ones at the bottom have long turned to
humus, a process that seemed to imply a fiction of
selfhood in which every person made up his own self,
imagining himself playing a role for better or worse,
which would make the possession of character mainly a
matter of putting on a good act ...[2]

Both Hochhuth and Walser thematize a concept of narrative, as
does Dürrenmatt, which fits the Lacanian scheme of metonymy as
deferred integration; the narrator of Hochhuth's *Atlantik-Novelle*
addresses the problem of history as an assemblage of facts with no
guarantee of overview or accurate interpretation: "Since it (history) as a
whole is indeed beyond our grasp and comprehension, it is alive only
where, from within its tumult, individuals still gaze at us and speak to
us."[3] The narrator goes on to describe a particular historical occurrence

---

[2] Friedrich Dürrenmatt, *The Assignment or On Observing the Observer of the
Observer* translated from the German by Joel Agee (New York: Random
House, 1988) pp. 24-25 *("... aber sie interessiere, was er über den Menschen
gesagt habe, dem er jede Identität mit sich selber abgesprochen habe, da er
immer ein anderer sei, hineingeworfen in die Zeit, ... was aber bedeuten würde,
daß es kein Ich gebe, besser, nur eine zahllose Kette von aus der Zukunft
auftauchenden, in der Gegenwart aufblitzenden und in der Vergangenheit
versinkenden Ichs, so das denn das, was man sein Ich nenne, nur ein
Sammelname für sämtliche in der Vergangenheit angesammelten Ichs sei,
ständig anwachsend und zugedeckt von den aus der Zukunft durch die
Gegenwart herabfallenden Ichs, eine Ansammlung von Erlebnissen und
Erinnerungsfetzen, bei dem die untersten Blätter längst zu Humus geworden
und der durch das frisch fallende und heranwehende Laub immer höher steige,
ein Vorgang, der zu einer Fiktion eines Ichs führe, indem jeder sein Ich
zusammenfingiere, sich in eine Rolle dichten würde, die er mehr oder weniger
gut zu spielen versuche, demnach komme es auf die schauspielerische Leistung
an ...)"* Friedrich Dürrenmatt, *Der Auftrag oder Vom Beobachten des
Beobachters der Beobachter: Novelle in vierundzwanzig Sätzen* (Zürich:
Diogenes, 1986) pp. 28-29. Subsequent quotations are from these editions.
[3] *"Da sie [die Geschichte] doch als Ganzes so ungreifbar wie unbegreifbar ist
- lebt sie nur, wo einzelne uns noch anschauen, noch zu uns sprechen, aus
ihrem Wirrwarr."* Rolf Hochhut, *Atlantik-Novelle* (Reinbek bei Hamburg:
Rowohlt, 1985) p. 22. Subsequent quotations are from this edition.

in the North Atlantic during the Second World War, but states that his narrative purpose is well served through a description of the events as mediated through the dreamwork of the unconscious: "Since sleep transcends time and space - I became an eyewitness" (p. 23).[4] The main character of Walser's *Runaway Horse*, Helmut Halm, has this to say about his attempt to write his father's biography:

> Helmut was disgusted when he found himself gluing together scraps of memory, coloring them, breathing onto them, inventing texts for them. He was too old for this puppet show. Surely to breathe life into the past meant resurrecting an event in a pseudo-vividness that simply denied the pastness of the past.[5]

Walser, Dürrenmatt and Hochhuth also include the perspective of the dyadic configuration of *Eros* and *Thanatos* in their novellas. The central figure in Walser's *Jenseits der Liebe*, Franz Horn, conjures up in a dream the image of a business associate whose health is in a state of rapid deterioration. In the narrator's dreamwork the latter describes his infected urinary tract as a variety of flower known as cowslip: "Oh yes, go ahead and have another look at this beautiful cowslip blossom. A more beautiful depiction of a festering urethra isn't possible."[6] Similarly Helmut Halm, the narrator of *A Runaway Horse*, finds himself drowning and crying out in the same fashion as he has done when having sexual relations with his wife:

---

[4] *"Da der Schlaf Räume und Jahre überbrücken kann - wurde ich Augenzeuge ..."*

[5] Martin Walser, *Runaway Horse* trans. Leila Vennewitz. (New York: Holt, Rinehart and Winston, 1980) pp. 15-16. (*"Helmut hatte sich geekelt, als er sich erlebte, wie er die Gedächtnisfetzen zusammenleimte, wie er sie anmalte, behauchte, Texte erfand für sie. Für dieses Puppentheater war er zu alt. Etwas von früher lebendig zu machen, hieß doch, es auf eine Weise komplettieren, daß das Vergangene in jeder Pseudoanschaulichkeit auferstand, die den Vergangenheitsgrad des Vergangenen einfach verleugnete."*) Martin Walser, *Ein fliehendes Pferd* (Frankfurt: Suhrkamp, 1978) p. 29. Subsequent quotations are from these editions.

[6] *"Ach ja, werfen Sie ruhig noch einen Blick auf diese Schlüsselblume. Schöner kann man die Harnröhrenvereiterung nicht darstellen."* Martin Walser, *Jenseits der Liebe* (Frankfurt: Suhrkamp, 1979) pp. 76-77. Subsequent quotations are from this edition.

Had he ever felt so utterly shattered? He gave a great wail.
During those last few months, when he had still been having sex
with Sabina, he had experienced exactly the same sensation, that
of being destroyed. [...] Each time he had wailed like that. A
long-drawn-out, steadily rising wail (p. 87).[7]

The cameraman Polyphemos of Dürrenmatt's *The Assignment*
shows his captive F. a "film portrait" of her fellow journalist whose fate
F. has been trying to unravel. The film shows her rape and murder with
some very unexpected close-up shots:

... she saw Jytte Sörensens's face before her, a twisted
grimace of lust, and then, for a moment, as the huge
hands wrapped themselves around her throat, her features
looked proud, triumphant, willing, the Danish woman had
wanted it all, her rape and her death ... (p. 120).[8]

Hochhuth's   *Atlantik-Novelle*   contains   a   poem   entitled
"*Matrosen*," a mariner's and submariner's rhyme in which sexual
relations and the act of firing and being targeted by torpedoes are
juxtaposed:

How invulnerable my body is through yours,
Two wisping flames, you and I - the wind
snuffs them out in an instant, when we unite them,
rather than burn until we are no more!
Birth addiction drives you on, the barbarity of being
even now in your womb I taste my ocean grave.
A question of time, 'till the shout: "torpedo fired"
rips me away with the float I have lost (p. 16).[9]

---

[7] "*Er heulte auf. In den letzten Monaten, in denen er noch geschlechtlich mit
Sabine verkehrt hatte, hatte er genau dieses Gefühl erlebt, das Gefühl,
vernichtet zu sein. [...] Jedes Mal hatte er so geheult. Ein lang gezogenes,
immer höhere Töne erreichendes Heulen.*" (p. 122).

[8] "*... sie sah das Gesicht der Jytte Sörensen vor sich, lustverzehrt, und dann,
wie die riesigen Hände ihre Kehle umschlossen, auf einen Moment, bevor es
sich entstellte, stolz, triumphierend, willig, die Dänin hatte alles gewünscht,
was ihr widerfuhr, die Vergewaltigung und den Tod ...*" (p. 124).

[9] *Wie unverwundbar wird mein Leib durch deinen.*
  Zwei schwache Fackeln, du und ich - der Wind
  verlöscht sie rasch, auch wenn wir sie vereinen,

The first line of the first stanza of *"Matrosen" "Vernutzt vom Krieg - 'jenseits des Lustprinzips'"* literally names *Beyond the Pleasure Principle* as a key to interpreting the tenor of the poem.

As do Walser and Hochhuth, Dürrenmatt employs mythological anchoring as a way of exploiting the metaphoric potential of the paradigmatic axis. Mythological figures are the prototypes for two of the novella's characters: the cameraman Polyphemos and his charge Achilles. Rolf Hochhuth's story *Die Berliner Antigone*, contains a less than oblique reference to the daughter of Oedipus, and Martin Walser's novella *Runaway Horse* implicitly invokes the images of Pegasus and his progenitor Poseidon.

The major premise in all of the textual analyses of this monograph is that the accentuation of the metaphoric potential of novellas and/or short stories is concomitant with, and may be engendered by the greater succinctness and limited scope of a shorter text's metonymic foundation. The elements contributing to concision, functionality and economy of means, as well as to a text's thematic plurivocality are: a restricted number of thematically interlocking motif complexes; cyclical, parallel and repetitive structure; a truncated line of cause and effect; verisimilitude predicated upon ellipsis and ambiguity; intertextuality and metatextuality. In order to investigate the significance of differing generic labels, quantatively similar texts by the same author will be compared with a view to establishing the formal and thematic implications of such differences.

-statt daß sie brennen, bis wir nicht mehr sind!

Treibt dich Gebärsucht, Daseins-Barbarei
- schmeck ich mein Meergrab schon in deinem Schoß.
Zeitfrage bis der Ruf: "Torpedo frei"
mich wegreißt samt verlorenem Floß.

Chapter One

Contemporary Poetics

The use of genre as a point of departure for analysing and comparing texts may seem questionable in a post-modern era, but it is a term which is not self-explanatory or self-evident. Although historically, definitions of general types and sub-types have been used to proscriptive ends, the realization that texts and text sytems are open-ended communication acts has necessitated a concept of genre that is descriptive and hypothetical in nature, one which admits to the inevitability of its own obsolescence as new texts are added to the corpus. Also, when used as a heuristic device, a concept of genre can provide a recognition of the literary historical antecedents shaping a text. Whether this relationship is one of accommodation or subversion, it offers a diachronic and synchronic overview of a text within a system of texts.[10] As noted by Northrop Frye, "The purpose of criticism by genres is not so much to classify as to clarify traditions and affinities, thereby bringing out a large number of literary relationships that would not be noticed as long as there were no context established for them."[11] Gérard Genette employs the terms "genericity" and "architextuality" to describe how a text is imbedded within a continuum of many transtextual ties. These include: paratextuality (a text's relationship to its title, its sub-title, epigraphs, date of publication, i.e. its external context); intertextuality (quotation, allusion); hypertextuality (relationships between texts in terms of imitation/transformation as well as between a text and a style); metatextuality (relationship between a text and its commentary). The metatextual aspect thus takes into account the role of critical commentary as a vital element in a text's interpretation. This is the framework or context of generic development to which Jean-Marie Schaeffer refers when he states:

> Genericity occurs whenever a text, contraposed with its
> literary context, in a broad sense conjures up an implicit

---

[10] John Reichert, "More than Kin and Less than Kind: The Limits of Genre Theory," *Theories of Literary Genre* ed. Joseph P. Strelka (University Park and London: The Pennsylvania State University Press, 1978) p. 57.
[11] Northrop Frye, *Anatomy of Criticism* (Princeton: Princeton University Press, 1957) p. 247.

framework which binds together a class of texts relative
to which the text in question has come to be: either it will
disappear within this framework or it will distend or
dismantle it; it will always assimilate itself to these
parameters or it will itself assimilate them.[12]

Genre provides author and reader with "a set of conventionalized
features" which permit information to be encoded and decoded against a
framework of "parameters of expectations," but by the same token, having
provided a point of orientation, it also affords the possibility of variation
and violation of its own conditions.[13]

The literary genre ... represents the most constant ...
tendencies of literary evolution. In the genre there are
always preserved ... elements of archaic character. But
these archaisms are retained in the genre only thanks to
their constant renewal, their so to speak
contemporanization. A genre is always that and not that,
it is always both old and new simultaneously. The genre
is reborn and renewed in each new stage of the
development of literature and each individual creation of
a given genre. Thus is expressed the life of a genre. That
is why archaic elements retained in the genre are not
dead, but remain eternally alive, that is, they remain
capable of renewal. A genre lives in the present, but
always with the memory of its past, of its beginnings.
Genre is the representative of creative memory in the
process of evolution of literature. It is for this reason that
the genre is capable of assuring the unity and
uninterruptiveness of this development.[14]

---

[12] "Il y a généricité dès que la confrontation d'un texte à son contexte littéraire
(trame qui lie ensemble une classe textuelle et par rapport à laquelle le texte en
question s'écrit: soit qu'il disparaisse à son tour dans le trame, soit qu'il la
distourde ou la démonte, mais toujours soit s'y intégrant, soit se l'intégrant."
Jean-Marie Schaeffer, "Du texte au genre," *Théorie des genres*, ed. Gérard
Genette and Tsvetan Todorov (Paris: Édition du Seuil, 1986) p. 204.
[13] Thomas G. Winner, "Structural and Semiotic Genre Theory," *Theories of
Literary Genre* ed. Joseph P. Strelka (University Park and London: The
Pennsylvania State University Press, 1978) p. 265.
[14] Mikhail Bakhtin, *Problemy poètiky Dostoevskogo* (Moscow: Sovetskij
pisatel, 1963) pp. 141-42, as quoted in Winner, p. 265.

The most recent discussion of the concept of genre occurs within the framework of a semiotic application of structuralist poetics. Bakhtin's analogy of genre to memory as constituted by the structure of language, posits a relationship between grammar and genre, inasmuch as genres are "mutable systems within systems (i.e., within the system of verbal art), ... codes or subcodes, models for the organization of texts (Winner, p. 266)." The process employed to deduce the structure of language can be seen as analogous to constructing hypotheses about literature, inasmuch as the point of departure in formulating the grammar of a language is the meanings of utterances or sentences in which there are implicit rules for generating those meanings. Similarly in literary discourse, the interpretation of a text is dependent upon an awareness of a convention of structural properties (not present in language per se) which can only be adumbrated on the basis of a model constructed of previously encountered tenor-vehicle relationships.[15] It would seem that there is no guarantee that a structure so derived is actually inherent in the phenomenon being observed. But that is a restriction implicit in the term 'convention' which is more a function of the commensurability of meanings and their derivation rather than their true and ultimate revelation. To interpret a text is to achieve a synthesis at a level of abstraction where the sometimes disparate elements of the vehicle of content can be made to cohere; this tenor must bear critical scrutiny as a plausible correlate of its vehicle, an exponent of literary convention and innovation and a derivation of empirical reality. Although the *prima facie* identity of and interest in a text is the statement it makes about reality, it is itself a fiction of reality. It is only in the awareness of its constructedness as a system of signs and symbols built on language, with its own distinct profile of structural properties, that the act of interpretation can be explained. The conventions of genre contribute to the process of synthesis through abstraction by providing a measure of contrast and comparison of various types of fictive constructs. Common to all of them is the component of

---

[15] David Lodge indicates the origin of these concepts: "Terms coined by I.A. Richards in *The Philosophy of Rhetoric* to distinguish the two elements in a metaphor. In 'Ships ploughed the sea,' 'Ships' movement' is the tenor and 'plough' the vehicle." David Lodge, *The Modes of Modern Writing* (Chicago: The University of Chicago Press, 1988). p. 75. As Paul Ricoeur explains, "... tenor and vehicle designate the conceptual import and its pictorial envelope." Paul Ricoeur, "The Metaphorical Process," *On Metaphor* ed. Sheldon Sacks (Chicago and London: The University of Chicago Press, 1979) p. 147.

empirical experience as an ultimate referent, which is precisely the reason
why that component cannot serve as a prime distinguishing feature.

The element of narrative discourse which sets it apart from other
types of literature is the presence of a narrative agent or agents. Their
function is to focus on a series of more or less logically and
chronologically related events caused or experienced by characters
bearing social, cultural and psychological traits in accordance with the
segment of empirical reality after which they and the events they
participate in, or generate, are modelled.[16] In fulfilling the mimetic
contract to which narrative discourse is committed, the minimal units of a
text which have "a specific effect or function different from that of
neighbouring stretches of text" bear a relationship to one another
according to the principles of logic applied to establish similarity, contrast
and contiguity. The selection of those minimal units which play a
functional as opposed to a referential and/or symbolic role in the the
progression of events determines the contours of plot. The sequence of
these functional units is reciprocally and teleologically determined. The
prima facie logic of the sequence is, however, determined by what Genette
calls

> ... that paradoxical logic of fiction which requires one to
> define every element, every unit of the story, by its
> functional qualities, that is to say among other things by
> its correlation with another unit, and to account for the
> first (in the order of narrative time) by the second, and so
> on.[17]

Jonathan Culler cites Greimas and Lévi-Strauss in their criticism
of Vladimir Propp's *Fairy Tale Transformations* as formulating such
basic functions "too close to the level of empirical observation."[18]
Greimas formulates a more fundamental structure which describes
thematic modification as a move from a negative contract to a positive
one, or vice versa, occurring between an initial and a final situation
(Culler, pp. 213 f.). Yet what accounts for a reader's ability to identify
which minimal narrative elements make up the structure of the plot is not
the equation of actions and conditions with a fixed set of plot-generating

---

[16] Mieke Bal, *Narratology. Introduction to the Theory of Narrative* (Toronto:
University of Toronto Press, 1985) pp. 18 f.
[17] Gérard Genette, *Figures II* (Paris: Seuil, 1969) p. 94, as quoted in Culler, p.
210.
[18] Jonathan Culler, *Structuralist Poetics* (London: Routledge and Kegan Paul,
1975) pp. 213 f.

functions, but rather the ability to assemble a structure on the basis of previous experience with the process, of which Roland Barthes has noted the following:

> [it is] a certain power of reading, which seeks to name with a sufficiently transcendent term a sequence of actions, which have themselves issued from a patrimony of human experience; ... the typology ... of these proairetic [plot-building] units seems uncertain, ... at least we can give them no other logic than that of the probable, of the organized world, of the *already-written*; for the number and order of terms are variable, some deriving from a practical store of trivial behaviour (to knock at a door, to arrange a meeting), and others taken from a written corpus of novelistic models.[19]

Barthes distinguishes between plot-building or distributional and integrative units. The former are in sequence on a horizontal syntagmatic plane, whereas the latter are "grouped with analogous items in paradigm classes which receive a meaning at a higher level of integration" (Culler, p. 203). Although cultural models may provide some indication as to how one determines which units are distributional, and which are integrative, it is the manner of closure of a narrative text, the way in which the sequence is brought to a conclusion, that provides the key to its structure.

> The reader must organize the plot as a passage from one state to another and this passage or movement must be such that it serves as a representation of theme. The end must be made a transformation of the beginning so that meaning can be drawn from the perception of resemblance and difference. And this imposes constraints on the way in which one names beginning and end. One can attempt to establish a coherent causal series, in which disparate incidents are read as stages towards a goal, or a dialectical movement in which incidents are related as contraries whose opposition carries the problem that must be resolved .... In composing an initial and final state the reader will draw on a series of actions which he can organize in a causal sequence, so that what is named as the state which the larger thematic structure requires is

[19] Roland Barthes, *S/Z* (Paris: Seuil, 1970) p. 209, as quoted in Culler, p. 221.

itself a logical development, or he may read a series of
incidents as illustrations of a common condition which
serves as initial or final state in the overall structure.
(Culler, p. 222).

An important point would seem to be that in many instances,
particularly in contemporary fiction, there is no possible immediate
distinction between plot-building, minimal units and integrational ones. In
other words, it becomes necessary to extrapolate through the operations of
a symbolic code a statement of theme from a chain of motifs or motif-
clusters which offers little direct indication of the tenor it projects as a
vehicle. Symbolic recuperation not only permits a reader to preserve "a
semantic or contextual coherence according to the thematic conditioning
of plot and character,"[20] but can also be the operation required simply to
establish any coherence of plot and character.

Although the tropological structure of narrative is foregrounded in
contemporary fiction and literary theory, the notion that rhetorical
figuration or trope, is a major constituent of language and *a fortiori* of
literary language, is a concept expressed by Nietzsche. Nietzsche also
expresses the belief that "truth statements cannot announce a
transcendental condition or state of logical certainty," since

the synthetic quality of human judgement, which
describes things according to the contingent quality of
their appearances, and then generalizes and identifies
them as essential qualities, is really only a rhetorical
process, a metonymic and metaphoric process, of false
substitutions.[21]

---

[20]   Alan Singer, *A Metaphorics of Fiction* (Tallahassee Fla.: Florida State
University Press, 1983) p. 39.
[21]   Ramon Saldivar, *Figural Language in the Novel* (Princeton: Princeton
University Press, 1984) p. 17. Saldivdar provides the following quotation as an
illustration of Nietzsche's treatment of the "now familiar question": "What
therefore is truth? A mobile army of metaphors, metonymies,
anthropomorphisms: in short, a sum of human relations which become
poetically and rhetorically intensified, metamorphosed, adorned, and after long
usage seem to a nation fixed, canonic and binding; truths are illusions of which
one has forgotten that they *are* illusions; worn-out metaphors which have
become powerless to affect the senses; coins which have their obverse effaced
and now are no longer of account as coins but merely as metal." Friedrich
Nietzsche, "On Truth and Falsehood in Their Extra-Moral Sense," *The*

The realization that truth cannot be proven to be more than shared subjectivity does not call the figurative legitimacy of the art work into question, since it understands that it is "based on the priority of tropological structures." (Saldivar, p. 18): "Art, therefore, treats *appearance* as *appearance*; it precisely does *not* intend to deceive, and is, consequently, *true*."[22] Another proponent of this argument is the Italian philosopher Ernesto Grassi who sees language expression as falling into two categories: on the one hand there is the rational or logical type, deductive in nature, and "limited to discovering what is already contained in the assumed premises."[23] The other type is the language of rhetoric, not a "technique of exterior persuasion" (Gregg, p. 16) but rather a source of analogical knowledge and "at the basis of rational thought" (Gregg, p. 16). As Grassi further observes,

> This form of expression provides us with insight through the presentation of images that bring out the similarities among phenomena by revealing relationships that we did not see before. It is the language of creation; the relationships created by its imagery constitute its "demonstration" (Gregg, p. 16).

Echoing Bakhtin, fiction for Alan Singer "... is conceived as a rupture of the contextual semes binding established discourse" (Singer, p. 25). Similarly, Paul de Man argues that

> Rhetoric radically suspends logic and opens up vertiginous possibilities of referential aberration. And although it would perhaps be somewhat more remote from common usage, I would not hesitate to equate the rhetorical, figural potentiality of language with literature itself.[24]

Complete Works of Nietzsche vol. 2 *Early Greek Philosophy* ed. Oscar Levy, trans. Maximilian A. Mügge (London: T. N. Foulis, 1911) p. 180, as quoted in Saldivar, p. 17.

[22] Friedrich Nietzsche, *Gesammelte Werke* vol. 6 (Munich: Musarion, 1922) p. 98, as quoted in Saldivar, p. 18.

[23] As quoted in Richard B. Gregg, *Symbolic Inducement and Knowing* (Columbia: University of South Carolina Press, 1984) p. 15.

[24] Paul de Man, *Allegories of Reading* (New Haven and London: Yale University Press, 1979) p. 10.

Although de Man designates metonymy as a trope of "syntagmatic structure based on contingent association," (de Man p. 15) therefore in his terms a grammatical, not a rhetorical structure such as metaphor is, he nevertheless sees both figures as complementary or dyadic rather than oppositional or polar (de Man, p. 16). Paul Ricoeur makes the same point by way of criticism of Roman Jakobson's subordination of the syntagmatic to the paradigmatic axis. He writes:

> ... for ... [Jakobson] the metaphoric process is opposed to the metonymic process ... What must be understood and underscored is a mode of functioning of similarity and accordingly of imagination which is non-immanent - that is, nonextrinsic - to the predicative process itself. In other words, the work of resemblance has to be appropriate and homogeneous to the deviance and the oddness and the freshness of the semantic innovation itself.[25]

The suspension of the referential or denotative sense of language is the condition for the emergence of a connotative, imaginative sense (Ricoeur, p. 152). Rather than a solipsistic, operation, this suspension of ordinary reference is one of production and projection "... of deeply rooted potentialities or reality to the extent that they are absent from the actualities with which we deal in everyday life under the mode of empirical control and manipulation" (Ricoeur, pp. 152-153). The novel and its related genres disseminate analogical, directive (as opposed to conventionally contiguous, denotative) knowlege through their subversion of the common currency of traditionally accepted or given symmetries by pointing towards new configurations of thesis and antithesis.

In his work *The Dialogic Imagination,* Bakhtin defines novellistic discourse as a tension between the centripetal or unifying forces of language as determined by a literary and social status quo and the centrifugal or destabilizing forces of a new prose genre in close affiliation with rhetorical forms (journalistic, moral, philosophical prose) whose centre was a dialogue of "concrete utterance[s] of ... speaking subject[s]."[26] The fundamental condition, that which makes a novel a

---

[25] Paul Ricoeur, "The Metaphorical Process," *On Metaphor* ed. Sheldon Sacks (Chicago and London: The University of Chicago Press, 1979) p. 145.
[26] M. M. Bakhtin, *The Dialogic Imagination* (Austin: University of Texas Press, 1981) p. 272.

novel, that which is responsible for its stylistic uniqueness, is the "speaking person and his discourse ... artistically represented ... by means of (authorial) discourse" (Bakhtin, p. 332). The speaking person or the rendition of his discourse is always the rendition of an ideology in the sense that any "particular language in a novel is always a particular way of viewing the world, one that strives for a social significance" (Bakhtin, p. 333). The intersection, opposition and hybridization of these "languages" Bakhtin refers to as "heteroglossia."[27] The artistic reworking of heteroglossia in the novel has a refractingly and mutually illuminating impact on all of its facets: the discourse of characters, authorial narration and incorporated genres (Bakhtin, p. 324). Novelistic prose is inherently heterogenic and protean.

Of considerable impact in the post-structuralist/ deconstructionist discussion are the writings of Jacques Lacan. Lacan draws upon Freud's theory of the Oedipus complex and his work *Beyond the Pleasure Principle,* Saussure's concept of signifier and signified and Jakobson's theory of the metaphoric and metonymic bipolarity of language in order to define his new concept. Lacan sees the successful negotiation of the Oedipus complex and the acquisition of language as complementary and convergent processes. As Elizabeth Wright notes:

> Lacan begins with the infant in an amorphous state, with no boundaries to its experience or sense of need ... [...] Lacan calls this pre-linguistic, pre-oedipal stage the realm of the 'Imaginary.' [...] What is imagined in particular is ... the 'Desire of the Mother' ... The child becomes all that would satisfy the mother's lack, ... all that would complete her desire. ... Second, the 'Desire of the Mother' is the child's own desire for the mother, as the part of the experience which has been prompt to satisfy its needs.

---

[27] "At any given time, in any given place, there will be a set of conditions - social, historical, meteorological, physiological - that will ensure that a word uttered in that place and at that time will have a meaning different than it would have under any other conditions; all utterances are heteroglot in that they are functions of forces practically impossible to recoup, and therefore impossible to resolve. Heteroglossia is as close a conceptualization as is possible of that locus where centripetal and centrifugal forces collide; as such, it is that which a systematic linguistics must always suppress." Glossary, *The Dialogic Imagination*, p. 428.

> ... The gap [in this illusory state] appears with the
> initiation of the child into the order of language, what
> Lacan calls the 'Symbolic Order.' The structures of
> language are marked with societal imperatives - the
> Father's rules, laws and definitions, among which are
> those of 'child' and 'mother.' Society's injunction that
> desire must wait, that it must formulate in the constricting
> word whatever demand it may speak, is what effects the
> split between conscious and unconscious, the repression
> that is the tax exacted by the use of language (Wright, pp.
> 108-109).

Lacan uses the Saussurian formula s/S, where s stands for the
part of the sign which is the concept referred to, the signified, and S
represents the word-sound enabling that reference, the signifier, but
inverts the formula to S/s to indicate the primacy of the signifier. What
may seem to be a sign with a fixed meaning is a completely arbitrary
combination whose referential function will vary according to context and
individual use. (Wright, p. 109). This inversion shows the primacy of
signifiers: language at the conscious level relegates the Cartesian
"cogito," the conscious ego to the status of a composite of signifiers
without any ascertainable centre, since every signifier indicates the
absence of what it stands for. "Language imposes a chain of words along
which the ego must move while the unconscious remains in search of the
object it has lost" (Wright, p. 111). The subject or ego can only present
itself, or more appropriately re-present itself through language, a chain of
signifiers which stand in only for the reality to which they refer. Lacan
terms this the symbolic mode, or "the discourse of the Other," a system of
signs imposed from without, appropriating the subject, eliminating its
unity but simultaneously, albeit allegorically, constituting it. The
Symbolic adds a linguistic dimension to Freud's concept of the ego and
super-ego; the id, including the basic drives of *Eros* and *Thanatos*, is
subsumed by the Imaginary in the Lacanian topology. Thus the subject is
determined by a discordant dynamic of consciousness and
unconsciousness, of the Symbolic and the Imaginary, the latter attempting
to affect a reappropriation of non-differentiation and/or stasis, the former
imposing a system of signification, differentiation and contiguity.
Language is the generating moment which both enables self-awareness
and cancels it out as a certainty.[28] Every signifier is a trope, the original

---

[28] Lacan notes: "The signifier, producing itself in the field of the other, makes
manifest the subject of its signification. But it functions as a signifier only to

trope being the metaphoric substitution of the metonymic "law of the father" for the "desire of the mother" Lacan borrows Jakobson's prime constituents of language, metaphor and metonymy, revises the distinction between the two in terms of an absolute opposition, a bi-polarization, "into an opposition between two superimposed axes - one horizontal (metonymic), the other vertical (met-aphoric) - in such a way that the two forms of discourse ... are always co-existant."[29]

Of particular importance in the Lacanian scheme is Freud's *Beyond the Pleasure Principle*, a work which quickly became controversial and was ultimately rejected by the psychoanalytic establishment. In it Freud hypothesizes that there is concurrent with the basic drive of *Eros* a death drive, *Thanatos*. Peter Brooks provides a cogent description of these drives which are seemingly at odds and yet complementary; he also illuminates the analogy drawn between the elusive and ongoing desire for integration at the level of ideas and the desire for physical union:

> Hence one can consider "binding" to be a preliminary function which prepares the excitation for its final elimination in the pleasure of discharge. In this manner, we could say that the ... death instinct serve[s] the pleasure principle; in a larger sense, the pleasure principle, keeping watch on the invasion of stimuli from without and especially from within, seeking their discharge, serves the death instinct, making sure that the

---

reduce the subject in question to being no more than a signifier, to petrify the subject in the same movement in which it calls the subject to function, to speak, as subject. [...] You will also understand that, if I have spoken to you of the unconscious as something that opens and closes, it is because its essence is to mark that time by which, from the fact of being born with the signifier, the subject is born divided. The subject is this emergence which, just before, as subject, was nothing, but which, having scarcely appeared, solidifies into a signifier." Jacques Lacan, *The Four Fundamental Concepts of Psychoanalysis*, ed. J. A. Miller, transl. Alan Sheridan (New York: Norton, 1978) pp. 207-208 as quoted in Régis Durand, "On Aphanisis: A Note on the Dramaturgy of the Subject in Narrative Analysis," *Lacan and Narration: The Psychoanalytic Difference in Narrative Theory* (Baltimore and London: Johns Hopkins University Press, 1983) pp. 860-865.

[29] Maria Ruegg, "Metaphor and Metonymy," *Glyph 6*, ed. Rodolphe Gasché, Carol Jacobs, Henry Sussman (Baltimore and London: The Johns Hopkins University Press, 1979) p. 147.

organism is permitted to return to quiescence. The whole
evolution of the mental apparatus appears as a taming of
the instincts so that the pleasure principle - itself tamed,
displaced, - can appear to dominate in the complicated
détour called life which leads back to death. [...] The
organism must live in order to die in the proper manner
.... We must have the arabesque of plot in order to reach
the end. We must have metonymy in order to reach
metaphor.[30]

This aporia projects psychoanalytic discourse beyond the realm of
the referential discourse of science, even though, strictly speaking, "there
is a fictive moment at the genesis of every science, a generative fiction (a
hypothesis) at the foundation of every theory."[31] It is no longer a
description of observables, but rather an allegorical, mythical
circumlocution of the truth. Freud leaves no doubt about this:

The theory of the instincts is so to say our mythology.
Instincts are mythical entities, magnificent in their
indefiniteness.   In our work, we cannot for a moment
disregard them, yet we are never sure that we are seeing
them clearly.[32]

The ultimately mythical status of psychoanalytic theory as posited
by Freud is entirely commensurate with Lacan's own position. The
emergence and disappearance of the subject through language, the
interplay of the Symbolic and the Imaginary, the superimposed axes of
metonymy and metaphor, are all concepts whose constituents are non-
bistable, dissymetrical, evanescent. The implication is, however, not that
truth is an illusion, only that it is mediated:

---

[30] Peter Brooks, "Freud's Masterplot," *Literature and Psychoanalysis* ed.
Shoshana Felman (Baltimore and London: The Johns Hopkins University
Press, 1985) p. 295.
[31] Shoshana Felman, "Beyond Oedipus: The Specimen Story of Psycho-
analysis," *Lacan and Narration*, ed. Robert Con Davis (Baltimore and London:
The Johns Hopkins University Press, 1983) p. 1050.
[32] Sigmund Freud, *The Standard Edition of the Complete Psychological
Works of Sigmund Freud*, vol. XXII, translated from the German under the
General Editorship of James Strachey (London: The Hogarth Press and the
Institute of Psychoanalysis, 1964) p. 95 as quoted in Felman, p. 1044.

> Between reality and the psychoanalytic myth, the relation
> is not one of opposition, but one of (analytic) dialogue:
> the myth comes to grips with something in reality that it
> does not fully comprehend, or master, but to which it
> gives an answer, a symbolical reply. [...] In much the
> same way as the gift of speech of the analytical
> interpretation ... acts not by virtue of its accuracy but by
> virtue of its resonance (whose impact is received in terms
> of the listener's structure) ..., that is, by virtue of its
> openness to a linguistic passage through the Other, so
> does the psychoanalytic myth, in resonating in the Other,
> produce a truthful structure (Felman, pp. 1044-45).

Literary narrative, like psychoanalytic dialogue, subdues that which is in constant motion,[33] reorders, stabilizes "past contingencies by conferring on them the sense of necessities to come."[34] The argument, then, for considering the analysis of the structure of the psyche and of fiction-making through the common denominator of language as rhetoric is certainly plausible, not least because "... much of Freud's [and Lacan's] understanding of interpretation and the construction of meaning is grounded in literature."[35]

---

[33] Ronald Schleifer, "The Space and Dialogue of Desire: Lacan, Greimas and Narrative Temporality," *Lacan and Narration* ed. Robert Con Davis (Baltimore and London: The Johns Hopkins University Press, 1985) pp. 888f.
[34] Jacques Lacan, *Écrits: A Selection*, trans. Alan Sheridan (New York, 1977) p. 48, as quoted in Schleifer, p. 889.
[35] Peter Brooks, "The Idea of Psychoanalytic Criticism," *Discourse in Psychoanalysis and Literature* ed. Shlomith Rimmon-Kenan (London and New York: Methuen, 1987) p. 16.

Chapter Two

Theory of the Novella

A majority of theorists investigating the origins of the genre cite Boccaccio's *Decameron* as its most palpable point of emergence. Bakhtin refers to the period of the late Middle Ages and the Renaissance (Boccaccio's *Decameron* appeared in 1353) as a period of the novelization of literature, at a time of disintegration of hierarchical and epic distance in which "the object of artistic representation was being degraded to the level of a contemporary reality that was inconclusive and fluid" (Bakhtin, p. 39). This new development was both synthetic and iconoclastic in nature as it drew upon the forms of the existing literary canon as well as extra-literary forms such as the letter, the philosophical tract and moral confession (Bakhtin, p. 33), yet set its discourse to reflect the contemporary vernacular as well as a narrated time of an inconclusive present. Socio-historical categories are no longer able to represent the individual in her or his entirety; "there always remains an unrealized surplus of humanness" (Bakhtin, p. 37). In his book *Boccaccio und der Beginn der Novelle*, Hans-Jörg Neuschäfer casts the novella in a similar light with respect to its literary heritage:

> It is precisely the undifferentiated inner person in the medieval predecessors of the novella which demonstrates an otherwordly system of references, of value-determining norms and event-shaping forces; this undifferentiated person is the object of and representative for these forces within the sphere of lived experience. This person is dependent either upon providence, or fate, or subject to the categorial demands of supra-personal ideas and norms. The dyadic inner person has the complementary and opposite pole no longer beyond, but within the world of lived experience, that is, within himself. He bears responsibility for himself, is no longer the object of a supra-personal course of events, but himself becomes a generating subject.[36]

---

[36] *"Gerade die Einpoligkeit der Person in den mittelalterlichen Vorläufern der Novelle verweist auf ein außerweltliches Bezugssystem wertsetzender Normen*

14

Neuschäfer and Bakhtin are referring to the same phenomenon: the emergence of prose narrative. From the perspective of German literature, the fictional mode often foregrounded by virtue of its status as an area of recognized achievement is the novella. Whatever discernable difference may exist between novel and novella, as exponents of one and the same historical point of issue, they have in common an innovative, protean and iconoclastic disposition. As Bakhtin expresses it, it is a concept of the individual within an inconclusive, ambiguous environment, necessitating the "incongruity of a man with himself" (Bakhtin, p. 37). Neuschäfer formulates the incongruity as external norms at odds with individual needs. The *Decameron* on the whole takes aim at a cultural mold requiring the individual "... to satisfy requirements which do not address real, human potential" ("... *Forderungen zu erfüllen, die an den realen menschlichen Möglichkeiten vorbeigehen"*) (Neuschäfer, p. 108). When Boccaccio's novellas lead from the norm to the exception, "human reason has no ultimate answer."[37] Bakhtin and Neuschäfer do not present fundamentally different aguments: Neuschäfer's external factor is one of moral conventionality, whereas Bakhtin stresses a broader social sphere. This tension between the individual and institutions is an aspect underlined in two significant monographs. Roger Paulin in his work *The Brief Compass* relates the "unusual event" to the "awareness that changes in fortune are attendant on our general state of human frailty" (Paulin, p. 14). Paulin characterizes Kleist's *Erdbeben in Chile* as "a story about those who seek to draw their own conclusions from events," (Paulin, p. 46) and Hoffmann's *Das Gelübde* and Kleist's *Die Marquise von O* are rendered as works in which "there can be no appeal to an *exemplum*," (Paulin, p. 57) but only to "that which is inside, which has validity for the inner eye ..." as the "... authority for the interpretation of the outside world" (p. 57). Similarly, Walter Silz underlines the value placed on the

---

und geschehnisbewegender Kräfte, deren innerweltlicher Repräsentant und deren Objekt die einpolige Person ist; sie ist abhängig, sei es von der Providenz, sei es von einem Fatum, sei es vom kategorischen Anspruch überpersönlicher Ideen und Normen. Die doppelpolige Person hat den ihr zugehörigen Gegenpol nicht mehr außerhalb, sondern innerhalb der wirklichen Welt, ja in sich selber. Sie kann deshalb auch für sich selbst aufkommen, ist nicht mehr Objekt eines überpersönlichen Geschehens, sondern wird ... selber zum Subjekt." Hans-Jörg Neuschäfer, *Boccaccio und der Beginn der Novelle* (München: Wilhelm Fink, 1969) p. 108.
[37] Roger Paulin, *The Brief Compass* (Oxford: Clarendon Press, 1985) p. 41.

individual beginning with the Renaissance.[38] His introductory remarks
lead into a discussion of nineteenth-century novellas, but one of the
constants he proposes from the Renaissance to his particular focus is the
element of lived experience, of the relationship of individual personality
and "the reality of existence" (Silz, p. 16) ultimately resulting, as he puts
it, in "literature's increased awareness ... that the only real realities are the
persuasions of the human mind" (Silz, p. 16). The novel and the novella
may be characterized as favouring a thematic constellation which
undermines established views, popular beliefs and rigorously held
dogmata. Rolf Schröder makes this point in his monograph of the novella
in the Biedermeier period:

> The flood of prose and novellas observed in the
> Biedermeier decades also meant the beginning of a
> comprehensive humanization of spiritual life. This,
> above all else, was what replaced dogmatic rigorism. [39]

Schröder stresses the view of the period that novel and novella did not
constitute substantially different categories. On this point he quotes
Friedrich Sengle: "Their common character as forms of prose was more
keenly felt than how they differed.[40] Furthermore, since at least the label
Novelle, if not the preponderance of the shorter prose form is in full
evidence, it would seem erroneous to suggest, as does Wolfgang Kaiser,
that the period of the Restoration made the novel "... the prevalent literary
form."[41] On the contrary, as Paulin states, "it would seem that the
Novelle in the pre-1848 years had usurped much of the function enjoyed
by the novel in other literatures" (Paulin, p. 63).

---

[38] Walter Silz, *Realism and Reality* (Chapel Hill: University of North Carolina
Press, 1954) p. 1.
[39] *"Die Prosa- und in den Biedermeierjahrzehnten die Novellenhochflut, die
wir beobachten, bedeutete zugleich doch auch den Ansatz zu einer
umfassenden Humanisierung des geistigen Lebens: sie war es vor allem, die
den dogmatischen Rigorismus ... ersetzen konnte."* Rolf Schröder, *Novelle und
Novellentheorie in der frühen Biedermeierzeit* (Tübingen: Niemeyer, 1970) p.
224.
[40] *"Ihr gemeinsamer Charakter als Prosa wurde ... stärker empfunden als ihr
Unterschied."* Friedrich Sengle, "Der Romanbegriff in der ersten Hälfte des
19. Jahrhunderts," *Arbeiten zur deutschen Literatur* (Stuttgart: 1967) p. 190,
as quoted in Schröder, p. 211.
[41] Wolfgang Kayser, Geleitwort zu *Annette von Droste-Hülshoff: Sämtliche
Werke,* 1939, pp. 97 f, as quoted in Schröder, p. 214

The nineteenth century is for the novella a most prolific era both in terms of production as well as theory. Indeed, these are the concepts, sometimes at variance with actual practice, that have become part of an established canon of theory. It is therefore important to know the sources and contexts of major theoretical items such as "*eine unerhörte Begebenheit*" (an unprecedented event), "*Wendepunkt*" (turning point), "*Mittelpunkt*" (central point), "*Falke*" (falcon), "*Silhouette*" and "*Symbol*"; the best procedure would seem to be a chronological one, whereby a first grouping of nineteenth and earlier twentieth-century theory statements serves as the established corpus with which the second grouping of more recent proposals contends.

According to this scheme, the first attempts to establish a theory come from Friedrich Schlegel. He underlines the novella's objectivity, which is to say the realistic, lived-experience nature of its content, as well as its subjectivity, or the "dramaturgy" of the author. It is both general and specific, "real" and fictive in configuration: general and "real," in the sense that the reader-listener may relate to it, specific and fictive, in that it must nevertheless project a newness from within its "factual" foundation:

> The novella is an anecdote, a story as yet unheard, which must be inherently interesting, ... therefore a story, which in a narrow sense, does not belong to history ... Since it must be interesting, it must contain something within its form which has the potential to captivate or entice ... told in such a way as one would relate a story within a gathering ... portrayed in a subjective mood and from a subjective point of view, indirectly yet symbolically ... perhaps it is especially adept at this indirect and hidden subjectivity, because it leans towards the objective.[42]

---

[42] "*Es ist die Novelle eine Anekdote, eine noch unbekannte Geschichte, die an und für sich schon einzeln interessieren können muß, ... eine Geschichte also, die streng genommen nicht zur Geschichte gehört ... Da sie interessieren muß, so muß sie in ihrer Form etwas enthalten, was vielen merkwürdig oder lieb sein zu können verspricht ... so erzählt, wie man sie in Gesellschaft erzählen würde ... eine subjektive Stimmung und Ansicht ... indirekt und gleichsam sinnbildlich darzustellen ... zu dieser indirekten und verborgenen Subjektivität eben vielleicht darum besonders geschickt, weil sie sich übrigens sehr zum Objektiven neigt.*" Friedrich Schlegel, *Jugendschriften* ed. Jakob Minor, vol. II,

The arguments of this excerpt of the *Nachricht von den poetischen Werken des Johannes Boccaccio* (1801) (cf. Paulin, p. 132) are echoed in August Wilhelm Schlegel's *Geschichte der romantischen Literatur* (1803); the novella portrays every-day occurrences which nevertheless go against the norm, if not question the norm. These facts are fictitious, are to be dealt with succinctly, and, for the first time, the term *Wendepunkt* (turning point) makes its appearance:

> The novella needs decisive turning points, so that the main contours of the story become clearly visible ... In order to narrate a novella well, one must treat the every-day occurrences entering into the story as succinctly as possible, without buttressing them in an unnecessary way, dwelling only on that which is singular and extraordinary, yet here also not providing any analysis of motive ... rather depicting things positively and credibly ... The novella is a story outside of history, consequently it narrates curious occurrences which happened, as it were, behind the back of bourgeois ways of thinking and creating order.[43]

Goethe's much-cited *"unerhörte Begebenheit"* (an unprecedented event) is from a letter to Eckermann dated 25 January,1827. Although not the first word on the subject, it has had a tendency to become the last, and perhaps most misrepresented one. This may be due to the omission of subsequent remarks relating "the event" to the *Elective Affinities*, which surely is a series of events, just as Goethe's *Novelle* is:

1882, pp. 411 f, as quoted in Ivo Braak, *Poetik in Stichworten*, (Würzburg: Universitätsdruckerei H. Stürtz, 1974) pp. 216 f.

[43] *"Die Novelle bedarf entscheidender Wendepunkte, so daß die Hauptmassen der Geschichte deutlich in die Augen fallen ... Um eine Novelle gut zu erzählen, muß man das alltägliche, was in die Geschichte mit eintritt, so kurz als möglich abfertigen, und nicht unternehmen es auf ungehörige Art aufstutzen zu wollen, nur bey dem Außerordentlichen und Einzigen verweilen, aber auch dieses nicht motivierend zergliedern ... sondern es eben positiv hinstellen, und Glauben dafür fodern ... Die Novelle ist eine Geschichte außer der Geschichte, sie erzählt folglich merkwürdige Begebenheiten, die gleichsam hinter dem Rücken der bürgerlichen Verfassungen und Anordnungen vorgefallen sind."* August Wilhelm Schlegel, *Vorlesungen über schöne Literatur und Kunst*, 3. Teil (1803/04), as quoted in Paulin, pp. 135 f.

Do you know what, we'll call it the novella; for what is a novella but an unprecedented event which has occurred. This is the real definition, and so much of what goes under the title "novella" in Germany is not a novella at all, but rather just a story or whatever else you want to call it. In that original sense of an unprecedented event, the novella is also present in the *Elective Affinities.*[44]

Of central concern to Ludwig Tieck are the blending of the realistic and the unexpected, hence in Goethe's terms *"sich ereignet"* (occurred) but also *"unerhört"* (unprecedented), a well focused execution of story-line consisting of *"eine Begebenheit,"* (an event) which, however, may be of greater or smaller proportion, as well as a *"Mittelpunkt"* (central point) which Tieck considers synonymous with peripiteia or *"Wendepunkt"* (turning point):

An occurrence should be told differently than an *Erzählung*; the latter should not be the same as a story, and the novella according to this pattern should above all else distinguish itself by the way it focuses intensely one great or modest occurrence, which, however easily it can happen, is yet wonderful, perhaps unique. This turning point in the plot - at which the story so unexpectedly changes direction, while yet developing the consequences with a certain naturalness, according to character and circumstances - will imprint itself the more strongly on the reader's imagination because the central concern, for all of its wonder, could, in other circumstances, equally well be a commonplace. [...] In each novella by Cervantes there is such a central point. ... Bizarre, whimsical, phantastic, somewhat jocular, garrulous, entirely taken up with descriptions even of minor matters,

---

[44] *"Wissen Sie was, wir wollen es die Novelle nennen; denn was ist eine Novelle anders als eine sich ereignete unerhörte Begebenheit. Dies ist der eigentliche Begriff, und so vieles, was in Deutschland unter dem Titel Novelle geht, ist gar keine Novelle, sondern bloß Erzählung oder was Sie sonst wollen. In jenem ursprünglichen Sinne einer unerhörten Begebenheit kommt auch die Novelle in den Wahlverwandtschaften vor."* Johann Wolfgang von Goethe, *Johann Peter Eckermann. Gespräche mit Goethe* letter of 29 Jan. 1827 (München: Karl Hanser Verlag, 1986) vol. 19, p. 203.

tragic as well as comic, profound as well as amusing, all these colours and characters are permitted by the real novella, only it will have that conspicuous turning point which differentiates it from all other genres of the *Erzählung*.[45]

It is interesting to note that Tieck is able to advocate a sharp focus as well as compatibility with a virtual host of subsidiary detail. Although it is not impossible to reconcile the two (by means of the concept of expanded motif complex, to be discussed within the second theory-grouping as described above), this seeming contradiction may be explained as the result of the basically inductive nature of the exercise: to devise a theory about an entire category of texts which is constantly expanding. The process can never be truly deductive, only hypothetically so, because of the ongoing accumulation of evidence and debate over the admissability of previous evidence. Nevertheless, some of the most significant elements in the history of the definition of the genre are determined here, even if the attempt to synthesize and integrate is not made. As the statements of these first critics accumulate, it can be clearly seen how establishing a framework becomes a somewhat elusive goal, especially when the insight has not yet been reached that a concept of genre must take into account a diachronic as well as synchronic continuum with an incumbent, essentially inductive method of inquiry. Expressed in spatial imagery, theory stagnates in a circular or concentric pattern when it fails to reflect the spiraling motion of its object. Boccaccio, the Schlegels, Goethe and Tieck are the major precedent-

---

[45] *"Eine Begebenheit sollte anders vorgetragen werden, als eine Erzählung; diese sich von Geschichte unterscheiden, und die Novelle nach jenen Mustern sich dadurch aus allen andern Aufgaben hervorheben, daß sie einen großen oder kleinern Vorfall in's hellste Licht stelle, der, so leicht er sich ereignen kann, doch wunderbar, vielleicht einzig ist. Diese Wendung der Geschichte, dieser Punkt, von welchem aus sie sich unerwartet völlig umkehrt, und doch natürlich, dem Charakter und den Umständen angemessen, die Folge entwickelt, wird sich der Phantasie des Lesers um so fester einprägen [...] In jeder Novelle des Cervantes ist ein solcher Mittelpunkt. ... Bizarr, eigensinnig, phantastisch, leicht witzig, geschwätzig und sich ganz in Darstellungen auch von Nebensachen verlierend, tragisch wie komisch, tiefsinnig und neckisch, all diese Farben und Charaktere läßt die ächte Novelle zu, nur wird sie jenen sonderbaren auffallenden Wendepunkt haben, die sie von allen anderen Gattungen der Erzählung unterscheidet."* Ludwig Tieck, *Schriften* Vorbericht zum 11. Band (Berlin: G. Reimer, 1829) pp. lxxxvi f.

setting theorists; Paul Heyse, although advocating some questionable items, does reflect and expand upon promising ones. The terms *"Silhouette"* and *"Falke,"* which are more often than not cited as his contribution to the standard corpus of novella theory, clearly illustrate a deference to tradition and the pitfalls of an inductive method which is not aware of itself. By *"Silhouette"* he means the reduction of the string of motifs to a brief and succinct description of its trajectory, or as he puts it, "if the attempt to recapitulate its content in a few lines is successful, in a way in which the old Italian masters gave their novellas short headings ..."[46] Using the example of Boccaccio's *Falkennovelle*, he cites the plot-résumé which precedes the text, singles out the motif of the falcon as "the specifics that make this story different from a thousand others ... "[47] Although *"Falke"* and *"Silhouette"* are presented as metaphors for the same concept, or more aptly put, of the same train of thought, they are two different things. *"Silhouette"* describes the main plot constituents or plot-building units, whereas *"Falke"* denotes a single particularly striking key motif. Hermann Pongs and Benno von Wiese will later seize upon the latter; Pongs refers to it as *"Dingsymbol,"* (inanimate object-symbol) entrenching it in its status as major genre-constituent. Under more critical scrutiny made possible by a vantage point much further on in the continuum, *"Falke"* and *"Silhouette"* will prove inadequate as genre-markers, since they are individual characteristics specific to a particular text, author and epoch; there is also no reason why they could not be present in the novel, lyric or drama, and they do not always occur in novellas which make up the accepted canon. Nevertheless, Heyse does discuss characteristics not bound to a particular period, not specific to an individual author or text, not restricted to a prescribed set of themes, and most importantly, he reflects upon the difference between novel and novella in terms of the latter's reduced proportions and perspective:

> Since long and short are concepts that are relative ... if there is to be more to it than labels, there must be something in the topic, in the problem, in the undeveloped kernel, which necessarily leads to one form or another. [...]

---

[46] *"ob der Versuch gelingt, den Inhalt in wenige Zeilen zusammenzufassen, in der Weise, wie die alten Italiener ihren Novellen kurze Überschriften gaben ...."* Paul Heyse, preface to *Deutscher Novellenschatz*, 1871, as quoted in Paulin, p. 149.
[47] *"das Spezifische, das diese Geschichte von tausend anderen unterscheidet ..."* Heyse, as cited in Paulin, p. 150.

Whereas the novel develops an extensive image of culture
and society and a small world-picture, actually intending
to show various groupings of overlapping or concentric
life spheres, the novella has as its task the portrayal of a
single conflict in a single sphere, a concept of fate or of
morality or of a clearly distinguished character image,
and within such a sphere to allow the relationships of the
individual characters to their world to shimmer through in
an abbreviated, allusive fashion. [...] Indeed here too
there will be no lack of hybrid forms. [...] Even our
greatest teller of stories with good reason let a novella-
like topic increase in proportion to become a novel, in
that he placed a significant problem within a richly
complex social life, although four people on a desert
island would have been just as able to experience the
forces of this natural law.[48]

Although couched in imagistically stylized language, several
important considerations emerge from this statement. It raises the
question of the tenor-vehicle relationship in texts which are quantitatively
dissimilar; it alludes to the possible thematic implications of a smaller
vehicle: more connotative than denotative; it sees the difference between

---

[48] *"Da lang und kurz relative Begriffe sind ... so muß, wenn es sich um mehr
als Namen handeln soll, schon im Thema, im Problem, im unentwickelten Keim
etwas liegen, das mit Notwendigkeit zu der einen oder anderen Form
hindrängt. [...] Wenn der Roman ein Cultur- und Gesellschaftsbild im
Großen, ein Weltbild im Kleinen entfaltet, bei dem es auf ein gruppenweises
Ineinandergreifen oder ein concentrisches Sichumschlingen verschiedener
Lebenskreise recht eigentlich abgesehen ist, so hat die Novelle in einem
einzigen Kreise einen einzelnen Conflict* [and not an "einzelne Begebenheit"],
*eine sittliche oder Schicksals-Idee oder ein entschieden abgegrenztes
Charakterbild darzustellen und die Beziehungen der darin handelnden
Menschen zu dem großen ganzen des Weltlebens nur in andeutender
Abbreviatur durchschimmern zu lassen. [...] Freilich wird es auch hier an
Übergangsformen nicht fehlen. [...] Hat doch unser größter Erzähler in
seinen Wahlverwandtschaften ein echt novellistisches Thema mit vollem Recht
zum Roman sich auswachsen lassen, indem er das bedeutende Problem mitten
in ein reich gegliedertes sociales Leben hineinsetzte, obwohl vier Menschen
auf einer wüsten Insel eben so gut in die Lage kommen konnten, die Gewalt
dieses Naturgesetzes an sich zu erfahren."* Heyse, as cited in Paulin, pp. 148 f.

small and large as a scale consisting of the same basic contituents with a flexible area of demarcation; it recognizes certain themes as inherently more amenable to a particular setting on the scale, but also realizes that another theme-type may generate either an expanded or contracted system of motifs in accordance with authorial intention; it admits the possibility of text-types which take up their places at various points along the scale without any attendant aesthetic depreciation. Heyse also reaffirms the predominant view that prose fiction in its best manifestations questions conventional wisdom, undermines entrenched views and moralities:

> The compendium of moral duties is by no means complete with the ten commandments; there is much that is not written, for which the scales of common morality are not sufficient, where a comic could instruct a vicar.[49]

In terms of chronology, this position is taken up first by A.W. Schlegel. Heyse is also aligning himself with Tieck on the question of thematic versatility at the expense of ignoring the constraints of established mores; Tieck's words are: "To the novella goes the privilege of overstepping accepted boundaries, depicting anomalies that are not directly in harmony with moral sensibilities" (Tieck, pp. 86 f.).[50] Heyse states that any topic which illuminates the "human condition" is admissable: "Every motivating factor of the human condition enters the sphere of creative possibility - the novella must remain true to this characteristic feature without restriction."[51] It is a view with which more recent critics such as Bakhtin, Neuschäfer, Schroeder and Silz still concur. The last point to be touched upon in Heyse's remarks is the insight he offers into the reasons for which prose in its more abbreviated and elliptic form outshone its epic counterpart in nineteenth-century Germany. Aside from a very distinct novella-tradition, Heyse points

---

[49] *"Der Kreis der sittlichen Aufgaben ist mit den zehn Geboten nicht abgeschlossen; Vieles ist, was nicht geschrieben steht, wofür die Pfundwage der alltäglichen Moral nicht ausreicht, und wo ein Komödiant einen Pfarrer lehren könnte."* Paul Heyse, An Frau Toutlemonde in Berlin, 1869, as quoted in Paulin, pp. 142 f.

[50] *"[Es ist] dieser Form der Novelle vergönnt, über das gesetzliche Mass hinweg zu schreiten, und Seltsamkeiten ... darzustellen, die nicht mit dem moralischen Sinn ... unmittelbar in Harmonie stehen."*

[51] *"Alles, was eine Menschenbrust bewegt, gehört in meinen Kreis - dieser Loosung wird die Novelle mit vollster Unumschränktheit treu bleiben müssen."* Heyse, pp. vii - xx, as quoted in Paulin, p. 147.

towards the gathering of empirical evidence in the sciences, the greater interest in particular facts in seeking out accurate sources for historical accounts, as well as the increasing opportunities for publication afforded by newspapers and journals as factors contributing to a type of literature which reflected a more cautious, tentative and pragmatic outlook. More important than the plausibility of each point is Heyse's recognition of a broad spectrum of possible reasons which would in concert favour one form of artistic expression over another. Schröder's criticism of E.K. Bennett, who ascribes the popularity of the shorter form to reduced leisure time, is well taken: "One must not be satisfied with lone assertions" (Schröder, p. 222).[52]   This holds true for the view that Germany, which did not become a nation state until 1871, lacked large urban cosmopolitan centres serving as a cultural focal point and catalyst, thus rendering a substantial, well-defined and broadly based cultural self-image as the requisite of the truly epic novel an impossibility. A simple equation of cause and effect misrepresents the complexity of cultural, social, historical and literary-historical conditions which have given rise to a literary artifact.

The final contribution to the theory of the novella which completes this overview of nineteenth-century theorists are comments made by Theodor Storm in 1888:

> The contemporary novella in its best manifestation is the epic sister of the drama and the most highly crafted form of prose writing. Similar to the drama, it deals with the most profound problems of human existence. In a similar way, in order to be complete, it requires a conflict as its central focus, which then determines the shape of the entire work; as a result, it requires the most unified of forms and the elimination of all that is extraneous to it. It is not only compatible with the the the highest artistic requirements, it demands that they be met.[53]

---

[52] "Man darf sich nicht mit einzelnen Feststellungen begnügen."
[53] "Die heutige Novelle in ihrer besten Vollendung ist die epische Schwester des Dramas und die strengste Form der Prosadichtung. Gleich dem Drama behandelt sie die tiefsten Probleme des Menschenlebens; gleich diesem verlangt sie zu ihrer Vollendung einen im Mittelpunkt stehenden Konflikt, von welchem aus das ganze sich organisiert, und demzufolge die geschlossenste Form und die Ausscheidung alles Unwesentlichen; sie duldet nicht nur, sie stellt auch die höchsten Forderungen der Kunst." Briefwechsel zwischen Theodor Storm und Gottfried Keller: Theodor Storm. Brief vom 14. August

Twentieth-century theorists latch on to most of the ideas of their nineteenth-century counterparts with varying degrees of success. Paul Ernst's remarks follow closely those of Storm and his predecessors inasmuch as he defines the genre as one which "...does not provide breadth and fullness ... but rather accomplishes its effect through unity and a highly integrated structure."[54] Ernst, apart from sharing Storm's view of the novella's kinship with the drama, further describes it as deciding a human fate "... in a single area" presenting its material "so to speak in abbreviated form" (p. 71).[55]

Hermann Malmede's *Wege zur Novelle* (Approaches to the Novella), a significant monograph which will be discussed here at some length, endorses this position, even to the point of echoing the title of Ernst's book *Der Weg zur Form* (An Approach to Form). Although Malmede presents some very compelling and carefully argued analyses, putting to rest some of the most confusing and contradictory spin-offs of the nineteenth-century canon of theory, he himself does not venture far from this orbit. Before reviewing the conclusions he reaches, a brief outline of his discussion of the major theorists is in order.

Malmede accomplishes this task through an organization of material into two categories, the first consisting of the more notable examples of inadequacy or *Typen der Verfehlung* (types of misconception), the second presenting what he considers to be more useful endeavours, or *Ansatzpunkte und Vorüber-legungen*. These attempts to define the genre are unsuccessful, as Malmede notes, because they apply criteria derived from other disciplines and areas of knowledge directly to texts. Having set aside or put to rest many untenable but more or less widely accepted assumptions, Malmede proceeds to secure the foundations for his own proposals. In this regard Robert Petsch is a major source.[56] Although the latter is said to have dispersed the formal characteristics amongst thematic and content-related observations,

---

1881 und "Vorrede," 1904, ed. Albert Köster, p. 119, as quoted in Braak, p. 218.
[54] *"... gibt nicht Breite und Fülle ..., sondern ... das Notwendige (,) und erzielt ihre Wirkung durch Geschlossenheit und strenge Fügung."* Paul Ernst, *Der Weg zur Form* (München, 1928) p. 391, as quoted in Hermann Malmede, *Wege zur Novelle* (Stuttgart: Kohlhammer, 1966) p. 139.
[55] *"... in einem einzigen Punkt ... gewissermaßen mit Kurzschrift."*
[56] Robert Petsch, "Epische Grundformen," *GRM* 16 (Heidelberg, 1928) and "Wesen und Formen der Erzählkunst," *Deutsche Vierteljahrsschrift für Literaturwissenschaft und Geistesgeschichte* vol. 20, Halle, 1942.

Malmede is able to assemble a catalogue of items which, in his view, are all form- or structure-related. Malmede writes:

The novella takes up a middle position between short and long narratives. Its contents therefore are "occurrences ... of considerable compactness," which can be "clearly discerned" within the "real overall scheme of events," which is itself "portrayed in a connotative and allusive fashion." [1942, 437] In accordance with its "small-stage proportions," events are played out in a "somewhat contracted way," therefore, at times, the narrator interjects in order to explain what has taken place" [1928, 382]; in the same vein: "the art of the novella-writer" expresses itself "through a certain conciseness" of the events portrayed [1928, 387]. Nevertheless, "events can easily stretch out over longer periods of time" and therefore highlight "several peaks, between which some of the valleys will remain in darkness (in contradistinction to the novel!)." [1942, 437] For this reason, the novella has "a linear configuration," requiring "the clarity of context" [1942, 438] and is limited to "the development of a single main motif." [1942, 441] It requires "rapid exposition, a compelling and convincing inner development, albeit with narrative gaps, and closure that is concise and significant: all in contradistinction to the actual long forms of narrative."[1942, 439] Thus the novella stands in close proximity to the drama (cf. [1942, 428]), and the novella-writer is really a "seer of scenes" [1942, 440] (Malmede, p. 96).[57]

---

[57] *"Die Novelle hat eine 'Mittelstellung zwischen Kurz- und Langerzählung.' Ihr Inhalt sind daher 'Vorgänge ... von merklicher Gedrungenheit,' die sich aus einem realen 'Gesamtgeschehen,' das in ihr nur 'mitempfunden und andeutend gestaltet' wird,' reinlich ablösen lassen.' [1942, 437] Ihrer 'kleinen Bühne' entspricht es, daß sich die Vorgänge 'mit einer gewissen Verengung abspielen' und darum zuweilen 'Zwischenbemerkungen des Epikers ... nachträglich ... auf den Sinn des Geschehens hinweisen' [1928, 382]; ebenso, daß 'die Kunst des ... Novellendichters' sich 'in einer gewissen Knappheit' der Darstellung äußert [1928, 387]. Trotzdem können die Vorgänge sich 'leicht über längere Zeiträume ausdehnen' und so 'mehrere Gipfel, zwischen denen manche Täler im Dunkel bleiben (im Gegensatz zum Roman!),' hervorbringen. [1942, 437] Aus diesem Grunde ist die Novelle*

By agreeing with this inventory, Malmede is agreeing with Paul Heyse and Theodor Storm, who, without any doubt, are the source of this material. The other major works cited by Malmede which advance similar if not identical hypotheses are those of Hans Heinrich Borcherdt[58] and Walter Silz. The former's comments show their lineage quite directly: "a greater or lesser occurrence is placed in the right light." The composition of the novella must be more deliberately crafted: "within its (the novella's) composition 'a certain occurrence becomes ... of central interest ... where all narrative strands merge and subsequently diverge (6)'" (Malmede, p. 136).[59] This is Storm's concept of a main event which serves as the organizing principle of composition. Silz is entirely forthcoming about his sources:

That the distinction between the Novelle and the novel is not simply one of length but of inner organization has been pretty generally recognized. The Novelle cannot be panoramic and leisurely; it must be concentrated and intensified, limited to one central conflict of crucial importance. Heyse had demanded this *"einzelner Konflikt;"* Storm reiterated it when he wrote to Erich Schmidt (October 9, 1879) that, in contrast to the novel, the Novelle calls for a stricter, more compact form and a conflict around which the whole is organized.

Time has a different value in the two narrative forms. The novel has more time at its disposal, and it tells its story in "historical," chronological order, at an unhurried pace: it hastens toward a climax, it tends to be

---

'*linear ausgedehnt*,' *bedarf der Klarheit der Zusammenhänge*' *[1942, 438] und ist auf den 'Entwicklungsraum eines einzigen Hauptmotivs' [1942, 441] beschränkt. Sie 'verlangt raschen Einsatz, eine sprungweise, doch hinreißende und überzeugende innere Entwicklung und einen knappen, vielsagenden Abschluß, alles im Gegensatz zu den eigentlichen Langformen' [1942, 439]. Sie steht so dem Drama nahe (vgl. [1942, 428]), und der Novellist ist recht eigentlich ein 'Szenenseher' [1942, 440].*
[58] Hans Heinrich Borcherdt, *Geschichte des Romans und der Novelle in Deutschland* I. Teil (Leipzig, 1926), as cited in Malmede, p. 202.
[59] "'ein kleiner oder großer Vorfall [wird] ins rechte Licht gestellt,' (p. 6) ... in ihr [der Komposition] tritt 'eine bestimmte Begebenheit ... in den Mittelpunkt ..., zu dem alle Fäden hinführen, von dem alle Fäden sich abspinnen.'"

all climax, without the before and after of the novel. Instead of unrolling past, present, and future in sequence, it seizes upon a fateful moment of dramatic presentness from which the past and the future are illuminated in a flash ... As to subject matter, the novel prefers the typical and social, the Novelle the singular and isolated. (Silz, pp. 6 f.).

The final aporia to be tackled is that of symbol and symbolism. Malmede develops a line of argument which he employs against Petsch, Hermann Pongs[60] and Benno von Wiese.[61] It conveys the position that it is false to speak of the symbolic potential of a genre - Petsch uses the term "*Symbolkraft*" (Malmede, p. 97): to do so is to include within one's concept of structure the thematic layer, the tenor, whereas Malmede restricts his definition of structure to the order of motifs within the vehicle: "... we restrict the term "structure" to the order of motifs within the content or plot-stratum" (Malmede, p. 97).[62] Any projection from the chain of motifs making up the vehicle is termed "background stratum," "strata structure," "stratification" and "vertical structure"; involvement with this area is an act of interpretation, a matter of dealing with specifics, whereas a discussion of genre must only concern itself with the non-specific: "Whatever strata are projected from the horizontal structure plane is a question of interpretation which targets specific information; it has nothing to do with genre" (Malmede, p. 99).[63] Nevertheless, the statement is also made that a symbol is indeed of relevance as it takes its place as a motif within the "horizontal structure" of the vehicle, projecting a thematic level which in turn may be the key to the organization of that same vehicle:

---

[60] Hermann Pongs, "Aufsätze zur Novelle," *Das Bild in der Dichtung Bd. II, Voruntersuchungen zum Symbol* (Marburg, 1939) pp. 97 ff., as cited in Malmede, p. 203.
[61] Benno von Wiese, *Die deutsche Novelle von Goethe bis Kafka, Bd. I, Interpretationen* 2nd. ed. (Düsseldorf: n.p., 1957); *Die deutsche Novelle von Goethe bis Kafka Bd. II* (Düsseldorf: August Bagel, 1962); *Novelle*, 2nd ed. (Stuttgart, 1963) as cited in Malmede, p. 204.
[62] "... *wir [beschränken] den Terminus Struktur auf die motivliche Ordnung innerhalb der Inhaltsschicht.*"
[63] "*Welche Schichten über die Strukturebene sich erheben, ist eine Frage der Werkinterpretation, die auf Bestimmtes zielt; eine Gattungsfrage ist es nicht.*"

Only when the thematic stratum evoked by the symbol becomes a form-determining principle, that is, when it requires a certain configuration of the relationship of motifs, which then creates a novella-typical structure, only then can one speak of the symbol as having generated the form of a novella; this is not a function of the symbol qua symbol, but of the symbol as motif. At the same time, this means that the genre is not defined by the mere presence of a symbol (Malmede, p. 97).[64]

It is erroneous to maintain that the meaning of a concatenation of dialogues, situations, scenes, actions, episodes and authorial mediation does not require an act of interpretation. For this statement suggests that to read a text is to observe an object which presents itself as a clearly defined, unmistakeably perceptible entity. It therefore also implies that it is possible to reconstruct accurately the process of an author's conception and execution of a given narrative strategy. "Following a story is not like following an argument: successful following does not entail the ability to predict the deductive conclusion, but only a sense of its rightness and acceptability ..." (Culler, *Structuralist Poetics,* p. 224). Ultimately, plot-building elements are a "temporal projection of thematic structures [...]; 'to make sense of their span they need fictive concords with origins and ends.'"[65] Malmede himself states, with respect to "foreground" and "background" constructs that "Symbols within a structure can determine in part or entirely the 'single-strand characteristic' of the chain of motifs" (Malmede, p. 156).[66]

In his book's concluding chapter entitled *"Folgerungen"* (Conclusions), Malmede, as a preamble to his own definition, makes the following statement:

---

[64] *"Allein wenn die vom Symbol angespielte thematische Schicht zu einem formgebenden Prinzip wird, indem sie eine bestimmte Verhältnissetzung von Motiven verlangt, die dann eine typisch novellenhafte Struktur erzeugt, kann das Symbol eine Novellenform hervorbringen; aber eben nicht als Symbol schlechthin, sondern als ein motivlich bestimmtes. Womit zugleich gesagt ist, daß durch die bloße Tatsache eines Symbols die Gattung nicht definibel ist."*
[65] Frank Kermode, *The Sense of an Ending: Studies in the Theory of Fiction* (New York: Oxford University Press, 1967) p. 7.
[66] *"Symbolbezüge können teilweise oder gänzlich die Einsträngigkeit ihrer Motivkette herstellen."*

On balance one draws the following conclusions: the concept "novella" can be and must be derived *a priori* as a category of the epic; only the area of possibilities within which the abstract basic form is to be threshed out - only this area in all its diversity is to be examined empirically (Malmede, p. 153).[67]

That is undoubtedly correct, but the parameters of this "area of possibilities" which Malmede designates, are too narrow. According to his conception of a genre definition, it must enable a clear perception of what constitutes its uniqueness when compared with neighbouring genres, yet he makes no mention of the short story, nor does he elaborate upon the term *"das Epische."* It might be argued that as it is one of the most elementary categories of literary theory, it requires no elaboration. Yet such a term may encompass texts as different as *Ulysses* and the *Iliad.* Although Malmede can hardly be taken to task for a lack of awareness of a debate occurring primarily after the date of publication of his monograph, his deliberations suffer from the omission of the novel and the short story as related text types within the contingent of modern prose narrative. Certainly, the near hegemony of the short story as the most popular form of short to medium-length fiction in post-war German literature, often touted as the successor to the novella, is an area which deserves more attention. In fact all of the theory and its empirical corroboration are restricted largely to pre-twentieth-century sources. Malmede does not address the relationship between novella and short story, and his discussion of the designation *Erzählung* is of a somewhat abbreviated nature:

> *"Erzählung"* (story) says nothing more, but that something is being narrated, indicating only the most general formal characteristics without providing any further determinants. [...] The requirement that the novella be given parameters that set it apart from the *"Erzählung"* is therefore an invalid one; rather, the

---

[67] *"Das Fazit: der Begriff Novelle kann und muß, als ein Unterbegriff des Epischen, apriori gebildet werden; allein der Möglichkeitsbereich, in dem die abstrakte Grundform umspielbar ist, ist in seiner Mannigfaltigkeit empirisch zu untersuchen."*

former is a special type of the latter" (Malmede, p. 154).[68]

In spite of the amputation of the vertical from the horizontal axis and the lack of a clearly defined rubric under which the novella would be subsumed as a particular sub-class, Malmede proceeds with a definition of that sub-class, parts of which do not bear critical scrutiny and others which do.   The first criterion is that of the single event, the *"Einzelereignis"* or *"Begenbenheit."* Goethe's modifier *"unerhört"* is rejected on the basis of Boccaccio's formulation "*Novella o favola o parabola o istoria*" (novellas or fables or parables or stories) which would scale down the "novelty"-requirement from one of near incredulity to the more general "worthy of being heard." (*Sie soll bloß ... hörenswert sein.*).   The assertion "*Daß dieser 'unerhört' sein soll, ist nirgends verlangt.*" (That this ought to be something unheard-of or not yet heard of, is not required anywhere) is a curious statement, since Malmede is searching the "area of possibilities" (*Möglichkeitsbereich*) as constituted by the theoretical canon for those elements which he has not yet eliminated.   Of necessity, *"unerhört"* is eliminated, along with the questioning of conventional wisdoms elucidated by August Wilhelm Schlegel or Paul Heyse, since, from Malmede's vantage point, such thematic and interpretative considerations cannot be expressed in terms of abstractions of form.

The requirements of a *"Vorgeschichte"* and where given, a *"Nachgeschichte"* are treated as part of the requirement that all narrative must be, by definition, comprehensible.   It is not clear why these expositional and closural strategies are particular to the novella, nor is it clear why a novella could not begin *in medias res* or finish in the same way, and be incomprehensible.   It is also not clear how *"Vorgeschichte"* and *"Nachgeschichte"* are intrinsically related to the novella's abbreviated structure.[69]   Malmede goes on to say: "The genre already has its basic

---

[68] "'*Erzählung' besagt nicht mehr, als daß überhaupt erzählt wird, und gibt allein die allgemeinsten Formbestimmtheiten ohne jede Festlegung an. [...] Die Forderung, die 'Novelle' gegen die 'Erzählung' abzu-grenzen, als wären beide gleichartige Gattungen, besteht demnach zu Unrecht; vielmehr ist jene eine Sonderform von dieser.*"

[69] Theodor Fontane's *Schach von Wuthenow* may be cited as an example of a novella which begins with the initial representation of a full-fledged scene. Thus the "antecedents indispensable to the understanding of the story" permitting that the reader "be informed of the time and place of the action, of the nature of the fictive world peculiar to the work or in other words, of the

form determined through the comprehensible narration of one, single occurrence (p. 155)."[70] But "*eine Begebenheit*," if one re-examines Goethe's definition, is used to describe the events of the *Elective Affinities*. The first part of the core of Malmede's definition is the implementation of statements previously credited to Petsch, Borcherdt and Silz:

> The novella follows a line leading to a central occurrence [...] and from here the line, of which there is only one, not several, may be drawn away, tracing effects and consequences. Its sharp focus and single-strand configuration, employed to delineate one occurence, the resulting relative brevity and elimination of extraneous subsidiary material (unless the latter is clearly a functional element of the overall structure) differentiate it from the novel and other epic genres, which, in their respective individual components, contain surplus material that is not a direct function of structure (Malmede, p. 155).[71]

Malmede further elaborates the proposed model through a more precise description of textual components comprising the novella's linear disposition:

> One can therefore recognize a novella through a chain of motifs that moves towards a central occurrence and, wherever applicable, away from this central event.

---

canons of probability operating in it; of the history, appearance, traits and habitual behaviour of the dramatis personae; and of the relations between them" are provided through an expositional strategy of distribution within the opening pages of the work. Meir Steinberg, *Expositional Modes and Temporal Ordering in Fiction* (Baltimore: Johns Hopkins University Press, 1978) p. 40.

[70] "*Durch das verständliche Erzählen lediglich einer Begebenheit ist die Grundform der Gattung bereits festgelegt.*"

[71] "*Die Novelle verfolgt eine zu dem Mittelpunktsereignis [...] hinführende und gegebenenfalls seine Folgen ausziehende Linie, nicht mehrere Linien. Ihre an ein Ereignis gebundene Einsträngigkeit und Zielstrebigkeit, deren Folge ihre relative Kürze und die Ausschaltung von Nebenhandlungen, es sei denn in strenger Funktionalität, ist, unterscheiden sie vom Roman und andren epischen Gattungen, die in ihren Einzelteilen jeweils, funktional gesehen, Überschüssiges enthalten.*"

Furthermore, the parts of the chain are not autonomous, but rather - and this a contradiction of the epic principle - are functional elements. They can, however, due to thematic or mimetic considerations, become more or less independent. If, in doing so, they exceed proportional limits, they exceed the limits of the genre. [...] Increasing the proportions yet maintaining a balance can be accomplished through the technique of *leitmotif* and *leitsymbol.* Even individual motifs can become more extensive and subsume other motifs, especially if they themselves must be conveyers of theme. In such a case one speaks of motif-complexes.[72]

As Malmede is wont to disprove a number of theoretical utterances on the basis of one example of a novella which does not conform to the theory, it can in like manner be shown that Brentano's *Geschichte vom braven Kasperl und dem schönen Annerl* may be seen to invalidate the concept of a single occurrence as a fundamental characteristic. It is interesting to note that Malmede mentions Boccaccio's *Falkennovelle* as an unusual example of the genre, inasmuch as two chains of motifs lead to the central occurrence of the scene of courtly hospitality and sacrifice of the falcon. In Brentano's novella, the Annerl and Kasperl-segments never come together; they are within the same motif-, leitmotif- and symbol-complex, yet remain insular with respect to one another as cause-and-effect sequences. Nevertheless, the Malmede-model offers a foundation and a point of departure and comparison in considering subsequent monographs dealing specifically with the novella, as well as with the theory of the short story qua narrative prose as produced by Anglo-American scholars.

---

[72] *"Man kann also die Novelle daran erkennen, daß in ihr eine Motivkette zum Mittelpunktsereignis hin- und von ihm gegebenenfalls wieder fortführt. Dabei haben die Glieder der Kette keine Selbständigkeit, sondern eine, dem epischen Prinzip angeblich widersprechende, Funktionalität, können sich aber zugunsten der Thematik oder Realistik mehr oder minder verselbständigen. Werden dabei die Proportionen gesprengt, so auch die Gattung. [...] Die Verschiebung der Proportionen kann durch Leitmotiv- und Leitsymboltechnik ausgeglichen werden. Aber auch die einzelnen Motive können umfangreicher, in sich gegliederter werden, besonders dann, wenn sie selbst thematische Bezüge in sich aufnehmen müssen. In solchem Fall sprechen wir von Motivkomplexen."*

In bringing this final portion of the discussion on theory to a conclusion, two works which fall into the former category, those of Judith Leibowitz[73] and Martin Swales[74] offer valuable insight into the viability of an extension of Malmede's proposal; the theory of the short story will be represented by a collection of articles by Charles E. May,[75] by Norman Friedman[76] and Valerie Shaw.[77] Lastly, a typology of literary discourse which addresses the structural relationship between content and form as described by David Lodge[78] will be considered as a solution to the Malmedian hiatus between the vertical and horizontal axes of texts.

Leibowitz chooses novellas which are decidedly at the longer end of the scale in order to develop her theory: among others these include *Der Tod in Venedig, Der Schimmelreiter, Bahnwärter Thiel, Kleider machen Leute,* and *Die Geschichte vom braven Kasperl und dem schönen Annerl.* For these and other novellas, the concept of "*Einsträngigkeit*," of single-strand-narration, if interpreted as a line of cause-and-effect rather than thematic cohesion, can prove somewhat daunting to apply, yet that does not negate its appropriateness to many other examples of the genre. Leibowitz' basic premise is that "the techniques of the short story and the short novel, even when they coincide, serve a different narrative purpose from that of the novella" (p. 19). This narrative purpose is one of intensity and expansion:

> Whereas the short story limits material and the novel extends it, the novella does both in such a way that a special kind of narrative structure results, one which produces a generically distinct effect: the double effect of intensity and expansion. Since the motifs in a novella are usually part of a closely associated cluster of themes, the same material remains in focus, while in the novel the central focus shifts. By means of this treatment of theme,

---

[73] Judith Leibowitz, *Narrative Purpose in the Novella* (The Hague, Paris: Mouton, 1974).

[74] Martin Swales, *The German Novelle* (Princeton: Princeton University Press, 1977).

[75] Charles E. May, ed., *Short Story Theories* (N.p.: Ohio University Press, 1976).

[76] Norman Friedman, *Form and Meaning in Fiction* (Athens: University of Georgia Press, 1975).

[77] Valerie Shaw, *The Short Story* (London and New York: Longman, 1983).

[78] David Lodge, *The Modes of Modern Writing. Metaphor, Metonymy, and the Typology of Modern Literature* (Ithaca: Cornell University Press, 1977).

which I call *theme-complex*, all the motifs are interrelated, permitting the novella to achieve an intensive and constant focus on the subject. At the same time, since the implications of each motif are suggested but not developed, the novella is eminently a narrative suggestion. This outward expansion from a limited focus is the effect of the typical plot construction of the novella. [...] The action is generally compressed by means of repetitive structure ... [whose] ... use enables the author to rework or redevelop themes and situations he has already developed. The repetition may consist of parallel situations which are counterparts to those already presented, or parallel motifs which represent different aspects of the theme complex (pp. 16f.).

This approach owes much to Malmede, or certainly is foreshadowed by his work, as does the position taken with respect to the traditionally accepted characteristics of the genre (p. 26). Leibowitz correctly sees that it is impossible to speak of a cluster of motifs without the organizing principle of theme and theme-complex to guide the interpretative procedure of this culling and sorting into groups. She also offers a more differentiated description of narrative sequences, but in doing so, cannot account for many examples of the novella which do not exhibit a more complex and extensive structure; these, it would seem, must now be called short stories. Nevertheless, Leibowitz does offer a system of comparison which allows short story, novella and novel to be considered as variants resulting from different combinations and proportions of the same narrative constituents.

The typical novella structure first builds to a revelation or recognition of a character or situation, but then achieves an effect of greater intensity by redevelopment. In continuing to develop the situation, the novella also reinforces the motifs already established. Instead of portraying an isolated truth, the novella expands the short story's revelation, so that the characters and situation are also seen evolving ... [...] Without undertaking the extensive development of the novel, the novella still develops its material, rather than merely presenting it. In its presentation and further examination of something problematic, the novella uses a structure particular to

itself. The novella's double aesthetic goal is to be both
micro- and macrocosmic, to go beyond revelation to a
testing out, to a novelistic treatment (in microcosm). [...].
The novel uses a series of complications. This is clearly
evident in the picaresque novel ... But other types of
novels may substitute for the separate encounters of the
picaro, different angles of vision, a multitude of
characters, or re-examination of a situation from different
points of view. [...] Because of these various
subordinate resolutions, the novel produces an effect of
diffuseness. [...]. The short story works toward a single
resolution; hence its effect of limitation (pp. 78 f.).

The caveat which ought to accompany this statement is that a
comparative treatment of the German and Anglo-American short prose
canons and theories reveals that short story and novella are virtually
interchangeable terms. Some theorists translate the German *Novelle* into
the English "short story."[79] In addition, there is considerable evidence to
show that a comparison of the theories of both traditions will result in a
much higher proportion of similarity than difference,[80] in spite of attempts
to prove otherwise.[81]

---

[79] Harry Steinhauer in his article "Towards a Definition of the Novella,"
Seminar, Vol. VI, No. 2, June 1970, makes reference to some of the criteria set
forth in defining the short story by Edgar Allan Poe as an example of the "vast
theoretical writing on this subject." (p. 155).
[80] In her monograph *Die Kurzgeschichte*, Ruth Kilchenmann initially attempts
to establish a difference between short story and novella: "The dense, logical,
cause-and-effect formal structure of the novella is clearly different from the
surface-skimming, arabesque-like expansiveness or haste and leaving of blank
spaces of the short story." (*"Die dichte, kausal und logisch aufgebaute Form
der Novelle hebt sich deutlich ab von der oft sprunghaften, oft arabeskenhaft
erweiterten oder gerafften und aussparenden Gestaltung der Kurzgeschichte"*).
Perhaps aware of the "shakiness" of the argument, she goes on to say: "... it is
rather difficult and hardly possible to define clearly the boundaries between
them." (*"...es [ist] schon schwierig und kaum möglich, Novelle und
Kurzgeschichte voneinander klar abzugrenzen ..."*). Ruth Kilchenmann, *Die
Kurz-geschichte* (Stuttgart: Kohlhammer, 1971) pp. 17 f.
[81] A good number of German critics have extended the traditional methodology
applied to the novella to define the short story. Thus Erna Kritsch Neuse in her
monograph *Die deutsche Kurzgeschichte* (Bonn: Bouvier, 1980), makes
sweeping statements about two genres in the most arbitrary manner: "The

short story narrator no longer interprets the world directly but rather indirectly; this he does by gathering together all of the building blocks of his world and erecting a building before the reader, who must then decide whether the building is habitable (p. 224). Here the novella takes the opposite path. Its characters are for the most part extensively portrayed [!], so that their actions ultimately appear to be motivated and psychologically grounded" (p. 226). ("*Der Kurz-geschichtenerzähler deutet die Welt nicht mehr direkt, sondern indirekt, indem er alle Bausteine seiner Welt zusammenträgt und vor dem Leser das Gebäude errichtet, aber diesem die Entscheidung überläßt, ob es bewohnbar ist*" (p. 224). "*Die Novelle nimmt hier den umgekehrten Weg. In ihr werden die Figuren meistens ausführlich charakterisiert [!], so daß ihre Handlungen schließlich motiviert und psychologisch begründet erscheinen*" (p. 226). She goes on to say that: "In contradistinction to the novella, the portrayal of atmosphere and mood recede to the background (p.237)". ("*Im Gegensatz zur Novelle tritt die Darstellung der Atmosphäre, der Stimmung in den Hintergrund*") (p. 237). Reference is also made to Klaus Doderer's Definition: "It (the short story) is the artistic depiction of a particular segment of time in a person's life, in which the orderly sequence of events of that life are disrupted by an unforeseen occurrence. This disruption (turn of fate) places the hero in an exceptional situation to which he must react" (Doderer, p. 40 f.). ("*Sie [die Kurzgeschichte] ist die künstlerische Gestaltung eines bestimmten Zeitabschnittes aus dem Leben eines Menschen, in dem der gesetzmäßige Ablauf dieses Lebens durch ein unverhofftes Ereignis gestört wird. Diese Störung (Schicksalsbruch) stellt den Helden in eine Ausnahmssituation, auf die er reagieren muß*"). Klaus Doderer, *Die Kurzgeschichte in Deutschland*, (Darmstadt, 1972) pp. 40 f. The latter also maintains that "The short story differs from the novella, roughly speaking, in that any attempt to recapitulate it in a few lines almost always fails" (p. 154). ("*Die Kurzgeschichte unterscheidet sich, grob gesagt [!], von der Novelle dadurch, daß bei ihr der Versuch, sie in wenigen Zeilen zusammen-zufassen, fast immer mißlingt*") (p. 154). Manfred Durzak sees the difference as socially and politically determined: "The mediation between the reality portrayed in the short story and the reader's experience of reality, which must be possible, should also be the given prerequisite for the reader's ability to identify with the short story characters. This is why the short story, in vivid contrast with the novella, is a democratic literary form of the present [!], obtaining its material from the reader's experience of reality, introducing individualized characters with which the reader can identify" (p. 307). ("*Die Transmission, die zwischen der Realitäts-darstellung der Kurzgeschichte und der Realitätserfahrung des Lesers möglich sein muß, sollte auch als Identifikationsvoraussetzung zwischen Leser und Personal der Kurzgeschichte gegeben sein. Von daher erklärt es sich, daß die Kurzgeschichte in deutlichem Unterschied zur Novelle eine*

*demokratische   Gegenwartsform   ist   [!],   ihre   Stoffe   aus   der
Wirklichkeitserfahrung des Lesers nimmt und individualisierte Personen
vorführt, in denen sich der Leser wiederzuerkennen vermag")* (p. 307). There
are also major differences when comparing style and technique: "Summarizing
this down to a formula, one could say that the short story, in terms of language,
does not provide an extensive, but rather an intensive artistic form. It does not
expand its language structures, but rather condenses and reduces them, thereby
charging them with meaning. An indication of the brilliance of this literary
form is the manner in which it thus opens itself more readily to the reader's
understanding, the latter easily recognizing its transparent surface and making
a gradual discovery of the formal foundations beneath this surface - all this in
contrast with the novella, which requires that the reader be bourgeois-educated
and possess a good knowledge of literature; the novella artificially restricts its
effect-potential through the language techniques it employs" (p. 308).
*("Formelhaft zusammengefaßt, könnte man sagen, daß die Kurzgeschichte
nicht extensiv sprachlich gestaltet, sondern intensiv: sie dehnt die
sprachlichen Strukturen nicht aus, sondern komprimiert, verknappt sie und lädt
sie dadurch mit Bedeutung auf. Daß sie sich dadurch dem Verständnis der
Leser annähert, der ihre einfach scheinende Oberfläche leichter erkennt und
erst allmählich die Systeme der formalen Unterkellerung, die sich darunter
befinden, entdeckt, ist ja eher ein Zeichen ihrer formalen Brillanz im
Unterschied zur Novelle, die den bildungsbürgerlichen, literaturkundigen
Leser voraussetzt und ihr Wirkungspotential durch ihre sprachlichen
Techniken künstlich eingrenzt")* (p. 308). Finally, Ludwig Rohner defines the
"*Kurzgeschichte*" as comprising 500 to 1500 words; the "*Erzählung*" 1500 to
15,000, the "*Novelle*" 15,000 to 50,000 and the novel anything beyond. He is
also more specific: "One can call the novella a dramatic anecdote, in which
case one must be aware of the considerable over-simplification in doing so. [!]
One cannot trace any line of development from the dramatic anecdote and the
novella [presumably one is now dealing with not one but two genres] to the
short story. The short story has nothing in common with the novella, they are
in no way related. [...] The contrast is obvious. At most one can speak of
them as being in the same neighbourhood: in the literary history of the
narrative, the short story has taken over from the novella, taking up the space
left vacant. The short story can do without the point or denouement (*die
Pointe*). When one does find a point or denouement, then this almost always
turns out to be of a stylistic nature." *("Man kann die Novelle als dramatische
Anekdote bezeichnen, wobei man sich der beträchtlichen Vereinfachung
bewußt sein muß. Von der dramatischen Anekdote und der Novelle fährt kein
Entwicklungsstrang zur Kurzgeschichte. Die Kurzgeschichte teilt nichts
Gemeinsames mit der Novelle, sie steht mit ihr in keinerlei Verwandtschaft.
[...] Der Gegensatz ist offenkundig. Man kann höchstens von einer*

Norman Friedman's definition of "what makes a short story short" is of particular interest, as it parallels Malmede's approach. With respect to the reasons for which a writer would favour a shorter prose-form, Malmede states: "The novella format is brought about in each instance either as a result of the particular structure of the topic, or because of (a writer's) preference for the novella format"(p. 148).[82] Friedman cites "Two fundamental reasons: the material itself may be of small compass; or the material, being of broader scope, may be cut for the sake of maximizing the artistic effect" (p. 170). He also distinguishes between simple changes and static actions on the one hand, and complex changes and dynamic actions on the other:

> ... a static story simply shows its protagonist in one state or another and includes only enough to reveal to the reader the cause or causes of which this states [sic] is a consequence, while a dynamic story brings its protagonist through a succession of two or more states, and thus must include the several causal stages of which these states are the consequences. Thus a static story will normally be shorter than a dynamic one. (pp. 174 f.).

The more expansive complex change or dynamic action requires the following parts:

> (1) a precipitating cause to bring him [the protagonist] into his first state, (2) a counterplot action to represent the consequences of that state, (3) an inciting cause which will serve to bring him out of the counterplot and on towards the opposite state, (4) a progressive action to represent him in the process of change, and (5) a culmination where the process is completed (p. 180).

Nachbarschaft sprechen: die Kurzgeschichte hat die Novelle in der Geschichte der Erzählformen abgelöst und die freigewordene Stelle besetzt. Die Kurzgeschichte kann auf die Pointe verzichten. Wenn man in ihr eine Pointe findet, dann enthüllt diese sich fast immer als Stilpointe"). Ludwig Rohner, *Theorie der Kurzgeschichte* (Frankfurt: Athenaum, 1973) p. 119.

[82] *"Das Zustandekommen der Novellenform hängt also im Einzelfall entweder von der zu ihr hindrängenden Eigenstruktur des gewählten Inhalts; oder von der Neigung zur verselbständigten Novellenform ...[ab]"*

Friedman's first criterion corresponds to Malmede's *"Vorgeschichte,"* the fifth to the *"Nachgeschichte"*; the terms plot, counterplot, opposite state and progressive action are commensurate with Malmede's positing of *"verschiedene Gipfel,"* (different peaks) albeit subject to the principles of *"Einsträngigkeit,"* (one, single chain of motifs) and *"Ziels-trebigkeit"* (sharp focus). Friedman's concept is one which describes the short story as comprising an "action," always in the singular, therefore equatable to Malmede's *"Mittelpunktsereignis"* (central occurrence). Friedman stresses "... the optimal degree of intelligibility ... in combination with the greatest economy of means" (p. 179). Malmede speaks of "a single event together with elements necessary for its comprehension"[83] as well as the functional nature (*Funktionalität*) of every element in the narrative sequence (p. 155).

The two definitions also have in common the weakness of not being able to account for texts which do not present a discursive sequence of causes and effects, "where objects are not determinate and the surfaces are not organized according to representational outline" (Shaw, p. 12).

Much that has been said of the novella within the German tradition has also been said about the short story by Anglo-American scholars. Shaw points to at least two possible short story configurations: one in which the striking image of one phase of a process or action is created, (p. 14) the other which makes use of repetitive structure. (p. 74). It is no coincidence that Leibowitz and Shaw share this latter view, even if they are describing allegedly different genres, since their common source of material is Henry James' reflections on the nature of the shorter prose text.

Of the novella E.K. Bennett has said: "... it is noticeable that all the finest examples of the Novelle in German literature stand at the very boundaries of the form and strain it to the utmost."[84] Shaw speaks of the "individual talent that unsettles the short story out of a tired formula and back into the experimentation which is its forte" (p. 19). Although it has already been shown that this strong proclivity towards innovation and experimentation is a characteristic of all modern prose narrative, the position has also been taken that the shorter form provides an even greater measure of flexibility and potential to this end:

> Certainly the short story has always been more flexible
> and open to experiment than the novel. [...] the strongest

---

[83] *"Ein einziges Ereignis samt dem zu seinem Verständnis nötigen Zubehör."*
[84] E.K. Bennett, *A History of the German Novelle* 2nd ed. (Cambridge: Cambridge University Press, 1965) p. 160.

convention of the novel, prolonged coherence of tone, to which even the most experimental novels must conform unless it is to fall apart, is false to the nature of whatever can be grasped of human reality. [...] The short story, as a form and as a *kind of creative vision* must be better equipped to attempt the capture of ultimate reality at a time when (whichever way you choose to see it) we are drawing nearer to the mystery of life or are losing ourselves in a bellowing wilderness of mirrors, as the nature of reality becomes more fully understood or more bewilderingly concealed by the discoveries of science and the proliferation of communication media outside the printed word.[85]

This would seem to suggest that thematic and structural coherence is more manifest in the novel: the greater the volume of material, the greater the amplitude and therefore more numerous the points of disclosure of its underlying rules of production, of sense-giving reference and of creative trajectory. Paul Heyse's remarks on the novella's specular quality are strikingly similar to Gordimer's, made a century later:

At a time when politics and philosophy were once again becoming more factually grounded, a time in which the writing of history was based upon the research of source material and in which physics and chemistry had their methods based on experimentation - this also had to be a time favourable to artistic texts in which the occurrence, the event, the particular case would permit this type of writing to come into its own in a variety of ways - without any higher claim to absolute moral or poetic value.[86]

---

[85] Nadine Gordimer, "'The Flash of Fireflies,'" *Short Story Theories* ed. Charles May, p. 179.
[86] *"Eine Zeit, die in Politik und Philosophie sich zunächst wieder auf den Boden des Tatsächlichen stellte, in der Geschichtsschreibung die Quellenforschung, in Physik und Chemie das Experiment ihrer Methode zu Grunde legte, mußte auch einer Dichtungsart günstig sein, in der die Begebenheit, das Ereignis, der einzelne Fall so vielfach ohne alle höheren Ansprüche auf absoluten sittlichen und dichterischen Werth zu ihrem Rechte kommen."* As cited in Paulin, p. 147.

Heyse also refers to the dissemination of information, but in the sense of a direct impact of the newspaper format on literature as well as with reference to an increase in the number of facts and the "news" made available to a reading public. Martin Swales, in remarks leading up to a discussion of Kleist's *Erdbeben in Chile* and *Die Marquise von O* writes of an interpretative tension that is central to the novella:

> I would argue that the mainspring of much novelle writing is the contact between an ordered and reliably interpreted universe on the one hand and an experience or set of experiences that would appear to conflict utterly with any notion of order or manageable interpretation on the other (Swales, p. 28).

This "*Schein und Sein*" dichotomy is referred to by Valerie Shaw as the "Chestertonian paradox"; she quotes Chesterton on the relationship between this motif and the short story: "Our modern attraction to the short story is not an accident of form; it is a sign of a real sense of fleetingness and fragility: it means that existence is only an impression, and, perhaps, only an illusion" (Shaw, p. 17). Swales also describes this tension as one between the subjective and the objective, between the poetic and the prosaic, common to all realistic fiction with a distinction only in degree (p. 37).

Swales speaks of the "hermeneutic challenge that is at the heart of the nineteenth-century novelle"; (p. 44). Malmede takes issue with the use of symbol as a genre constituent, yet theorists are, more often than not, drawn to this characteristic: Swales interprets the "symbolic disposition of the genre" as "the interpretative gamble [which] does not readily yield an image of an intact world" (p. 44). Richard Kostelanetz makes similar claims about the short story, and, it must be noted, classifies such attributes as exclusively "American," just as some German scholars have thought of the novella as an exclusively German literary phenomenon:

> But in America, as nowhere else, short story writers from the times of Washington Irving, Hawthorne, Poe and Melville to the present have always discarded realism for the elliptical and symbolic representational styles. To this day, the best American short stories have presented (1) experiences which are not typical but so extreme that they strain the reader's 'willing suspension of disbelief,' and (2) actions which are not explained by the author but

are presented without editorial comment for the reader's interpretation. The author depicts in depth rather than in breadth, and the world described is not varied and definable but narrow, disordered and ambiguous. What American short story writers have always offered is a vision of life that must transcend reportage with metaphor if it is to succeed as literature.[87]

Kostelanetz also claims that the short story as a medium is "more metaphoric than the novel" (p. 214).

David Lodge uses artistic prose to demonstrate the corollary he develops to Jakobson's definition of the poetic function: whereas Jakobson states that "the poetic function projects the principle of equivalence from the axis of selection into the axis of combination," this describes the function of metaphor in poetry. Jakobson defines prose as a metonymic mode; although metonymy is a tropological figure of non-logical deletion, it is, as he states, "the appropriate medium with which to describe logical relationships between concepts or entities or events" (p. 88). Lodge is able to demonstrate the metaphoric potential of prose with a corresponding "weakening of metonymic or syntagmatic relationships - i.e. the relationships of contiguity in time and space, and of cause and effect" (Lodge, p. 104). To this end, Lodge uses D.H. Lawrence's short story *The Rainbow*, in which metaphor "feeds on" metonymy (p. 164). Lodge shows how realistic particulars are turned into symbols and how descriptive metaphors become thematic ones. It must be noted, however, that he does not restrict his analysis to shorter prose pieces.

Both the German novella and the American short story have, in their respective traditions, been defined in terms of the succinctness of a metonymic foreground-vehicle which, in its singular and limited scope, exploits the figurative potential of the thematic, metaphoric axis. This is the fundamental structure of the model to be applied to the texts in the following discussion. As noted in the Introduction, the specifics of this model are: a restricted number of thematically interlocking motif complexes; cyclical, parallel and repetitive structure; a truncated line of cause and effect; verisimilitude predicated upon ellipsis and ambiguity; intertextuality and metatextuality. In each of the following chapters, a novella will be compared with a text of similar length by the same author but with a differing generic label, i.e. *Erzählung, Roman*, in order to determine the significance of these differences. With the exception of the

---

[87] Richard Kostelanetz, "Notes on the American Short Story Today," *Short Story Theories*, ed. Charles E. May, p. 215.

second Dürrenmatt text in the following pairs, these are, as cited above: *Atlantik-Novelle* and *Die Berliner Antigone* by Rolf Hochhuth; *The Assignment* and *Der Sturz* by Friedrich Dürrenmatt;[88] *Runaway Horse* and *Jenseits der Liebe* by Martin Walser.

---

[88] Friedrich Dürrenmatt, *Der Sturz* (Zürich: Diogenes, 1985). Subsequent quotations are from this edition.

Chapter Three

Rolf Hochhuth's Atlantik-Novelle

This collection of shorter prose texts first published in 1985 carries the title of the lead text of the anthology. The other work of this compilation which bears any reference to this particular generic affiliation is *Grüninger-Novelle*; *Die Berliner Antigone*, having first appeared in 1958, received a sufficient degree of acclaim for the words of its reviewers to be included on the jacket of this new anthology. George Steiner mentions this work in his monograph on the Antigone-theme, referring to it as a novella, as does the information on the jacket.[89] As the collection, in addition to taking its title from the lead text, also carries the designation *"Erzählungen"* and contains pieces specifically referred to as novellas, anecdotes, a letter, and in one case a monologue written in free verse, it is plausible to argue that any piece not otherwise defined is an *"Erzählung."* There is also evidence to suggest that each text is tied in to the collection through a set of themes and motifs anchored in the first text of the anthology. It remains to be determined to what extent, if any, the presence or lack of such labels is a significant indication of varying structural possibilities generated by a given theme or theme-complex or by a given, traditional narrative structural scheme.[90]

Each of the texts to be considered here deals with the topic of death precipitated in an arbitrary manner by the perils of war, specifically by events of the Second World War. The texts contain references to documents and statements made by historical figures as well as occurrences whose facticity may be verified. In the case of the lead text, *Atlantik-Novelle*, the narrator uses the term *unerhörte*

---

[89] George Steiner, *Antigones* (New York and Oxford: Oxford University Press, 1984) p. 143.

[90] The question is also raised about the significance attached to such labels by authors and publishers, especially if two generic labels are assigned to one and the same text, as is the case with Birgit Pausch, *Die Schiffschaukel* (Hamburg: Rowohlt, 1984). This text is referred to on the cover as a novel, *"Roman,"* yet on the title page the term *"Novelle"* appears.

Begebenheit (p. 23) in the one of several explicit references to Goethe to describe the uneven, unpredictable process of historical events in general and the particular event of a maritime disaster which serves as the focal and culminating point of the story. As depicted in the novella, (pp. 24ff.) this incident occurred on October 2, 1942, as the cruiser *HMS Curaçao* was escorting the passenger ship *Queen Mary* on the final leg of its journey as a troop transporter to the Clyde; the cruiser assumed a zig-zag course, intersecting the passenger liner's direct course as a precaution in the event of submarine attack. Although the liner's speed was its best defence, the probability of an air attack became greater as shipping approached the European coast. According to the *Dictionary of Disasters at Sea during the Age of Steam,*[91] a *U-Boot* sighting caused confusion, setting the ships on a collision course, resulting in the smaller *Curaçao* being impaled on the *Queen Mary*'s bow with both halves of the cruiser briefly hanging there before sinking into the sea. The liner nevertheless maintained its course with little damage done. As a rescue attempt would have meant a reduction in speed, hence a greater vulnerability to attack, none was undertaken by the liner. These facts are taken up into the fiction of *Atlantik-Novelle*, with the omission of the submarine sighting as the precipitating factor. This omission is indicative of a major theme of the novella: the absence of any clearly discernable line of cause and effect in recording historical data: the reliance on eye-witness accounts which are as individual and non-objective as the indivuals who make them. Yet this "unheard-of event" is described only on the last five pages of the twenty-five-page novella; it cites the Admiralty as its source for the final lines of its closing paragraph:

> The Admiralty would then very calmly summarize: "What would have indeed happened, had the *Queen* cut into the *Curaçao* amidships in the munitions magazine!" Only two destroyers turn back to fish out bodies and people. 72 sailors survive. 72 out of 410 (p. 33).[92]

---

[91] Charles Hocking, *Dictionary of Disasters at Sea during the Age of Steam* Vol. 1 (Sussex: Lloyd's Register of Shipping, 1969) p. 172.

[92] *"Die Admiralität wird denn auch sehr gefasst resümieren ... 'Was wäre erst geschehen, hätte die 'Queen' die 'Curaçao' genau mittschiffs zerschnitten - in der Munitionskammer!' Nur zwei Zerstörer wenden, um Menschen und Leichen zu fischen. 72 Matrosen überleben. 72 von 410."*

The lack of a clearly focused series of causes and effects as a
major theme is reflected in the juxtaposition of scenes and episodes
which, at first glance, form an unlikely and confusing sequence. If one
compares the opening lines of the novella with those cited above, in
order to stake out the parameters of an interpretation, keeping in mind
that a suggested strategy is to posit that "the end must be made a
transformation of the beginning so that meaning can be drawn from the
perception of resemblance and difference," (Culler, p. 222) the
relationship is not readily perceived:

> Fritz, my two-year-old second child, the one who wakes
> me up in the morning, usually comes up to the bed with
> a statement or a question: Yesterday he claimed ...
> "Men get sons and women get daughters." Today he
> asked: "Can you go driving with your bed?" (p. 8).[93]

To the exchange of this initial scene the narrator adjoins a
paragraph on the topic of dreamwork as a valid correlate of reality,
drawing upon the image of the bed as that which enables dreams to
occur, which in turn function more effectively than any concrete vehicle
in overcoming the boundaries of space as well as time. The answer to
the child's question "bed is the only way I can go driving" is preceded
by a reflection of the embarrassing semantic potential of the word
Führer in *Führerschein* (driver's permit): " ... now we're at a point that
we're ashamed if we haven't managed to get a *Führer's* permit";[94]
followed by references to Kant and Lichtenberg as part of a discussion of
the relationship between reality and dreaming:

> "Only the organizational context of ideas according to
> the laws of causality differentiates dreams from life."
> Nothing other than that? Don't anyone dare complain
> that Kant is difficult! ... And although an arch-
> rationalist, Lichtenberg went so far as to say that dreams

---

[93] *"Fritz, mein zweijähriger Zweiter, der mich morgens weckt, tritt meist sofort
mit einer Behauptung oder einer Frage ans Bett; gestern stellte er fest ...
'Männer kriegen Söhne und Frauen Töchter.' Heute fragte er ... 'Kannst du
mit deinem Bett Auto fahren?'"*
[94] *"Nur mit meinem Bett kann ich Auto fahren." [...] "...so weit sind wir
gekommen, daß wir uns schämen, wenn wir es noch nicht zu einem 'Führer'-
Schein gebracht haben.."*

which change our decisions, free from "the constraints of oftentimes artificial reasoning" could "safeguard our moral foundations more than any teachings that reach our hearts the roundabout way ..." But how could Lichtenberg claim to know that "oftentimes artificial reasoning" is not the underlying factor of dreams also? (p. 8).[95]

The third paragraph relates the narrator's impressions of ocean voyages on the *France* and the *United States,* the former being a stabilized vessel with only two classes, the latter having been built as a troop ship, now offering four classes. Because of the lack of stabilizers, a voyage from New York to Bremerhaven is a day faster than the competition, albeit with side-effects: "... but for that the passenger is swung around so that he pukes from New York to Bremerhaven, since these sea journeys I often dream of ships, of waves"[96] (p. 9). The expositional strategy is completed with the fourth paragraph; here the distinction that one is careful to make between narrator and author is blurred by the narrator's referring to his publisher, Ledig-Rowohlt, the actual publisher of *Atlantik-Novelle,* as well as to himself as a dramatist who has been writing a play about Churchill. The narrator then says of his publisher that he never resembled Churchill so much as when warned by the publisher not to underestimate the difficulties in portraying Churchill. In other words, he is most like the other when he negates the possibility of grasping the other, the signifier which both indicates the signified, as well as its absence (standing in for something that is of necessity not actually there itself).

This novella can be seen to have as one of the overall designations of its theme complex the affirmation of the Imaginary, of metaphor, of the vertical, paradigmatic axis as the corollary of the

---

[95] *" 'nur der Zusammenhang der Vorstellungen unter sich nach dem Gesetz der Kausalität unterscheidet das Leben vom Traum.' Sonst nichts? Da soll noch einer mäkeln, Kant sei kompliziert! ... Und obgleich Erzrationalist, ging Lichtenberg so weit zu sagen, Träume, die Entschlüsse verändern, frei vom 'Zwang der oft erkünstelten Überlegung' könnten unseren 'moralischen Fond mehr sichern als alle Lehren, die durch einen Umweg ins Herz kommen' ... Woher aber wollte Lichtenberg wissen, ob nicht auch den Träumen oft 'erkünstelte Überlegungen' zugrunde liegen?"*
[96] *"... doch dafür wird der Passagier darin geschaukelt, daß er kotzt von New York bis Bremerhaven, seit diesen Meerfahrten träume ich oft von Schiffen, von Wogen."*

Symbolic, of metonymy, of the horizontal, syntagmatic axis which in "
... commonsense view ... is the appropriate medium with which to
describe logical relationships between concepts or entities or events"
(Lodge, p. 88). It juxtaposes dreamed experience or non-empirical
reality with lived experience: "A light quilt: our flying carpet! It
carries us everywhere more quickly even than a plane. Since I crossed
the Atlantic in both directions by ship, ... I often dream of ships ...";[97] it
contrasts the abstract with the physical, the spiritual with the profane
(Kant and Lichtenberg versus Hitler) and "so that he pukes from New
York to Bremerhaven." This antithetic structuring is employed
beginning with the first paragraph of the text: the narrator's youngest,
"mein zweijähriger Zweiter," makes the statement "Men get sons and
women get daughters." The narrator thus highlights a child's reasoning
at this early stage of development more as a function of the Imaginary
than the Symbolic, grouping things paradigmatically, making
substitutions on a vertical axis without a full awareness of contiguity and
sequence. On the other hand, the noun *"Zweiter"* (second child) and its
attribute *"zweijährig"* (two-year old) are morphological and phonemic
categories "brought into relations of contiguity according to the
principles of similarity and contrast,"[98] and as this is an artistic text in
which "the perceiver is drawn to the artistic structure *qua* structure," the
morpheme *"zwei"* in the compound *"zweijährig"* can be seen as standing
in a mutually generative relationship with the noun *"Zweiter"*; one
paradigm thus generates another very similar paradigm adjacent to it in
the sequence. This is a conventional operation in a poetic text, yet in the
child's case, it contradicts established knowledge. Similarly, the word
for a driver's permit, *"Führerschein,"* an association the narrator makes
tangent to the response *"Nur mit meinem Bett kann ich Auto fahren,"*
(Bed is the only way I can go driving) is an instance of exploiting the
semantic polyvalency of the paradigm to evoke an entire nexus of
historical events which are not readily assimilable to the immediate
sequence from which they are projected. On the other hand, the narrator
next sets his position on dreams in contiguity with Kant and
Lichtenberg; this is but yet another instance of thesis/antithesis, since the

---

[97]   *"Eine leichte Steppdecke ... unser fliegender Teppich! Der trägt uns
rascher überall hin als sogar Flugzeuge"* versus *"Seit ich den Atlantik in
beiden Richtungen zu Schiff überquerte, ... träume ich oft von Schiffen ..."*
[98]   Roman Jakobsen, "Linguistics and Poetics", *Style in Language*, ed. T.
Sebeok (Cambridge: Massachusetts Institute of Technology Press, 1960) p.
358.

former posits as the only difference between dream and reality the
elimination of the law of causality ("*das Gesetz der Kausalität*"), and the
latter sees dreams in the light of their more compelling, closer link to a
moral foundation ("*moralische[r] Fond*"). Scanning back over this
second paragraph, the contours of a larger opposition become
discernable: the allusion to Hitler in the preamble to the affirmation of
the ability to drive a car with one's bed leads into the image of
travelling, albeit within a dream, and this is connected to the situation of
an "LSD trip." "Ultimately one needs neither four wheels nor LSD to
take trips, the term the medical profession uses to name this high-flying
condition" (p. 8).[99] With the reference to Kant and Lichtenberg, a
polarity emerges with The Third Reich juxtaposed with both positive,
creative ("*Steppdecke/Reisen*"- light quilt/travelling) and negative ("*lila
Zustand/LSD*"- high-flying/LSD) dreaming on the one hand, and the
Enlightenment (Lichtenberg) and Kant on the other, with the latter also
deconstructing into dreaming anchored in morality, hence a positive
activity, and dreaming (in view of Kant's solipsistic "*Ding an sich*" - the
thing unto itself) not necessarily anchored anywhere and not necessarily
positive. Adjoined to this are the third paragraph with its stabilized and
non-stabilized vehicles, and the fourth paragraph with the boundaries
between author and narrator, historical, real and imaginative figures
removed. The thematic range staked out thus far in the text comprises
the following components: the paradigmatic/ syntagmatic duality/unity
of the antinomic psyche as the underlying factor of dreaming, thinking,
of the ability to establish context, to write history, to write a story, to
define identity; as a result, the possibilty of any direct line of cause and
effect in fictive narration, both in general and in this specific attempt to
render a documented maritime disaster against the background of the
Second World War, is made tenuous.

The themes, motifs and images introduced thus far in the text are
expanded upon according to the principles of parallel, repetitive and
antinomic structuring. In the fifth paragraph the narrator examines his
relationship with his publisher, portraying him both as a protector and an
oppressor, one who needs less sleep and therefore causes the narrator to
get less than his requirement (" ... for Ledig the travel companion sees
to it that one suffers from sleep deprivation, because this sixty-year-old

---

[99] "*Denn schließlich bedarf man weder der vier Räder noch des LSD, um auf
Reisen zu gehen, wie die Mediziner den lila Zustand nennen.*"

needs less sleep than others who are age thirty-five"),[100] but also the Churchill figure, the protector with drawn sword, one step ahead and to the right of his charge.

> ... if there was something I felt, then once again it was how reassuring it was to have this man at your side. More precisely, to your right and a half a step ahead, this publisher with a broad back bent forward like a man on skis, one who protects you from a savage public as effectively as flexible armour plating. He strides into its hungry jaws with that walk I had already known from long before, even before I saw Ledig for the first time: namely in newsreels featuring Churchill.   ... the umbrella isn't taken along because of the rain ... rather it's due to our boring style in men's clothing that no longer permits rapiers in public (p. 10).[101]

The imagery and comparisons of this sequence of reflections on the part of the narrator may be construed to have a humourous bent. Churchill/Ledig is portrayed as an almost legendary knight, only on skis, and the shining armour appears to be an English fabric, probably somewhat unshiny, in all likelihood an unobtrusive navy-blue or conservative gray. A propensity for tears is also not what is usually associated with a mythical hero. Although flexible armour plating corresponds to current military technology, it seems, on the surface of things, to be an oxymoron. In the next paragraph, Churchill is quoted as having made a remark to Eisenhower that the Normandy-invasion had a fifty-percent chance to succeed, "of course in tears" (*"natürlich unter Tränen"*) (p. 10). The figure of Churchill-Ledig also introduces the motif of the modern man, whose most well-known prototype is Hamlet,

---

[100]   *"... denn der Reisebegleiter Ledig sorgt für Schlafentzug, weil der Sechzigjährige weniger davon braucht als andere mit fünfunddreißig."*
[101]   *" ... wenn ich ein Gefühl hatte, dann wieder einmal dies ... Daß es ruhig macht, diesen Mann neben sich zu haben. Genauer ... zur Rechten einen halben Schritt vor sich zu haben, diesen Verleger mit breitem, skifahrerhaft vorgebeugtem Rücken, der einen wie eine flexible Panzerplatte abschirmt gegen die Bestie Öffentlichkeit, in deren hungrige Fresse Ledig in jener Gangart hineinläuft, die ich lange schon kannte, bevor ich Ledig zuerst sah ... nämlich aus Wochenschauen, die Churchill zeigen. ... der Schirm [wird] nicht eigentlich gegen den Regen mitgenommen ... sondern weil unsere langweilige Männermode nicht mehr gestattet, mit Degen auszugehen."*

plagued by doubt, oscillating between strength and weakness, swept up by events rather than forging them after his own design. In this context the narrator describes Churchill seeking refuge behind a pillar whenever standing on a railway platform while trains thunder past. In counterbalance to this idiosyncracy is the description of his gait which shows the victory of resolve over hesitation.

> When those who are sensitive, dreamers, those who are fearful - and Churchill never waited on a platform without taking up position behind an iron pylon when a train roared by - when they "take steps" to act, then the way they move expresses the resolve necessary to go forward. This is also true in Ledig's case. The uninhibited man of action, unconstrained by reflection, doesn't walk the way Churchill walked, the way Ledig walks - without a doubt one can rely more on a companion who walks with you, *in spite of everything*, a companion who must tread down his own apprehension with his first steps (p. 10). [102]

The images and motifs surrounding the Churchill-Ledig figure are suggestive of Hamlet, although an explicit reference (explicit intertextuality is a major characteristic of Hochhuth's fiction) is not made. The portraying of reality as a mediated construct determined in no insignificant measure by dreamwork,[103] the co-ordinates of land and sea as the geographic setting of the narration, the trait of melancholia

---

[102] *"Wenn Sensible, Verträumte, Ängstliche - und Churchill wartete nie auf einem Bahnsteig, ohne sich hinter einen Eisenpfeiler zu stellen, wenn ein Zug vorbeisauste - zu Taten 'schreiten', dann drückt ihre Gangart aus, daß ein Entschluß dazu notwendig war. So auch bei Ledig. Der ungehemmte Täter, den keine Reflexion bremst, geht nicht, wie Churchill ging, wie Ledig geht - aber mehr Verlaß, zweifellos, ist auf einen Gefährten, der trotzdem mitgeht; dessen erste Schritte die eigenen Hemmungen tottreten müssen."*
[103] "... for there is nothing either good or bad that thinking makes it so ... O God, I could be bounded in a nutshell and count myself a king of infinite space, were it not that I have bad dreams." Hamlet, Act II, Scene II, *The Complete Works of William Shakespeare*, ed. William George Clark and William Aldis Wright (New York: Grosset and Dunlap, 1911) p. 1022. Commenting on a statement atributed to Churchill by the narrator, the latter quotes Ledig on this topic as having said "But in dreams too, history always becomes a nightmare" (*"Aber Geschichte wird auch in Träumen stets zum Alptraum"*) (p. 26).

and the accusatory visitation from the father ("a generation after his death, his father returned to interrogate him about his professional incompetence, whereas he, in the meantime, had been victorious in the struggle to defeat Hitler"),[104] and the amalgam Ledig/Churchill, the initially hesitant, yet ultimately resolved publisher/ man of action,[105] all point to a probable example of intended intertextuality with the Shakespearian text. Admittedly, the parallel drawn in this way requires some conjecture, yet that is precisely the tenor of the narration highlighted in particular by this character-synthesis and by the overall narrative fabric of this text: it leads the reader to extend the paradigm, to further explore the axis of substitution and selection, to proceed metaphorically, creatively, yet somewhat subjectively and ultimately precariously, if the metonymic foundation is not sufficiently considered.

This open-ended facet of language and thinking, thematized in the text as a product of both the private act of dreaming, itself breaking down into condensation and displacement, metonymy and metaphor, as well as an aggregate of information about the past, assembled from texts which are both contradictory as well as complementary, objective and subjective, can also be examined from the perspective of myth. In elucidating this concept, Joseph Campbell has said that "the myth is the

---

[104] *"Der Vater kam ein Menschenalter nach seinem Tode, um den inzwischen zum Sieger über Hitler gewordenen Sohn wegen dessen beruflicher Untauglichkeit zu verhören".*

[105] In the soliloquy at the end of Act II, Scene II, Hamlet reflects on his strategy to have a play performed for Claudius as a means to indict and challenge him, taking himself to task for not acting directly, but rather more cautiously relying on the medium of words, as he is not completely convinced of the true nature of his father's apparition ... " ... for it cannot be / But that I am pigeon-liver'd and lack gall / To make oppression bitter ... Why, what an ass am I! / This is most brave, / That I, the son of a dear father murder'd, / Prompted to my revenge by heaven and hell, / Must, like a whore, unpack my heart with words ... ... I'll have these players / Play something like the murder of my father / before mine uncle ... I'll observe his looks; / I'll tent him to the quick ... if he but blench, I know my course. The spirit that I have seen / may be the devil ... and the devil hath power / To assume a pleasing shape; yea, and perhaps / Out of my weakness and my melancholy, / As he is very potent with such spirits, / Abuses me to damn me ... I'll have grounds / more relative than this ... the play's the thing / Wherein I'll catch the conscience of the king" (p. 1025).

public dream, and the dream is the private myth."[106]   Myths are "magnified dreams ... a manifestation in symbolic images, in metaphorical images of the energies of the organs of the body in conflict with each other" (p. 39). Mythology exists in dreaming when a dream "... talks about permanent conditions within your own psyche as they relate to the temporal conditions of your life right now" (p. 39). The narrator in *Atlantik-Novelle* adheres to this scheme. He characterizes his own narration and the narrative of history as a product of the human psyche, in that he disrupts the linearity of the narration of the collision at sea of the *Queen Mary* and the *Curaçao* by merging it with a narration of the circumstances of its own germination as a fiction in his own psyche. He explicitly draws his characters according to the metaphorical

---

[106] Joseph Campbell, *The Power of Myth* (New York: Doubleday, 1988) p. 40. Campbell delineates a psychological grounding in his definition. The more conventional understanding is examined by John H. White, *Mythology in the Modern Novel* (Princeton: Princeton University Press, 1971). White mentions Thomas Mann's amplification of the concept to include not only the psychological basis but also legend, history and literary tradition (p. 68). He quotes Richard Chase's *Quest for Myth* (Baton Rouge: n.p., 1949) which discusses the standard definition ... "The division of Greek mythological literature made by Heyne and Herder has become more or less standard in modern times. Sir James Frazer carries this definition to its logical conclusion. Myths proper, he writes, are concerned with the origins of the world and man, the motions of the stars, the vicissitudes of vegetation, weather, eclipses, storms, the discovery of fire, the invention of useful arts, the mystery of death. Legends are 'traditions, whether oral or written, which relate the fortunes of real people in the past, or which describe events, not necessarily human, that are said to have occurred at real places.' (p. 74)" (p. 68). White does not see any useful application of this taxonomy which "differentiates between euhemerisms (myths that have arisen from the stylization of actual historical events and characters), and cosmogonic and aetiological myths (fictive explanations of natural phenomena, origins and causes)." As is the case with allusions to and quotation of other works of fiction, mythological allusions expand and make transparent the tenor of a text. On this point he quotes Herman Meyer's *The Poetics of Quotation in the European Novel* (Princeton: n.p., 1968) p. 6: "In general it might be maintained that the charm of the quotation emanates from a unique tension between assimilation and dissimilation: it links itself closely with its new environment, but at the same time detaches itself from it, thus permitting another world to radiate into the self-contained world of the novel."

structure of myth.[107] He includes in his narration a poem whose central theme is Freud's *Beyond the Pleasure Principle*, citing this work explicitly, developing imagery anchored in the basic drives of *Eros* and *Thanatos*, "energies ... in conflict with each other." Although these specifics will be examined presently at greater length, their general character is one which has been designated as "metafictional."

Metafictional novels tend to be constructed on the principle of a fundamental and sustained opposition: the construction of a fictional illusion (as in traditional realism) and the laying bare of that illusion. In other words, the lowest common denominator of metafiction is simultaneously to create a fiction and to make a statement about the creation of that fiction. The two processes are held together in a formal tension which breaks down the distinction between 'creation' and

---

[107] The narrator draws the comparison between Ledig and Churchill so closely, that they merge ... " ... who said that, Ledig or Churchill, I no longer know." ("... *wer hat das gesagt, Ledig oder Churchill? Ich weiß es nicht mehr.*") (p. 25). This movement away from the notion of an encapsulated, unique personality to identification with an archetype or antecedent is, according to Thomas Mann, the basic formula of myth. In *Freud und die Zukunft*, as quoted in *Mythology in the Modern Novel*, John J. White, he writes ... "The ego of antiquity and the way it conceived of itself differs from our way of thinking. It was less exclusive, less sharply delineated. It was, so to speak, open-ended towards the past, it incorporated much of what had been, repeating it in its own present, existing with it once again. [...] This "imitation" is much more than is presently meant by this word; it is the mythical identification which was especially familiar in antiquity, but has continued to play a role into the modern era *and at all times remains a spiritual possibility.* It has often been pointed out that Napoleon's character bore the stamp of antiquity. ... later ... he explained ... 'I *am* Charlemagne.' Take note - this was not ... 'I evoke him;' nor was it: 'I am as he was'; but rather simply: 'I *am he.*' This is the formula of myth." ("*Das antike Ich und sein Bewußtsein von sich war ein anderes als das unsere, weniger ausschließlich, weniger scharf umgrenzt. Es stand gleichsam nach hinten offen und nahm vom Gewesenen vieles mit auf, was es gegenwärtig wiederholte, und was mit ihm 'wieder da' war. [...] Dies 'Nachahmen' aber ist weit mehr, als heut in dem Wort liegt; es ist die mythische Identifikation, die in der Antike besonders vertraut war, aber weit in die neue Zeit hineinspielt und seelisch jederzeit möglich bleibt. Das antike Gepräge der Gestalt Napoleons ist oft betont worden. ... später ... erklärte er ... 'Ich bin Karl der Große.' Wohl gemerkt - nicht etwa: 'Ich erinnere an ihn'; Auch nicht: 'Ich bin wie er'; sondern einfach: 'Ich bin's.' Das ist die Formel des Mythos.*") p. 19.

56 THE POST-WAR NOVELLA

'criticism' and merges them into the concepts of 'interpretation' and 'deconstruction.'[108]

One means employed in the text to deconstruct the fixed value that might be assigned to any lexical item is the exploitation of its semantic polyvalency, especially by favouring items which can be re-motivated to create an opposition within the item itself, or to juxtapose items which may be assigned opposing values. This is the technique used in the case of the noun "*Führerschein*," where the notion of possessing the means of embarking on a journey, of expanding one's horizons, albeit within the frame of reference of dreamwork, is counteracted with the meaning of "a trip" as induced by hallucinogens as well as the historical trip of madness induced by Hitler. Churchill, the latter's historical counterpart, continues to be portrayed in the same antithetic vein as indicated above (cavalier/bourgeois, courageous man of action/ hesitant neurotic) with the next antithesis constituted by a reference to his native practical wit (*Mutterwitz*), Churchill is quoted as having said

> The unrelenting pressure of circumstance, the acute pain of misfortune, the incentive deriving from contempt and derision in early years are necessary ... to conjure forth that sense of purpose and unwavering native practical wit ... (p. 10).[109]

This statement on failure as the means to success, itself consonant with the antinomic mode of portrayal of the character to whom it is attributed, is elaborated upon through narrative commentary of the personal disposition of Ledig-Rowohlt, further contributing to a merging of these two identities. "Churchill said it, Ledig confirmed it." ("*Churchill hat es gesagt, Ledig hat es bestätigt.*") (p. 10). The narrator focuses on the compound "*Mutterwitz*," performing the same operation as in the case of "*Führerschein*" inasmuch as he diverts from the standard lexical value assigned to the compound (native wit), in order to consider the meanings of each of its parts when taken separately:

---

[108] Patricia Waugh, *Metafiction: The Theory and Practice of Self-Conscious Fiction* (London and New York: Methuen, 1984) p. 6.

[109] "*Es braucht den unerbittlichen Druck der Umstände, die stechenden Schmerzen des Unglücks, den Ansporn der Geringschätzung und des Hohns in frühen Jahren, um jene ... Zielstrebigkeit und jenen beharrlichen Mutterwitz hervorzubringen ...*"

"'*Mutterwitz*' - actually a rather silly word, in Ledig's case entirely inappropriate, since he inherited melancholia from his mother, his native wit from his father" (p. 10).[110] The narrator describes having gained this understanding of the personality of his publisher during a voyage to New York on "De Gaulle's new flagship, the *France*" on his way to the Broadway premiere of his play *The Deputy (Der Stellvertreter)* (p. 10). It is not entirely appropriate to refer to the following scene, in which Ledig relates an anecdote - proof of his wit - as flashback or analepse,[111] as the narrative present fluctuates among the New York hotel room on the eve of the performance of *The Deputy*, the *France*, the *Queen Mary* in 1942 (later in the text) and a vantage point to which all of the above are anterior, staked out by the opening lines of the text through the narrator's exchange with his second eldest. The anecdote, as is the case with many other motifs, images and instances of intertextuality in this narrative, would seem to be less than a component which is integral to the thematic and structural trajectory of the text; it follows a tangent initiated by the notion of native wit, inasmuch as it is meant to serve as an example of such wit. The hat which Ledig wears on the *France* is not his usual bowler, but rather "a gray, multi-coloured checkered linen hat" (*"ein grau-bunt gewürfeltes Leinenhütchen"*) (p. 11). The hats themselves form an opposition between formal and informal, rigidity of shape and relative shapelessness, and the modifiers "*grau-bunt*" and "*gewürfelt*" are indicative of paradox (colourful in a gray manner) and of that which is aleatory (*gewürfelt* - dice and the throwing of dice). The anecdote is as follows:

> Lost, recently, at an English country seat during a scene caused by a fit of jealousy. At the time I was sitting quite sedately with the lady in the garden ... through this garden there flows a narrow but quickly moving rivulet. What's that floating along, I suddenly remark to myself. My hat! In a rage, the master of the house had ripped it apart at the hat-stand and thrown it into the water ... I then obtained a new one, the finest imaginable in London's Savile Row. I sent it to the brute with my

---

[110] "... '*Mutterwitz*' - ein ziemlich blödes Wort übrigens, im Falle Ledig ganz unzutreffend, denn von der Mutter kommt ihm die Melancholie, der Witz vom Vater - ..."

[111] Seymour Chatman, *Story and Discourse* (Ithaca and London: Cornell University Press, 1978) p. 64.

card, on which I had written: "Something to throw into
the river" (p. 11).[112]

This scene is assimilable to the theme of the writing of texts and
their publication, in particular to the performance of *"Der Stellvertreter."*
The publisher is the instance by which an author's text becomes
available to the public, possibly being carried to prominence by a
"stream" of reviews and criticism. *Hoch"huth"* and *"Bowler-Hut"* are
the key to the metaphor. As well as a reference to criticism, the modifier
"zerfetzt" could also connote the truncated version of *The Deputy*
necessitated by an actual performance of a work of such considerable
length.[113] In terms of its immediate textual environment, the image of a
hat cast into a river, a text being released to the public, follows closely
on the motive of the launching of a new ship. Taken at this level, the
modifier *"zerfetzt"* prefigures the fate of passengers on ships sunk in
times of war. Each level of meaning has in addition the common

---

[112]   *"Abhanden gekommen, neulich, bei einer Eifersuchtsszene auf einem
englischen Landsitz. Dabei saß ich völlig sittsam mit der Dame im Garten ...
durch diesen Garten treibt ein schmales, aber wildes Flüßchen. Was kommt
denn da geschwommen, denke ich plötzlich. Mein Hut! Der Hausherr hat ihn
aus Wut in der Garderobe zerfetzt und ins Wasser geworfen. ... Ich holte dann
in London einen neuen, den denkbar feinsten, in der Savile Row. Den schickte
ich an den Wüterich, mit meiner Karte, auf die ich schrieb ...* 'Something to
throw into the river.'"
[113]   "'Too long to be good' - I recently read this headline over a revue of a
performance that lasted three hours! On the question of Hochhuth's play I
would rather say ... 'Too good, to be too long!' Nevertheless, even though a
performance spread out over two or three evenings would be the most adequate
- some parts will have to be cut ... In any case, I have reached an agreement
with the publisher Rowohlt whereby the play will be available to the public in
print at the same time as the Berlin premiere - as a necessary foundation and
supplement." (*"Zu lang, um gut zu sein' -- las ich jüngst als Schlagzeile über
der Besprechung einer Aufführung, die dreieinhalb Stunden dauerte! Ich
möchte lieber, was Hochhuths Stück betrifft, sagen: 'Zu gut, um lang zu sein!'
Trotzdem - wiewohl eine Aufführung an etwa zwei oder drei Abenden das einzig
Angemessene wäre - werden Striche vorgenommen werden müssen ....
Jedenfalls habe ich mit dem Rowohlt Verlag vereinbart, das gleichzeitig mit
der Berliner Uraufführung die Buchausgabe an die Öffentlichkeit gelangt als
notwendige Unterstützung und Ergänzung."*) Erwin Piscator, Preface to *Der
Stellvertreter* (Hamburg: Rowohlt, 1963) p. 10.

element of a patriarchal figure as an initiating instance: Ledig-Rowohlt, de Gaulle and Churchill. The image of a narrow, rushing stream coursing through and intersecting what must be an ample and substantial estate garden, presided upon in this scene by a woman, certainly the more solid and stable partner in a relationship characterized here by an outburst of childishness and aggressivity of her male counterpart, can be seen to anticipate the imagery and themes of the poem *"Matrosen,"* included in the second part of the novella. There the polarity woman-earth-stability/man-fluidity-instability is paralleled with a similar set of oppositions:

> Land! What blockades and mines deny us,
> a girl can give that dares
> to ground the lightening ripping us apart,
> to love us 'till the light.[114]

Here too, the male is connoted by an unrestrained, narrow torrent of energy which is absorbed and contained by the earth, a metaphor for woman,[115] yet the opposition and its dissolution are constantly repeated. "A question of time, 'till the shout: "torpedo fired" rips me away with the float I have lost." (*"Zeitfrage, bis der Ruf: "Torpedo frei"/ mich wegreißt samt verlorenem Floß."*). The compulsion to destroy and to self-destruct, to discharge, is ever present as the other aspect of the desire to complement and merge and regenerate. Ledig's response to the incident in the garden is to provoke the belligerent party by providing him with the means to repeat his aggression. Both in the anecdote and in the poem, there is strong evidence of the phallic design of the imagery along with the language- and psyche-related polarities associated with this ultimate symbol. It is

---

[114] *"Land! - was Blockade, Minen uns verwehrten,*
kann ein Mädchen geben, das es wagt,
um den Blitz, der uns zerreißt, zu erden,
uns zu lieben, bis es tagt."

[115] "Our conventional zigzag symbol of lightning descends from the phallic **sceptres** of ancient sky gods, whose bright spirits were supposed to come down from heaven in this way to fertilize Mother Earth, or the **womb** of the abyss ... [...] Like other phallic symbols, the lightning bolt was often used as a weapon. [...] The Greek name for lightning, Keraunos, meant a destroyer and was personified as a god." Barabara G. Walker, *The Woman's Dictionary of Symbols and Sacred Objects* (San Francisco: Harper Collins, 1988) p. 343.

the ultimate antinomic referent determining the oppositional, contradictory configuration of the majority of textual components.

For the remainder of this first of three sub-sections of the novella, the narrative maintains the locus of the New York hotel room as the background for preparations being undertaken for the performance of *The Deputy*. Ledig is both overbearing "... There, in the New York hotel, I had wanted only to have breakfast with him and had no intention to attend his Highness' levee, but he wouldn't let me go"[116] and protective in his intention to confirm security arrangements for the premiere. The person connected with the publishing house responsible for such matters, assigned the name Greenburger, is of Jewish heritage, yet his physiognomy is described through a comparison with an artefact of Egyptian culture, the yoke from which the Jewish people had to free themselves according to the Old Testament; more recent historical events in the Middle East make the comparison just as dichotomous: "... a man with a Ramses-like head and such sorrowful eyes, as if the thousand-year-long persecution of the Jews were reflected in them ..." (p. 11).[117] He is to arrange police protection in anticipation of an expected demonstration by two groups normally expected to occupy opposite sides in any issue of common concern: Nazis and Jesuits. This is a reflection of the impact achieved by the play in its criticism of the complacency and apathy of Pius XII with respect to the atrocities perpetrated by the fascist regimes of Germany and Italy. The narrator counters Ledig's remark that it is less than a compliment to require police protection through the comment that as an instrument used in a democratic society, it is an acceptable restriction. In a totalitarian context, the same instrument is used to achieve the opposite effect: "One may ally oneself with democratic police, just as I had to in Basel; on the other hand, *The Deputy* is forbidden by the police in Spain and Russia" (p. 11).[118] The countries mentioned also formed opposite poles of the political spectrum for much of the twentieth century. The motif of a supportive and a detrimental role played by an organ ensuring state security prefigures the defensive course taken by the *Curaçao* and its

---

[116] "... *Da, im New Yorker Hotel, hatte ich nur bei ihm frühstücken wollen und nicht die Absicht, seinem Lever beizuwohnen, aber er ließ mich nicht gehen.*"
[117] "... *ein Mann mit Ramses-Kopf und so traurigen Augen, als spiegele sich in ihnen die jahrtausendalte Geschichte der Verfolgung der Juden ...*"
[118] "*Mit demokratischen Polizisten darf man sich doch verbünden, das mußte ich auch in Basel; zum Ausgleich wird 'der Stellvertreter' in Spanien und Rußland von der Polizei verboten.*"

culmination in a collision course with a civilian vessel appropriated for military use. In terms of the immediate textual environment, the opposition protector/oppressor is a value assigned to both the publisher and police presence. For the remainder of this segment, the narration is carried by this dialogic discourse of statement and counter-statement on certain aspects of the narrator's literary output. The transition is made from the topic of opposition to the play's performance through Ledig's obviously spurious comment that the demonstrators object to the author's reliance on historical figures as the vehicles of his creativity. "The common man's anger is aroused, because you let yourself be so taken-up with historical figures ... In these times history ought to be illustrated without using names, for example, the unknown soldier ..." (p. 11).[119] In another instance of intertextuality, Ledig mentions Samuel Beckett's *Endgame* as an example of the final situation, *"die Endsituation,"* Although not elaborated upon in the text, *Endgame* and *Atlantik-Novelle* have similar dimensions with regard to the ability to ascertain meaning:

> *Endgame* deals with the end of the human race - no more procreation; ... The play also ridicules and undermines any serious and sustained effort at the characters finding or constructing meaning among themselves. ... It is as if the characters (or playwright) concede the truth of certain psychoanalytic propositions that aspects of thinking, such as establishing meaning, significance and connection at even an abstract level are closely tied up with establishing personal significance and meaning at the level of human contact.[120]

The narrator, however, sees a distinction between this work dealing with a situation beyond the end of time, with the protagonist anxious to ensure that the process does not begin again, and his own intention to show the difficulty in articulating the almost inconceivable awareness of the individual that time will cease at the point of death

---

[119] *"Die Volkswut kommt auf, weil Sie sich von historischen Figuren hinreißen lassen ... Heute müßte doch Geschichte am Namenlosen exemplifiziert werden, am unbekannten Soldaten ..."*

[120] Bennett Simon, "Tragic drama and the family: the killing of children and the killing of storytelling," *Discourse in Psychoanalysis and Literature* ed. Shlomith Rimmon-Kenan (London & New York: Methuen, 1987) pp. 163 f.

which is imminent. The opposition is one in which the former wants
time to remain at the end already reached, whereas the latter cannot cope
with the notion that it soon will be at an end. In the narrator's words,
Beckett

> ... shows the leftovers of humanity, that which is post-
> historical. But a human being in the midst of history,
> still realizing that he is being sent to the slaughter and
> still nearly able to articulate this, even though
> defenceless to prevent it, - that is to say, an exemplary
> situation of the individual at a time of compulsory
> military service: this has, to my knowledge, not yet
> been portrayed (p. 12).[121]

In a general sense the narrator is describing the tenor of the
novella with this remark: to draw the individual, *"der einzelne,"* (the
German has the connotation of isolation, of aloneness), marginally able
to grasp her or his position in a continuum of history which at this
juncture conscripts its participants as combatants, and to do so in the
context of an exemplary situation, unique yet representative, in other
words in the context of the *"zum Aufmerken veranlassende Begebenheit"*
(event that causes one to take notice).

The human situations which most readily provide models for the
narrator's fiction are those of the individual subjected to chaos, upheaval
and destruction. The best subjects are historical figures, as these are the
most prominently visible exponents of the historical process; their
depiction, or that of figures connected with them, will have considerably
more impact:

> Benn also did not "believe" in history, though he did say
> that duchesses =6
> were more evocative than potato peel. Perhaps more can
> be shown of the instruments of history as well as its
> victims - usually the two are identical - even in epic
> portrayals, only when, at minimum, the base of the ivory

---

[121] *"...zeigt die Menschenreste, die nachgeschichtlichen. Aber der Mensch
inmitten der Geschichte, der noch begreift, daß er verheizt wird, es fast noch
artikulieren kann, wenn er auch wehrlos dagegen ist - also der einzelne in der
exemplarischen Situation des Zeitalters der Wehrpflicht: . wurde meines
Wissens noch nicht dargestellt."*

tower containing the decision makers has been reached. One can show Felix Hartlaub in the *Führer's* headquarters writing his journal entries on the *Wehrmacht's* leadership, but not in the streets of Berlin where he ultimately perished (p. 13).[122]

Together with the central concept of paradox and the paradoxical as the underlying characteristic of every context, these reflections create a profile of an artistic programme strikingly similar to that of Kleist, albeit with a valorization of the actual historical occurrence:

In every one of them [Kleist's *Erzählungen*] the settled order of things, the normal routine, is disturbed by some disaster or unforseen event that makes a mockery of conventional human responses and places men and women in situations alien to their normal range of experience. These situations are *"unerhört"* in every sense of the word and amply bring out the novel element implied in the word Novelle .... Throughout the *Erzählungen* there runs the theme of truth and knowledge, the deceptive nature of appearances and the reality that may underlie them. His stories are constant variations on this theme, his characters have continually to grope their way through a confusing tangle of misleading appearances, finding out in the process that they are unable to trust the evidence of their senses and unable to rely on the operation of their rational faculties to provide answers to the riddles with which they are so unexpectedly faced .... The paradox is Kleist's basic means of expression, it is the form of statement most basic to his thinking. He sees life, whether it be universal metaphysical problems or the riddle of the

---

[122] *"Auch Benn hat ja nicht an Geschichte 'geglaubt,' aber doch gesagt, an 'Herzoginnen' lasse sich mehr ausdrücken als an Kartoffelschalen. Vielleicht kann sogar in epischen Schilderungen das Werkzeug der Geschichte, auch ihr Opfer - die sind ja meist identisch -, erst dann gezeigt werden, wenn es wenigstens bis an den Rand des grünen Tisches vorgedrungen ist. Felix Hartlaub können Sie im Führerhauptquartier darstellen, wie er dort das Tagebuch der Wehrmachtführung schrieb - aber nicht in den Straßen Berlins, in denen er zuletzt verlorenging."*

human personality, in terms of opposition, of plus and minus, of a *"Polarverhältnis."*[123]

Yet another paradox: the most significant or dramatic event in the lives of ordinary individuals, as the narrator's quote from the *Odyssey* would suggest, is death. "'Thus it came to pass that the sailor Elpinor met his death, / his death being the only chance to mention him. / For he never distinguished himself, neither through courage nor through wit'" (p. 13).[124] This intertextual link is appropriate as a corroboration of the narrator's concept of fiction, as a topos called forth in part by one of the physical loci of the creative process (the *France* en route to new York) as well as by the maritime disaster marking a core idea in the germination of the text (as ostensibly indicated by the title *Atlantik-Novelle*) which also turns out to be its culminating episode. Because of its origin, the topos also reflects the significance of myth both as a stabilizing factor (everything has an archetype, an ultimate origin) and a destabilizing one (one is still within the hermeneutic circle).

The narrator refers to the ocean voyage just completed as the motivating instance for remembering the fate of sailors trapped in sunken ships during the war. He goes on to reflect on the dichotomy of the suspension of real time in the case of a reader's involvement with a text or an audience's involvement with a performance of a play, versus the narrator's intention to demonstrate an acute awareness of the passage of each minute as one of the last to be experienced.

Ledig asserts that the true reason for prefering historical figures is the narrator's opposition to the Marxist concept of history: his concept is one in which individuals determine its random direction, as opposed to a human collectivity advancing towards an ineluctable state of complete social hence individual harmony. The image of Ledig emerging naked from his bath causes a reflection on this breach of the convention (the use of a towel) and the assumed unconventionality of Churchill in the same situation: "Churchill would never have covered his nakedness in a conventional manner." (*"Nie würde sich Churchill konventionell 'bedecken'"*). The mythological merging of these figures

---

[123]   Denys Dyer, *The Stories of Kleist* (New York: Holmes and Meier, 1977) pp. 151 ff.

[124]   "'*Da geschah es, daß der Matrose Elpenor zu Tode kam,/ Die einzige Gelegenheit, ihn zu erwähnen. / Denn nie tat er sich hervor, weder durch Mut noch durch Klugheit.'*"

is again forefronted: "Now a servant ought to appear with a towel, shaking his head, saying: 'Sir, you are to dine with the king in twenty minutes'" (p.14),[125] yet the narrator wishes to avoid the use of a towel in the stage production he envisages, because it would resemble a toga, the implication being that he would thus be cast in a mythical light: " ... that can be conspicuous, that can be reminiscent of a toga" (" ... *das kann ins Auge gehen, kann an eine Toga erinnern*" (p.13). This first segment of the novella draws to a close with yet three more instances of intertextuality which establish literary antecedents with similar thematic content. The first is made in the context of Ledig's ongoing telephone conversation with Greenberger, in which it is established that the police protection will be provided by mounted police: "So, on horseback, that's pretty good too ..." ("*So, berittene, das ist doch och mal ganz schön ...,*") an anachronism as a shield for the play's iconoclasm. The conversation turns to the topic of legal matters involving Rowohlt and the estate of Robert Musil. This is an oblique reference to the difficulties encountered in publishing *The Man Without Qualities*. In this work, the narrator describes historical events as follows: "This history of ours looks pretty unsafe and messy, when looked at from close hand, something like a half-solidified swamp ..."[126] While Ledig performs his toilet, he criticises the narrator for not having a living model for his Churchill figure, unwittingly providing that very model. The narrator speculates on the possibility of including such a scene in his Churchill play, " ... but unfortunately, the way a prominent person dresses is no longer a fresh image: Brecht has already stolen that from *Leonce and Lena* for his *Galilei*" (p. 14).[127] In this play by Georg Büchner, King Peter states:

"When I speak so loudly I scarcely know who it
is who's speaking, myself or another, it frightens me.
[...] I am I. [...]What do you think of that, my Lord

---

[125] "*Jetzt müßte der Kammerdiener mit einem Badetuch kommen und kopfschüttelnd sagen ... 'Sir, Sie essen in zwanzig Minuten beim König.'*"
[126] Robert Musil, *The Man without Qualities* vol. 2 (London: Secker and Warburg, 1954) p. 68.
[127] "*... aber leider, wie ein Prominenter sich anzieht, das ist abgebraucht: Brecht hat das für den 'Galilei' schon bei 'Leonce und Lena' gestohlen ...*"

President?[...] Your Majesty, it may be so, and then
again it may also not be so."[128]

Consonant with the *V-Effekt*, the thematic trajectory of Brecht's
play is to a significant extent determined by the insight that all
perceptions and assumptions must be challenged and re-interpreted:
"The millennium of faith is ended, said I, this is the millennium of
doubt. [...] The sayings of the wisemen don't wash any more.
Everybody, at last, is getting nosey."[129] The remark "that is no longer a
fresh image" (*"das ist abgebraucht"*) stands in strong contradiction to
the thematic common denominators brought to light by an investigation
of the numerous cases of intertextuality. The narrator thus calls into
question the veracity or face value of his own commentary, which is
entirely consistent with, and the ultimate implication of, the
deconstructive configuration of this text.

The second segment of *Atlantik-Novelle* opens with the time of
narration set on the *France*. As in the first section, the technique of a
close reading is the only appropriate method to reveal the close
integration of theme, motif and lexical item of a textual structure
projecting the initial impression of a somewhat random sequence of
experiences, much akin to lateral thinking and stream of consciousness.
The first paragraph will be quoted in its entirety, as it is a compact
repetition of the expositional strategy of the preceding segment.

The tablets I take for seasickness along with the alcohol,
which of course one should not drink when taking them,
but nevertheless does - being a passenger with no
responsibilities and consuming larger quantities of it - a
reflection of the land-to-water ratio - these tablets have,
in an alliance with the sea itself and with readings on
naval warfare, for which there is an endless amount of
time on board, led to the following: they give rise to
dreams, but with such an intensity, that these dreams
even have an influence well into the day. Dreaming,
being awake, where does one end and the other begin,

---

[128] Georg Büchner, *Complete Plays and Prose: Leonce and Lena*. Translated
and with an introduction by Carl Richard Mueller (New York: Hill and Wang,
1963), p. 79.
[129] *Seven Plays by Bertolt Brecht*. Edited and with an intoduction by Eric
Bentley (New York: Grove Press Inc., 1961), p. 335.

looking into the expansive, swirling wake, reading,
dozing, writing, speaking, for my publisher is lying next
to me once again, as I am, wrapped up securely against
the wind by sailors' expert hands. The February air,
carnation-stem-gray, is even more humid than it is cold
(p. 15).[130]

A repeated use of images, motifs and theme constituents begins
to evolve into a distinct pattern of parallels and leitmotif. The use of
medication to counter sea-sickness along with the consumption of
alcohol is the first factor mentioned as a cause of a higher level of
dreamwork on this voyage. This repeats the motif of the LSD "trip" in
the opening lines of the novella and re-states the elements of the sea and
sea-sickness as conducive to dreaming. Another initiating cause is the
horizontal position in which passengers spend much of their time
dozing, wrapped up in blankets on deck chairs, the latter having been
mentioned in the first instance in precisely the same context: "Of course
in these dreams I experience countless interesting things, more so than
what I have seen simply while I lay in deck chairs"(p. 9).[131] This also
echoes the lines "A light quilt, our flying carpet" ("*Eine leichte
Steppdecke: unser fliegender Teppich*"). The publisher's presence as a
mentor-"provocateur" is also re-introduced. The imagery of water, first
used as a metaphor in the third paragraph for everyday coincidences "the
brackish water of everyday chance occurrences") ("*das Brackwasser
alltäglicher Zufälligkeiten*") reappears here as "the broad frothy
turbulence of the ship's wake" ("*[das] breite weißwirbelnde
Kielwasser*"), an extension of the metaphor to the more turbulent,
convoluted reality of dreams from the placid, stagnant blend of the

---

[130] "*Die Tabletten, die ich gegen Seekrankheit nehme, dazu der Alkohol, den
man natürlich nicht dazu trinken sollte, den man aber doch auf See ungefähr in
so viel höheren Quanten trinkt als pflichtloser Passagier, wie man mehr
Wasser dort sieht als Land - sie haben, im Bunde mit der See selber und mit
Seekriegs-Lektüre, zu der so unendlich viel Zeit ist an Bord ... Träume, in einer
Intensität hervorgerufen, daß diese Träume sogar den Tag noch stundenweise
mitbestimmen. Träumen, Wachen - wann beginnt was, wenn man ins breite,
wirbelnde Kielwasser blickt, lesend, dösend, schreibend, sprechend, denn mein
Verleger liegt wieder neben mir, wie ich, wie wir alle winddicht verpackt von
kundigen Matrosenhänden. Ist doch die Februarluft, nelken-stengelgrau, noch
feuchter als sie kalt ist.*"

[131] "*Und erlebe natürlich in diesen Träumen unendlich viel Interessantes, als
ich nur auf Deckliegestühlen gesehen habe.*"

reality of consciousness. The compound "carnation-stem gray" ("*nelkenstengelgrau*") calls to mind the earlier description of Ledig's hat as "gray, multi-coloured) ("*graubunt*"). The modifier evokes a perception of moisture and colour with its first component "carnation" ("*nelken*"); this coincides with the humidity ascribed to the February sea air, and in terms of colour and shape to the frothy whiteness of the ship's whirling wake. "Gray," not an unusual description for a bleak month, is the negative complement to the positive value established by "*nelken*," forming another link in the oppositional chain. A possible implication of "*Stengel*," the German word for stem, is the semantic variation in the expression *vom Stengel fallen* meaning "to suffer from a sudden feeling of weakness" or "to be surprised." This would be another example of the lateral thinking or "*Assoziationsschübe*" (p. 15) as in "*Führerschein*" and "*Mutterwitz*," only the narrator does not explain the anomaly. It is left to the reader to draw a connection between the theme of altered or unusual states of perception and a redirected semantic value of "*Stengel*" in order to bring disparate categories into more meaningful proximity.

The second paragraph begins with the sentence "One is not seated - one is bedded down on the deckchairs" (*Man sitzt nicht - gebettet ist man in den Deckstühlen*") (p. 15). The image of the location and its accoutrements (bed, deck chair, blanket) in which dreamwork most frequently occurs is not only taken up a third time, it is also italicized. Nevertheless, the thematic direction is once again indicated with the next, somewhat laconic statement "One often dreams" ("*Man träumt oft*") and yet again with the following sentence: "And the waking state is often determined by association-shifts first brought forth by dreams, who knows from what realms of fear![132] The rhetorical "who know's" ("*wer weiß?*"), the exclamatory banality and repetitive monotony of this statement within a text exhibiting such a high and esoteric level of intertextuality (the narrator plainly knows and has explicitly stated what his sources are) necessarily project a sardonic tone and raise the question of an intent to allegorize the entire process of creation, interpretation and generic affiliation.

Similarly, the rhetorical question which follows seems to be a redundant and overly simplistic transition to the verse "*Matrosen*," of which the narrator, in position on the stern of the ship, says that it has so to speak come into being on its own, when the verse itself has as its key an understanding of the psychic dynamics of the conscious and the

---

[132] "*Und das Wachsein ist auch noch bestimmt durch die Assoziationsschübe, die erst die Träume heraufbrachten, wer weiß, aus welchen Angstzonen!*"

subconscious: "Why else would these memorial verses come into being on their own here on the stern ..." (*"Warum sonst diktierte sich hier am Heck das Gedenkblatt sozusagen von selber ..."*) (p. 15). The narrator can thus be seen as successful in including his own commentary and reflections within the network of dichotomy and incertitude as the prevalent feature of this work.

The paradigmatic narrow vision of children is taken up again within the context of the narrator's own childhood experiences and reminiscences of the war. He chides his own lack of a sense of contiguities as a ten-year-old who idealized war heroes, not unlike the narrator's own adult and prevalently idealistic musings on Churchill and Ledig. As in the first section, where this faulty paradigmatic thinking was juxtaposed with an example of this operation as inherent to a poetic text, "my two-year-old second eldest" (*"mein zweijähriger Zweiter"*) the narrator now presents the poem he has written to commemorate two submariners in particular, whose description is also drawn along oppositional lines. One of these is referred to as "sub-navy-lieutenant Breitenstein" (*"Leutnant zur See Breitenstein"*), the other as "leading seaman Schlunk" (*"Obermatt Schlunk"*) hence an upper and a lower ranking mariner, whose names, with slight phonetic modification to the latter, suggest the opposition broad and thin, *breit* and *schlank*. The narrator remembers the impressive manner in which Breitenstein "... would lightly cast his hand away from the black visor of his white cap-" (" ... *leger die Hand vom schwarzen Schirm seiner weißen Mütze wegstieß - "*). The latter cut an imposing figure "... whenever he would proudly pass by us when on furlough" (" ... *wenn er im Urlaub stolz an uns vorbeiging"*), whereas Schlunk was reticent about his experiences, "... told sparingly (of his tours of duty), and incidentally, only when we really pressured him to ... " (*"sparsam erzählte, übrigens nur, wenn wir ihn sehr darum bedrängten ... "*) (p. 15). The rhymed verse and troping of *"Matrosen"* is immediately preceeded by statistical facts about war casualties: "Of 39,000 German submariners, 27,212 lost their lives, most of the remainder were captured") (*"Von 39000 deutschen U-Boot-Fahrern sind 27212 gefallen, die weitaus meisten anderen gefangen worden"*) (p. 16). In one paragraph there are four manifestations of binary terms: upper rank/lower rank, robust/frail, black/white, fact/fiction.

As indicated in the Introduction, the poem names *Beyond the Pleasure Principle* in the first line of the first stanza, in which Freud postulated that there was in addition to libidinal impulsion another basic drive, the death drive, whereby the human organism in its drive to eliminate any unpleasant stimuli, specifically the existential isolation every individual seeks to overcome through union with another, could also be seen in the light of the tendency of all organisms to revert to an initial, less differentiated state. The first two lines of the first stanza "Depleted by war - / 'beyond the pleasure principle' / Sleep unto death tempts nearly as much as a bed!" ("*Vernutzt vom Krieg, - 'jenseits des Lustprinzips': / Schlaf bis zum Tod lockt fast schon wie ein Bett!*") indicate that the external experience of war obscures the boundary between the internal proclivity to retreat from existence permanently and the regeneration of a temporary retreat from consciousness. In spite of a resulting inner meaninglessness and emptiness ("though lifeless, caught in the jostle on board a murder machine") ("*Entseelt zwar dank des Bord- und Mordbetriebs*") the body drives on, as a consolation to its own carnality, until nothing remains, ("lurking to kill / yet driving relentless, this flesh / To comfort itself / 'till fish gnaw it away from our bones") ("*treibt doch, bis uns die Fische zum Skelett / Abnagen, unser Fleisch zum Trost der Fleischlichkeit*"). "*Unser Fleisch*" can be both, in apposition to "*uns*" the object of "*abnagen*" as well as the subject of "*treibt*," thus bringing into immediate proximity the body as that which is to be destroyed and that which must continue to exist. A furlough provides an escape from the darkness of an underwater vessel to the darkness lived even far removed from the sea; "and an entire darkness" ("*und eine ganze Dunkelheit*") can refer either to the perilous underwater conditions on board a submarine as well as to a leave from duty perceived as a desirable type of obscurity: "Furlough again from Atlantic-gray / coffins of steel, and an entire darkness / oceans away, a human existence, for women / Protect like a pier against foe and tribunal!"[133]

Yet even the safe haven of sexual intimacy and union also bears the stamp of destruction and disunion: "I taste my watery grave in your womb" ("*schmeck' ich mein Meergrab schon in deinem Schoß*"). The last stanza juxtaposes the firing of a torpedo with sexual intercourse, itself described as "the barbarity of being" ("*Daseinsbarbarei*"). Coming as it does at the beginning of this second segment of the novella, in which the narrator for the most part reflects upon reality and history as a sequence of events with no discernible pattern of cause and effect, in which every major or striking occurrence can be nothing more

---

[133] "*Einmal noch Urlaub vom atlantikgrauen / Stahlsarg - und eine ganze Dunkelheit / meerfern wie Menschen leben, weil uns Frauen / Vor Feind und Kriegsgerichten schützen wie ein Kai!*"

than an "*unerhörte Begebenheit,*" the poem suggests through its theme of the ultimate myth that human thinking, determined by an antinomic psyche, must perceive everything in antinomic terms. The human propensity to see things paradigmatically, mythically and metaphorically is both a creative ability towards insight as well as an obstacle to any unmediated perception of pure logic or sense of contingencies uncontaminated by metaphor. This is the narration's primary thematic concern - to demonstrate the primacy of the paradigm over that of the sequence, of dreamwork over consciously perceived reality, of the poetic text over the logical discourse of history. In accordance with this configuration, it is therefore consistent that the metonymy of a prose text be undermined to the extent that the cornerstone or the ultimate stopping place for the stream of oppositions be contained within the type of poetic text in which metaphor and the paradigm tends to be valorized over metonymy and the sequence. The poem consolidates the major themes and theme-bearing motifs introduced thus far in the novella: that of sleep and dreamwork as the access to an antinomic psyche, of the resulting mythical, non-objective aspect of all human thinking, with particular reference to the experience of the solitary individual attempting to survive in and render meaning to a cataclysmic environment. The initiating moment of the poem, the wake of the ship, undergoes a transformation in the next paragraph from that which encourages creativity to that which is reminiscent of death and decay: "In this way I cast my rhymes, gazing into the ship's wake that is as white as the lime thrown onto mass graves"(p. 17).[134] This is the transition employed to lead into the several paragraphs in which the narrative returns to the motiv of death at sea as a result of hostilities between warring nations. Included are statistics on the survival rate of sailors in the British merchant marine during the war (three out of four), the fact that submarines would only rarely rescue victims due to a lack of space, details on the types of death: exposure, a fiery death in the case of torpedoed oil tankers, slow asphyxiation in the case of sailors trapped in air pockets of sunken vessels. Quoting Churchill, the narrator refers to the allied loss of "four million six hundred thousand tonnes of shipping in the 'Battle of the Atlantic'" ("*vier-millionensechshunderttausend Tonnen Schiffsraum in der 'Schlacht um den Atlantik'* ... ") (p. 17). This is the factual counterweight to the poetic and philosophical discourse on cataclysmic death in times of war taken

---

[134] "*So reime ich hier, den Blick ins Kielwasser gerichtet, das so weiß, wie jener Kalk ist, den man auf Massengräber wirft.*"

up by the poem *"Matrosen."* It goes on to include the tonnages of the *Queen Mary* (81,235) and the *Queen Elizabeth* (83,673) as the largest liners pressed into troop transport service. The actual speed of these ships, 28 knots, hence their ability to out-maneuvre any other vessel, along with the need for reduced speed and therefore an escort in coastal areas, are some of the few items directly relating to the circumstances of the collision of the *Curaçao* and the *Queen Mary.* The rendition of other remarks made by Churchill about wartime shipping statistics reverts to the pattern of binarity as the prevalent method of establishing coherencies. In this vein, whatever tactics are adopted by the allied powers are described as being met by enemy counter-measures to eliminate their efficacy: "'The enemy repeatedly changes his method of attack in order to render our countermeasures ineffective'"[135] (p. 18). Similarly, the advantage of the free flow of information afforded by democratic institutions is shown to be a considerable vulnerability, a disadvantage as it relates to the publication of statistics on sunken tonnage, thereby providing the enemy with proof of success or failure of its tactics: "'... Our struggle to survive is indeed harsh enough, without we ourselves becoming an efficient branch office of the German news agency'"(p. 18).[136] As the narrative moves closer to its final segment culminating in the collision episode, a transition is made from an emphasis on the psychic apparatus, of the human possibilities of perception and expression, to the object of these perceptive and expressive abilities. The reflections on the concept of cause and effect, of the possibility to organize the material of reality into meaningful categories or paradigms are made with respect to both "logical" as well as poetic discourse; the reasons for this assumption are twofold: in addition to the use of the term *"Wendepunkt,"* (p. 19) a high-profile term in novella theory in discussing the aleatory nature of such turning points, the narrator, as pointed out in the discussion above, quotes Goethe's definition of the novella: "Goethe translated 'novella' from the Italian as 'an unheard-of occurrence'" (*"Novelle übersetzte Goethe aus dem Italienischen: 'unerhörte Begebenheit'"*) (p. 23). Secondly, in another example of intertextuality, the narrator can be seen implicitly to criticize

---

[135]   "'*Der Feind ändert unablässig seine Angriffsmethoden, um unsere Gegenmaßnahmen unwirksam zu machen.*'"
[136]   "'*... Unser Kampf ums Dasein ist wahrhafig hart genug, ohne das wir selber zu einem leistungsfähigen Zweig des deutschen Nachrichtendienstes werden.*'"

apparently unbridled data accumulation which is, however, the very hallmark of his own fiction:

What an excruciating discrepancy - no one has ridiculed this as convincingly as the Spaniard Ortega y Gasset - between the entirely deficient philosophical (but also practical and technical) yield of the transcription of history on the one hand, and the industrious, mindless, bee-like amassing of facts on the other: though there is much that history knows and recognizes, there is little in what it produces which can be called science or ethology! (p. 22).[137]

The significance of the paradigm, of metaphor to creative insight does not necessarily guarantee an accurate vision of objective reality, whatever that may be. Whereas the obstruction has been treated primarily from the point of view of the subject of observation, the inherent inobservability of its object is now considered. History does not lend itself to paradigmatic categorization:

Only if battles fit paradigms, does it make sense to ponder them; for example, when their outcome has not been determined by coincidence, but rather point to a historical constant ... In the elimination of Hitler's U-boats in the Atlantic, I find there are none (p. 19).[138]

Goethe is also the source of a further intertextual component, which is included to corroborate this view. He is quoted as restricting his interests to historical events which bore a connection to laws of nature, "Only where he had already ascertained the possibility that

---

[137] *"Was für ein quälendes Mißverhältnis - niemand hat das so überzeugend wie der Spanier Ortega y Gasset bespottet - zwischen dem so dürftigen philosophischen (und auch praktisch-technischen) Ertrag der Geschichtsschreibung selbst einerseits - und ihrer so bienenfleißigen, bienenstumpfigen Aufhäufung von Fakten andererseits ... So unendlich viel sie auch kennt, die Geschichte - wie wenig doch gibt sie her als Wissenschaft, als Ethologie!"*
[138] *"Über Schlachten nachzusinnen kann einen Sinn haben dann, wenn sie paradigmatisch sind. Zum Beispiel nicht nur durch Zufälle in ihrem Verlauf bestimmt wurden, sondern historische Konstante aufzeigen ... ich finde hier, in der Beseitigung der U-Boote Hitlers im Atlantik keine."*

individual occurrences could be seen to result from natural laws ... " (p.
20). [139] Leading up to this statement is a reference to Goethe's interest in
the repetition compulsion observable in nature and therefore also
conceivably in history. This "repetition compulsion"
("*Wiederholungszwang*") (p.20), a concept which Goethe " ... had also
already reached" (" ... *auch schon vorgedrungen war*") (p. 20), is
attributed to Spengler, a scholar who had come into Goethe's sphere of
influence. The impetus for Freud's *Beyond the Pleasure Principle* was
precisely the observation of a repetition compulsion, specifically the
compulsion to repeat unpleasant dreams. This brings to light another
aspect of the inescapable presence of the paradigmatic axis of all
language and thinking: another characteristic inherent to its both
creative and "seeing" as well as distortive and "unseeing" potential, it
implies an affinity not only to a bringing into meaningful proximity
those things whose interrelation had gone unnoticed, but also a
dependency on those categories which have long been established. Even
though Freud considered the theory of repetition compulsion within the
context of the psychic mechanism, as an internal property of the subject
rather than the object of perception, the concept was already in place,
already had a tradition. This reaching back while simultaneously
reaching forward is paralleled in this text by the mythological
characterization of Ledig-Churchill, a creative amalgam of ostensibly
factual ingredients. As well, the numerous instances of intertextuality,
both constitute as well as provide insight into this narrative's
unconventional, non-linear and seemingly additive fabric. If tradition is
broken with, it does not happen in a vacuum without reference to
antecedents. As opposed to the opening of this novella segment with its
commemorative "memorial page" ("*Gedenkblatt*") which nevertheless
departs from a particular situation to wider reaching implications, the
closing paragraphs of this second subsection present the tradition-bound,
"unseeing" aspect of paradigmatic thinking, also in the form of a
commemorative gesture. This episode both completes an oppositional
pattern and, through a return to the same thematic categories of the
primacy of the paradigm and the commemorative gesture, achieves a
type of circularity. It also constitutes a narrative strand of historical,
external origin to complement the personal, internal experience of the
narrator's own experience of a sea voyage, completing the store of
antecedents to the episode of the final novella segment.

---

[139] *"Nur dort, wo er die Möglichkeit schon erkannt hat, Einzel-ereignisse als
Resultate von Naturgesetzen zu durchschauen ..."*

The destruction of the most powerful British battle cruiser, the *Hood* on May 24, 1941 in the Straits of Denmark, was a repetition - almost down to the day a quarter of a century later - a precise repetition of every detail and of the cause, of the destruction of the battle cruiser und flagship *Invincible* under Admiral Hood ... on May 31, 1916 in the Skagerrak, blown to pieces by one salvo from the German ship *Derflinger.* The British had neglected the horizontal armoured plating of their battle ships - ... This is precisely what happened a quarter of a century later, when the British flagship *Hood* under Admiral Holland ... was blown out of the water only six minutes after having engaged the *Bismarck,* because a salvo had struck through the once again completely inadequate armour deck-plating over a munitions magazine ... [...] What a price to pay for the snootiness of some chief engineer of the British navy: three thousand men blown up in the explosions of three battle cruisers in one battle was not a sufficient "caution," at least now, in the planning stages, to equip the new battle ship, which would enter service in 1918 after a christening by the late Admiral Hood's widow, with resistant horizontal armour over the magazines (pp. 21f).[140]

---

[140] "*Wiederholt hat sich - fast auf den Tag genau ein Vierteljahrhundert später -, exakt sogar wiederholt in allen Details und in seiner Ursache, mit der Vernichtung der 'Hood,' des stärksten Schlachtkreuzers der Briten, am 24. Mai 1941 in der Dänemarkstraße - die Vernichtung des Schlachtkreuzers 'Invincible' 1916 am Skagerrak, als Admiral Hood am 31. Mai mit diesem Flaggschiff ... in die Luft flog, nach einer Salve der deutschen 'Derflinger.' Die Briten hatten die Horizontal-Panzerung ihrer Schlachtschiffe vernachläßigt - ... Genau dies ereignete sich ein Vierteljahrhundert später, als das britische Flaggschiff 'Hood' des Admirals Holland ... nur sechs Minuten nach Beginn des Gefechts mit der 'Bismarck' in die Luft flog, weil eine Salve den ebenfalls wieder völlig unzureichenden Panzerschutz des Decks der 'Hood' über einer Munitionskammer durchgeschlagen ... hatte. [...] Welcher Preis für die Hochnäsigkeit irgendeines Chefingenieurs der britischen Marine: Daß diesem Mann die ... Explosion dreier Schlachtkreuzer 1916 ... doch nicht genug waren als 'Belehrung', jetzt wenigstens das in der Planung befindliche neue Schlachtschiff, das 1918 in Dienst gestellt und nach dem soeben*

As inconceivable as this re-occurrence is the collision of the
Queen Mary and the *Curaçao* in the next segment, with the loss of only
the latter ship; the point of impact on the *Curaçao* was two thirds of the
way along the length of its hull, not in its characteristically vulnerable
midship-section. This episode illustrates the narrator's assertion that to
understand history is to appreciate the overriding role played by
coincidence and pure chance. Even observable contingencies may be
obscured by established categories. The narrator describes history as a
"a whirling flow of details" (*"ein Strudel flußabwirbelnder Details"*) (p.
21), a convolution of facts turning in upon themselves. His own
narration in this middle segment begins by demonstrating the
assimilation of real historical time and space to the creative dream, to the
"private myth," of an historical past to a conscious and unconscious
present, and concludes by showing the assimilation of creative insight to
the myth or "public dream" of tradition and history, of the conscious and
unconscious present to the historical (and literary historical) past.

The third segment begins with a reiteration of the "unseeing,"
static and precedence-bound aspect of dreamwork: "dreams also have a
condensing dynamic" (*"Komprimieren tun sie auch, die Träume"*) (p.
23). "Condensation, it will be recalled, belongs to the metonymic axis
in Jakobson's scheme" (Lodge, p. 86). Freud's designation of the
fundamental structures of condensation and displacement in dreamwork
are not inherently positive or negative, but the textual environment of
this third segment suggests that consendation is, in this particular
context, a manifestation of the death instinct, of the compulsion to revisit
images portending destruction:

> There (in dreams) it becomes so irrelevant that we are
> not headed for England, that we are not at all crossing
> the Atlantic on a zig-zag course from New York to the
> Clyde, zig-zaging to avoid German torpedoes, but in fact
> boarded the *France* in Le Havre ... (p. 23).[141]

---

*gefallenen Admiral 'Hood' von dessen Witwe getauft werden sollte, mit einer
widerstandsfähigen Horizontal-Panzerung über den Munitionskammern
auszurüsten!"*
[141] *"Wie unerheblich wird in ihnen [den Träumen], daß wir nicht unterwegs
nach England sind, überhaupt nicht auf West-Passage von New York in den
Clyde zickzacken - Zickzackkurs, um deutschen Torpedoes auszuweichen,
sondern daß wir uns in Le Havre auf der 'France' eingeschifft haben ..."*

Dreamwork can illustrate the displacement of established categories through creative vision, but its function here is to express a change-resistant, paradigmatic stasis. The image of the sea is employed to evoke the paradox of an organism which is both moving and unmoving:

> Astonishing! Even in a typhoon the roll of the waves, ten thousand tonnes of water, does not move forward, rather it rages up and down, spasms without a purpose, release through exhaustion; astonishing, that the seas even in hurricane squalls swell up on the spot, climb, rise up, only to cave back in on themselves - without any relationship to a whole, to an overall sequence of events - as seldom a thing in nature as it is in history (p. 29).[142]

The analogy between the sea and history is explicitly made, drawing the perception of the external forces of history and nature within the same circle of indeterminacy as is present within the psyche, all in parallel with the movement of the narrative itself. A by-now-familiar cycle of motifs, images, narrative reflections and intertextuality is re-developed, re-initiating the narrative inventory of the first and second segments. The motif of sea-sickness, of alcohol consumption and lapses of consciousness along with the presence of Churchill-Ledig is repeated: "Frightening, this surging and this night - my travelling companion is right - the bar is a better place than bed to put oneself into safekeeping" (p. 24).[143] Similarly, the narrator includes lines of verse in this segment: "His shadow hovered, unknowable/ on the evening of my room." ("*Sein Schatten weilte unbegreiflich / auf dem Abend meines Zimmers.*") (p. 27). This repeats the theme of incomprehension and darkness of

---

[142] *"Erstaunlich! Daß demnach selbst bei Taifunen noch die Wellen-walzen, zehntausendtonnenschwer, nicht 'voran'-kommen, sondern sich, Spasmen ohne Endzweck, Entkrampfung durch Erschöpfung, Spasmen ohne Endzweck, nur hoch- und abtoben; daß die Seen noch bei Orkanböen auf der Stelle anschwellen, steigen, sich bäumen, um in sich selber zusammenzubrechen - durchaus ohne Beziehung zu einem Ganzen, einem "Gesamtablauf," den es offenbar in der Natur so wenig gibt - wie in der Geschichte ..."*
[143] *"Unheimlich ist es, dieses Rollen und diese Nacht - besser als im Bett, da hat mein Gefährte recht, ist man an der Bar aufbewahrt."*

"Matrosen." It is another instance of intertextuality, whose source the
narrator both denies and states: "I'm sure I won't remember where these
lines are from (Lasker-Schüler on Trakl)" (*"Bestimmt entsinne ich mich
jetzt nicht des Standorts dieser Zeilen [Lasker-Schüler über Trakl]) ... "*
(p. 28). This echoes the disclaimer made at the beginning of the second
segment: " ... who knows from what realms of fear!" (" ... *wer weiß aus
welchen Angstzonen"*).   The narrator pursues the same idolizing
tendency and lack of a sense of contiguities exhibited by children (in this
case of his own fiction) by stating of Churchill that " ... only the sea
could intimidate him" (*"..nur das Meer konnte ihn einschüchtern"*) (p.
30), whereas he has previously made reference to a fear of quickly
moving trains while standing on platforms.   These are two further
instances of the narrator's including his own assertions within the realm
of   the   contradictory.   The   modifier   "carnation-stem-gray"
(*"nelkenstengelgrau"*) is paralleled by the description of the elements in
this third segment: "I ... see before us ... seas the colour of dried
flowers ..." (*"Ich ... sehe vor uns ... die immotellenfarbenen Seen ..."*)
and "The crests shine bright" (*"Die Kämme leuchten"*) (p. 28). The sky
is also rendered according to the pattern of light and dark: ("Now the
sun begins to peer over a cloudbank, pale as a thin broth ... ") (*"Wie
blasse Bouillon kündigt jetzt über einer Wolkenbank die Sonne sich an ...
"*) (p. 30).   The associative thinking or *"Assoziationsschübe"* of the
previous segments are also built in to this third segment. A description
of the instruments on the bridge of the *Queen Mary* in the hours before
twilight exhibit features similar to the description of twilight itself: The
ship is referred to as "the sunship" (*"[das] Sonnenschiff"*) (p. 27),
whereas in the preceding sentence "Only the faint glow of the screened
compass light brings twilight to the bridge ...   (*"Nur das matte
Kompaßlicht, abgeschirmt, gibt der Brücke Dämmerhelle ... "*).
        The protective and oppressive paternal figures represented by
Ledig-Churchill and de Gaulle also reoccur in this third segment. The
surrounding textual elements in the first segment were the embarking on
a journey on de Gaulle's new flagship, the anecdote told by Ledig
relating the episode of the battered hat in the narrow, rushing stream,
followed by remarks about protective and oppressive police. In the third
segment a similar configuration appears, beginning with a nearly
verbatim repetition of phrases of the first segment: " ... he does not
suspect that ... his back, to the right and a half a step ahead, has a surge-
calming effect on me" (*"... er ahnt nicht, daß ... sein Rücken, rechts,
einen halben Schritt vor mir, eine wogenglättende Wirkung auf mich
haben"*) (p. 25 - cf. p. 9). Ledig's superior taste as a consumer, as

evidenced by the purchase of a hat in Savile Row, is alluded to again through his statement " ... I eat only the best") (" ... *ich esse nur das Beste*") (p. 25). The anxiety at being thrust into a narrow, threatening unknown is rendered here through the narrator's being led by Ledig-Churchill through a narrow maze of steps and corridors on board ship: "No steps, only a ladder in front of a locked iron door. Climbing back, trudging back, the passage is even more narrow than on the way in; he comes across passages to the left, passages to the right." (p. 24)[144] De Gaulle, his flagship, and the subversion of democratic institutions by one of the bodies established to protect those institutions is also taken up again:

> Have you read what de Gaulle said about Kennedy's assassination - and de Gaulle is said to have a very efficient secret service which certainly has, here too on the flagship ... bugged some of the luxury suites; de Gaulle said: "Kennedy's murder ... the police carried it out, or ordered it to be carried out ..." (p. 25).[145]

The imagery of water (brackish water, a ship's whirling wake, a stream) ("*Brackwasser*," "*wirbelndes Kielwasser*," "*Fluß*") and its attendant symbolism figures even more prominently in this predominantly fictional-historical segment, as a more subtle and integrated way of carrying the theme of the "slip and slide" of all discourse and perception; in spite of the lower frequency and lesser disruptive degree of metafictional self-consciousness, the explicitly intertextual underpinning of the novella is shown in this segment as well:

> Only the Friesian Jaspers saw the sea as: "demanding that one persevere, with no solid ground in sight, and the essence of things emerge precisely because of this."

---

[144] "*Keine Treppe, nur eine Leiter vor einer Eisentür, die verschlossen ist. Zurückklettern, zurückstampfen, der Gang ist noch enger als auf dem Herweg, er stößt auf Gänge links, auf Gänge rechts.*"
[145] "*Haben Sie gelesen, was de Gaulle zur Ermordung Kennedys gesagt hat, und de Gaulle soll einen sehr tüchtigen Geheimdienst haben, der sicherlich auch hier auf seinem Flaggschiff einige Luxuskabinen ... verwanzt hat; de Gaulle sagte ... 'Die Ermordung Kennedys ... Die Polizei hat die Tat ausgeführt, oder sie hat den Befehl dazu gegeben....'*"

And it wasn't a coincidence that Goethe, who also saw
the sea, illustrated the senseless, the completely
senseless waste of energy of the Napoleonic era through
"streams," "currents," "rivers," and "floods" [146] (pp.
29f.).

The topographic dominance of the sea in this segment affords
the opportunity to enable a condensation of many previous
manifestations of water imagery and the metaphors it generates, thereby
achieving a final saliency of this troping, a completion and summing-up
of the scheme of reference between tenor and vehicle as well as their
more palpable integration. Scanning over the progression of references
to the sea which accomplish this task, one encounters the sea as
evocative of the aimlessness of historical events and the progression of
time, of the solely vertical motion of a horizontal axis:

In fact the towering masses of water are waves *which
do not move forward*, as appearances would have it, but
rather arch up and breathe out in a stationary position.
The ocean is a filled vessel whose contents are in motion
horizontally at the surface only due to currents and tides
... (p. 29). [147]

The inability to move along a horizontal axis, to establish a true
sense of contiguity or the ultimate absence of true contiguity possesses
the corollary of a sense of the mythical, an inclination to see sameness,
the indebtedness of creativity to tradition. Hence the description of the
waves evocative of the war-time environment as "phalanx on phalanx"
(*"Phalanx vor Phalanx)"* (p. 28), "an ancient Greek and Macedonian

---

[146] *"Nur dem Friesen Jaspers stellt das Meer ... 'Die Forderung, es aushalten
zu können, daß nirgends der feste Boden ist, aber gerade dadurch der Grund
der Dinge spricht.' Und Goethe, der auch das Meer gesehen hat, illustrierte
nicht zufällig an 'Bächen,' an 'Strömen,' an 'Fluß' und 'Überschwemmung'
den sinnlosen - den absolut sinnlosen - Potenzverschleiß der Napoleonischen
Ära ..."*
[147] *"Tatsächlich sind die aufgetürmten Wassermassen Wellen, die sich nicht
vorwärts bewegen, wie es den Anschein hat, sondern sich stets an der Stelle
wölben und ausatmen. Der Ozean ist eine gefüllte Schale, deren Inhalt sich an
der Oberfläche nur dank Strömungen und Gezeiten in den Horizontalen bewegt
..."*

battle formation."[148] The sea is also described in terms of the Eros-Thanatos contradiction intoned in *"Matrosen"*: it is on the one hand " ... a decorative bunting of sperm-white ejaculate" *("... ein spermaweiß bewimpeltes Ejakulat"* (p. 29); the wake of the *Queen Mary* and the *France* is "... the usual, broad train, long, beautiful, 'innocent,' like bridal tulle. Or like lime chaff - lime on the graves of the men of the *Curaçao.*"[149] The narration of the final episode, accomplished primarily in the narrative present, re-establishes the dream-framework of its germination, just at the time of collision of the two ships:

> I see the ship's wake - is it flowing towards me or away from me, I don't know, it's flowing over Schlunk's face, over my face, washing us towards each other, and, jumping overboard, he pulls me down with him and I scream as does he and all the others - and then I'm awake. And when Ledig, packed into the deckchair next to me on the wind-sheltered stern of the *France* puts his hand on my wrist and asks in a fatherly, bemused way: "Sleep well?" To this date the following has never been recorded in the annals of seafaring: the passenger liner guillotined the cruiser! (p. 33).[150]

As at the beginning of this third segment, the analogy is drawn between the convolutions and fluidity of dreaming and those of the ship's wake. This final intersection of dreamwork and reality coincides with the final words in the portrayal of this "unheard of event." The last three sentences of the novella are "Only two destroyers turn back to fish

---

[148] *Collins Dictionary of the English Language* ed. Patrick Hanks (London & Glasgow: Collins, 1979) p. 1098.
[149] *"... die übliche breite Schleppe, lang, schön, 'unschuldig', wie bräutlicher Tüll.   Oder wie eine Kalkspreu - Kalk auf dem Grab der Männer der 'Curaçao.'"*
[150] *"Ich sehe Kielwasser - läuft es auf mich zu, läuft es von mir her, ich weiß es nicht, es läuft über Schlunks Gesicht, läuft über meins, spült uns zueinander, und er zerrt mich, über Bord springend, mit sich hinab, und ich schreie wie er und wie alle - und bin wach. Und als Ledig, im Liegestuhl neben mir verpackt auf dem windgeschützten Heck der 'France' seine Hand auf mein Handgelenk legt und väterlich belustigt fragt ... 'Schön geschlafen?' da ist in den Annalen der Seefahrt, bis dato niemals zu verzeichnen, folgendes einzutragen ... Der Passagierdampfer hat den Kreuzer guillotiniert!"*

out bodies and people. 72 sailors survive. 72 out of 410" ("*Nur zwei Zerstörer wenden, um Menschen und Leichen zu fischen. 72 Matrosen überleben. 72 von 410)*" (p. 33). The alliteration of "*zwei Zerstörer*" (two destroyers) recalls the phonemic parallelism of "*mein zweijähriger Zweiter*" (my two-year-old second eldest) of the opening sentence of the novella. In that context, it was seen to stand for the affirmation of the imaginary, of metaphor as a counter-value to metonymy as the "appropriate medium with which to describe logical relationships between concepts or entities or events." Thus the closural strategy initially seems to favour the contiguous over the paradigmatic of the opening strategy, albeit repeating similar phonemic and lexical categories.   In both instances, the immediate textual environment includes a paternal presence. In the opening sequence, it is the child who interrupts the father's sleep, "Fritz ... who wakes me in the morning ..." ("*Fritz, ... der mich morgens weckt ...* ," whereas in the closing sequence it is the paternal figure who interrupts his charge: ." "... Ledig ... puts his hand on my wrist ... " ("*... Ledig ... [der] seine Hand auf mein Handgelenk legt ...*") calling to mind Lacan's scheme of the "*Non/Nom du père*" ("no"/name of the father) as that which launches the child on its journey of deferment of the Imaginary. Finally, the circle is drawn closed as the narrator ends his narration in the same position in which he began it, that is to say, in the horizontal position most conducive to sleep, to dreamwork and flights of the imagination.

Die Berliner Antigone

The title of this text incorporates a play from Sophocles' trilogy (composed of *Antigone, Oedipus Rex* and *Oedipus at Colonus*) as a trope and prefiguration of its content. In his discussion of this work and numerous others which have drawn on its theme, George Steiner speaks of its basis in foundational myths, (p. 158) and the "principal constants of conflict in the condition of man," (p. 231) or "elemental antinomies": (p. 234)

> The polarities of masculinity and femininity, of ageing and of youth, of private autonomy and of social collectivity, of existence and mortality, of the human and the divine, can be crystallized only in adversary terms (whatever the many shades of accommodation between them). To arrive at oneself - the primordial journey - is to come up, polemically, against 'the other'. The boundary conditions of the human person are those set by gender, by age, by community, by the cut between life and death, and by the potentials of accepted or denied encounter between the existential and the transcendent (pp. 231-232).

Each of the texts under discussion in this chapter realizes the valorization of the metaphoric and allegoric potential of prose to a high degree through mythological themes. Steiner indicates the versatility of myth in this respect when he states that

> Myth embodies the potential of finality while postponing, through ambiguity, error, and conflict, its fulfilment. In myth there is always an 'awaiting of meaning ...' [...]
> But it is myth and its commitment to transcendence which generate, which compell, the dynamics of recursion, of repetition (that 'asking again') across time (p. 303).

For this reason, myth is an apt device for the shorter prose form of the novella and short story, if one defines these as achieving within limited quantitative proportions "an effect of greater intensity by redevelopment," to be "both micro- and macrocosmic" (Leibowitz, pp.

78f.) or as "a highly compressed form of narration" dealing "with some central issue in human relationships ... that go far beyond the particular context of the story ..." (Dyer, p. 10).

In the case of *Die Berliner Antigone*, the significance of intertextual expansion of the tenor is established even before the text begins. In Sophocles' text, Creon, the despotic king of Thebes declares that any attempt to bury Polyneices, fallen in a struggle against his own city of Thebes, will be considered as heinous a crime as murder. Antigone, Polyneices' sister, defies the edict, buries her brother, citing her duty to her family and to divine law. Condemned by Creon as a traitor herself, she dies by her own hand.

The central figure of *Die Berliner Antigone*, Anne, is tried by a military court in Berlin for having stolen her brother's body from a dissection lab and providing him with a proper burial. This had been denied him after conviction and execution for a treasonous offence. At Hitler's own order Anne is to be executed for her undertaking. The officer presiding over the trial is the father of Anne's fiancé. For fear of alienating his son and his wife, he interprets Hitler's words to the effect that Anne should "'... reimburse the anatomical institute for the corpse in person'" ("'*in eigener Person der Anatomie die Leiche zurückerstatten*'") (p. 204) to mean that she must replace the body, not substitute her own. He threatens to carry out the order as it was meant if she does not reveal its location. Although the authorities are successful in intimidating her, her decision to live comes too late; her fiancé, learning of her perilous situation, has commited suicide. The grief-stricken father is absent for several days, during which the process leading to Anne's execution runs its course with no intervention.

The deictics of the opening sentence begin the exposition *in medias res*. The first motif is a familiar one: the inability to establish agency in the case of an occurrence for which definitive proof cannot be obtained from the only reliable source - its likely agent:

> Since the accused had already been convicted on *one* count of perjury, the presiding judge believed he could save her: Anne claimed to have removed her brother - or as the state prosecutor said as often as he could - "the corpse of the hanged man" from the anatomical institute and brought it to the *Invaliden*-cemetery immediately following the air raid - without the help of a second party. And in fact a handcart and a shovel had been stolen. Also in that night the fire brigade, soldiers and

Hitler-Youth had secured the bodies of victims, lining them up in a gym and along the cemetery's main driveway. Yet two gravediggers ... denied convincingly to the court that they had seen the unclothed body of a young man amongst the 280 victims who had asphyxiated or burned to death. Their statements were taken as conclusive. They were able to describe with precision the details of having personally placed the fifty-one dead in their graves three days later, bodies that no next-of-kin could identify nor had sought to claim ... (p. 202).[151]

This passage contains motifs which are a chilling contradiction of standard Western societal and interpersonal norms of interaction. Above all else is the paradox that a court should be concerned with the prevention of the burial of a body. That the evidence provided by grave diggers claiming to remember every corpse they had handled (at the rate of roughly three hundred killed in one night, this would amount to 2100 a week) is considered admissable, defies comprehension and impugns the motives of such an assembly. To speak of those deceased whose burial *is* sanctioned as *"geborgene Opfer,"* secure victims, is a contradiction of terms and as such a description consonant with the grotesquely paradoxical nature of its textual surroundings. The corollary to this paradox is that those who are still alive are not secure, that protection lies in death. This is precisely how this motif is developed in the text. The passage in which Anne draws this conclusion also

---

[151] *"Da die Angeklagte einer falschen Aussage bereits überführt war, glaubte der Generalrichter, er könne sie retten: Anne behauptete, ihren Bruder, den Gehenkten, wie der Staatsanwalt möglichst oft sagte - sofort nach dem Fliegerangriff ohne fremde Hilfe aus der Anatomie herausgeholt und auf den Invalidenfriedhof gebracht zu haben. Tatsächlich waren ein Handwagen, aber auch eine Schaufel ... entwendet worden. Auch hatten in dieser Nacht ... Feuerwehr, Hitlerjungen und Soldaten ... die geborgenen Opfer in einer Turnhalle oder entlang der Hauptallee des Friedhofs aufgereiht."*

Vor Gericht aber hatten zwei Totengräber ... überzeugend bestritten, unter den 280 Verbrannten oder Erstickten, ... den unbekleideten ... Körper eines jungen Mannes gesehen zu haben. Ihre Aussagen hatten Beweiskraft. Sehr präzise vor allem in den Nebensächlichkeiten gaben sie an, persönlich jeden einzelnen der 51 Toten, die weder zu identifizieren gewesen noch von Angehörigen gesucht worden waren, drei Tage später in die Grube gelegt zu haben ..."

incorporates the motif observed in *Atlantik-Novelle* of the individual experiencing the last minutes of life with little hope of survival, of the dialectic of the creation of life and its destruction, as well as that of the prone sleep-position and the reversed expectation that night and darkness are where existence is nurtured, away from the light of reality:

> Sometimes the loved-ones who had died, her fiancé, her mother, her brother, snatched her from her fear, enabled her to imagine the unimaginable, - her own death, not with a sense of terror but as the only true, dependable freedom. During these moments, she was prepared. At night, when she lay prone, the desire to remain alive was predominant.

> During the day, tortured by the sounds of the prison ... she tried ... to turn her attention away from ... the hands that wanted to strangle her - these hands had been grasping at her since the trial. She tried to escape to the realization that only death can protect us from harm (p. 212).[152]

The human crisis portrayed in these lines calls to mind the words of the first stanza of the poem *"Matrosen"* in *Atlantik-Novelle*: "Sleep unto death tempts nearly as much as a bed! / though lifeless, caught in the jostle on board a murder machine ..." (p. 16).[153] In the second stanza, darkness is the place of union with another, away from the differentiation and alienation of daylight: "Furlough again ... / ... and an entire darkness / oceans away .../ Protect like a pier against foe and tribunal!" (*"Einmal noch Urlaub .../...-und eine ganze Dunkelheit/ [...] Vor Feind und Kriegsgerichten schützen wie ein Kai!"*) (p. 16).

---

[152] *"Manchmal entrissen ihre Toten, der Freund, die Mutter, der Bruder, Anne ihrer Angst und bewirkten, daß das Unvorstellbare, ihr eigenes Totsein, vorstellbar wurde ohne Entsetzen, ja eben als die wahre verläßliche Freiheit. In solchen Momenten war sie bereit. In den Nächten, wenn sie lag, überwog ihre Daseinsbegierde."*
Am Tag, unter der Folter der Zuchthausgeräusche ... versuchte sie ... sich abzuwenden ... von dem Kübel und den Würgehänden, die sie seit der Gerichtsverhandlung nach sich greifen sah - und in die Einsicht zu flüchten, daß allein der Tod uns beschützen kann."
[153] *"Schlaf bis zum Tod lockt fast schon wie ein Bett! / Entseelt zwar dank des Bord- und Mordbetriebes ..."*

Similarly, the cemetery under the cloak of night where Anne buries her brother is portrayed as a safe haven against the fiery and destructive brightness of reality:

> ... Anne let herself be drawn into the whirl ... The now phosphorescent *Friedrichstraße* had bolted up in a wind of fire, violently spewing itself into the sky, an explosion of light, a fading away, a sparking flag of destruction. And then, like an island of peace, oceans away from this orgiastic, burning madness, the dark plot lay there .... (p. 207).[154]

The metaphor *"meerweit"* also has its counterpart within a similar context in the second stanza of *"Matrosen"*: and an entire darkness / oceans away, a human existence ... (*"... eine ganze Dunkelheit / meerfern wie Menschen leben ..."* (p. 16). In *Atlantik-Novelle*, the sea is a trope for the convolutions of the interaction of inner and outer reality; crisis situations bring the dual relationship of opposition and alliance between Eros and Thanatos to the surface. Emancipation from the isolation of the self can be reached either through an extension by means of union with others, and when that is not possible, through a reduction of the self to nothingness. Anne's act in the cemetery is both of these - it is the final act of restoration of her brother to nothingness, and in doing so, she is joining him in taking the same path away from a turbulent consciousness with its internal and external currents, hence the water metaphors (whirl [*"Wirbel"*] and oceans away [*"meerweit"*]) to her own state of non-consciousness. Her fiancé, Bodo, will join her in the same way. Of the first Antigone, George Steiner writes,

> Antigone envisions herself as entering either upon blank and inconceivable extinction - something like Baudelaire's *'grand trou / Tout plein de grand horreur, menant on ne sait où'* [great hole / filled entirely with great horror, leading to the unknown] - or as seeking uncertain reunion with the clan of the self-destroyed and

---

[154] *"Anne ließ sich einfach mitreißen von dem Wirbel ... Die phosphoreszierte Friedrichstraße hatte sich brechend und verglühend im Feuerwind gegen den Himmel gebäumt, eine flackernde Fahne der Verwüstung. Und dann, wie eine Friedensinsel, so meerweit getrennt von der orgiastischen Brandwut, lag der dunkle Acker da."*

fratricidal dead. No Elysium beckons, no Socratic grove
(Steiner, p. 281).

The passage from *Die Berliner Antigone* quoted above contains
the parallel metaphors "a sparking flag of destruction" and "the orgiastic
burning madness." These also express the *Eros/Thanatos* ambivalence,
drawn into greater prominence by the phallic symbolism of the flag.
There are three other occurrences of this combination of the colour red
(predominant in the flag in question), the phallic symbol, and the notion
of darkness, of the oblivion of death. The first is the presence of flag
bearers at the common grave sight as quoted above (p. 202); the second
and third, in order of appearance in the text, are a description of objects
in the court upon which the chief justice fixes his gaze:

> He stared at a water stain that was now coming through
> the wall just above a bust of the *Führer*, looking like a
> larger-than-life finger print. The colossal bronze figure
> had remained unshakeable on its pedestal, although the
> air pressure produced by the previous night's bombing
> had even ripped pipes out of the wall in the courtyard ...
> [...] ... the water stain over the *Führer's* bust standing
> before the long rage-red banner darkened and ate into
> the wall more and more ... (pp. 203f.).[155]

Thus a symbol of absolute patriarchal hegemony, cast in the
mythical proportions of a larger-than-life bronze figure, is counterpoised
with symbols which would mitigate its impact: that of night and
darkness, the escape and threat of *Thanatos*, and the symbol of an
immanent deluge in the circular configuration of water, a trope for the
uncontrollable flow of events, ideas and basic drives.

Another motif common to both texts is that of the mass burial
site and the ritual used to mark the passing from life. In *Atlantik-
Novelle*, the narrator writes a poem as an epitaph: "In this way I cast my
rhymes, gazing into the ship's wake that is as white as the lime thrown

---

[155] *"Er sah sich fest an einem Wasserfleck, der jetzt wie ein überlebensgroßer
Fingerabdruck die Wand über der Büste des Führers durchdrang. Die
kolossale Bronze war unerschütterlich auf ihrem Sockel geblieben, obgleich
der Luftdruck des nächtlichen Bombardements selbst Rohre im Gerichtshof aus
der Wand gerissen hatte ... [...] ... der Wasserfleck über der Büste des Führers
vor dem langen wutroten Fahnentuch [fraß] weiter und dunkler um sich ..."*

onto mass graves" (p. 17). In *Die Berliner Antigone*, this motif is used to reflect an ideology which distorts reality by favouring the paradoxical euphemism "communal grave" ("*Gemeinschaftsgrab*") over the banned term "mass grave" ("*Massengrab*"), evoking the notion that death is also a locus of social intercourse to be afforded the same ideological trappings that accompanied life:

> The term "mass grave" had been forbidden. The government of the *Reich* was in the habit of laying the dead of a communal grave to rest with particular effort to provide solace: not only were there clergy of both confessions on hand and a well-known Party orator, there were also standard bearers and a platoon band of the guard-batallion (p. 202).[156]

Here the basic antinomy of life and death is linked to that of the opposition between society and the individual, and, through the reaction to the description of this ritual of one of those sitting in judgment, it is also connected to the tensions between masculine and feminine, youth and aging:

> An associate judge of the military court, a grandfatherly, warm-hearted general ... was so touched by the description of the burial ceremony that he recommended to the accused in a tone of gentle officiousness that she finally tell the truth about her brother's "whereabouts" (p. 203).[157]

This motif of empathy and concern of the victimizer for the victim, runs through the text as a leitmotif, whose manifestation three times includes the male/female polarity. The first instance of this occurs

---

[156] "*Die Bezeichnung Massengrab war verboten worden. Die Reichsregierung pflegte die Toten eines Gemeinschaftsgrabes mit besonders tröstlichem Aufwand beizusetzen: nicht nur waren Geistliche beider Konfessionen und ein nahmhafter Parteiredner, sondern auch noch ein Musikzug des Wachtbataillons und eine Fahnenabordnung hinzugezogen worden.*"

[157] "*Ein Beisitzer der Reichskriegsgerichtes, ein großväterlich warmherziger General ... war so gerührt durch die Schilderung der Totenfeier, daß er der Angeklagten mit milder Zudringlichkeit empfahl, endlich die Wahrheit zu sagen über den 'Verbleib' ihres toten Bruders.*"

after a sequence of flashback and reflection on the part of the "chief justice," in which his son's intransigence on the matter of his plan to marry Anne and his wife's insistence that he intervene to save his prospective daughter-in-law is treated, immediately followed by the recollection of a scene in which Hitler insists on an expeditious and ruthless suppression of Anne's act of dissent ("How could he have, under Hitler's Rasputin-like, coercive, bone-chilling stare, made the impossible confession that this girl, this sister of an archtraitor, was secretly engaged to his son ..." (p. 204).[158] Here the male/female polarity stands as a motive which seems to outweigh the relationship between individual and collective, as it does in the case of the sentimental admiral. The chief justice does not accept these proportions easily: "Bodo, - and not even his mother - seemed to have any sense of what it had cost him to twist the *Führer's* words, only so that this rebellious minx be spared the executioner's axe" (p. 204).[159] In spite of Hitler's intimidation, he nevertheless decides to attempt to save Anne's life. He takes the same risk that Anne has taken, in defiance of the state, and is indeed characterized in the narration himself as a prisoner: "The chief magistrate ... had murmured through frozen lips 'Yes, *Führer*,' and later, as if a blind prisoner, he could not find his way to his car" (p. 204).[160] The chief justice falls into the same tone as the elderly admiral: "Sweating under his cap, he fell into the same personal, unprofessional tone as the elderly admiral, promising the accused, almost as if she were someone in whom he could confide, that he would allow for such mitigating circumstances" (p. 204).[161] He also couples this kind tone with the threat of decapitation, should the accused not see fit to divulge the location of the body within twenty four hours. Once again, the admiral's predisposition to Anne is figured in the narrative: "...the

---

[158] *"Wie hätte er denn in Hitler's kaltblaue, rasputinisch zwingende Augen hinein, das unmögliche Geständnis ablegen können, dieses Mädchen, die Schwester eines Hochverräters sei heimlich mit seinem Sohn verlobt ..."*
[159] *"Bodo schien kein Gefühl dafür zu haben, auch seine Mutter nicht, was es ihn kostete, ... dem Führer das Wort im Munde umzudrehen, nur damit dieses aufsäßige Frauenzimmer vor dem Beil bewahrt blieb."*
[160] *"Der Generalrichter ... hatte mit erfrorenen Lippen 'Jawohl, mein Führer' gemurmelt und später, ein geblendeter Gefangener, nicht mehr zu seinem Wagen hingefunden."*
[161] *"Jetzt verfiel er, Schweiß unter der Mütze, in den unsachlich persönlichen Ton des betagten Admirals und versprach der Angeklagten fast vertraulich mildernde Umstände."*

admiral caressed this half-expired 'marvel of a girl' with the wistfully pleasured gaze common in old men" (p. 205).[162] Towards the end of the text, this motif is again taken up: the individual who cuts Anne's hair in preparation for execution is attracted to her and uses the same familiar tone as does the admiral; the impending decapitation is evoked by the flashing of scissors:

> Anne did not resist ... when they bound her feet with a short chain and drove her with six other women ... to the *Plötzensee*. There a half-idiotic, retired cobbler, who had zealously maintained this privilege for years, ceremoniously cut the hair from the backs of their necks, full of kindly chatter and with a lecherous, frightened look in his eyes; while doing this, he grinned, wrapped the hair around the bare skin of his forearm and performed a little dance around his captive, continuously opening and closing the scissors as he danced, until they whistled him out like a dog (p. 213).[163]

The final example of this leitmotif of personal involvement of the victimizer with the victim is found in the last sentence of the text. Anne has died at the hands of the executioner who would also put to death those responsible for the assassination attempt against Hitler on July 20, 1944. These executions were filmed and shown to Hitler's staff. When the chief justice had coupled his kind persuasion with a death threat, the reason he had given was that in such a time of "total war," the court had no time to waste with such drawn-out matters: "'At this time of total war, the court cannot waste its time with exhaustive enquiries'" ("'*An langwierige Nachforschungen kann das Gericht zu diesem Zeitpunkt des Totalen Krieges keine Kräfte verschwenden*'") (p.

---

[162] "*...der Admiral [tätschelte] mit dem wehmütigen Wohlgefallen alter Männer diese halberloschene 'Pracht von einem Mädel ...'*"
[163] "*Ohne Auflehnung ließ Anne ... sich auch noch die Füße an eine kurze Kette legen und mit sechs anderen jungen Frauen ... zum Auto nach Plötzensee bringen, wo ihnen ein halbidiotischer Schuster, der seit Jahren als Rentner dieses Privilegium eifrig hütete, mit verschreckt geilen Augen und zutraulichem Geschwätz umständlich das Haar im Nacken abschnitt; dabei ... wickelte [er] ihr Haar grinsend um einen seiner nackten Unterarme und tänzelte, die Schere unaufhörlich öffnend und schließend, um die Gefesselte herum, bis man ihn hinauspfiff wie einen Hund ...*"

205). The concept of "total war" was introduced by the minister for propaganda, Joseph Goebbels in the *Berliner Sportpalast* on July 20, 1944 after German forces had been repulsed at Stalingrad.[164] Thus the text ends with this ironic situation: the author of the concept of total war, of which the court, its philosophy and the fate it imposes upon its victims are an exponent, shudders at the effect of his own edict:

> A state official made it known that even Hitler's satanic party associate, the Minister of Propaganda, several times held his hands before his eyes as the film was screened (p. 214).[165]

The name of the executioner is given as "the horse meat butcher Röttger" (*"der Pferdeschlächter Röttger"*) (p. 214). It corresponds to another leitmotif, that of the reduction of the victims of the Nazi regime to the status of animals being prepared for slaughter. After sentence has been passed, Anne is referred to by those who administer the penal system as a "package" of flesh ready for state use: "Package meant: written off as a legal entity, released for decapitation and officially monitored cadaver dissection" (p. 211).[166] "Packages" are also deprived of food, reduced to the level of animals whose main concern is to obtain nourishment to maintain a basic level of subsistence: "The pain of hunger reduced her to an animal state ..." (*"Der Hungerschmerz reduzierte sie auf ihre Animalität ..."* (p. 213). Under these conditions of captivity, Anne is described in terms strongly reminiscent of Rilke's poem *Der Panther*: "Her gaze fluttered back and forth, fell back wounded as it struck the walls, became entangled in the bars as the daylight burst through" (p. 210).[167] The first stanza of Rilke's poem is as follows: "His eye has grown so weary with passing by the bars / that it holds nothing more. He feels as though there were a thousand bars /

---

[164] *Meyers Großes Universal Lexikon*, vol. 6, p. 11.
[165] *"Ein Staatssekretär hat überliefert, daß selbst der satanische Partei-genosse Hitlers, sein Propagandaminister, während der Filmveran-staltung sich mehrmals die Hand vor die Augen hielt."*
[166] *"Paket besagte: als juristische Person abgebucht, zur Dekapitation und behördlich überwachten Kadaververnutzung freigegeben."*
[167] *"Ihr flatternder Blick stieß sich wund an den Mauern und verfing sich an den Gitterstäben, durch die der Tag hineinprahlte."*

and behind these thousand bars no world."[168] A fellow prisoner is also to be executed for having become desperate for food: "The displaced person from Lodz had secretly eaten her fill in a bakery in Dresden during an air raid warning; she was therefore to be decapitated for looting" (p. 209).[169] Those used by the victimizers to reduce their victims to prey are portrayed in similar terms (cf. the cobbler who cuts Anne's hair being whistled out like a dog). If there is to be any symmetry made out of this low point on the scale of human existence, its high point in Hochhuth's fiction is not constituted by the idea of a benevolent and anthropomorphic deity. In *Atlantik-Novelle*, the narrator states: "Human beings know that their heritage is divine, since they cannot have made themselves. That also applies to their dogs and to the birch trees in their gardens" (p. 19).[170] The need to transcend the status of human animal is referred to by the narrator as "Hallucinations of salvation, insane images, whose attainment has led the religious or ideologically motivated to spill more blood than for any earthly short-term goal ..."(p. 20).[171] In Hochhuth's *Grüninger-Novelle*, the attorney's wife makes the observation - and the paradox could not be more sharply stated - that rather than Father Christmas, the more appropriate metaphor for God would be the great white shark (p. 102). This motif occurs in *Die Berliner Antigone* in the flashback in which Anne calls to mind her brother's grave. The stone she had chosen to mark the sight bore a Latin text with the inscription "*Apost. 5, 2.*" (p. 206). Significantly, the stone is described as being cracked and worn down by the elements, "...wept upon by snow and rain, torn ....." ("*ausgeweint von Regen und Schnee, zerrissen ...*"), and the words of this inscription are to remain a cryptic

---

[168] "*Sein Blick ist vom Vorübergehen der Stäbe / so müd geworden, daß er nichts mehr hält. "Ihm ist, als ob es tausend Stäbe gäbe / und hinter tausend Stäben keine Welt.*" *Twentieth Century German Verse*. Introduced and edited by Patrick Bridgewater (Harmondsworth, Middlesex: Penguin Books, 1968) p. 36.

[169] "*Die Verschleppte aus Lodz hatte sich heimlich, während eines Fliegeralarms, in einer Dresdener Bäckerei satt gegessen und sollte deshalb als Plünderer geköpft werden.*"

[170] "*Zwar weiß er [der Mensch], daß er göttlicher Herkunft sein muß, da er sich ja nicht selber gemacht haben kann. Das trifft auch zu auf seinen Hund oder auf die Birke in seinem Garten.*"

[171] "*Heils-Halluzinationen, Wahnbilder, zu deren unmöglicher 'Erreich-ung' der Mensch als Religiöser oder Ideologe mehr Blut vergossen hat als für jedes irdisch-erreichbare Teil-Ziel ....*"

reference in the novella: the chaplain who has visited Anne during her confinement may have translated the passage for her, but any significance it may have is deliberately questioned as Anne is led to her execution: "If Anne could now remember the words of Apostles 5:29 ... we don't know" (*"Ob Anne sich jetzt des Wortes Apostl. 5:29 erinnern konnte ... wir wissen es nicht"* (pp. 213f.). This quotation from the New Testament, when it is ascertained, assures that in addition to itself another text is called to mind - Brentano's *Geschichte vom braven Kasperl und dem schönen Annerl*. The following citation is from *The Acts of the Apostles*, and verses 27 through 29 show more clearly why this inscription is appropriate to Hochhuth's text:

> 27 And having brought them, they set them before the Sanhedrin. And the high priest questioned them, 28 saying, "We strictly charged you not to teach in this name, and behold, you have filled Jerusalem with your teaching, and want to bring this man's blood upon us." 29 But Peter and the apostles answered and said, "We must obey God rather than men."[172]

The ultimate stopping place, the foundation of security for this Antigone is not the rock of Peter, but the rock itself, the natural environment from which human beings emerge and to which they are re-integrated. The first example of this motif is found in the reminiscence of the cemetery scene itself:

> And at least within herself, she escaped from the walls and the bars, away from the cell - and was free, as long as she thought of the strip of earth outside, the old, pagan strip of earth ... [...] Berlin's most magnificent, regal trees form an arch as high as a cathedral over the few grave stones ... - and on that afternoon she had chosen one of the stones, a strong shield of peace, to mark her brother's grave (p. 206).[173]

---

[172]   *Saint Joseph Edition of the Holy Bible* (New York: Catholic Book Publishing Company, 1963) p. 129.

[173]   *"Und wenigstens innerlich riß sie sich los von Wand und Gitter, heraus aus der Zelle - und sie war frei, solange sie draußen an den Streifen Erde dachte, an den heidnisch alten ... [...] Die mächtigsten, die königlichen Bäume Berlins wölbten sich dort domhoch über die wenigen Grabsteine ... .und einen der*

Within this context is the related motif of the gothic lancet arch, also observed in *Grüninger-Novelle* in the paradoxical situation of being present only in the lower portion of a building. It is also employed in this text, but its symbolic impact is once again held earth-bound through the parallel symbolic description of trees as *"domhoch,"* as tall as cathedrals. "Protected from the street by wild-growing forsythia, protected by the Gothic niche behind her, she dug without haste ..." (*"Vor der Straße durch verwilderte Forsythien geschützt, geschützt im Rücken durch die gotische Nische, grub sie ohne Hast ..."*) (p. 207). Such imagery casts nature as the locus of the experience of transcendence more commonly associated with consecrated places of worship. The comfort afforded is very concretely of a tactile, visual and corporeal nature, rather than a spiritual experience: "Minutes passed before tears and the touch of the earth rid her of her numbness ..." (*"...Minuten vergingen bis Tränen und ihre Berührung der Erde dieses Erstarrtsein von ihr nahmen ..."*) (p. 207). This motif is once again called up when Anne remembers a particularly happy evening spent with her fiancé, and writes of this in her last letter, albeit in the awareness that this metaphysical surrogate is an attempt to establish constancy where indeed no evidence of it exists:

> She had to find some small consolation - even if it were
> a lie - some thought that would remain with him, and as
> she saw a star through the bars, one she did not know,
> and then another, she thought of something they had
> agreed upon on their last vacation while sailing on a
> brilliant, star-lit night: to always think of each other,
> when, in the evening, they saw the Great Bear ... In
> closing she wrote: "I can see our Great Bear through the
> bars, that's why I know that you are thinking about me
> now ... Bodo, dear Bodo, I entrust it with all of my
> thoughts and wishes for you, for ever ..."(p. 208).[174]

Steine, einen starken Schild der Ruhe ... hatte sie an jenem Nachmittag zum Grabstein des Bruders bestimmt."

[174] *"Sie mußte einen kleinen Halt, ein einziges Wort, das ihm blieb, hineinlügen - und da sie einen Stern durchs Gitter sah, den sie nicht kannte, und noch einen, so fiel ihr ein, was sie im letzten Urlaub verabredet hatten, beim Segeln in einer hohen hellen Nacht: immer aneinander zu denken, wenn sie abends den Großen Wagen sähen ... Und sie schloß ... 'Ich sehe durchs*

Earlier in the letter, Anne calls on Bodo to place birch branches from the banks of the river Havel as an act of remembrance of her brother: "... Later, when you look for me again, take a few branches from our birch on the Havel and place them on his grave ..." ("...*wenn Du mich später wieder suchst, so nimm ein paar Zweige von unserer Birke an der Havel und leg sie auf sein Grab* ...") (p. 206). This complement of natural objects is portrayed as a surrogate device, consciously employed as a symbol to constitute the most central meaning that things may have. Although the narration includes the main character's observation that this is done out of the necessity not to lose hope altogether, the natural elements which figure here evoke a sense of durability, of timelessness, of the never-ending cycle. The ancient stone of the tomb-marker, the spring-blossoming forsythia, the towering trees and the night lighted by a dome of stars are metaphors for eternity. Also a part of this motif complex is the scene in which Anne is given an apple by her guard as a compensation for having removed a shard of glass, which could have been used as an instrument of suicide: "... she ... was so frightened seeing tears in Anne's eyes for the first time, that she quickly went to fetch an apple." ("...*sie ... erschrak so sehr, als sie zum erstenmal, in Annes Augen Tränen sah ... daß sie schnell ging, einen Apfel zu holen*") (p. 213). In Northern myth, the apple is a symbol of death, but also of rejuvenation; "As a symbol of consummation, it is the opposite of the egg of initiation."[175] The birch tree, the Great Bear - the most important constellation of the Northern hemisphere, ("*Der große Wagen*") and the river Havel are all particularly apt symbols in this regard, since, when taken together, they foreshadow a new cycle of political and social contingencies which result from the chaos and death of the Second World War.[176]

Gitter unseren goldenen Wagen, und da weiß ich, daß Du jetzt an mich denkst ... Bodo, lieber Bodo, alle meine Gedanken und Wünsche für Dich vertrau ich ihm an, für immer ...'"

[175]   Ad de Vries, *A Dictionary of Symbols and Imagery* (New York and Amsterdam: North Holland Publishing Company, 1974) p. 18.

[176]   As "the earliest forest tree to put out leaves," the birch has long been a symbol of the beginning, of re-generation and re-birth (De Vries, p. 46). Two of its characteristics which would make it an appropriate symbol for Hochhuth's fiction are the colour contrast of its bark (" ... recognizable ... by the light and dark peeling bark of the common Birch ..." (p. 46) and its solipsistic method of self-generation ("unisexual catkins") (p. 46). It is also connected with the idea of the apocalypse: "around the birch the last world-

If, in interpreting this text, one attempts to apply Hermann Malmede's or Norman Friedman's scheme of a clearly discernable, linear chain of motifs constituting a singular event, the outcome would be, as with Atlantik-Novelle, the same non-applicability of the model. Anne's fate in *Die Berliner Antigone* is determined not by one, but by several factors. It may be said that she has sealed her own fate by undertaking to subvert the brutal authority of a dictator who does not subscribe to the conventions of civilization. Even when offered a reprieve, she does not grasp at the chance soon enough. It can also be argued that the need to restore her brother and herself to the earth are the result of built-in psychological and mythical patterns very difficult to ignore. When she is finally driven to ignore them, she is no longer at one with herself: "She no longer understood the girl that had buried her brother - did not want to be that girl, wanted to take it back. This

---

battle will be fought (Norse)" (p. 47). The birch is one of Russia's most prodigious trees: "...Russia ... remarkable for its endless birch woods.") (p. 46). The Great Bear is the constellation mentioned by the biblical figure of Job (Chapter 9, 9) ... "He made the Bear and Orion." In verse 22 he states: "Both the innocent and the wicked he destroys." The Great Bear also marks the cycle of the seasons ... "...its tail turns in the directions of the seasons connected with them: in Spring to the East, in Summer to the South, in Autumn to the West, and in Winter to the North" (p. 38.). It too is connected with the apocalypse: "...in some myths a stag, pursued by the Polar Star, which is the Hunter; when the stag is killed, the end of the world will come" (p. 39). As it is "the most important constellation of the Northern hemisphere," it can be seen in this context to be readily associated with the country which occupies the largest and most northern land-mass of the Northern hemisphere. Most obviously, the bear is a widely recognized symbol for Russia. The Havel runs through West Berlin, west to a confluence with the Elbe, a major natural boundary for the states of East and West Germany, considered until recent times to be the most likely starting place for a nuclear conflagration. The symbolic act of placing branches from the birch, taken from the banks of the Havel, on the grave of a soldier who had rebelled against and had fallen victim to the barbarism of those he served, suggests both the emergence of a new political and social reality as well as a re-enactment of the myth of planting cultures. As Joseph Campbell observes ... "...in the forest and planting cultures, there is a sense ... that death is required for new life. And the individual isn't quite an individual, he is a branch of a plant. Jesus uses this image when he says, 'I am the vine, and you are the branches.' [...] The motif of the plants that you eat having grown from the cut-up and buried body of a sacrificed deity or ancestral personage occurs all over the place, but particularly in the Pacific cultures" (p. 102).

destroyed her" (p. 210).[177] The actual chance for averting death is the
result of the chief justice being able to take advantage of the
ambivalence of language - exploiting an ironic statement by choosing its
face value over its real intent. Anne is initially given twenty-four hours
to divulge her secret. This is extended to eleven days when, through
chance, the court-building is razed in an air-raid: "A powerful airburst
had levelled the law court, extending Anne's time to reconsider to eleven
days" (*"Die Planierung des Gerichthofs durch eine Luftmine
verlängerte Annes Bedenkzeit auf elf Tage"*) (p. 209). Anne's letter to
Bodo precipitates his suicide; his grief-stricken father is absent from the
court for several days, permitting the machinery of "the law" to take an
irreversible course. On this point the text makes even the possibility of
intervention ambiguous: the chief justice's motive to save Anne
disappears with his son's death, and he is decorated by Hitler for
subordinating family interests to those of the state:

> The chief magistrate had not explicitly withdrawn his
> offer, but would ... possibly no longer have been in a
> position to snatch the delinquent from the mechanism of
> annihilation that had already begun to run its course (p.
> 211).[178]

Thus any linear chain of cause and effect is subverted by chance,
ambiguity, the transparency of language, a complex of contingencies and
the filter of eye-witness accounts (the chaplain who ministered to Anne
refuses to provide details about her execution: "Spare yourself the
technical details, my hair turned white over it" (*"Ersparen Sie sich die
technischen Einzelheiten, mein Haar ist darüber weiß geworden"*) (p.
214). The circularity observed in the other novellas under discussion
here is also present in *Die Berliner Antigone*. As mentioned above, the
chief justice issues his threat at the beginning of the text, citing the
propaganda minister's call for "total war" as a legitimation of swift and
unrelenting action. The closural strategy consists in part in portraying
the propaganda minister cringing while being subjected to filmed

---

[177] *"Sie begriff das Mädchen nicht mehr, das seinen Bruder bestattet hatte -
wollte es nicht mehr sein, wollte es zurücknehmen. Damit war sie vernichtet."*
[178] *"Der Generalrichter hatte sein Angebot nicht ausdrücklich widerrufen,
wäre aber ... vielleicht auch nicht mehr imstande gewesen, die Delinquentin
aus der angelaufenen Vernichtungsmaschinerie zurückzureißen."*

executions, carried out by the same person who executed Anne. In addition, the text includes the following epitaph on its last page:

> Epitaph/The Berlin Anatomical Institute /during the years 1939 -1945 received/ the bodies / of 269 executed women / Professor Stieve in Parliament / on July 20, 1952, / the 8th anniversary /of the unsuccessful attempt to assassinate / Hitler (p. 214).[179]

Thus the text closes with a commemoration of victims of atrocities made in an assembly convened as an instrument of law, whereas it began with the indictment of one of those victims, also by an assembly convened as an instrument of law(lessness).

---

[179] *"EPITAPH / Die Berliner Anatomie / erhielt in den Jahren 1939 - 1945 / die Körper / von 269 hingerichteten Frauen / Professor Stieve im 'Parlament' / am 20. Juli 1952, / dem 8. Jahrestag / des gescheiterten Attentats / auf Hitler."*

Chapter Four

Friedrich Dürrenmatt's The Assignment

First published in 1986, Dürrenmatt's novella has as its full title *The Assignment: Or On the Observing of the Observer of the Observers (Der Auftrag oder Vom Beobachten des Beobachters der Beobachter: Novelle in vierundzwanzig Sätzen).*[180] The first date of publication of *The Coup (Der Sturz)* is 1971; in the edition used for this analysis, the original German text appears with three others under the designation *"Erzählungen"* (stories*).*

A résumé of the plot of *The Assignment* is possible if events are summarized according to their chronology within the text: it is not possible to propose a definitive causal sequence, since given instances of cause and effect frequently appear with an alternative cause-and-effect-sequence. F., a film-journalist, is commissioned by a psychiatrist, Otto von Lambert, to investigate his wife's disappearance and murder in a North African desert. The text presents alternative reasons for her initial disappearance. F. accepts the assignment, flies to the North African country and is given a tour of the crime scene (the desert ruins of Al-Hakim) by the authorities. She is permitted to interview several suspects whose accounts have been rehearsed, and must witness the execution of the alleged murderer. Finally, she has her film material replaced by the authorities' own doctored and self-congratulatory version and is ordered to leave the country with her film team immediately. Before this happens, she is enlisted by the head of the country's secret service to pursue, under his protection, the true nature of the circumstances surrounding Tina von Lambert's death. He does not believe that the murder was a retaliation on the part of certain international interests for von Lambert's refusal at an anti-terrorist conference to brand Arab "freedom-fighters" as terrorists. F. is housed in a deserted hotel at the edge of a wasteland, where she discovers that Tina von Lambert is still alive, never having left Switzerland, and that in fact the woman who was murdered was a Danish journalist, Jytte Sörensen. Sörensen had borrowed Tina's passport and red fur coat, since the only way to enter the country was to conceal her journalistic intent with a false identity. F. herself has happened upon a

---

[180] In translation the original "Novella in twenty-four sentences" is omitted, although the translator maintains the format of twenty-four long sentences.

100

red fur coat in the market place and buys it, believing it to be a link to the murder victim. (All four young female characters in *The Assignment*, Tina von Lambert, Jytte Sörensen, F., and the woman assigned by the chief of the secret service to impersonate F. appear in red fur coats). Having entered the desert, F. falls into the hands of Polyphemos, a cameraman who had originally been assigned to an underground observatory. This was in a part of the desert where a secret weapons-testing-ground has been established by anyone with a stake in the arms' race. Polyphemos reveals to F. that the head of the secret service intends to expose his country's sponsorship of this highly lucrative weapons-experimentation in a coup attempt. Since Polyphemos has become a redundant recorder of information, having been replaced by a network of computerized satellites which observe the testing ground as well as each other, an attempt is being made to eliminate him. The explosions of ICBMs draw nearer as he speaks, and the power to the underground cavern has been cut off. As one who has observed what each party concerned wishes to conceal, Polyphemos has no place to which he may retreat. He has permitted Jytte Sörensen to be raped and murdered by his insane charge, Achilles, a former American bomber pilot and professor of Classics at a "hillbilly" university, so that he may photograph the proceedings. These frozen, static moments of death give him a sense of power over time:

> ... a metaphor of global catastrophe, because the purpose of the camera was to arrest time, ..., to stop time by destroying time, film too, he said, only seemed to reproduce reality when it was run through a projector, it created the illusion of process when actually it consisted of successive still shots, ... he had felt like a god with his camera, but ..., he himself was being observed as he observed ..., a god who was observed was no longer a god, ... (pp. 108-109).[181]

---

[181] ... "... *ein Gleichnis der Weltkatastrophe, denn die Kamera sei dazu da, ... die Zeit aufzuhalten, indem sie die Zeit vernichte, auch der Film gebe ja die Wirklichkeit, lasse man ihn ablaufen, nur scheinbar wieder, er täusche einen Ablauf vor, der aus aneinandergereihten Einzelaufnahmen bestände ... er habe sich mit seiner Kamera wie ein Gott gefühlt, ... aber .. ein Gott, der beobachtet werde, sei kein Gott mehr ...*" (pp. 112-13).

F. is about to suffer the same fate as her Danish colleague when Polyphemos and Achilles are shot by observers hiding in wrecked military vehicles. The text concludes with a remark made to F. on her good fortune: "... goddamn, were you lucky" (p. 129) (*"Donnerwetter, hast du aber Glück gehabt."*) (p. 133).

The epigraph of *The Assignment,* Kierkegaard's *Either/Or,* also cited by one of the novella's characters (p. 74) speaks of a nexus of contingencies to which the speaker sees his or her existence consigned:

> What will come? What will the future bring? I do not know. I have no presentiment. When a spider plunges from a fixed point to its consequences, it always sees before it an empty space where it can never set foot, no matter how it wriggles. It is that way with me: before me always an empty space; what drives me forward is a consequence that lies behind me. This life is perverse and frightful, it is unbearable (p. 2).[182]
>
> Kierkegaard

In his study *Novelle und Kriminalschema,*[183] Rainer Schönhaar has pointed out that ambiguity, a high-profile term in contemporary literature, is also a characteristic of German literature after 1800. To what degree this is so is not a question to be dealt with in this context; of major significance for his monograph, however, is the work of Kleist, which has already been mentioned in this study. Schönhaar's examination of the formal implications of the criminality pattern (*"Kriminalschema"*) and his suggestion of an attendant existentialist aspect of the tenor of this vehicle are of particular interest for the text in question here, since the narration of *The Assignment* is propelled, if not by a question-and-answer structure, by a progression through a maze of questions and only partial answers, frequently presented as an "either-or" choice, showing the

---

[182] *"Was wird kommen? Was wird die Zukunft bringen? Ich weiß es nicht, ich ahne nichts. Wenn eine Spinne von einem festen Punkt sich in ihre Konsequenzen hinabstürzt, so sieht sie stets einen leeren Raum vor sich, in dem sie nirgends Fuß fassen kann, wie sehr sie auch zappelt. So geht es mir; vor mir stets ein leerer Raum; was mich vorwärts treibt, ist eine Konsequenz, die hinter mir liegt. Dieses Leben ist verkehrt und grauenhaft, nicht auszuhalten" (p. 7).*
[183] Rainer Schönhaar, *Novelle und Kriminalschema* (Bad Homburg v.d.H., Berlin, Zürich: Verlag Dr. Max Gehlen,1969) p. 198.

intertextual epigraph to be an appropriate expositional strategy. As Schönhaar observes,

> A primary essential characteristic of the narrative of the detective story is the ongoing search for hidden and underlying causes, the search for unknown circumstances and unknown perpetrators, for motives, opportunities, for those bearing responsibility, in short, the search for the criminal, and therefore how one can combine all of these individual questions into a heuristic concept-model (p. 193).[184]

This is indeed the question which is asked at the beginning of the text of F., a television journalist, who is enlisted by a psychiatrist, von Lambert, to investigate his wife Tina's apparent rape and murder in a North African country, most likely Morocco, referred to in the text as M., with the point of entry for F. being the city C., it must be assumed, Casablanca. A body has been discovered in the desert, where Tina von Lambert is reported to have been seen wearing a red fur coat. The reason for her presence in M. is, in her husband's eyes, her attempt to flee his psychiatric observation of her depressed condition:

> ... he was guilty of his wife's death because he had always treated the heavily depressed woman as a case instead of as a person, until she had accidentally discovered his notes on her sickness and, according to the maid, left the house straight away, a red fur coat thrown over her denim suit, ... (p. 7).[185]

---

[184] *"Ein erstes wesentliches Kennzeichen detektorischen Erzählens ist das ständige Fragen nach verborgenen Ursachen und Hintergründen, nach unbekannten Sachverhalten und nach unbekannten Tätern, nach Tatmotiven, Tatgelegenheiten und Tatverantwortlichen, die 'Kriminal-frage' nach dem Täter also, wie all diese Einzelfragen sich in einem heuristischen Hilfsbegriff zusammenfassen ließen."*

[185] *"... er sei am Tod seiner Frau schuldig, weil er die oft unter schweren Depressionen Leidende immer mehr als Fall statt als Frau behandelt hätte, bis sie, nachdem ihr seine Notizen über ihre Krankheit durch Zufall zu Gesicht gekommen, kurzerhand das Haus verlassen habe, nach der Meldung der Hausdame nur in ihrem roten Pelzmantel über einen Jeansanzug geworfen ..."* (p. 13).

F., on the other hand, does not believe that the reason for Tina
von Lambert's sudden departure was her husband's treating her more as a
case than as a wife, but rather her sordid, detailed account of her
husband's physical and personal habits falling into his hands. As F.
observes,

> Tina von Lambert had portrayed her husband as a
> monster, but gradually, not immediately, virtually peeling
> off pieces of him, facet by facet, examining each one
> separately, as if under a microscope, constantly
> narrowing and magnifying the focus and sharpening the
> light, page after page about his eating habits, page after
> page about the way he picked his teeth, page after page
> about how and where he scratched himself, page after
> page about his coughing or sneezing or clearing his throat
> or smacking his lips, ... [...] Tina had found out that von
> Lambert had read her journal, obviously a much more
> shattering discovery ..., since, for one who secretly hates
> and suddenly learns that the hated one knows it, there
> could be no other way out than to flee, ... (pp. 10-12).[186]

Nevertheless, F. does not postulate this reversal of observer and
observed, the first manifestation of the motive of seeing and being seen to
which the title of this work refers, as the complete truth. She remarks on
the one hand that it was probably not von Lambert's abstractly
professional diagnosis of his wife's depression as the debilitating insight
into the senselessness of existence, which, having been made known to
her, would have caused her to flee; Tina von Lambert's written
exclamation of "I am being watched"(p. 12). ("*Ich werde beobachtet*") (p.

---

[186] "*Tina von Lambert habe ihren Mann als ein Ungeheuer beschrieben, aber
allmählich, nicht sofort, sondern indem sie eine Facette dieses Menschen um
die andere von ihm gleichsam losgelöst, dann wie unter einem Mikroskop mit
immer steigernder Vergrößerung und in immer schärferem Licht betrachtet,
seitenlang beschrieben habe, wie er esse, seitenlang wie er in den Zähnen
stochere, seitenlang wie er sich und wo er sich kratze, seitenlang wie er
schnalze oder sich räuspere, huste, niese ... [...] Tina sei dahinter gekommen,
von Lambert hätte ihr Tagebuch gelesen, dieses sei ungeheuerlich ... und für
jemanden, der im Geheimen hasse und plötzlich wisse, der Gehasste wisse es,
gebe es keinen anderen Ausweg als die Flucht ...*" (pp. 14ff.).

16) in her own diary could hardly have been sparked by such an impersonal document:

> ..., they weren't observations at all but literally an abstraction of her humanity, defining depression as a psychosomatic phenomenon resulting from insight into the meaninglessness of existence, ... which made it seem inconceivable to her that Tina had fled as a result of having read these pages ... (p. 13).[187]

Although the greater likelihood in F.'s eyes is the revelation of Tina's own unpleasant observations of her husband which caused her to flee, the true cause of her leaving remains unclear: "...there still was the riddle of what could have driven Tina into the desert, ..."(p. 13) ("... *es bleibe rätselhaft, was Tina in die Wüste getrieben habe* ...") (p. 16). Thus begins a main characteristic of Dürrenmatt's text, already observed to be a prominent feature of Hochhuth's fiction, of subverting assumptions of causality without any resolution of the ambiguity. Attendant to this thematic-structural similarity is the motif of the shortcomings of human rational faculties in solving the riddles and paradoxes of reality, of which Kleist has been shown to be a major proponent and source (cf. chapter three of this study). The criminality pattern and the significance attributed to paradox are certainly not restricted to this one text of Dürrenmatt's production. In an appendix to his play *The Physicists*, entitled *21 Points to the Physicists* the author makes the following observations about the nature of chance and paradox:

> 8. The more human beings proceed by plan the more effectively they may be hit by accident. [...] 19. Within the paradoxical appears reality. 20. He who confronts the paradoxical exposes himself to reality. [188]

---

[187] "... *nicht ein Beobachten, sondern ein Abstrahieren vom Menschen sei hinter diesen Notizen zu lesen, die Depression definiert als psychosomatisches Phänomen, ausgelöst durch die Einsicht in die Sinnlosigkeit des Seins ... weshalb es ihr gänzlich unmöglich sei zu glauben, Tina sei geflüchtet, weil sie diese Notizen gefunden hätte ..." (p. 16).*

[188] Friedrich Dürrenmatt, *The Physicists* translated from the German by James Kirkup (New York: Grove Press, 1964) 95/96 ("8 / *Je planmäßiger die Menschen vorgehen, desto wirksamer mag sie der Zufall treffen.* [...] 19 / *Im Paradoxen erscheint die Wirklichkeit. 20 / Wer dem Paradoxen*

The documents of von Lambert and his wife are indeed cast as a paradox: "... and if Tina's description of her husband was grotesque in its exaggeration and excessive concreteness, von Lambert's notes were equally grotesque in their abstraction, ..."(p. 12) *("... sei die Schilderung Tina's über ihren Mann ins Übertriebene, ins allzu Anschauliche geraten, so die Notizen von Lamberts ins allzu Abstrakte ...")* (p. 16). As to von Lambert's motivation for a journalistic investigation into his wife's death, F. speculates that although von Lambert seems truly to love his wife, the emotion of love of another person is a projection of self-love: "... it was all too easy to imagine that one loved someone, and that basically one loved only oneself, ..." (p. 11) *("... man bilde sich allzuleicht ein, jemanden zu lieben und liebe im Grunde nur sich selber ...")* (p. 15). In her discussion of Lacan and Freud, Elizabeth Wright has observed: "The lover is narcissistically projecting an image of a desire that ... completes his own, that looks at him from a place where he wishes to be ..." (Wright, p. 117). The spectacular funeral von Lambert had arranged (the coffin is flown from M., suspended from a helicopter, to the gravesite in Switzerland and is lowered directly into a grave as F.'s film crew records the event) (p. 9) would indicate a need for publicity. Not only does von Lambert wish to discover the truth, he wants to publish the results: "... he regarded it as his duty to find out the truth, and beyond that, to make it available to science, ..." (p. 8) *("... [er] ... erachte es für seine Pflicht, die Wahrheit zu erfahren, mehr noch, sie der Wissenschaft zugänglich zu machen, was sich ereignet habe ...")* (p. 12). Thus F. speculates that perhaps (she uses the words "why not" to punctuate her train of thought) von Lambert's motivation is less the discovery of the truth, than being seen and recognized for having done so, less a matter of achieving an epitaph of truth for his wife than attaining one of recognition for his own achievements and self-realization:

> ... the spectacular funeral had made her suspect that its purpose was to cover up his hurt pride, why not, and as for the assignment to hunt for the circumstances of her death, he was probably trying, albeit unconsciously, to build a monument to himself, ... (pp. 11-12).[189]

---

gegenübersteht, setzt sich der Wirklichkeit aus.") Friedrich Dürrenmatt, *Die Physiker* (Zürich: Diogenes, 1985) pp. 92f.

[189] *"... die spektakuläre Beerdigung habe sie mißtrauisch gemacht, die kaschiere seinen Stolz, warum nicht, und mit dem Auftrag, nach den*

Von Lambert's emotional attachment to his wife and his professional intention to establish the truth describe a way of coming to terms with empirical reality that is determined largely by an internal, libidinal impulse - the basic drive of Eros. It is also determined by the requisite assimilation of this desire to the discourse of culture (as a result of the Oedipal phase) - creating a concept of self through its concretization as a signifier, the pronoun "I" standing in for a constantly emerging consciousness, becoming "... objectified in the dialectic of observation with the other ...."[190] The extended title of this work, "on observing the observer of the observers," describes a predominant leitmotif, of which this reversal of the subject-object relationship is the first manifestation, as a dynamic of observing subject projecting its objects in assimilation to itself, but also of a subject which has to become the object of this process for other observing subjects. This, along with a leitmotif of disorientation, is how the aporia and paradoxical alternatives of lived experience are rendered in the text: the first instance of this motif demonstrates a disequilibrium, in that the observing subject does not interact with its object to, in turn, itself become an object: von Lambert interprets his wife's behaviour as a function of his psychiatric observation of her, and F., it may be postulated, attributes to Tina von Lambert her own journalistic experience of having to overcome the unpleasantness of being seen by the observed to be the observer. Further instances of this motif are designed to show how technology intervenes to exacerbate the difficulty in bridging the gap between subjects who must interact, unless the solitude inherent in being a subject is to become absolute.

The plot covered thus far represents the first four segments or, indeed, sentences of the total twenty-four which comprise the novella. It has been noted of Kleist's style that a predominance of hypotactic sentence structure corresponds to a concept of reality as an endless web of contingencies (Malmede, p. 65). Without a doubt, Dürrenmatt's twenty-four sentences also constitute a discourse of contingencies and concatenations which the author himself characterizes as not emanating from an objectively visible, logically controlled and executed core idea, but more as assuming the form of spoken language, of a spontaneous speaking-while-thinking, of one voice answering another, and to this end

---

Umständen zu forschen, die zum Tode seiner Frau geführt hätten, versuche er, wenn auch unbewußt, vor allem sich selber ein Denkmal zu setzen ..." (p. 15).
[190] Jacques Lacan, "The Mirror Stage as Formative of the Function of the I as Revealed in Psychoanalytic Experience," *Critical Theory Since 1965* (Tallahassee: Florida State University Press, 1986) p. 735.

being inspired by the statement and counterstatement of the music of
Bach:

> ... the ancient epic was the spoken word ... it was my aim
> to discover a type of prose which would once again out of
> necessity have to be spoken, in order to be controlled. I
> substituted sentence for verse, inspired by Johann
> Sebastian Bach's "The Well-Tempered Clavichord." Yet
> I experienced an unusual adventure: *I* was not the one
> leading the sentences where *I* wanted, the sentences led
> me where *they* wanted.[191]

More analogically descriptive than logically analytical, such a
statement is an extension of the narrative to which it refers rather than an
exegesis of the narrative process. It reflects epistemological uncertainty
and should preclude any expectation of a definitive answer as to how a
text comes into being or what a given passage or sentence "really means."
Much contemporary fiction deflects this question through its very
inclusion within the fictive structure, either metafictionally and
thematically, as in the case of Hochhuth, or as with Dürrenmatt's *The
Assignment*, as an integral thematic component, suggesting the fictional
nature of reality while maintaining the artifice of realism. It is,
nevertheless, a subversion of syllogistically developed plots and characters

---

[191] " ... *die Epik der alten Zeit war gesprochenes Wort ... es ging mir darum,
eine Prosa zu finden, die wieder zwangsläufig gesprochen werden muß, um sie
kontrollieren zu können. Ich ersetzte den Vers durch den Satz, angeregt durch
'Das wohltemperierte Klavier' von Johann Sebastian Bach, doch erlebte ich
ein Abenteuer besonderer Art: Nicht ich trieb die Sätze, wohin ich wollte, die
Sätze trieben mich, wohin sie wollten."* Dürrenmatt as quoted on the rear
jacket of the original German edition cited in this study. The question of the
centre of form or the realization of authorial intention to develop a construct
based on a sharply focused centre is by no means a contemporary problem.
Henry James comments as follows on a work whose date of publication is 1889:
"If it ever be of interest or profit to put one's finger on the productive germ of a
work of art, and if in fact a lucid account of any such work involves that prime
identification, I can but look on the present fiction as a poor fatherless and
motherless, a sort of unrecognized and unacknowledged birth. I fail to recover
my precious first moment of consciousness of the idea to which it was to give
form ..." Henry James, *The Art of the Novel*, p. 79, as cited in Carroll, p. 61.

which culminate in a decisive ending and afford universal insight.[192] As F. observes of herself at the end of the fourth sentence, there is no assurance that the "truth" can be discovered: "... it was all beginning to make her feel like one of those probes they shoot out into space in the hope that they will transmit back to earth information about its still unknown composition" (p. 13).[193] Tina von Lambert's true motives are not ever explicitly dealt with in the text, although the events of the unfolding plot and the unexpected turn-around of her not ever having been in the desert, not having been raped and murdered, but rather having been re-united with her husband and giving birth to his child, provide the groundwork for reader-speculation, but nothing more. " ... D. read ... of the birth of a healthy baby boy to Otto and Tina von Lambert, the fulfillment of a long-cherished wish for the well known physicist and his wife, who had once been thought dead and buried, ..."[194] This information is provided a little more than half way through the text in the fourteenth sentence, where F. is handed a newspaper clipping by the head of the secret service, showing Tina von Lambert reunited with her husband:

> ... "Return from the Dead," the wife of the famous psychiatrist had fallen into a depression and gone into hiding in the studio of a deceased painter, her passport and her red fur coat had been stolen, which had evidently led her to being confused with that woman who was murdered near the Al-Hakim ruin, the riddle now being not only the murderer's identity but also that of the deceased woman, ... (p. 73).[195]

---

[192] Eileen Baldeshweiler, "The Lyric Short Story: The Sketch of a History," *Short Story Theories*, ed. Charles May, p. 202.

[193] "... *die F., komme sich wie eine jener Sonden vor, die man ins All schieße, in der Hoffnung sie könnten Informationen zurück zur Erde senden, deren Beschaffenheit man noch nicht wisse*" (p. 17).

[194] "... *er ... las, ... Otto und Tina von Lambert sei ein langgehegter Wunsch in Erfüllung gegangen, indem die schon Totgeglaubte und beerdigte einem gesunden Knaben das Leben geschenkt habe ...*" (p. 132).

[195] "... *sensationelle Rückkehr einer sensationell Beerdigten, die Gattin des bekannten Psychiaters habe sich infolge einer Depression im Atelier eines verstorbenen Malers versteckt gehalten, ihr Paß und ihr roter Pelzmantel seien gestohlen worden, was offenbar dazu geführt habe, daß sie mit jener Frau verwechselt worden sei, die bei der Al-Hakim-Ruine ermordet wurde, wobei man nun nicht nur vor dem Rätsel stehe, wer der Mörder, sondern auch wer die Ermordete sei ...*" (p. 77).

This information answers one question and raises others. F. had
been puzzled by an address found in Tina's diary; she ascertains by
visiting that location that it is the studio of a celebrated artist, recently
deceased, who had left the city several years before his death.
Nevertheless, the studio looks to be in present use, indeed this artist's
paintings are in evidence throughout the room, as are opened tubes of
paint and portions of leftover food. A description of these paintings
indicates that the artist's intentions run parallel to those of F.'s
undertaking of a grand portrait of the world, inasmuch as his choice of
subjects points to an additive, eclectic depiction of the seamier side of
reality - an apt description of F.'s own filming of Tina von Lambert's
helicopter burial as part of a heterogeneous montage:

> ... large-scale portraits, ... the con men, the winos, the
> professionally unemployed, bagmen, street preachers,
> pimps, smugglers, and other artists of life, most of them
> under the ground now, no doubt less ceremoniously
> interred than the painter, whose funeral she remembered,
> conceivably some weeping prostitutes had come, ... (pp.
> 28-29).[196]

The answer to this question of the atelier's being in active use is
provided at the end of this seventh sentence: these are all props for a film
crew doing a piece on the artist's life. Another question is raised about
Tina von Lambert's association with this project, especially in view of the
presence of a portrait of a woman wearing a red fur coat, observed by F.
on her first visit to the studio, but no longer there when she returns to find
the film crew at work. If Tina was in fact one of these artist's subjects,
she has not been in conventionally acceptable company; in this context,
the fact that she actually owns a red fur coat and that her preoccupation
with her husband focuses to such a high degree on his physical attributes
could indicate that she would have been one of the ladies crying at the
burials of outcasts in the text cited above. As an alternative, or perhaps
as an additional conjecture to that of a past life on the fringes of society,
her depression could be associated with her pregnancy: the revulsion she

---

[196] *"... großformatige Porträts, ... Pumpgenies, Quartalsäufer, Clochards,
Straßenprediger, Zuhälter, Berufsarbeitslose, Schieber und andere
Lebenskünstler, die meisten unter der Erde wie der Maler, nur nicht so
feierlich wie dieser, bei dessen Begräbnis sie dabeigewesen war, höchstens daß
bei jenen einige weinende Dirnen zugegen gewesen waren ..." (p. 32).*

experiences over her husband either would indicate that he is not the father, or that he is the father and the reality of bearing his child is overwhelmingly threatening to her. This is a gap in the text which is left for the reader to fill through the weighing of alternatives, accomplished by means of the structure of speculation - yet another manifestation of the "either-or" motif.

The fifth and sixth sentences of the novella are constituted primarily by the theoretical musings of the logician D., whom F. has sought out for any enlightening observations on the task she has accepted to pursue. True to the unity of effect or economy of means observed as a trait of the shorter prose form, the logician D. and the psychiatrist von Lambert, (cf. F.'s and the artist's parallel mimetic intentions and F.'s and von Lambert's subjective interpretation of Tina's motivation) share similar attributes: The latter is described as being "... extraordinarily childlike and helpless in a way that reminded her of many scientists, ..."(p. 12).[197]   The logician D., characterized as an apparently helpless individual, provides F. with analytic insight of the same solipsistic configuration into the impossibility of the human endeavour to establish meaning, as von Lambert has proposed in diagnosing his wife's crisis, but F. has labeled such an obstruently abstract discourse as "this sort of idiocy"(p. 12) *"immer derselbe Quark."*(p. 16). Similarly, she does not initially consider D.'s analyses in an entirely serious light:

> ... F. ..., drove into town, ..., where she encountered the logician D., whose lectures at the university were attended by two or three students - an eccentric and sharp-witted man of whom no one could tell whether he was unfit for life or merely pretended to be helpless, who expounded his logical problems to anyone who joined him at his table in the always crowded restaurant, and this in such a confused and thoroughgoing manner that no one was able to understand him, not F. either, though she found him amusing, liked him, and often told him about her plans, ... (pp. 9-10).[198]

---

[197] *"... er habe etwas ungemein Kindliches, wie viele Wissenschaftler, und Hilfloses ..."* (p. 15).

[198] *"... die F. ... fuhr in die Stadt ... zum Logiker D.., dessen Vorlesung auf der Universität von zwei, drei Studenten besucht wurde, zu einem scharfsinnigen Kauz, von dem niemand wußte, ob er dem Leben gegenüber hilflos war oder diese Hilflosigkeit nur spielte, der jedem, welcher sich in dem stets überfüllten Restaurant zu ihm setzte, seine logischen Probleme erklärte, derart wirr und*

This character develops a line of thought analogous to the Lacanian *aphanisis* or disappearance of the subject, (cf. chapter 1 of this study) as well as the Lacanian concept of the "gaze," yet the validity of these significant psychoanalytic ideas is subverted by the tenuous credibility of their vehicle within the fiction. Such a destabilization of scholarly or scientific discourse is however entirely consonant with the Freudian insight into the mythical nature of the theory of identity and instincts, but there is an additional *caveat* to be observed in applying this theory to F.'s "analysis" by D..: the structure of the psyche as delineated by Freud and Lacan proposes a model which has come under increasing scrutiny as a possible exponent of misogynist cultural tendencies.

As cited in the introduction to this study, D. calls into question the concept of identity based on a stable, integral and central core. F. recapitulates D.'s ideas as follows:

> ... man's not ever ... identical with himself because he was always an other, thrown into time, ... which, however, would mean that there was no self, or rather, only a countless chain of selves emerging from the future, flashing into the present, and sinking back into the past, so that what one commonly called one's self was merely a collective term for all the selves perpetually growing under the constant rain of selves drifting down through the present from the future, an accumulation of shreds of experience and memory, comparable to a mound of leaves that grows higher and higher under a steady drift of other falling leaves, while the ones at the bottom have long turned to humus, a process that seemed to imply a fiction of selfhood in which every person made up his own self, imagining himself playing a role ... (pp. 24-25).[199]

---

gründlich, daß sie niemand zu begreifen vermochte, *auch die F. nicht, die ihn jedoch amüsant fand, ihn mochte und ihm gegenüber oft ihre Plane erläuterte ..." (p. 14).*
[199] *"... er [habe] jede Identität mit sich selber abgesprochen ..., da er immer ein anderer sei, hineingeworfen in die Zeit, ... was aber bedeuten würde, daß es kein Ich gebe, besser, eine zahllose Kette von aus der Zukunft auftauchenden, in der Gegenwart aufblitzenden und in der Vergangenheit versinkenden Ichs, so daß denn das, was man sein Ich nenne, nur ein Sammelname für sämtliche in der Vergangenheit angesammelten Ichs sei, ... eine Ansammlung von Erlebnissen und Erlebnisfetzen, vergleichbar mit einem Laubhaufen, bei dem*

As discussed in the first chapter of this study, Lacan sees the emergence of language and the deferral of desire occurring at the Oedipal stage of development as convergent processes. Language makes identity possible, but it is only a symbolic representation and a repression of incipient amorphous consciousness. Alan Singer's description of this theory provides a succinct rendition of the major points to be called to mind while considering Dürrenmatt's text and specifically the discourse of the logician D..:

> ... the Oedipal stage occurs as the result of the interposition of a "third term" (the-name-of-the-father) into the circuits of the child-mother communication. The child's unrationalized desire for meaning (the illusory self-presence of Lacan's *imaginary* stage of consciousness) yields to a complex substitutional logic (what Lacan calls the *symbolic* stage). The insufficiency of every signifier to the inciting desire (for presence) guarantees a metonymic concatenation of substitutive terms that propel the speaking subject into cultural life. [...] The source of meaning (the unrelocatable referent), however, remains an endlessly deferred question. In fact, the identity of the subject is constituted in this deferral (Singer, p. 142).

The undifferentiated relationship of the infant to woman-as-mother is one of physicality and its nurture and gratification as the first human experience. Tina and Otto von Lambert are *dramatis personae* who are drawn in the archetypal image of these roles of father and mother: Tina's concerns are described as entirely corporeal, and her role within this fiction is to bear a child. Her husband performs the function of providing the *"nom (non) du père"* both as father and in his role as a psychiatrist who is intent on making a *name* for himself by propagating the most abstract of discourses, that of psychoanalysis, in which he postulates that the ultimate meaning is that there is no ultimate meaning, hence calling forth the *"non"* as well as the *"nom."* F.'s acceptance of von Lambert's mandate to investigate the circumstances of his wife's

---

die untersten Blätter längst zu Humus geworden und der durch das frisch fallende und heranwehende Laub immer höher steige, ein Vorgang, der zu einer Fiction eines Ichs führe, indem jeder sein Ich zusammenfingieren, sich in eine Rolle dichten würde ..." (pp. 28f.).

death are interpreted by D. as yet another extension of the metonymic
chain of deferrals of meaning, as the desire to play a new role, one which
is the opposite of that of an observer: "... she should (sic) go to the desert
because she was looking for a new role, her old role had been that of an
observer of roles, and now she wanted to attempt the opposite, ..." (p.
26).[200] F. has gone through a transition from the position of one who had
set as a goal the creation of a journalistic master-portrait of totality: "F.,
... was pursuing the still vague idea of creating a total portrait, namely a
portrait of our planet, by combining random scenes into a whole ..." (p.
5),[201] to one in which the observer must be aware that through the act of
observation she herself determines that which is observed. As D. states,
F. will become the object of the portrait:

> ... and now she wanted to attempt ... not portraiture,
> which presupposed a subject, but reconstruction, raking
> together scattered leaves to build up the subject of her
> portrait, never being sure, all the while ... whether, in
> fact, she wasn't ultimately making a self-portrait, ... (pp.
> 29-30).[202]

According to Lacan and Sartre, the subject can only define its
object in terms of its own perception of the object, yet the subject's
perception of itself is also the definition it has acquired as an observed
object of other subjects:

> In *L'être et le néant* Sartre describes and interprets the
> "regard" [the gaze] as basic to human relations. For
> Sartre, because I cannot at one and the same time remain
> subject and seize myself as an object, I am dependent
> upon the other to testify to my existence as something

---

[200] "... *sie wolle in die Wüste gehen, weil sie eine neue Rolle suche, ihre alte
Rolle sei die einer Beobachterin von Rollen gewesen, nun beabsichtige sie, das
Gegenteil zu versuchen ..." (p. 30).*
[201] "... *sie [hatte] sich vorgenommen ..., ein Gesamtportrait herzustellen ...
unseres Planeten nämlich ... durch ein Zusammenfügen zufälliger Szenen zu
einem Ganzen ..." (p. 10).*
[202] " ... *nun beabsichtige sie ..., nicht zu porträtieren, was ja einen Gegenstand
voraussetze, sondern zu rekonstruieren, den Gegenstand ihres Portraits
herzustellen, damit aus einzelnen herumliegenden Blättern einen Laubhaufen
anzusammeln, wobei sie nicht wissen könne ... ob sie am Ende nicht sich selber
porträtiere ..." (p. 30).*

other than pure subjective consciousness. However ...
because the other must by definition seize me as an object
when gazing at me, the other has access to me from
which I am forever barred. [...] This dialectic of
otherness is reversible, of course, but that cannot mitigate
its being fundamentally symbiotic and alienating at the
same time.[203]

The new role to be played will be F.'s own construct, but
nevertheless relative to its observers or a context of other role-players,
which the term "role" implies. The seventh sentence containing the
episode of the artist's studio would seem to re-state the motif of the
infinite process of substitution of one role or signifier of a whole
unblemished identity for another: the image presented in the text at first
calls to mind Freud's and Lacan's mirror stage,[204] which begins with the
child's first image of itself as a whole entity, marking the first stage in a
metonymy of metaphors which will be its fictional construct of identity.
As F. has been made conscious of this process to some extent by D., she

---

[203] Ronnie Scharfman, "Mirroring and Mothering in Simone Schwarz-Bart's
Pluie et vent sur Télumée Miracle and Jean Rhys' *Wide Sargasso Sea*," *Yale
French Studies*, 62 (1981) p. 90.
[204] Robert Con Davis has described Freud's discussion of the dynamics of
visual experience treated in *Instincts and Their Vicissitudes* as a process
isomorphic with the dynamics of the acquisition of language. The epiphany of
language occurs at the point of repression of the first libidinal relationship
(with the mother); "... desire exists, in Freud's view, in the province of the
unconscious, in the very system of substitutions and shifts ..." (Davis, p. 998).
Lacan posits seeing as "... a function in a largely unconscious discourse that
can be glimpsed in what Lacan calls ... the "Gaze" - the functioning of the
whole system of shifts. [...] The subject who looks, in Lacan's scheme, is
precisely the one who is "seen" - that is, implicated - by the desire of [his own]
unconscious discourse" (p. 987). The desire is for a sense of wholeness, whose
first manifestation is described by Lacan in an act of seeing a unified image
(the mirror stage) where there is in fact no unity; it is the first metaphor, the
first signifier for an elusive signified determining the spiral of experience, the
ever-deferred meaning that confers significance on life, "... to achieve proper
integration in the course of life and death." Peter Brooks, "Symbolization and
Fiction-Making," *Explorations in Psychohistory*, ed. Robert Jay Lifton (New
York: Simon and Schuster, 1974), p. 219. Both in the case of seeing subject
and the subject as signifier, the intention is to obtain a coherent representation
of the self and its environment.

has become receptive to seeing herself as a decentered set of positions, thus leaving behind the illusory position of observer as an entirely self-generating subject, observing things in their isolated, additive and primarily metonymic, hence more detached than unified totality; the new position posits identity as an intersubjective experience, it includes a higher degree of similarity with difference, metaphor with metonymy, the constant interplay of the Imaginary with the Symbolic:

> ... F. ... found herself standing before a painting of a woman in a red fur coat, which F. at first took for a portrait of Tina von Lambert, but which turned out not to be Tina after all, it could just as well be a portrait of a woman who looked like Tina, and then, with a shock, it seemed to her that this woman standing before her defiantly with wide-open eyes was herself, ... (p. 29-30).[205]

In his article *"Beobachtete Beobachter"* (Observed Observers) in *Die Zeit* (12/12/86), Jürgen Manthey has written that Dürrenmatt's novella highlights the human need to see and to be seen: technology has short-circuited this process which has its beginnings in the mirror-phase: "... one thinks of Lacan's mirror stage and its significance for the formation of consciousness. For one experiences a social rebirth - repeatedly and continuously - in the reflection of the eyes of 'the Other.'"[206] He also points out that F. may be meant to represent an archetype, a symbol for that which is female as being better able to control technology: "Is film in better hands in female hands? Do female and film stand for future (= F)? Is that the 'assignment,' as suggested by the title, to which 'woman' has agreed?[207] If this is so, then one must confront the major weakness of Lacanian theory, namely that woman is relegated to the position of an

---

[205] *"... die F. ... stand vor dem Portrait einer Frau im roten Pelzmantel, daß die F. zuerst für das Bildnis Tina von Lamberts hielt, dann aber war es wieder nicht jenes der Tina, es könne ebensogut das Portrait einer Frau sein, die Tina ähnlich war, doch zuckte sie plötzlich zusammen, es schien ihr, diese Frau, die trotzig vor ihr stand mit weit aufgerissenen Augen, sei sie selber ..."* (pp. 33f.).
[206]   *"... (an Lacans Spiegelstadium und seine Bedeutung für die Bewußtseinsbildung ist zu denken.). Denn seine soziale Wiedergeburt erlebt er, und zwar ständig neu, im Reflex der Augen des/der anderen."*
[207] *"Ist der Film in weiblichen Händen in besseren Händen, stehen Frau und Film zusammen für Future (=F)? Ist das 'der Auftrag', den die Frau laut Titel übernimmt?"*

object or a "predicate to the male subject."[208] "... Within the phallic definition, the woman is constituted as 'not all' in so far as the phallic function rests on an exception - the 'not' - which is assigned to her."[209] As Flieger observes, "... Lacan insists on assigning woman to an objective role - the role of the excluded term ..." (p. 961). As a corrective to this inadequacy, the work of Julia Kristeva has been considered as particularly relevant, inasmuch as she has elaborated her theory in conjunction with Freud's and Lacan's theory of the unconscious. As Alice Jardine has described it, it is

> ... a theory of the speaking subject which, escaping the Cartesian boundaries, becomes a subject in process / in question ... [...] In opposition to traditional Marxist thought, she emphasizes the individual development of the speaking subject within particular ideological / political / artistic practices. She also takes exception to Lacan in her emphasis on the period before the mirror stage within that individual trajectory or, more precisely, on the work of differentiation, stratification and confrontation practiced in language before being posited by a speaking subject in a grammatically structured, communicative chain. This space before the sign, the *semiotic*, has been and continues to be coded in our culture as feminine; the space of privileged contact with the mother's (female) body.[210]

Ronnie Scharfman has suggested that Lacan bypasses a *reciprocal* mirroring relationship of an infant with the mother-figure. She cites D. W. Winnicott, who has asked

> ... what a baby sees upon looking at the mother's face. "I am suggesting that, ordinarily, what the baby sees is himself or herself. In other words, the mother is looking at the baby and *what she* [the baby] *sees is related to what she* [the mother] *sees there*." In *The Reproduction*

---

[208] Jerry Aline Flieger, "The Purloined Punchline: Joke as Textual Paradigm," *Lacan and Narration* ed. Robert Con Davis, p. 961.
[209] *Feminine Sexuality*, eds. Juliet Mitchell and Jacqueline Rose (New York and London: W.W. Norton, 1982) p. 49, as cited in Flieger, p. 961.
[210] Alice Jardine, "Pre-Texts for the Transatlantic Feminist," *Yale French Studies*, 62 (1981), p. 228.

of Mothering Chodorow argues repeatedly that, because
they share the same gender and position in society,
mother and daughter also share the dual unity in the pre-
Oedipal period which is of enduring consequence and sets
the pattern for all other experiences of relatedness.[211]

Seeking her new role, F. sees her own image in that of Tina von
Lambert, who is to become a mother and has removed herself from a
situation in which both she and her husband had been the objects of each
other's observation rather than interacting subjects. This forms a parallel
with F.'s own former role of journalist as observer, which will now
change to one of creative and intuitive involvement, also in parallel with
Tina von Lambert's role as a "symbol of immanence, expressed by her
central involvement in that life-giving but involuntary process which
perpetuates the species."[212]   Sandra Gilbert describes the situation of a
woman-writer's self contemplation which begins "... with a searching
glance into a male-inscribed text ...," and culminates in "... her refusal to
be fixed or 'killed' by an author/owner." (pp. 493-494). This is
analogous to F.'s contemplation of the artist's depiction of a woman in a
red fur coat, Tina von Lambert's removing herself from the position as an
object of her husband's psychoanalysis and F.'s refusal to submit to the
fate suffered by her Danish colleague. In this context Gilbert cites a poem
by Mary Elizabeth Coleridge, "... central to female (and feminist)
poetics," to illustrate this experience. It will be rendered here in its
entirety, because it bears a striking similarity to F.s gazing at what she
initially considers to be a portrait of a depressed, rebellious, very aware,
vital and iconoclastic, yet absent Tina von Lambert.

I sat before my glass one day,
And conjured up a vision bare,
Unlike the aspects glad and gay,
That erst were found reflected there-

---

[211]   D. W. Winnicott, "Mirror-role of Mother and Family in Child
Development," *Playing and Reality* (New York: Basic Books, 1971), p. 112,
and Nancy Chodorow, *The Reproduction of Meaning* (Berkeley: University of
California Press, 1978), as cited in Ronnie Scharfman, "Mirroring and
Mothering in Simone Schwarz-Bart's Pluie et vent sur Télumée Miracle and
Jean Rhys' Wide Sargasso Sea," *Yale French Studies*, 62 (1981) p. 91.
[212]   Sandra M. Gilbert, "Literary Paternity," *Critical Theory Since 1965*, ed.
Hazard Adams and Leroy Searle (Tallahasee: Florida State University Press,
1986) p. 493.

The vision of a woman, wild,
With more than womanly despair.

Her hair stood back on either side
Her face bereft of loveliness.
It had no envy now to hide
What once no man on earth could
    guess.
It formed the thorny aureole
Of hard unsanctified distress.

Her lips were open - not a sound
Came through the parted lines of red.
Whate'er it was, the hideous wound
In silence and in secret bled.
No sigh relieved her speechless woe,
She has no voice to speak her dread.

And in her lurid eyes there shone
The dying flame of life's desire,
Made mad because its hope was gone,
And kindled at the leaping fire
Of jealousy, and fierce revenge,
And strength that could not change nor tire.

Shade of a shadow in the glass,
O set the crystal surface free!
Pass - as the fairer visions pass -
Nor ever more return, to be
The ghost of a distracted hour,
That heard me whisper, 'I am she!'[213]

Of this poem Gilbert observes that "it suggests that women themselves have the power to create themselves as characters, ... the power to reach toward the self trapped on the other side of the mirror/text and help her to climb out." (p. 494). In terms of Dürrenmatt's novella, Tina von Lambert's disappearance, re-appearance and giving birth is the inciting moment and the framework for the story, yet the main narrative of

---

[213] Mary Elizabeth Coleridge, "The other Side of a Mirror," *Poems by Mary Coleridge* (London: Elkin Mathews, 1908) pp. 8-9, as cited in Gilbert, pp. 494-495.

F.'s investigation will develop a trajectory away from the narrative strand of domestic confrontation and individuation to one of collusion and intrigue between warring nations, whose aim is to maintain the massive production and testing of armaments. This would reinforce the assertion made in this study that the "single-strand" narrative ("*Einsträngigkeit*") is not necessarily pertinent to every example of the genre, or that a discussion of genre and text interpretation are processes which must be kept apart. The only way to relate the chain of motifs constituting the story of Tina von Lambert and that of F.'s perilous odyssey through the testing-ground-desert of Northern Africa is to do so on a thematic level of abstraction, at the level of a common tenor to strands of a narrative vehicle which do not intersect once they emerge and take divergent directions. The connection between the micro- and macrocosmic spheres (to use Leibowitz' terms) is to be found in this text in the common theme of women's creating their own autonomy through their resistance to being fixed or "killed" by the pen of artistic paternity, or indeed by the actual weapons used by the human male, whose "... 'transcendence' of nature is symbolized by his ability to hunt and kill ..." (Gilbert, p. 493). Tina's role as a mother - the essential contributor to the continuation of the life-cycle and her escape from the role of observed object to generating subject is mirrored in F.'s use of film to reflect things in their motion and fluidity; she also attempts to overcome the stasis of a fixed position, although it is that of an observing subject, in order to integrate the position of subject and object - the necessary dialectical process for any evolving human being. This contrasts with Otto von Lambert's detached diagnosis of the "blank" of life, and with Polyphemos' still photographs of annihilation and death. As is the case with Hochhuth, the vertical, paradigmatic axis of interpretive transparency is reinforced through the use of mythological motifs. Polyphemos is an appropriate mythological aptronym for a figure obsessed with a view of reality provided through the single eye of a camera; although F. does not defeat him in a concrete sense, the constant flux and fluidity of film in parallel with her own viability within the evolutional dialectic of subject and object - being able to avoid the static positions of voyeur (mere looking) and exhibitionist (merely being seen) which are the resulting positions of stasis when the system of shifts from one position to another is not maintained,[214] form a counterpoise to Polyphemos' obsession / perversion. In addition, F. and Tina von Lambert, according to the Lacanian definition of woman, are the "not," the "absence of"; when asked for his name, Odysseus had replied "Noman is my name; Noman is what mother and father call me and all my

---

[214] Cf. Robert Con Davis, pp. 985-87.

friends." The Cyclopians hear Polyphemos' cries after Odysseus has driven a stake through his eye, but this ruse causes them to disperse: "Well, if no man is using force, and you are alone, there's no help ..."[215]

The motif of the red fur coat, so prominent in the text, can be seen to have a mythological-archetypal underpinning if considered in juxtaposition with other recurring motifs and as a functional element within the text's theme complex. F., drawn as a character whose aspirations are of a non-tactile, abstract, philosophical nature, nevertheless sets out on her search through the desert wearing the red fur coat, a trope for the more tactile, physical, vulnerable and emotional experience of Tina von Lambert and her position as an erotic object and target. In her mediation of these ostensible opposites, F. encounters the character of the old woman at the abandoned desert hotel. The latter is portrayed as both a caring, maternal figure who lovingly strokes the red fur coat and seems to care about the fate of Tina von Lambert, and as one who giggles and cackles grotesquely as she learns of Tina von Lambert's fate. The Danish journalist, Jytta Sörenson, has also worn this coat. She is portrayed in Polyphemos' film clips as having submitted to her rape and murder as an act of erotic submission. These figures bear a strong resemblance to the *Demeter/Kore/Hecate* archetype forming a part of a woman's "supraordinate self," described by Carl Jung:[216]

> I usually describe the supraordinate personality as the "self," thus making a sharp distinction between the ego, which, as is well known, extends only as far as the conscious mind, and the *whole* of the personality, which includes the unconscious as well as the conscious component. [...] ... the self is felt empirically not as subject but as object, and this by reason of its unconscious component, which can only come to consciousness indirectly, by way of projection (p. 187). [...] The figure corresponding to the Kore in a woman is generally a double one, i.e. a mother and a maiden. [...] The maiden's helplessness exposes her to all sorts of *dangers* for instance of being devoured by reptiles or ritually slaughtered like a beast of sacrifice. [...]

---

[215] *The Odyssey*, trans. W.H.D. Rouse (Winnipeg: The New American Library of Canada / Mentor Classics, 1966) pp. 107-108.

[216] C. G. Jung, *The Archetypes and the Collective Unconscious* Vol. 9 of *The Collected Works of C.G. Jung* translated by R.F.C. Hull (London: Routledge and Kegan Paul, 1959) pp. 184-188.

Sometimes it is a ... descent into Hades and a quest for
the "treasure hard to attain," occasionally connected with
orgiastic sexual rights or offerings of menstrual blood to
the moon (p.184)... [...] The figures corresponding to
Demeter and Hecate ... are over-life-size "Mothers"
ranging from the Pietà type to the Baubo type [old nurse
/female clown whose lascivious jokes made Demeter
laugh]. [...] I can recall only very few cases where
Demeter's own noble figure in its pure form breaks
through as an image ... I remember a case, in fact, where
a maiden-goddess appears clad all in purest white, but
carrying a black monkey in her arms. The Earth Mother
is always Cthonic [Hecate] ... In pictorial or plastic
representations the Mother is dark deepening to *black*, or
red ... and with a primitive or animal expression of face
... (p. 185). [...] Demeter and Kore, mother and daughter,
extend the feminine consciousness both upwards and
downwards. They add an "older and younger," "stronger
and weaker" dimension to it and widen out the narrowly
limited conscious mind bound in space and time, giving it
intimations of a greater and more comprehensive
personality which has a share in the eternal course of
things (p. 188).

Elsewhere Jung interprets a dream of a figure of a woman in a red
dress sacrificed on a stone cross as signaling a failure of the individuation
process in the female psyche: "But as long as a woman is content to be a
femme à homme (a man's woman), she has no feminine individuality. She
is empty and merely glitters - a welcome vessel for masculine
projections." (Jung, pp. 198-199).

Sandra Gilbert's article provides yet another insight into the
mythical aspect of *The Assignment* with respect to F.'s role in
constructing her identity. She cites a fictionalized Author's Introduction to
Mary Shelley's *The Last Man* in her discussion of literary paternity.
Shelley describes a visit to "'the gloomy cavern of the Cumaean Sibil.'
Entering a mysterious, almost inaccessible chamber, they found 'piles of
leaves, fragments of bark, and a white filmy substance ...'"[217] The
logician D. has used the analogy of a pile of leaves to describe all the
discarded roles of the "I," from which F. must construct her path, "...

---

[217] Mary Shelley, *The Last Man* (1826; reprint, Lincoln, Neb.: University of
Nebraska Press, 1965), pp. 3-4, as cited in Gilbert, p. 495.

raking together scattered leaves to build up the subject of her portrait, ..."(p. 30).

The underground installation to which Polyphemos brings F. repeats the motif of the abandoned artist's studio with its array of images and is presaged by the detention and interrogation areas of the police facilities in which the alleged murderer of Tina von Lambert is executed. This bunker-observatory is described as follows:

> ... the Land-Rover was already sinking beneath the ground, a roof closed over it, they were inside a subterranean garage, ... an iron door slid open, and he limped ahead of her ..., through cellarlike rooms that also had the look of a photographer's studio, the walls densely covered with tiny photographs, as if for some absurd reason someone had spliced whole rolls of developed film onto thousands of separate frames, several large pictures of destroyed armored cars in the midst of a wild mess of photography, books strewn across various tables and chairs, also reams of scribbled sheets of paper, mountainous stacks of film rolls, ... [...] ... she was in the closing jaws of a world-monster, ... (pp. 84-89).[218]

Gilbert describes the mythological figure of the Sibyl as "a prophetess who described her divine intuitions" on tender leaves and fragments of delicate bark ... who mythically conceived all women artists" (p. 495). Although the motif structure of the Dürrenmatt text is partially at variance with that of the Shelley text, to the extent that the hidden cavern is not the domain of a figure symbolizing the source of female artistry, the fragmentation does not significantly alter the motif of the bond between female artistry and the locus of female physical creativity (cavern/ womb); Polyphemos' and Achilles' activity consists in dismembering and violating the progression and flow of film and the

---

[218] *"... schon sank der Geländewagen nach unten, über ihm schloß sich eine Decke, wonach sie sich in einer unterirdischen Garage befanden ... eine Eisentür glitt auf, und er hinkte ihr durch ... halb keller-, halb atelierhafte Räume voraus, die Wände eng mit kleinen Photos bedeckt, als wären entwickelte Filmrollen absurderweise in lauter Einzelbilder zerschnitten worden, in einem wilden Durcheinander mit Stößen von Fotobüchern auf Tischen und Stühlen lagen Großaufnahmen zerschossener Panzerwagen herum, dazu Stöße vollgekritzelter Papiere, Berge von Filmrollen [...] ... sie war im Schlund eines Weltungeheuers, das seinen Rachen schloß ..." (pp. 88-93).*

progression and flow of life: Dürrenmatt's narrative style itself reflects
the fluidity of the medium of film and the primordial character of female
creativity through its design as twenty-four "movements" of discourse -
described by the author himself as a reflection of language in its incipient
dialogical spoken form and inspired by music which synthesizes and
harmonizes voice and countervoice. The number twenty-four evokes the
ongoing emergence and fading of night and day as one of the most basic
modulations in the flow of time, as an expression of its more cosmic or
monumental rather than its linear-historical aspect.[219] The following

---

[219]   Julia Kristeva elaborates on the concept of time within female subjectivity
as follows: "As for time, female subjectivity ['Subjectivity' here refers to the
state of being 'a thinking, speaking, acting, doing or writing agent'] would
seem to provide a specific measure that essentially retains repetition and
eternity from among the multiple modalities of time known through the history
of civilizations. On the one hand, there are cycles, gestation, the eternal
recurrence of a biological rhythm which conforms to that of nature and imposes
a temporality ... regularity and unison with what is experienced as
extrasubjective time, cosmic time, occasional vertiginous visions and
unnameable jouissance. On the other hand, and perhaps as a consequence,
there is the massive presence of a monumental temporality, without cleavage or
escape, which has so little to do with linear time (which passes) that the very
word 'temporality' hardly fits ... [...]
    The fact that these two types of temporality (cyclical and monumental) are
traditionally linked to female subjectivity insofar as the latter is thought of as
necessarily maternal should not make us forget that this repetition and this
eternity are found to be the fundamental, if not the sole, conceptions of time in
numerous civilizations and experiences ... The fact that certain currents of
modern feminism recognize themselves here does not render them
fundamentally incompatible with 'masculine' values.
    In return, female subjectivity as it gives itself up to intuition becomes a
problem with respect to a certain conception of time: time as project, teleology,
linear and prospective unfolding; time as departure, progression, and arrival -
in other words, the time of history. ... this kind of temporality is inherent in the
logical and ontological values of any given civilization, that this temporality
renders explicit a rupture, an expectation, or an anguish which other
temporalities work to conceal. It might also be added that this linear time is
that of language considered as the enunciation of sentences (noun + verb; topic-
comment; beginning-ending), and that this time rests on its own stumbling
block, which is also the stumbling block of that enunciation - death. A
psychoanalyst would call this "obsessional time", recognizing in the mastery of
time the true structure of the slave." Julia Kristeva, "Women's Time," *Critical
Theory Since 1965*, pp. 472-73.

passage from the Shelley text indicates the plausibility of an assumption of intertextuality:

> On examination, we found that all the leaves, bark and other substances were traced with written characters. What appeared to us more astonishing, was that these writings were expressed in various languages: some unknown to my companion ... We could make out little by the dim light, but they seemed to contain prophecies, detailed relations of events but lately passed ... Since that period ... I have been employed in deciphering these sacred remains ... I have been obliged to ... model the work into a consistent form ... (pp. 3-4).

The active male figure of Polyphemos as the destroyer of the medium which F. uses to construct her model of coherence is the added component in *The Assignment*. The motif of deciphering texts also features in the Dürrenmatt text; F. attempts to translate a text written and discarded by Jytte Sörensen who had occupied the same desolate hotel before entering the desert:

> ... only then did she notice ... a bunched-up piece of paper, which she unfolded and smoothed out, and on it, in a handwriting that was unfamiliar to her, was a statement ..., in a Nordic language, incomprehensible to her, but, stubborn as she was, she sat down at the desk and tried to translate the words, ..., but by midnight she felt she had solved the riddle ... (p. 70).[220]

The last sentence of this text, in which F. has used parentheses for lexical items she is not sure of, reads "'This life is backward (bagvendt) and puzzling (raedsomt?), intoler-able'"(p. 71). ("*Dieses Leben ist verkehrt (bagvendt) und rätselhaft (raedsomt?), nicht auszuhalten*'" (p. 75). This is the novella's epigraph excerpted from Kierkegaard's *Either/Or*, in which the Danish *raedsomt* indeed means "horrible,"

---

[220]   "*... dann erst bemerkte sie ... ein zerknülltes Papier, das sie auseinanderfaltete und glättete, in einer Handschrift, die sie nicht kannte, war etwas geschrieben, ... aber da es eine nordische Sprache war, verstand sie es nicht, hartnäckig wie sie war, setzte sie sich an die Schreibkommode, die sie heruntergeklappt hatte und versuchte zu übersetzen ... es war Mitternacht als sie glaubte, das Zitat enträtselt zu haben ...*" (p. 75).

(*grauenhaft*) rather than F.s translation of "puzzling" (*rätselhaft*). This may be taken as an indication that F. considers her situation as still viable, that the never-ending progression of riddles into an "empty space" of deferred answers is a condition of life she is willing to meet. The theme of the inability to understand a particular discourse, to interpret and to choose between alternatives is expressed in the text through a series of similar motifs, of which the translation of the Kierkegaard-text is an example. Another is the breakdown in communication between F. and the police escort to the Al-Hakim ruin:

... [F. would have preferred] ... to gather information first but had no way of explaining herself, because, whether by design or by negligence, no interpreter was present and the policeman accompanying her or rather bossing her around did not have the command of French one might have expected in this country, ... (p. 33).[221]

The victim of the execution witnessed by F., whose identity or role is not expanded upon in the text, must communicate with her through a foreign Scandinavian accent in a foreign language, English: "... he ... spoke English more or less the way Scandinavians speak English, ..."(p. 40). ("... er ... sprach Englisch wie etwa Skandinavier Englisch sprechen ...") (p. 44). The language of the woman who is the sole caretaker of the desert hotel is also not entirely comprehensible:

... F., ... asked in French if she could have some breakfast, which the old woman affirmed with several intense nods, ... then asked F. whether she was a friend [of Tina's], and when F said yes, she began to talk with great excitement, and what F. thought she was able to make out of this stuttering, garbled communication was that Tina had come here in a rented car (the woman repeated the word "alone" several times, and kept stammering something incomprehensible about the rented car), ... (pp. 62-63).[222]

---

[221] "... [die F. vermochte] ... sich aber nicht zu verständigen ..., weil, sei es aus Absicht oder aus Nachläßigkeit, kein Dolmetscher zugegen war und die sie mehr herumkommandierenden als begleitenden Polizisten nicht Französisch verstanden, was man doch in diesem Lande hätte voraussetzen können ..."(p. 37).
[222] "... die F. .... [fragte] auf französisch, ... ob sie frühstücken könne, was die Alte mit einem heftigen Nicken bejahte ... dann fragte, ob die F. eine Freundin

Associated with the repeated motif of the lacunae of language and communication is that of labyrinths, of the unknown space of passageways, of opened and closed doors, of the fork in the road. The first manifestation of this complex in the text occurs in the episode of F.'s visit to the artist's studio as she makes her way through the entrance: "... surprisingly, even the door was open, but the stairs led up into darkness, she searched in vain for a light switch, climbed the stairs, holding her hands out in front of her, ..."(p. 28).[223] As F. and her film team are being driven from M. to the Al-Hakim ruin in the desert in a police jeep, she is not able to ascertain how the convoy can navigate its way through the wasteland:

> ... then the motorcyclists came roaring by, ... making signs that were undecipherable to them, until suddenly they had left the stone desert and were tearing along a macadam road ... somehow, unaccountably, the driver had managed to find this road, even though it was partially covered over with sand, ... (p. 34).[224]

F. is led through corridors in the police facility to witness the execution of Tina von Lambert's alleged murderer. The description of this is accomplished through a repetition of the labyrinth motif:

> ... the investigating magistrate ... opened the door, ... led them through corridors, down a flight of stairs along further corridors, [opened an iron door with a key, led

---

[von Tina] sei und als diese bejahte, sich vor Aufregung in ihren Sätzen verhaspelnd berichtete, so weit es die F. zu verstehen vermochte, Tina sei mit einem gemieteten Auto allein hierhergekommen, wobei sie das "allein" mehrmals wiederholte, auch etwas Unverständliches über das gemietete Auto hervorstammelte ..." (p. 67).
[223] "... die Türe hinauf erwies sich zu ihrem Erstaunen unverschlossen, die Treppe verlor sich oben im Dunkeln, sie suchte vergeblich nach einem Lichtschalter, stieg hinauf, die Hände tastend vor sich ..." (p. 32).
[224] "... dann ratterten wieder die Motorradfahrer heran, machten Zeichen, die sie, an ihre Sitze geklammert, nicht begriffen, bis sie plötzlich in die Sandwüste gerieten ... dermaßen fegten sie mit ihrem Jeep über eine asphaltierte Straße, wobei rätselhaft blieb, wie es ihrem Fahrer ... möglich gewesen war, diese zu finden, war doch die Straße teilweise mit Sand bedeckt ..." (p. 38).

them through another corridor] narrower than the others, ... (p. 43).[225]

As F. attempts to explore a part of C. on her own, she finds herself in the narrow streets of the old city: "... jostled by [sweating] tourists, she arrived in the old city ... she moved through dark, cavernous streets ..."(p. 49) ("... *so war sie ... geschoben von schwitzenden Touristen, in die Altstadt geraten, ... sie bewegte sich durch dunkle schluchtartige Gassen* ...") (p. 53). After F. happens upon and buys a red fur coat in the bazaar, she must find her way back to the hotel: "..., without any idea of how she had found her way out of the old city or where she was, she found a taxi ..." (p. 5,) ("... *aus der Altstadt gelangt, sie wußte nicht wie und auch nicht, wo sie war, fand sie ein Taxi* ...") (p. 55). After arriving at the hotel on the edge of the desert, F. orients herself with her surroundings: "..., she went back along the road on which she had come, arrived at a stony plateau, the road forked, she chose a road that forked again after half an hour, she went back, ..." (p. 66).[226] Having discovered and been informed that the object of her search is not Tina von Lambert, but Jytte Sörensen, F. reflects on the circumstances that have led her to undertake this investigation:

> ... wandering through an uninhabited wasteland ..., without any idea of where the road she was senselessly, stubbornly taking would lead, ... she too felt as helpless as a spider falling into empty space, this road she was taking now, dusty, stony, ... and now she was walking along this road, reluctant and yet unable to do otherwise, carrying her suitcase like a hitchhiker ... (pp. 76-77).[227]

---

[225] The text within square brackets is my translation of the original German, a phrase not included in the Agee translation. "... *der Untersuchungsrichter ... öffnete die Türe ... schritt durch Korridore voran, dann eine Treppe hinunter, wieder Korridore, öffnete mit einem Schlüssel eine Eisentüre, wieder ein Korridor, schmäler als die anderen* ..." *(p. 47).*

[226] "... *sie ging den Weg zurück, den sie gekommen war, geriet auf eine steinige Hochebene, der Weg verzweigte sich, sie wählte einen Weg, der sich nach einer halben Stunde wieder verzweigte, sie ging zurück* ..." *(p. 71).*

[227] "... *sie ... [wählte] in der menschenleeren Einöde den Weg ... ohne Wissen wohin die Straße führte ... auch sie fühlte sich hilflos wie eine in den leeren Raum fallende Spinne, dieser Weg, den sie nun ging, staubig, steinig ... und nun schritt sie gegen ihren Willen diesen Weg entlang und konnte doch nicht anders, den Koffer in der Hand wie eine Autostopperin* ..." *(p. 81).*

In a bid to escape the bunker-observatory, F. again finds herself navigating an unknown course:

> ..., she stepped into the hallway, which was empty, stood still, suspecting a trap, heard someone hammering against an iron door somewhere, followed the sound, the doors sliding open as she approached them, walked hesitantly through the rooms she had already seen, found new corridors, bedrooms, technical labs ... [...] but what if it wasn't a trap at all, maybe she wasn't being watched, maybe she was free, ... ran along several passageways, entered a cell that at first she took to be hers but which wasn't, ... hurried back through the underground room, ... (pp. 88-89).[228]

After deciding against an escape in the all-terrain-vehicle which seemed to be at her disposal, F. spends the night, to be greeted the next morning by Polyphmos who appears briefly to invite her to breakfast. Once again, F. loses her way through this building: "... again the hammering and banging, then silence, she walked and lost her way, then some rooms she remembered, ..."(p. 92). ("... *wieder das Hämmern und Poltern, dann Stille, sie verlief sich, dann Räume, an die sie sich erinnerte ...*") (p. 95). The last two expressions of this leitmotif of disorientation locate it clearly within the contours of the subject/object dynamics of experience and awareness, although each occurrence of this motif has indeed been a function of this spiral; in each successive example, F. has willingly accepted the direction determined for her by all of the male agents in the text: Otto von Lambert, the head of the secret service in M. and, finally, Polyphemos and Achilles. These represent the external impetus in the progression of experience, but there is also the question of the internal momentum of the *Eros/Thanatos* ambiguity which the last examples of the disorientation-motif bring to light. The first is in the form of a dream -

---

[228] "... *sie [trat] ... in den Korridor, der war leer, sie witterte eine Falle, blieb stehen, irgendwo hämmerte jemand gegen eine Eisentüre, sie ging dem Geräusch nach, die Türen glitten auf ... sie ging durch Räume, die sie schon gesehen hatte, sie ging zögernd, immer neue Korridore, Schlafstellen, technische Räume ... [...] vielleicht war alles eine List, vielleicht wurde sie nicht beobachtet, vielleicht war sie frei, sie lief Irrwege, betrat eine Zelle, die sie zuerst für die ihre hielt, die jedoch nicht die ihre war, eilte wieder durch die unterirdischen Räume ..."(pp. 92-93).*

a displacement of the act of suicide which F. considers herself to have *perhaps* passively pursued: "..., perhaps she couldn't stand herself and her flight consisted of letting herself drift ..." (p. 121). ("... *vielleicht hielt sie sich selber nicht aus und die Flucht bestand darin, daß sie sich treiben ließ* ...") (p. 125). The dream is generated by F.'s having viewed Polyphemos' "film-portrait" of Jytte Sörensen, shown to have experienced sexual gratification as she was raped and murdered. As stated above, F. initially displaces through her dreamwork the prospect of her own trajectory of obstructions towards death into that of all those closest to her; the dream also connects the termination of existence with a state of euphoria present in Jytte Sörensen's death:

> ... she saw herself as a girl, standing by a mountain stream before it threw itself over the edge of a cliff, she had walked away from the camp and placed a small paper boat in the stream, and followed it, watched it getting caught by various stones and drifting loose again, and now it was sailing inexorably toward the waterfall, and the little girl watched with tremendous excitement and pleasure, for she had put all her friends in the ship ..., and above it, on top of two cliffs, squatted Polypheme [sic], and Achilles, ... (pp. 121-122).[229]

When F. herself is sent forth into the desert by Polyphemos as a target for Achilles, she is also reduced in this extreme life-and-death situation to a state of animality which valorizes the basic drives (cf. Hochhuth's *Atlantik-Novelle* and *Die Berliner Antigone*), yet where *Thanatos/Eros* had in the case of Sörensen surfaced under such extreme duress, F. has overcome the male-associated stasis of the subject-object polarity, and as the text would suggest, acquiesces in the process of subject emergence in its supra-individual sense: as a woman she contains

---

[229] "... *sie sah sich als Mädchen, an einem Bergbach stehend, bevor er sich über eine Felswand in die Tiefe stürzte, sie hatte sich vom Lager entfernt und ein kleines Papierschiff in den Bach gesetzt, war ihm dann gefolgt, bald wurde es von diesem Stein aufgehalten, bald von jenem, doch immer wieder befreite es sich und nun trieb es unaufhaltsam dem Wasserfall entgegen, und sie schaute zu, das kleine Mädchen, unbändig vor Freude, denn sie hatte das Schiffchen mit all ihren Freundinnen besetzt, mit ihrer Mutter und ihrem Vater, ... und ... wie es über die Klippe schnellte, hinab in die Tiefe, jubelte sie laut, ... und sie saß in diesem Schiff ... und über diesem, auf zwei Klippen, hockten Polyphem ... und Achilles ..." (p. 126).*

a natural, creative and re-generating potentiality whose proportions are those of cyclical and monumental time, a mythical, archetypal counter-balance (reflected in F.'s cognizance of the illusory, seemingly pre- and ahistoric topography of the scene) to the temporality of the individual, isolated subject whose ultimate parameters are the libidinal motor of the *Eros/Thanatos* tension. Thus F. is described in this scene as one who emerges from the position of object, which is in itself shown to be non-threatening, to becoming an active, non-static vital subject. Significantly, F. is clad only in the red fur coat, a symbol of her process of individuation with which virtually every other female figure in the text is associated:

> ... she was drenched with sweat, she took off her clothes, not caring that she was being watched, keeping only the fur coat on, and continued walking, the Land-Rover behind her, she walked and walked, ..., then she stopped thinking, because it was senseless to think of anything, in the wavering distance she could see bizarre squat rocks, ... she had always wanted to see a mirage, but as she approached them, already staggering, the rocks turned out to be a tank cemetery, burned out hulks standing around her like huge turtles, ..., and as Achilles stood before her, half-naked, covered with dust, as if he had just come out of the thick of battle, ..., his idiot's eyes wide open, she was seized by the enormous impact of the present and by a feeling she had never known, a desire to live, to live forever, to throw herself upon this giant, this idiot god, to sink her teeth into his throat, to change into a savage beast, devoid of all humanity, atone with him who wanted to rape and kill her, ..., but he seemed to evade her, turned in a circle, ... he ... stared at the ... steel corpses, from which life began to stir, bodies climbing from rusted tanks and shattered scout cars, cameramen with their equipment, like fantastic animals, silhouetted against the burning silver of the sky, ... (pp. 124-126).[230]

---

[230] "... sie war schweißüberströmt, sie zog sich aus, es war ihr gleichgültig, daß man ihr zusah, hüllte sich nur noch in den Pelzmantel, ging weiter, der Geländewagen hinter ihr, sie ging und ging ... dann dachte sie an nichts mehr, weil es sinnlos war, an etwas zu denken ... in der flirrenden Ferne tauchten bizarre niedere Felsen auf, sie hatte geträumt, eine Fata Morgana zu sehen ... doch als sie, schon taumelnd, näher kam, erwiesen sich die Felsen als ein Friedhof zerschossener Panzer, die sie wie schildkrötenhafte Riesentiere

In effect F., through her ability to be spontaneous, intuitive, to
live and to feel, has become the instrument of Polyphemos' and Achilles'
nemesis. She plays the role of a target/object in order to draw out and
ensnare two entities who represent the two opposed forms of hysteria
counterpoised by F.'s interpersonal capacity: the psychically numbed,
static Polyphemos and the frenzied motion of Achilles.

In his article "The Sense of Immortality," Robert Lifton has
described impaired psychic conditions which are very useful in
understanding Dürrenmatt's fictional characters. As Polyphemos relates
his past to F. he mentions a photographer-father murdered by gangsters
and his ensuing role as a cameraman-vigilante, embarking on a highly
prolific career of providing evidence of the most serious crimes. Once
politicians become implicated, Polyphemos retreats from enemies on all
sides to the employ of secret services and then to the arms industry (pp.
95-99) (pp. 99 -103). Polyphemos' background story, like that of
Achilles (a former bomber pilot in Vietnam) fits the profile of a person
experiencing psychic numbing on two counts: personal loss and a spate of
extreme situations which deaden moral sensitivity and interpersonal
capacities. As Lifton observes of this condition,

... hysteria tends to involve either this form of stasis
[deadening or numbing of various aspects of the psyche]
or its seeming opposite, exaggerated movement or activity
that serves as a similar barrier against feeling and living.
These patterns ... resemble those I encountered among
Hiroshima survivors.

In obsessional neurosis and obsessive-compulsive styles
of behaviour the stress is upon order and control. One

---

*umstanden ... und wie Achilles vor ihr stand, halb nackt, als käme er von einem
Schlachtgetümmel ... die Idiotenaugen weit geöffnet, wurde sie vom
ungeheuren Anprall der Gegenwart erfaßt, von einer noch nie gekannten Lust
zu leben, ewig zu leben, sich auf diesen Riesen, auf diesen idiotischen Gott zu
werfen, die Zähne in seinen Hals zu schlagen, plötzlich ein Raubtier geworden,
bar jeder Menschlichkeit, eins mit dem, der sie vergewaltigen und töten wollte
... doch er schien ihr zu entweichen, drehte sich im Kreise ... zu den ...
Stahlleichen glotzte ... Kameramänner tauchten gleich phantastischen Tieren
auf, hoben sich ab vom kochenden Silber des Alls ..." (pp. 128-130).*

tries to "stop time," to control its flow so as to order existence and block spontaneous expression ... [231]

Polyphemos describes his condition in the same terms: "... he was no longer human - since being human required the illusion of being able to experience something directly ..."(p. 108).[232] As cited at the beginning of the discussion of this text, Polyphemos uses a camera to control and hinder the flow of time: "... the purpose of the camera was to arrest time, ..., to stop time by destroying time, ..."(p. 108). ("... *die Kamera sei dazu da ... die Zeit aufzuhalten, indem sie die Zeit vernichte ...*") (p. 112). When Achilles is described, he is shown moving his body to the rhythm of Homeric verse: "... a bald-headed man who was scanning verses, Greek hexameters, Homer, swaying back and forth to the beat, ..."(p. 119) ("... *eine kahlköpfige Masse, Verse skandierend, griechische Hexameter, Homer, hin- und herwippend im Takt der Verse ...*") (p. 123). As F. is being pursued through the desert, she notices Achilles in the all-terrain-vehicle "... swaying from side to side, reciting the *Iliad*, ..."(p. 124) ("... *hin- und herwippend, aus der 'Ilias' zitierend ...*") (p. 128). The use of alcohol and narcotics to cope with the distress of these initially defensive and salvific but ultimately debilitating psychological structures is also a motif, used not only in conjunction with the portrayal of Polyphemos and Achilles, but as a repeated motif in the case of other subsidiary figures and of F. herself. Polyphemos remarks that in order to control Achilles, the use of a narcotizing substance is necessary: "... he had stuffed him full of Valium ..."(p. 119). ("... *er habe ihn mit Valium vollgestopft ...*") (p. 123). Before he is sent to kill F. he is described as "still half stunned" (p. 124) ("*immer noch halb betäubt*") (p. 128). Polyphemos is described in his first encounter with F. as being intoxicated: "... she ... sat down next to him, smelling an unmistakable whiff of whiskey ..."(p. 83) ("... *sie ... nahm neben ihm Platz, der nun deutlich nach Whisky stank ...*") (p. 86). As he leads her through the underground installation, his condition is confirmed:

> "... he mumbled something she could not make out, ... he limped ahead of her ..., through ... rooms ..., then a photo lab, ..., a corridor, until, perpetually lurching and

---

[231] Robert Jay Lifton, *Explorations in Psychohistory* (New York: Simon and Schuster, 1974) p. 285.
[232] "... *er sei kein Mensch mehr - da zum Mensch-Sein der Schein gehöre, die Einbildung eben, etwas direkt erleben zu können ...*" (p. 111).

swaying on his injured leg, he led her into a windowless
room ..."(p. 84).[233]

After he relates his background and explains the function of the
installation, he consumes more alcohol: "He ... pulled a bottle of whiskey
out ..., poured some whiskey into a glass ..., drank it all, ... poured himself
another whiskey, ..." (p. 106).[234] His explanation of the use of the camera
to destroy time is accompanied by the filling and re-filling of the glass,
until Polyphemos gulps directly from the bottle when F. asks how he has
come by his name. The following passage also describes the psychic
numbing mentioned above:

> He had drunk one glass of whiskey after another, he had
> ... turned back into ... an alcoholic with a furrowed face
> and small burning eyes that nevertheless appeared
> petrified, as if they had stared into some cold horror
> throughout eternity, and when she asked, ..., whose idea it
> had been to call him Polypheme, she sat back [sic], for
> she had scarcely uttered the question when he put the
> bottle to his lips ... (p. 111).[235]

The narcotization motif is, significantly, not restricted to these
pathological figures: almost every character in *The Assignment* is shown
consuming alcohol. This begins in the scene in which F. seeks the logician
D.'s advice: "D. had listened to F's report and absent-mindedly ordered a
glass of wine, even though it was just eleven o'clock, ..."(p. 14) ("*D. hatte
sich den Bericht der F. angehört und sich zerstreut ein Glas Wein
bestellt, obwohl es erst elf Uhr war* ..."(p. 18). The early hour does not
constrain F. either:

---

[233] "*... er ... antwortete etwas Unverständliches ... er hinkte ihr durch weitere
... Räume ... voraus, ... dann ein Fotolabor ... ein Korridor, worauf er sie, mit
dem hinkenden Bein immer wieder einknickend, so betrunken war er, in einen
fensterlosen Raum führte ...*" (p. 88).
[234] "*... er ... holte eine Flasche Whisky hervor, goß sich Whisky ins Glas ...
trank es aus ... schenkte sich neuen Whisky ein ...*" (p. 110).
[235] "*Er hatte ein Glas Whisky um das andere getrunken ... er hatte sich ...
verwandelt ... in einen Säufer mit einem durchfurchten Gesicht mit kleinen
brennenden Augen, die dennoch wie versteint wirkten, als hätten sie seit
Ewigkeit in ein Kaltes Grausen geblickt, und als sie fragte ... wer den Einfall
gehabt habe, ihn Polyphem zu nennen, stutzte sie-, kaum hatte sie die Frage
gestellt, setzte er die Flasche Whisky an den Mund ...*" (p. 114).

F., who had listened attentively to the logician and had ordered Campari, said she supposed D. wondered why she had accepted von Lambert's assignment, ... in the desert, she sensed, was a reality she would have to meet, ... it remained to be seen what it would be for her, and then, draining her glass of Campari, she asked D. whether he thought it was crazy of her to accept this assignment ... (pp. 24-26).[236]

The head of the secret service in M., in spite of his Muslim faith, more or less openly consumes alcohol: "... the investigating magistrate, dedicated himself assiduously to an Alsatian white wine ..., waved off the cameraman, ..., and explained at great length that he was a believing Moslem, in many respects even a fundamentalist ..."(p. 41).[237] The motif is repeated when the latter visits F. in her hotel room to offer her the task of investigating the true circumstances of the murder at Al-Hakim: "... next to the refrigerator was a bottle of whiskey, and when she said she preferred whiskey, he said he had thought so ..."(p. 54).[238] F.'s cameraman does not agree with her acceptance of this assignment: "... not until she had finished did he pour himself a whiskey, ..."(p. 57) ("... *erst als sie geendet hatte, schenkte er sich einen Whisky ein ...*") (p. 61). He will not be a part of this dangerous undertaking, withdraws and leaves her to continue packing: "... F. suddenly had the feeling she would never see him again, ... she furiously downed the glass of whiskey ..."(p. 59) ("... *der F. war es plötzlich, als ob sie ihn nie mehr sehen würde ... trank wütend das Glas Whisky aus ...*"(p. 63). This motif of narcotization underlines a dysfunctional capacity for observation and perception; dysfunction occurs when the usual interaction between persons, characterized by "the convergence and divergence of desires over what is taken to be the same knot of understanding" (Wright, p. 178) does not

---

[236] *"Die F., die dem Logiker aufmerksam zugehört ... [hatte] ... sich einen Campari bestellt ... [...] in der Wüste, liege eine Realität, der sie sich wie Tina stellen müsse ... was es für sie selber sein werde, wisse sie noch nicht, und dann fragte sie D.., den Campari austrinkend, ob sie nicht verrückt sei ..." (pp. 28-30).*

[237] *"... der Untersuchungsrichter, fleißig einem elsäßischen Weißwein zugetan ... dem Kameramann abwinkend ... [beteuerte] ... weitläufig, er sei ein gläubiger Muslim, ja in vielem geradezu ein Fundamentalist ..." (p. 45).*

[238] *"... neben dem Kühlschrank sei eine Flasche Whisky, und als sie sagte, sie ziehe Whisky vor, sagte er, das habe er gedacht ..." (p. 58).*

often result in some sort of negotiation of conflicting interpretations: in Dürrenmatt's text, ambiguity and uncertainty as a major attribute of human interaction are shown to be survivable, even if the alternative to stasis is a progression through a never-ending labyrinth, a conjecture based on a premise that always has an alternative, a path that must be chosen over a divergent path. The epigraph of *"Either/Or,"* the leitmotif of disorientation and the "criminality pattern" which is an exponent of the more universal pursuit of the cause behind the effect, are components employed to express this pervasive ambiguity and epistemological uncertainty. The process of "establishing a coherent field of meaning" (Lifton, p. 286) depends on the interaction of perceptually functional subjects. In the case of Polyphemos and Achilles, perception has become distorted, and there is an impaired, disconnected sense of reality which has been referred to here as psychic numbing. In both cases, a prolonged death anxiety has lead to this condition; this is shown in the text to be a function of technology both as an interposing barrier between subjects and in its ultimate destructive power in the form of its nuclear capability. Such a potential moves that which is bearably ambiguous - the natural cycle of life and death - into the realm of utter meaninglessness and unmitigated paradox. It is an existence where the only certainty is that it can atomize itself into extinction within minutes. Polyphemos and Achilles are extreme exponents of this sterility and stasis, but as the narcotization-motif demonstrates, the desire to alter the perception of such a threatening and alienating reality is pervasive. The most extensive leitmotif of the text is a vehicle of this theme of dysfunctional static subjects, restricted to an isolated observer-role in the observation of paradox and opposition. The first example of this motif, as mentioned above, occurs with the mutual observation of von Lambert and his wife. The logician D.'s observations present this motif very clearly:

> ... he had installed [a mirror telescope] in his house in the mountains, ... that he occasionally pointed at a cliff from which he was being observed by people with field glasses, ... the people observing him and discovering that he was observing them through a mirror telescope felt caught in the act, and since being caught in the act produces embarrassment [sic] and embarrassment frequently leads to aggression, more than one of these people, after retreating in haste, had come back to throw rocks at his

house as soon as he had dismantled the telescope ... (pp. 15-16).[239]

This excerpt describes a degeneration of a system of what should ideally be one of interacting subjects into a relationship between voyeurs. Technology is shown in its potential as an interposing factor in human interaction. It can easily distort social and cultural matrices meant to reconcile the disparate requirements of individuality with its instinctual vicissitudes and organic and psychic needs with those of communality and its inherent limitations of these. Technology presents the option of valorizing the latter at the expense of the former:

> ... a very suitable definition of contemporary man might be that he is a man under observation - observed by the state for one, with more and more sophisticated methods, while man makes more and more desperate attempts to escape being observed, which in turn renders man increasingly suspect in the eyes of the state and the state even more suspect in the eyes of man; similarly ... man, on another plane, is busy observing nature as never before, inventing more and more subtle instruments for this purpose, cameras, telescopes, stereoscopes, radio telescopes, X-ray telescopes, ... synchrotrons, ..., space probes, computers ... (pp. 16-17).[240]

---

[239] *"... er ... [besitze] ... doch in seinem Haus in den Bergen ein Spiegelteleskop ... das er bisweilen gegen einen Felsen richte, von wo aus er von Leuten mit Ferngläsern beobachtet werde ... die ihn beobachtenden fühlten sich dadurch, daß er sie durch sein Spiegelteleskop beobachte, ertappt, ertappt zu werden erwecke Schmach, Schmach oft Aggression, mancher, der sich verzogen habe, sei zurückgekehrt, wenn er, D., sein Instrument weggeräumt hätte, und habe Steine nach seinem Haus geworfen ..." (p. 20).* It would seem more semantically and psychologically accurate to translate the German *Schmach* with the English "humiliation."

[240] *"... der Mensch sei heute ein beobachteter Mensch, der Staat beobachte ihn mit immer raffinierteren Methoden, der Mensch versuche sich immer verzweifelter dem Beobachtet-Werden zu entziehen, dem Staat sei der Mensch und dem Menschen der Staat immer verdächtiger, ebenso beobachte wie noch nie der Mensch die Natur, indem er immer sinnreichere Instrumente erfinde, sie zu beobachten, wie Kameras, Teleskope, Stereoskope, Radioteleskope, Röntgenteleskope, Synchrotrone, Raumsonden, Computer ..." (p. 21).*

The text presents a viewpoint which is not critical necessarily of the actual development of an increasing capability to define natural phenomena, but rather of the way in which such knowledge is misused. Just as a concept of solipsistic individuality which does not see itself within the context of human developmental needs being met through interaction, leads to a dysfunctional system and dysfunctional individuals, the failure to recognize the viability of human existence as directly dependent on the viability of its natural environment leads to a state of *dis*integration.   Seen in this light, the text's anthropomorphism of environmental reactions to abuse is an appropriate adjunct to the basic theme of dysfunctional relationships resulting from the neglect of natural requirements:

> ... nature, for her part, was observing man and becoming
> aggressive, for what was the pollution of air, earth, and
> water, what were the dying forests, but a strike, ...
> precisely aimed defensive measures of observed nature
> against her observer, ... (p. 17).[241]

Having completed his observations on the delusory and voyeuristic position of the would-be invulnerable observer who aspires to complete control of his object, D. expands on the implications of the opposite condition becoming static, that of the need to be observed. D.'s musings are an expression of the motif of paradox and the propensity of human thinking to proceed on the basis of oppositional categories, but he is, significantly, not frozen into either of the alternative positions he delineates, rather he engages in a discussion of the epistemological uncertainty to which he sees human thinking relegated. Not only are his observations a manifestation of this motif of paradox and opposition, but he also represents, when he himself becomes an object of observation, a position which straddles the subject-object dialectic, seen as being both in control and vulnerable:

> ... an eccentric and sharp-witted man of whom no one
> could tell whether he was unfit for life or merely
> pretended to be helpless, who expounded his logical

---

[241] "... *die Natur beobachte nun ihrerseits den sie beobachtenden Menschen und werde aggressiv, bei der verschmutzten Luft, dem verseuchten Boden, dem verunreinigten Grundwasser, den sterbenden Wäldern handle es sich um einen Streik ... gezielte Abwehrmaßnahmen gegen das Beobachtet-Werden ...*" (p. 21).

problems to anyone who joined him at his table in the
always crowded restaurant, and this in such a confused
and thoroughgoing manner that no one was able to
understand him, not F. either, though she found him
amusing, liked him, and often told him about her plans, ...
(p. 10).[242]

Even though D.'s discourse is ambivalent and can be seen as the first
instance of the motif of incomprehensible discourse discussed above, it is
precisely because it is ambivalent in destabilizing other discourses which
are apodictic or monolithic, and above all else because it is dialogical and
therefore receptive to alternatives, that it is vibrant, non-static and human
in the best sense of the word. F.'s fondness for D. and her need to submit
her plans to his observation (F. as a subject focuses on D. as an object of
emotion, to become, in turn, an object of D.'s analysis), stand in contrast
to the static position of being observed which D. now describes as the
alternative opposite possibility of his argument:

... much the way D.'s mirror telescope and the rocks that
were thrown at his house were measures taken against
being observed, or, for that matter, von Lambert's
manner of observing his wife and her manner of
observing him, in each case a process of objectification
pursued to a degree that could only be unbearable to the
other, ...,but, he added, after suddenly bursting into
laughter and becoming serious again, what he was
constructing here was of course only one of two
possibilities, the other one being the precise opposite of
what he had described, ... this state of not being observed
would begin to torment him after a while, much more
than the knowledge of being observed had bothered him
earlier, ... because not being watched would make him
feel not worth noticing, ... being insignificant would make
him feel meaningless, ... other people suffered as much

---

242 *"... niemand wußte, ob er dem Leben gegenüber hilflos war oder diese
Hilflosigkeit spielte, der jedem ... seine logischen Probleme erklärte, derart
wirr und gründlich, daß sie niemand zu begreifen vermochte, auch die F. nicht,
die ihn amüsant fand, ihn mochte und ihm gegenüber oft ihre Pläne erläuterte
..." (p. 15).*

from not being observed, and that this was the reason why they all observed ... each other ... (pp. 17-19).[243]

The complementary pole to that of the disorder of the isolated subject is the negation of individuality and the pursuit of meaning as an object of a larger design, as a member of a national, political or religious group:

> ... humanity was about to return to its swaddling clothes, fundamentalists, idealists, moralists, and political Christers were doing their utmost to saddle unobserved humanity with the blessings of being observed, and therefore with meaning, for man, in the final analysis, was a pedant who couldn't get by without meaning ... (p. 22).[244]

D. is himself a paradox inasmuch as it is his academic training which enables him to avoid the pitfalls of pedantry, although he does admit that his career as an academic has been unsuccessful, (p. 19)(p. 23) an indication that there is a price to pay for challenging majority views and conventional wisdom. Here the paradox motif underlines the positive aspect of what may seem to be a stalemate of argument and counterargument in other contexts. It shows an ability to undermine the

---

[243] *"... so wie sein Spiegelteleskop und die Steine, die gegen sein Haus geworfen würden, Gegenmaßnahmen gegen das Beobachtet-Werden seien, desgleichen was zwischen von Lambert und dessen Frau abgespielt habe ... auch dort sei Beobachten ein Objektivieren und so habe denn jeder den anderen ins Unterträgliche objektiviert ... fügte aber hinzu, nachdem er plötzlich in ein Gelächter ausgebrochen war, wieder ernst geworden, was er da entwickelt habe, sei natürlich nur die eine Möglichkeit, die andere bestehe im puren Gegenteil dessen, was er ausgeführt habe, ... Unbeobachtet-Sein würde ihn mit der Zeit mehr quälen als das Beobachtet-Sein vorher, ... nicht mehr beobachtet käme er sich nicht beachtenswert ... bedeutungslos, sinnlos vor ... die Menschen ... litten unter dem Unbeobachtet-Sein wie er, auch sie kämen sich unbeobachtet sinnlos vor, darum beobachteten alle einander ..." (pp. 21-23).*
[244] *"... die Menschheit sei im Begriff, wieder zu den Windeln zurückzukehren, Fundamentalisten, Moralisten, Idealisten, Politchristen mühten sich ab, einer unbeobachteten Menschheit wieder eine Beobach-tung und einen Sinn aufzuhalsen, weil der Mensch nun einmal ein Pedant sei und ohne Sinn nicht auskomme ..." (p. 26).*

constraints of established "normalcy" and to experiment with untried ideas, hence his parting remarks to F.: "... in short, a crazy enterprise, but, on the other hand, so crazy that it wasn't crazy, and he wished her well"(p. 26).[245] Perhaps an indication that F. possesses a kindred unruly spirit is a narrative component of the following sentence that would otherwise be considered a simple vehicle of verisimilitude. In the context of D.'s way of thinking as well as in the context of a genre which, as theory would have it, stresses functionality, a perfunctory act can be seen as an expression of the motif of observation as paradox and opposition, here more precisely of rule and exception: "... she rolled up the top of her convertible just in time to avoid a downpour, through which she drove past the center of town to the old market and parked, ignoring a NO STOPPING sign, ..." (p. 27).[246] A further instance of this motif is the description of the head of M.'s secret service as a docile looking "pretty boy," "*ein sanfter Schönling.*" (p. 41)(p. 45). F.'s venture into the marketplace of C. after witnessing the execution incorporates this motif as well:

> ... a multiracial thicket of travellers all busily photographing and filming each other and forming an unreal contrast to the secret life inside the compound of the police ministry, like two interlocking realities, ... (p. 47).[247]

F.'s second unexpected encounter with the head of the secret service in her hotel room repeats the motif as well as the same lexical items used to describe him initially:

> ... there ... sat the gentle, pretty-faced man with rimless glasses, the investigating magistrate, who returned F.'s

---

[245] "*... Ein Unterfangen, das zwar verrückt sei aber wiederum so verrückt, das es nicht verrückt sei und er wünsche er ihr alles Gute*" (p. 30).
[246] "*... ein Platzregen setzte [ein], durch den sie ... zum Altmarkt hinunterfuhr und trotz des Verbots am Trottoirrand parkte ...*" (p. 31).
[247] "*..ein Völkerdickicht von einander knipsenden und filmenden Ferienreisenden ... [bildete] einen unwirklichen Kontrast zu den Vorgängen ... die sich im weißgetünchten Gebäudekomplex des Polizeiministeriums abgespielt hatten als ob sich zwei Wirklichkeiten durcheinanderschöben ...*" (p. 51).

long, wordless gaze, and then, with a movement of his
hand, invited her to sit down on the second armchair,
which she did mechanically, because it seemed to her as if
behind those soft, sentimental features she could discern
something hard and determined that had been previously
hidden, ... (p. 53).[248]

This character's explanation of the power struggle in M. describes a state
of mutual observation and opposing factions. The chief of police does not
know that his attempt to close the case of the murder at Al-Hakim has
been unsuccessful:

> ..., all the police chief wanted was to look like a strong
> man who could use the police as his private army, so that,
> once he took over, his power would look secure from the
> start, but he, the head of the secret service, intended to
> expose the chief of police, to show how he had corrupted
> the police and how weak his power really was, how
> unstable and already crumbling, ... (p. 55).[249]

The re-appearance of this figure in the deserted hotel on the edge
of the wasteland calls forth this motif yet once again, but this repeated use
of obvious contrast almost renders this character a caricature, particularly
the shift from spectacles without frames to sunglasses with massive
frames: "... The head of the secret service ..., dressed all in white with a
black cravat, wearing a pair of heavy-framed shades in place of the

---

[248] "... dort ... saß ... der sanfte Schönling mit der randlosen Brille, der
Untersuchungsrichter, der die ihn stumm betrachtende ebenfalls stumm
betrachtete, darauf mit der Hand auf den zweiten Lehnstühl wies, in den sich
die F. mechanisch setzte, weil es ihr schien, als ob beim Schönling hinter dem
Weichen, Sentimentalen etwas Hartes, Entschlossenes, bis jetzt Verstecktes zum
Vorschein komme ..." (p. 57).
[249] "... dem Polizeichef gehe es darum, als der starke Mann zu erscheinen, der
über die Polizei wie über eine Privatarmee verfüge, damit, wenn er die Macht
im Lande übernommen, diese als gesichert erscheine, ihm dagegen, dem Chef
des Geheimdienstes, gehe es darum, den Polizeichef bloßzustellen, zu zeigen,
wie dieser die Polizei korrumpiert habe und daß dessen Macht unsicher, labil
und schon am Zerfallen sei ..." (p. 59).

rimless glasses, ... stood up, ..." (p. 72).[250] It might be postulated that this transition reflects the change in the narrative from a situation with so many unknowns - the "docile pretty boy" brings news of Tina von Lambert's reunion with her husband and confirms F.'s discovery that the murder victim was Jytte Sörensen - from a mystery with almost no contours to one which will have truly massive international implications. If this is so, the functionality of every component of the genre would almost seem overplayed in this instance, hence a conjecture that the genre is being allegorized here. Similarly, F.'s last meal before leaving the hotel for her ordeal in the desert presents an oscillation between light and dark colours - from dark to light, back to dark and then back again to light, somewhat like a see-saw effect, but it also has a fairly obvious potential as an allegory of the most significant meal portrayed in the New Testament: "... lamb in a red sauce, white bread, and red wine, ..."(p. 67) ("... *Schaffleisch in einer roten Sauce und Weißbrot, dazu Rotwein ...*") (p. 72). These are the same foodstuffs (lamb, bread and wine) and this is the same sequence of their presentation as in the Passover meal consumed by Christ and the Apostles. (cf. Matthew 26). The elements of this motif are themselves a paradox when they are considered in their religious symbolic implications: they are both life-giving sustenance symbolizing spiritual sustenance and salvation, but are so because they represent (in the Catholic and Orthodox traditions they *are* body and blood) the ultimate sacrifice. Depending upon one's point of view or the fervency of one's belief, this could move an allegorical motif, in terms of its effect rather than its actual representation, into the realm of the grotesque, a characteristic often associated with Dürrenmatt's prose and drama which will be considered at a later point in the discussion. Even seemingly minor details such as the objects in F.'s hotel room are an expression of the leitmotif of points of view that are both alienating and symbiotic. Volumes of fiction by Jules Verne are juxtaposed with a picture of a colonial general: "..., a fireplace ..., some volumes of Jules Verne on the mantelpiece, above it the portrait of Marshal Lyautey, ..."(p. 65).[251] Verne stands at the beginning of a tradition of science fiction which describes odysseys to the centre of the earth as well as to the moon, among others. The common element between Verne and Lyautey would be that of colonisation and subjugation, Lyautey having enforced French

---

[250]   "... *Der Chef des Geheimdienstes, ganz in Weiß mit einem schwarzen Halstuch, an Stelle der randlosen Brille eine Sonnenbrille mit massiver Fassung ... erhob [sich] ..." (p. 76).*
[251]   "... *ein Kamin ... auf ihm einige Bände Jules Verne, über ihm wieder das vergilbte Bild des Mareschall Lyautey ..."p. 69).*

colonisation of territories in North Africa and Jules Verne envisioning
future human colonies on the moon. The oppositional relationship
between these two historical figures may be described as flights of the
imagination - a new vision - versus the last attempts to maintain an old
and static image of France as a colonial and imperialist power. This
example of the motif is a particularly salient one of the integration of
theme with an immediate textual environment. There is an allusion to
inward journey and outward journey, to subjugation and emancipation, to
technological progress and its inherent danger. It describes decay and
stasis but also presages the extra-terrestrial description of topography of
the desert into which F. will go, "..., into the stone desert, ... that looked
like a Martian landscape, ..."(p. 127) "... *hinein in die Steinwüste ... die
wie eine Marslandschaft schien* ..."(p. 87), and "... Polypheme ... was
herding her along ... through a pockmarked moon landscape of sand and
stone, ..."(p. 124). "... *Polyphem ... trieb sie ... in eine zernarbte
Mondlandschaft aus Sand und .Stein* ..." (p. 127). Another example of
contrast involving dark and light is the appearance of Polyphemos in the
same style of dress in which the head of the secret service had been
attired: "... He ... was wearing a clean white suit and a black shirt, ..." (p
91) "... *Er ... trug einen sauberen weißen Anzug und ein schwarzes
Hemd* ..." (p. 95). When Polyphemos demonstrates the range of the
monitors in the observatory, the black-and-white contrast is employed to
describe a relationship between a monolithic ideology, represented by the
Al-Hakim ruin,[252] and a centre of human habitation in the proximity of a
natural environment and natural phenomena:

> ..., a small black square by the left margin, the Al-Hakim
> ruin, the city on the top right, the mountain by the left
> margin, the cloud was still there, a blinding white cotton
> ball, at the center of the picture a small sphere with
> antennas, the first satellite as observed by a second
> satellite for the purpose of observing what it was
> observing, ... (p. 102).[253]

---

[252] This ruin is a monument to a Muslim historical holy figure, who is known
to have introduced discriminatory measures against other religious groups,
including the destruction of churches and synagogues. His fanaticism was also
a cause of suffering to other Muslims. The Druse sect sees in him the
embodiment of original divine power. (*Meyers Universallexikon*).
[253] "... *am linken Bildrand ein kleines, schwarzes Viereck, die Al-Hakim Ruine,
rechts oben die Stadt, am rechten Bildrand das Gebirge, immer noch die
Wolke, ein blendender weißer Wattebausch, in der Bildmitte eine kleine Kugel*

Technology is the interposing factor in this image, causing alienation and disjuncture of man as a natural entity and man seeking to define a meaningful existence. The logician D. has already alluded to this polarization: a greater understanding of nature through technology points to the non-existence of a personal God, the improbability of any providential observer, hence a fierce rekindling of traditional beliefs and absolute ideologies to counter the threat of a concept of human existence as a purely organic, natural and non-transcendent process. Whenever Al-Hakim is mentioned in the text, it is always as a low, dark spot within the brightness of a natural environment:

> ..., when all of a sudden the Al-Hakim ruin rose up before them from a depression into which they flew unexpectedly, straight toward the monument which loomed up before her ..., black, obscuring the sun, ... (pp. 34-35).[254]

F.'s vision of this monument from the hotel terrace repeats the same characteristics of darkness contrasting with light, a low black point in the landscape against the brilliance of the sun:

> ... now F. had a view of a gentle, still verdant hill ... far down to a shimmering whitish-yellow color, the desert, and it seemed to her that, at the outermost edge of the eye's reach, she could half discern, half surmise something black, the Al-Hakim ruin, ... (p. 63).[255]

The last example of detached observation through technology and resultant dichotomies completes the scale of application of this motif from the interpersonal sphere to one of macrocosmic proportions. Mutual observation makes a balance of terror possible and the sole guarantor of peace is the capacity to wage war:

---

mit Antennen, der erste Satellit von einem zweiten Satelliten beobachtet, um zu beobachten wie dieser beobachte ..." (p. 106).
[254] *"... doch unvermutet tauchte vor ihnen die Al-Hakim-Ruine auf, die in einer Mulde lag, in die sie unvermutet hinunterrasten, dem Monument entgegen, das, die Sonne verdunkelnd, schwarz vor ihr ... aufwuchs ..."* (p. 39).
[255] *"... so blickte nun die F. ... hinunter, ... bis es unten weißgelb hinaufschimmerte, die große Sandwüßte, auch glaubte sie am Ende des Sichtbaren etwas Schwarzes zu ahnen, die Al-Hakim-Ruine ..."* (p. 67).

..., the strategic conceptions of both sides required a careful inspection of the target precision of missiles, ... preserving world peace at the risk of killing both peace and the world, ... by relying too heavily on the intimidation of the enemy or on the computer or on an ideology or even on God, ... (pp. 102-103).[256]

In surveying the application of this leitmotif from the private to the general sphere, the element of the grotesque, although present in most of its manifestations, is more strongly sensed and can be justified as an appropriate term in certain examples. Critics have turned their attention to what some perceive to be a characteristic of Dürrenmatt's ouevre, but even a definition of the term is a matter of contention. Robert Helbling's article addresses this problem and provides some insight into the difficulties encountered within the discussion of the definition and application of this term.[257] According to Helbling, the critics "generally agree that the grotesque consists in sensing the ludicrous within the fearsome or horrific" (p. 177). Although he cites Wolfgang Kayser in his description of the psychological effect of the grotesque as "a heterogeneous mixture of instant fear and defensive or liberating laughter,"[258] Helbling extends the element of visceral laughter to include "intellectual elements of 'recognition' of the ludicrousness of human fears and attitudes" (177), suggesting that there is "a role for the *comic* in the grotesque" (p. 177). Helbling refers to Bergson's definition of the comic in the latter's *Le Rire*.

Comedy expresses a person's lack of adaptability to society, an 'inelasticity,' the comic character is a human type that monomaniacally goes his own way, out of touch

---

[256] "... *so sei es für die strategische Konzeption beider Seiten notwendig, die Zielgenauigkeit der ... Raketen zu überprüfen ... wodurch einerseits der Friede auf Erden erhalten werde, wenn auch auf die Gefahr hin ... die Erde würde ... damit zu Tode gerüstet, indem ... alzusehr auf die Einschüchterung des anderen oder auf den Computer oder auf eine Ideologie oder gar auf Gott vertraut werde ..."* (p. 106).

[257] Robert E. Helbling, "Dürrenmatt Criticism: Exit the Grotesque?" *Play Dürrenmatt*, ed. Moshe Lazar (Malibu: Undena Publications, 1983) pp. 175-188.

[258] Wolfgang Kayser, *The Grotesque in Art and Literature* Trans. Ulrich Weisstein (Bloomington: Indiana University Press, 1963).

with his fellow human beings ... It is undeniable that one can observe many forms of Bergsonian "automatism" and inelasticity in Dürrenmatt's dramatic characters ... the ossification of attitudes and stylized verbal expression in most of his *dramatis personae* (p. 179).

Citing Kayser once again, the grotesque is said to emerge from a "satiric world view" (p. 178). "Generally speaking, satire is of course a conscious criticism of human frailties, obtuseness or stupidity ..." (178). Philip Thomson observes that the present tendency "is to view the grotesque as a fundamentally ambivalent thing, as a violent clash of opposites, and hence, as an appropriate expression of the problematical nature of existence."[259] The grotesque is a favoured mode "prevalent in societies marked by strife, radical change and disorientation" (Thomson, p. 11). Thomson's basic definition of the grotesque is "the unresolved clash of incompatibles in work and response" (p. 27). As opposed to the derisive laughter of satire, the more ludicrous than disturbing quality of the farcical or bizarre or the predominantly disturbing quality of the macabre, the grotesque produces a confused reaction, is meant to disorient and overwhelm (p. 42). Similarly, irony must be distinguished from the grotesque, since the former "depends on the resolvability, intellectually, of a relationship (appearance/reality, truth/untruth, while the grotesque presents essentially the unresolvability of incompatibles" (p. 50). The opening scene of the novella which describes Tina von Lambert's helicopter burial is a prime example of the grotesque, in that the solemnity usually observed on the occasion of a burial of human remains is replaced with a sensationalism akin to that of a circus-act or a media event.

> ... the psychiatrist ... had the corpse transported by helicopter across the Mediterranean, suspended in its coffin by ropes from the bottom of the plane, so that it trailed after it slightly, over vast stretches of sunlit land, through shreds of clouds, across the Alps in a snowstorm, and later through rain showers, until it was gently reeled down into an open grave surrounded by a mourning party, and covered with earth ... (p. 3).[260]

---

[259] Philip Thomson, *The Grotesque* (London: Methuen & Co. Ltd., 1972) p. 11.

[260] "... *der Psychiater [ließ]* ... *die Leiche mit einem Helikopter über das Mittelmeer transportieren, der Sarg, worin sie lag, mit einem Tragseil unter der Flugmaschine befestigt, dieser nachschwebend, bald über*

The image of an object suspended from another, moving through the air evokes several associations: that of a rescue attempt of an injured person, of a trapeze artist performing stunts in a circus act, of an attempt to quickly remove dangerous materials, or even of the proverbial stork on its way to an expectant mother. (The last of these associations is not as improbable as it may seem, since the person assumed to be in the coffin is not dead and in fact gives birth to a child.). The clash is between one of efficient technology in its speedy dispatch of a corpse and the ritual of burial which is said to facilitate the difficult process of acceptance of death. A taboo is flouted, causing both tension, because the rules are broken, and delight, because a moment of liberation from the constraints of accepted social behaviour has been provided. (cf. Thomson, pp. 60-61). Similarly, the execution of the Scandinavian dwarf (a paradoxical and comical hybrid due to the contrasting physical characteristics of these types) is referred to in the text in a manner reminiscent of an operetta:

..., the Scandinavian stopped in front of the concrete wall facing the row of policemen, the officer walked back to his men and positioned himself next to the row, held the sword vertically in front of his face, just like a scene in an operetta, and as if to emphasize that, the rotund police chief came in, waddling laboriously, sweating, until he had reached the dwarfish, grinning man by the wall, stuck a cigarette in his mouth, ... the dwarfish man smoked, ... a dull thud followed, ... the dwarfish man reached for the cigarette with his manacled hands, dropped it, extinguished it with his foot, collapsed, and lay on the ground, motionless, blood flowing out of every part of his body toward the center of the courtyard, where there was a drain, ... (pp. 43-44).[261]

sonnenbeschienene unermeßliche Flächen, bald durch Wolkenfetzen flog, dazu noch über den Alpen in einen Schneesturm, später in Regengüsse geriet, bis er sich sanft ins offene von der Trauerversammlung umstellte Grab hinunterspulen ließ, das alsobald zugeschaufelt wurde ..." (p. 9).
[261] "... der Skandinavier stellte sich an die Betonwand der Polizeireihe gegenüber, der Offizier schritt zu ihr zurück, stellte sich neben die Reihe, hielt den Säbel steil vor sein Gesicht, alles wirkte wie eine Operette, der fette Polizeichef wälzte sich herein, was den Eindruck des Operettenhaften erhöhte, wälzte sich mühsam und schwitzend zum Zwerghaften, Grinsenden, steckte ihm eine Zigarette in den Mund ... der Zwerghafte rauchte, schien endlich zu

The comical element derives from stock characters and a stock situation, exaggerated human attributes and deformities. A balance is struck with this ludicrous scene through the impartial description of blood flowing massively from a bullet-riddled body into a drain designed for this purpose, thus creating an ambivalent reaction of both distress and amusement. The reaction of the elderly female caretaker of the desert hotel to the news of Tina von Lambert's assumed death is also an expression of this motif of the grotesque:

> ... Tina would not come back, ... she was dead, to which the old woman at first responded with indifference, as if she had not understood what she had heard, but suddenly she began to grimace, and to giggle to herself, in despair, as F. gradually realized, and, taking the old woman by the shoulder and shaking her, she demanded to be shown the room Tina had rented, whereupon the old woman, still giggling, mumbled something that sounded like "all the way up," and F. walked up the stairs, ignoring the sounds of the old woman's sudden sobs, ... (p. 64).[262]

The behaviour of this character indicates both awareness and disorientation: "... pointing at the red fur coat with a quivering hand, 'her coat,' babbling these words over and over, and obviously so bewildered ..."(p. 62).[263] She is also portrayed as a figure who feels a sense of concern and responsibility for F., "... as if to watch over her ..."(p. 63)

---

rauchen, die Polizisten wurden unruhig ... ein dumpfes Geräusch, der Zwerghafte griff mit den gefesselten Händen nach der Zigarette, ließ sie fallen, trat sie aus ... stürzte in sich zusammen ... lag unbeweglich am Boden, während Blut aus ihm floß, überall, gegen die Mitte des Hofes zu, wo sich ein Abflußgitter befand ... (pp. 48-49).
[262] *"... Tina werde nicht zurückkommen, sie sei tot, eine Nachricht, die von der Alten zuerst gleichgültig entgegengenommen wurde, so als hätte sie nicht begriffen, doch plötzlich fing sie an zu feixen, in sich hineinzukichern, aus Verzweiflung, wie es der F. allmählich aufging, und, indem sie die Alte bei der Schulter packte und schüttelte, verlangte sie, in das Zimmer geführt zu werden, das Tina gemietet hatte, worauf die Alte etwas murmelte, das, weil sie dabei wieder kicherte, wie "ganz oben" klang, und dann, wie die F. die Treppe hinaufging, in ein Schluchzen auszubrechen ..."* (p. 68).
[263] *"... auf den roten Mantel zeigend, 'ihr Mantel' plappernd, immer wieder, so offensichtlich durcheinander ..."* (p. 66).

("... *als müsse sie diese bewachen* ...")(p. 67). The reaction to her smirking and giggling at the news of Tina's death is to perceive its ineptitude and therefore its comic potential; on the other hand, F. understands this aberration as a sign of extreme distress, and since this figure has been entirely benevolent, the reaction is an ambivalent one of pity or concern as well as a perception of the comic element in this momentary departure from "sane" behaviour. As Thomson states, "Manifestations of insanity, particularly those involving maniacal laughter, are often grotesque, because insane behaviour is abnormal ...: it can be comic and frightening or pitiable at the same time." (p. 53). The scene in which F. is pursued by Polyphemos and Achilles also demonstrates the element of the grotesque deriving from insane behaviour:

> ... now nearly inaudible, now roaring toward her again, a monster playing with its victim, the Land-Rover, steered by Polypheme, next to him Achilles, still half stunned, swaying from side to side, reciting the "Iliad,"..., but Polypheme did not need to steer her, she walked and walked, ... then a laugh behind her ... (p. 124).[264]

The figure of Achilles provides the comical aspect to what seems to be imminent rape and murder, inasmuch as he is an automaton (cf. Bergson), "a bald-headed mass of flesh" (p. 118) (p. 122) exhibiting abnormally repetitive behaviour. Indeed, if different lexical items are used to render this scene, it sounds like the beginning of a joke. (Two insane people riding through the desert in a jeep are chasing a woman wearing nothing but a red fur coat ...).

The Assignment is clearly an example of a text in which the design of the relationship of every narrative component within a motif-complex to its thematic significance is meticulously conceived. The plot progression of scene, episode, the omniscient authorial rendition of character reflection and even subsidiary mimetic detail call on one or several leitmotifs: the lacunae and misinterpretation of language, the labyrinth of endless corridors, narcotization, the grotesque, paradox, the dialectic of subject/object as both an alienating and symbiotic relationship and the duality of male and female. These are interlocking components

---

[264] "... *bald nicht mehr hörbar, bald heranbrausend, ein Untier, das mit seinem Opfer spielte, der Geländewagen, von Polyphem gesteuert, neben ihm Achilles, immer noch halb betäubt hin und her wippend aus der 'Ilias' zitierend ... doch brauchte Polyphem sie nicht zu lenken, sie ging und ging ... dann ein Lachen hinter ihr ...*" (p. 128).

which emanate from a sharp focus on a limited sequence of experiences of only a few individuals, but enable, along with the use of symbol, intertextuality and mythological metaphor the emergence of a field of interpretation which has universally human implications.

All of the texts analysed in this study thus far demonstrate a highly tectonic and functional design, achieve thematic expansiveness yet restrict themselves to quantitatively limited proportions of human experience and are correspondingly on the shorter end of the prose-scale; they also have been directly or indirectly designated as members of a genre whose usage as a literary label has not been in strong evidence in this century. The next text to be analysed in this study, Dürrenmatt's *The Coup (Der Sturz,)* demonstrates the same incidence of parallel, repetitive structure, the same interlocking nexus of narrative components with thematically expansive implications, and possesses features that have been considered in the historical discussion of the novella and the short-story as constitutive of the genre. The differences that emerge in the course of the following portion of analysis indeed prove that proportions vary, that generic labels are best considered as a heuristic device, a framework of established variables upon which the salient features of a text may be delineated and from which they will most likely depart.

Friedrich Dürrenmatt's Der Sturz

It is just as daunting to read one's way into this text as it is for its
characters to speculate desperately on each other's true motivations for
having uttered a particular sentence or for having assumed a certain
posture or facial expression. The tenuous relationship between signifier
and signified, the slip and slide of language, the deferment of true meaning
and the constraints of the group on the expression of the basic instincts of
the individual are key thematic and structural elements of this story. The
language and conventions are those of ideology, yet paradoxically - also a
significant concept for the theme and structure of the Dürrenmatt texts
under discussion here - the players of the game are involved in a life-and-
death-struggle, whose outcome is the result of the inevitable vicissitudes
of instinct combined with the role of pure chance. As cited in the
preceding discussion of *The Assignment,* a basic tenet is in strong
evidence here, namely that the more deliberate the plan, the greater the
effect of the disruption of coincidence and chance upon that plan.[265] The
general Apollonian/Dionysian antinomy,[266] the related opposition of
ideology versus instinct, of teleology versus random occurrence and the
crisis of isolated, observing subjects locked into a treadmill of
abstractions, "'piling pleonasm on to an antonomasis' ... - that is,
multiplying language on a discourse which already misnames its object

---

[265] "The more human beings proceed according to a given plan, the greater
may be the effect of chance or coincidence when it strikes." (*"je planmäßiger
die Menschen vorgehen, desto wirksamer mag sie der Zufall treffen."*)
[266] "Nietzsche used the terms in *The Birth of Tragedy out of the Spirit of Music*
(1872). He was making a distinction between reason and instinct, culture and
primitive nature ... Apollonian is also often thought to signify 'sunny' and
'serene', whereas the Dionysian means 'stormy' and 'turbulent'." J.A. Cuddon,
A Dictionary of Literary Terms (Middlesex: Viking Penguin, 1985) p. 51. In
her monograph on Nietzsche's philosophy of art, Rose Pfeffer observes of the
central phenomenon of Dionysus that Apollonian measure, control and the
"organizing power of forms" are essential to the "primal chaos ... of savage
urges and orgiastic frenzy that threaten to destroy all forms ... Both the artistic
and natural forces create in the same manner, in the same tragic rhythm where
dialectical powers are constantly at work in eternal recurrence - creating and
destroying without purposes and goals ..." Rose Pfeffer, *Nietzsche, Disciple of
Dionysus* (Cranbury, New Jersey: Associated University Presses, Inc.: 1972)
pp. 220-221.

...,"[267] are the major thematic components of *Der Sturz*. A closer look at Lacan's terminology reveals that this oft cited phrase is aptly applied to Dürrenmatt's text: Pleonasm, the Greek for 'superfluity' is defined as "the redundant use of words," (Cuddon, p. 513) and antonomasis, the Greek 'naming instead' is accomplished through epithet, "a descriptive word or phrase added to or substituted for a person's name" (Collin's English Dictionary).

In all there are fifteen members of the Politburo with whom the reader must contend; such a large contingency of characters, made even more difficult to assimilate due to their representation by the first sixteen letters of the alphabet (J is omitted, a point to be considered later in the discussion) would seem to contradict the premise that the novella and short story favour limited proportions, particularly since not all of these play an active role in propelling the plot to its culminating point. Yet those who are both central to, and remain at the periphery of the action, are portrayed according to a repetitive structure constituted primarily by the Apollonian/Dionysian antinomy and a restricted number of interlocking motifs, including that of alternative interpretations of a given set of circumstances, the "either-or" syndrome already seen to be a major component in *The Assignment*. *Der Sturz* has a non-narrative, pictorial framework consisting of diagrams of letters of the alphabet, the first of which is illustrated after the title page. A in the upper centre is flanked by two rows of letters, with the alphabetical sequence alternating between the rows in descending order of power. On the last page of the text, the alphabetical sequence of the two rows is scrambled to reflect the change in the hierarchy of power: A is missing, since this is the figure who has been purged. The letters and epithets (the latter coined by the cynical A) and ministerial duties of the Politburo members will be provided here in a concordance in order to facilitate the discussion of these figures. A is the omnipotent dictator who has tagged his colleagues as follows: B, "*Eunuch*," and "*unser Genie*," eunuch and genius, foreign minister; C, "*Staatstante*," state aunt, head of the secret police; D., "*die Wildsau*," the wild sow, party secretary; E, "Lord Evergreen," minister of foreign trade; F, "*Schuhputzer*" and "*Arschlecker*," shoe-shine-boy and ass-licker, minister for heavy industry; G, "*der Teeheilige*," the holy teetotaler, head ideologue; H, one of the Genghis Khans, ("*Gin-gis-Khane*,") with special emphasis on gin, marshal of the armed forces; I, "*die Ballerina*," minister for agriculture; K, the other *Gingh*is Khan, president; L, "*das Denkmal*,"

[267] Jacques Lacan, *Écrits*: A Selection, trans. Alan Sheridan (New York, 1977), p. 136, cited by Ronald Schleifer, p. 872.

the monument, minister of transport; M, *"die Parteimuse,"* the party's source of culture and entertainment, minister of education and the only female member; N, postal minister with no "alias," due to his relative insignificance, a newcomer to the Politburo; O, the minister for atomic energy, also no "alias;" P, minister for youth affairs, no "alias." The two factions within this body are D, B, M and the marginal L, who are opposed by G, I, K and F. The names on A's liquidation list are G, F, D, M and H.

In his monograph on Dürrenmatt's prose, Peter Spycher refers to an attempt made by a specialist in Slavic studies to treat *Der Sturz* as one would a key novel, assigning a historical equivalent to each of the fictional figures - with a somewhat questionable degree of success.[268] In a global sense, there is an obvious historical parallel in the institutions of totalitarian and oligarchic states and of corporate hierarchies in which power- struggles and takeovers periodically occur. Although the connection between a work of art and empirical reality is always mediated, the accuracy of art's specular quality and prediction of lived experience is at times especially forceful: the democratization of the Russian political system in the late eighties calls to mind the reform proposed in *Der Sturz*, only the treadmill of untruths, fear and incompetence is so entrenched in its fictional form that the attempt to eliminate it meets with failure and the system perpetuates itself. Yet another historical occurrence which lends itself to a positivist treatment of *Der Sturz* are the commentaries on the lack of a response of the former East German government to the mass exodus which took place at the borders of Austria and Hungary. The rumoured impending death of chief of state Erich Honecker and the surprising absence of any measures to halt the flow sparked the following comments: "... the strict hierarchy of power within the party apparatus, and the desire to protect one's position in advance of a possible shakeup at the top, have kept potential reformers from speaking up ... state and party leadership is paralysed and above all

---

[268] With the exception of Stalin as a possible model for A, the remainder of the characters are difficult to assimilate to any historical counterparts. For example, D is said to resemble Malenkov in a "foggy" fashion; *"Parteisekretär D [erinnert] nebelhaft an Malenkow ...."* F is said to be partly based on Nikita Khrushchev: *"... F ... ist eine Kreuzung, aber mit deutlichen Zügen Chruschtschows ...."* The remainder of these comparisons are similarly inconclusive. Peter Spycher, *Friedrich Dürrenmatt. Das erzählerische Werk* (Frauenfeld und Stuttgart: Verlag Huber, 1972) pp. 346f.

preoccupied with the internal fight for power."[269] The fictional dictator A's cynical trait of mocking and denigrating fearful and subservient subordinates also has an interesting historical parallel; a reviewer of former Soviet foreign minister Andrei Gromyko's book *Memories* refers to the latter's admiration of politicians who showed no feelings, like himself, and cites Khrushchev's less than respectful remark on this characteristic: "If I ask Mr. Gromyko to take off his trousers and sit on a block of ice, he will obey and he will stay there until I tell him to move."[270]

Dürrenmatt's substitution of letters for names not only enables the reception of a more general rather than a specifically historical set of circumstances, it is also a formal technique which expresses an aspect of the theme: the inability to call things by their proper names, to speak of fear when there is fear, untruth and failure when these are at hand. In *The Assignment,* the logician D., theorizing on the improbability of ultimate truth, includes an excerpt from an oft cited passage in German literature: "Feeling is everything. Words are just sound and smoke, bedimming the light of heaven."[271] Faust's reply to Margarete when asked if he believes in God thus expresses "the inability of mere words and names to grapple with reality .... God is but a name to domesticate the mysteriousness of our strivings, anxieties, feelings."[272]

Not only does Dürrenmatt concretize his characters as minimally as possible through the use of letters, reminiscent of algebraic equations when they appear within the syntax of a sentence, he avoids the use of the letter J: the symbolic significance of this letter for anyone conversant with the Christian tradition does not require a major leap of the imagination, and in another short text, *Abu Chanifa und Anan ben David*, Dürrenmatt closes the narrative with the two protagonists seeing the object of their struggle and quest for the divine in each other. "*Jahwe* was Abu Chanifa and *Allah* was Anan ben David" ("*Jahwe ist Abu Chanifa und Allah*

---

[269] Robert J. McCartny, "East Germany Paralysed by Honecker's Illness," *The Montreal Gazette* 14 Sept. 1989: A8.

[270] Gregory Wirick, Rev. of *Memories*, by Andrei Gromyko. *The Montreal Gazette* 12 Aug. 1989: K4.

[271] Goethe, *Faust* Trans. Brarker Farley (University of Toronto Press, 1972) p. 60. ("*Gefühl ist alles; Name ist Schall und Rauch, Umnebelnd Himmelsgluth.*") Goethe, *Sämtliche Werke: Faust I* vol. 6.1 (München: Carl Hanser Verlag, 1986) p. 636.

[272] Jean Charles Seigneuret, ed. *Dictionary of Literary Themes and Motifs*, (New York: Greenwood Press, 1988) p. 890.

Anan ben David gewesen").[273] It is interesting to note that the simple omission of the letter J is able to generate a process of interpretation, leading to the hypothesis that the absence of this letter symbolizes the vacuity of any concept of providence meant to "domesticate the mysteriousness of our strivings ..." Similarly, the absence of O, minister for atomic energy, an energy source with numinous potential, launches a discourse of machination and analysis fuelled by the assumption that O has been purged; since his absence has a banal explanation as claimed by those assumed to have liquidated him (they speculate illness whereas he has simply mistaken the date of this assembly) the entire proceedings have been superfluous, in other words, a pleonasm caused by the interaction of characters who are rendered through the technique of antonomasia, without the identity of a name, spurred on by the *non*-presence of someone designated as "O," "Null," zero, in whose midst there is no J.

The prime focus for the narration is one of restricted omniscience describing N's speculations on the discourse of his colleagues. The opening scene describes the ritual of a cold buffet and stringent security measures observed as the preliminaries for each meeting of the Politburo. The extended distribution of expositional information in this scene relating to the backgrounds and traits of these characters essential to the narration takes up the first eighteen pages, almost a third of the text. There is no question of the conventional proportions expected of a *Vorgeschichte*, yet the characters are introduced according to an emerging pattern; each figure is in a fearfully precarious position, with swift liquidation an immanent possibility depending on what the leader deems politically correct in a given situation, that is, most expedient in maintaining his power-position. The crisis situation at the centre of the text, as mentioned above, is the absence of the minister O, who is assumed to have been purged, with a "ripple effect" being expected by those with whom this individual was aligned. Scanning this lengthy expositional segment reveals that the characters are introduced in six pairs: although three of these combine figures with prevalently similar traits and the remaining three introduce characters with opposite characteristics, the Apollonian/Dionysian antinomy is observable as a measure of contrast between the members of each pair. With the introduction of each set, the absence of O sets off a process of speculation whose vehicle is the "either/or" structure. The effect of the hiatus is twofold: it engenders fear and a resulting effort to conceal vulnerability through feigned indifference,

---

[273] Friedrich Dürrenmatt, *Abu Chanifa und Anan ben David, Werkausgabe in dreißig Bänden* vol. 23 (Zürich: Diogenes, 1985) p. 86.

or it leads to an offensive posture and an attempt to exploit the vulnerability of others. The epithets and letters used in the designation of the characters are repeated components, but to call them a leitmotif does not seem entirely justifiable; they are minimal naming devices, signifiers with a tenuous, abbreviated designatory relationship to the characters they signify, and they are a complement to the repeated use of slogans, ideological jargon, maxims devoid of meaning in the context in which they are used and the theme of the unstable relationship of discourse to meaning. In addition, there is once again the repeated motif of narcotization attendant to situations of prolonged and acute fear and anxiety as observed in the preceding analysis of *The Assignment*.

The first pair of figures to be introduced are N and L. Both have communications portfolios inasmuch as L is the minister of transport and N is the postal minister. Both have lower positions in the hierarchy, although L is a senior colleague, one of the original revolutionaries, "the monument" (*"das Denkmal"*) with a reputation for justice, a popular following and hence some degree of immunity to the periodic liquidations. The motif of fear of becoming the target of a purge is in evidence with both L and N. N's ascent to power has paradoxically made him more vulnerable than he ever was: "In spite of their junior rank as ministers in charge of the postal service, his predecessors had all disappeared without a trace within this mechanism of state" (p. 11).[274] L sees his position in the hierarchy as even more precarious than N's, since his longevity makes every new purge the more likely to signal his downfall: "The fear of an accusation undermined L's confidence. He knew that his overthrow must come eventually. Like both marshals H and K, he too was was often drunk" (p. 12).[275] Both L and N show indifference: "Even now he stank of champagne, yet his raw voice was calm, and his watery, blood-shot eyes gave a look of derision" (pp. 12-13).[276] N's reaction to L's remark that they are both doomed because O has not appeared (*"'Kamerad,' sagte er zu N, 'wir sind erledigt.'"*) (p. 13) also expresses indifference: "N didn't answer. It did not even give him a start. He pretended to be indifferent")

---

[274] "*... seine Vorgänger waren trotz der doch eher untergeordneten Stellung der Post innerhalb der Staatsmaschinerie verschollen ...*"
[275] "*Die Furcht vor einer Anklage unterhöhlte L. Er wußte, daß sein Sturz einmal kommen mußte. Wie die beiden Marschälle H and K war er oft betrunken ...*"
[276] "*Auch jetzt stank er nach Champagner, doch war seine rauhe Stimme ruhig, und seine wässerigen, blutunterlaufenen Augen blickten spöttisch ...*"

(p. 13).[277] The "either/or" structure signalled by the adverb "*vielleicht,*" the conjunction "*oder,*" and the use of conditional and concessive sentences occurs twice in the first three pages of the text. N remarks to himself that the officer who usually searched everyone for concealed weapons was not present on this day, leading him to speculate upon his fate: "The colonel ... must have been on vacation, or had been transferred, or removed from duty, or demoted, or shot" (p. 11).[278] His inner reaction to L's premonition of disaster repeats this exercise in speculation: "Perhaps O's arrest was a rumor, perhaps L was mistaken, and if L was not mistaken, then perhaps N's situation was not as hopeless as L's after all" (p. 13).[279]   N represents the Apollonian pole of the Dionysian/Apollonian antinomy: he reason for his appointment to the secretariat is his mastery of a particular discipline ("N was nothing but a specialist in his field") ("... *N [war] nichts als ein Spezialist in seinem Ressort*") (p. 17) and he is shown to be disinterested in the pornography sent to him by F and the crates of Bordeaux with which B periodically provides him: ("... wine meant nothing to him ... [...] Thus N, who was sober and had moderate erotic requirements, saw the pornographic material pile up") (pp. 20-21).[280] L's behaviour, on the other hand, is rendered through the narcotization motif and is shown to be unrestrained for this reason:

He was more drunk now than before. His words were a little slurred and he had to start over as he pointed out that O was missing and that consequently this meeting of the Politburo could not even be said to have begun. [...] "Sick," L now screamed out, leaning on the left armrest and thumping with his right fist on the table ... (pp. 31-33).[281]

---

[277] "*N antwortete nicht. Er zuckte nicht einmal zusammen. Er spielte den Gleichgültigen.*"

[278] "*der Oberst ... mußte im Urlaub sein, oder war versetzt, oder entlassen oder degradiert, oder erschossen worden.*"

[279] "*Vielleicht war O's Verhaftung ein Gerücht, vielleicht täuschte sich L, und wenn sich L nicht täuschte, so war N's Lage vielleicht doch nicht so hoffnungslos, wie jene L's ...*"

[280] "*... er [machte] sich aus Wein nichts ... [...] So häufte sich beim nüchternen und erotisch mäßigen N das pornographische Material an ...*"

[281] "*Seine Trunkenheit hatte offenbar zugenommen. Er wies darauf hin, leicht lallend und zweimal ansetzend, daß O fehle und daß darum die Sitzung des Politischen Sekretariats noch gar nicht habe beginnen können. [ ] "Krank"?*"

Although D and I are the next to make an entrance, full attention is focused on D when his colleague C, who is the next to appear, enters the room. The configuration of contrasting figures after L and N is then I and F, D and C. I's former position of attorney general also incorporates the motif of fear, as A at one point enlisted I to eliminate his son-in-law, reversed his decision, but not quickly enough. His subsequent appointment to a position of power carries with it the same higher degree of vulnerability and fear to which all members of this body are subject:

He had been named a member of the Politburo and thus was added to the most convenient of all possible hit lists .... A now had an official excuse to liquidate I, should he want to liquidate him at some point, and because A had never missed a chance to liquidate someone, I was not given any chance of survival. I knew this and behaved as if he didn't (p. 14).[282]

As with N and L, the motif of fear is coupled with that of feigned indifference. The introduction of this figure also presents the first example of superfluous jargon: I's agriculture portfolio could not be more ill-suited to this barrister and balletophile, who attempts to deflect attention from his ineptitude in agricultural matters through an informed commentary on the art of dance:

He was all too obvious in masking his insecurity. He was telling the party secretary about a performance of the ballet. At every meeting I talked about all of this prancing about, throwing out technical terms to describe the art of the dance, more so since he had taken over the

---

schrie denn auch L, sich auf den linken Vorderarm stützend und mit der rechten Faust auf den Tisch trommelnd ..."
[282] "Er wurde zum Mitglied des Politischen Sekretariats ernannt und damit auf die bequemste der möglichen Abschußlisten gesetzt ... .A besaß jetzt eine öffentliche Ausrede, I zu erledigen, wenn er ihn einmal erledigen wollte, und weil A noch nie eine Chance ausgelassen hatte, jemanden zu erledigen, gab man I keine Chance mehr. I wußte dies und benahm sich, als wüßte er es nicht."

agriculture ministry, although, as a lawyer, he understood
nothing about agriculture (p. 14).[283]

This paradoxical combination of professional responsibility and
personal disinclination is repeated with the other figure within this
particular example of the strategy of pairing, with each element of I's
configuration reflected by an opposing counter-element in F's situation. F
has a sketchy educational background, no interest in culture and a
particularly rural or agrestic stamp to his appearance and mode of
expression. His portfolio of heavy industry offers a set of responsibilities
for which his profile and qualifications could not be more ill-suited:

> Only F, the minister for heavy industry, who had grown
> up in a village, had cobbled together half of a raw and
> primitive education at some rural teacher's college,
> looked like a farmer and talked like a farmer, - only F
> talked about farmers in the Politburo (p. 15).[284]

The motif of fear and the effort to camouflage it are evidenced
with this figure well after the initial expositional material has been
provided, yet the pattern is the same. The following passage occurs after
A has announced his plan to democratize the party through the elimination
of the Politburo and L has attempted to declare the proposal as
inadmissible on the procedural grounds that O's absence means there is no
quorum. F attacks L to gain favour with A:

> The composure of the minister for heavy industry was
> deceiving. The shoe-shine boy was acting out of pure
> terror at L.'s behaviour. He could see A.'s rage pouring
> down on everyone ... As was his custom, he began with
> an endless string of farmers' sayings he had acquired, no

---

[283] *"Er versuchte allzu offensichtlich seine Unsicherheit zu verbergen. Er
erzählte dem Parteisekretär von einer Aufführung des Staatlichen Ballets. I
erzählte in jeder Sitzung von der Tänzerei und warf mit Fachausdrücken der
Balletkunst um sich, besonders, seit er noch das Landwirtschaft-sministerium
übernehmen mußte, obgleich er als Jurist von der Landwirtschaft nichts
verstand."*
[284] *"Nur der Minister für die Schwerindustrie F, der in einem Dorfe
aufgewachsen ... und eine von einem ländlichen Lehrerseminar roh und
primitiv zusammengezimmerte Halbbildung besaß, der wie ein Bauer aussah
und wie ein Bauer redete, erzählte im Politischen Sekretariat von Bauern ..."*

matter that they did not fit the circumstances. He said: "Before the fox attacks, the chickens get fresh." He said: "A farmer only washes his wife when the landowner wants to sleep with her." ... He said: "Even big farmers can fall into a pit of liquid manure"(pp. 38-39).[285]

Despite the clearly contrived nature of I's serenity and cultural leanings, these along with his educational background are Apollonian elements which contrast with the Dionysian F, who is described as "the instinctively devious practitioner of violence" (*"der instinktiv listige Praktiker der Gewalt"*) (p. 23). The next pair of opposites to be introduced are D and G As with the figures introduced thus far, D... also experiences fear, conceals it, and causes N to speculate on the various implications of O's liquidation for D..:

In spite of his political savy and all of his power within the party, the wild sow would certainly also be fearful, should the news of O's failure to appear be accurate, yet D controlled himself.   He never lost his relaxed demeanor. ... O's arrest (given the case that it was not just a simple rumor caused by his failure to appear) could be the prelude to an attack on D, because O was D's subordinate in the party; it could, on the other hand, also point to the overthrow of the chief ideologue G, since O was regarded to be his protégé: that O's liquidation, (should it happen) threaten both D and G simultaneously, although a possibility unto itself, was hardly probable (p. 15).[286]

---

[285] *"Die Ruhe des Ministers für die Schwerindustrie täuschte. Der Schuhputzer handelte aus purem Entsetzen über L's Vorgehen, er sah schon A.'s Zorn über alle herfallen ... Er begann nach seiner Gewohnheit mit den ewigen Bauernsprüchen, die er sich angeeignet hatte, gleichgültig ob sie paßten oder nicht. Er sagte: 'Bevor der Fuchs angreift, werden die Hühner frech.' Er sagte: 'Der Bauer wäscht sein Weib nur, wenn der Junker mit ihr schlafen will.' ... Er sagte: 'Auch ein Großbauer kann in die Jauchegrube fallen.'"*

[286] *"Bei all dessen Macht innerhalb der Partei und bei all dessen politischer Intelligenz empfand die Wildsau sicher auch Furcht, sollte die Nachricht von O's Nichterscheinen zutreffen, doch D beherrschte sich.   Er verlor seine Lockerheit nie. ... O's Verhaftung (falls sie nicht ein bloßes Gerücht war, das durch sein Nichterscheinen verursacht wurde) konnte einen Angriff auf D*

As with I and F, D and G form a pair of opposites which illustrate
the Apollonian/Dionysian antinomy. D is described as "energetic, a *bon-
vivant* and ladies' man" (*"vital, ein Genießer und Frauenheld"*) (p. 16)
whereas the chief ideologue maintains an abstemious lifestyle: "... he was
a teetotaller and an ascetic who wore a Byron collar, a gaunt introvert
who even in winter walked in sandals"(p. 16).[287] When challenged by F to
leave the room to prove that he has no fear of arrest, G dismisses F's
suspicions in the language of intellectual scorn he has used so successfully
to squash any opposition to his theories, but he also declines to leave the
room:

> "Nonsense," retorted the chief ideologue G, who then rose
> and went to the window. "Nonsense, pure nonsense," he
> said once again with his back to the others. "Then leave
> the room" came the challenge from F. The chief
> ideologue turned around and stared at him with suspicion.
> What was he supposed to do outside, he asked. The chief
> ideologue was also not going to risk leaving the room, F
> concluded in a relaxed tone. G, he said, knew exactly,
> that only here was he secure. "Nonsense, pure
> nonsense," came G's retort once again. "Then go out,"
> came the renewed challenge. G remained standing at the
> window (p. 45).[288]

The introduction of G and D, who have not been on speaking
terms, activates the motif of speculation and of weighing alternative

---

*einleiten, weil O in der Partei D unterstand, sie konnte jedoch auch auf den
Sturz des Chefideologen G hinzielen, als dessen persönlicher Schützling O
galt: daß O's Liquidierung, (falls sie eintraf) D und G zugleich bedrohte, war
an sich möglich, doch kaum wahrscheinlich."*
[287] *"Er war ein Abstinenzler und Asket mit Schillerkragen, ein hagerer
Introvertierter, der auch im Winter Sandalen trug."*
[288] *"'Unsinn,' entgegnete der Chefideologe G, erhob sich und ging zum
Fenster. 'Unsinn, purer Unsinn' sagte er aufs neue mit dem Rücken gegen die
anderen gekehrt. 'Dann verlaß das Zimmer,' forderte ihn F auf. Der
Chefideologe wandte sich um und starrte F mißtrauisch an. 'Was er draußen
solle,' fragte er. Der Chefideologe wage es auch nicht, hinauszugehen, stellte
F gelassen fest. G wisse genau, daß er nur hier sicher sei. 'Unsinn, purer
Unsinn,' entgegnete G wieder. 'Dann geh hinaus,' forderte er den Teeheiligen
aufs neue auf. G blieb am Fenster stehen."*

interpretations of interactional behaviour. N attempts to relate the fact that G now greets D. to the absence of O:

> Actually G did not greet D. any more. That the chief
> ideologue was now in fact greeting the party secretary, as
> N was shocked to observe, pointed to G's fear that O's
> disappearance was aimed at him; similarly, the
> circumstance of D's returning the greeting led to the
> conclusion that he also feared a threat. But that both
> were afraid meant that O really must have been arrested.
> Yet the fact that the teetotaller's greeting was, on the one
> hand, heartfelt, and the wild sow's was, on the other,
> merely pleasant, indicated that the threat to the chief
> ideologue was a shade more possible than the one against
> the party secretary (pp. 16-17).[289]

As the next minister to enter the room, E is categorized along with N as having been pushed unwillingly into a position of power by others who had tried too hard and fallen victim to each other's intrigues. He also shares another trait which the introductory pair of L and N have in common, namely occupying a seat in the Politburo on the basis of a particular area of expertise required by a given portfolio. L is one of the "founding fathers" of this system; N has been appointed postal minister because of his connection with a recently successful stamp design, and E is an expert in matters of foreign trade: "... as he was an expert, he had survived every purge, this had led to A's nicknaming him 'Lord Evergreen.'" (p. 18).[290] The pattern of opposing characteristics is, however, formed between E and the virtually identical H and K who are the next to be portrayed. Although seven characters are thus far introduced, the strategy employed to preserve the economy of form is to draw each figure using a restricted number of interlocking motifs (fear,

---

[289] *"Eigentlich grüßte G D nicht mehr. Daß der Chefideologe den Parteisekretär jetzt grüßte, wie N erschrocken bemerkte, wies auf G's Furcht hin, O's Verschwinden gelte ihm, so wie der Umstand, daß D. zurückgrüßte, auf dessen Furcht schließen ließ, er sei bedroht. Daß sich jedoch beide fürchteten, bedeutete, daß O wirklich verhaftet sein mußte. Die Tatsache aber, daß der Teeheilige herzlich, die Wildsau dagegen nur freundlich grüßte, deutete darauf hin, daß die Bedrohung des Chef-ideologen um eine Nuance möglicher war, als jene des Parteisekretärs."*
[290] *"... und so überstand E als Fachmann jede Säuberung, was ihm von Seiten A's den Spitznamen 'Lord Evergreen' eintrug."*

insecurity, feigned indifference and/or defensive aggression, speculation, competence/incompetence, narcotization, the use of vacuous jargons) and a relationship of similarity and contrast both with respect to the appropriate or inappropriate matching of personal background and professional responsibility, and on an interpersonal level within the pairs using the Apollonian/Dionysian antinomy. The text summarizes the narrowly focused conditions of interaction for its cast at this juncture of the half-way-point of their introduction:

> They had to see to being clever, perceive the opportunities, cower if needs be, and exploit the others' human weaknesses. They were forced to do much that was unworthy and laughable (p. 18).[291]

This is the description of an oligarchy whose operative conditions of confrontation and manipulation and extreme concentration of power distort human vulnerability and foibles into monumental liabilities: rational and political considerations are completely displaced by what is nearly portrayed as a group-psychosis: ("Their power, and thus their fear of one another was too great for them to be engaged purely in politics. Up against all of this, reason didn't stand a chance ") (p. 19).[292] In this way the macrocosmic character of national and international politics is rendered a function of the microcosm of intra- and interpersonal dynamics.

The next pair of figures, nearly indistinguishable from each other, illustrate this departure from reasoned, rational behaviour in optimal fashion. A majority of the motifs mentioned above are repeated in introducing these characters: fear, aggression to disguise fear, incompetence, vacuous jargon, narcotization and murderous intrigue comprise the attributes assigned to these caricature-like subsidiary figures:

> Of those who were not yet present, both the marshalls, the minister of defence and the president now entered. Old and sweating, both of them were pasty, bloated and stiff and were festooned with decorations and medals .... two sacks filled to bursting with fat, flesh, fear and urine.

---

[291] *"Sie hatten klug zu sein, die Gelegenheiten wahrzunehmen, sich im Notfall zu ducken und die menschlichen Schwächen der anderen auszunutzen. Sie waren zu vielem gezwungen, das unwürdig und lächerlich war."*
[292] *"Die Macht, und damit die Furcht voreinander - war zu groß, um reine Politik zu treiben. Die Vernunft kam dagegen nicht an."*

Alluding to their favourite drink, A had nicknamed them
the "*Gin*-ghis Khans" ... Marshall H, a paragon of
military incompetence .... had worked his way up like a
fungus, eliminating his predecessors one by one ... now
drew himself together once again before screaming,
goggle-eyed: "Down with the enemies in the bosom of the
party!" ... One had become used to the empty phrases that
fear squeezed out of him. With every meeting of the
Politburo he expected to be ousted and would launch into
self-accusations and furious attacks on someone else,
without ever stating precisely who that someone else was
(p. 20).[293]

The description of H and K employ the same Dionysian elements
used for L, namely unrestrained, alcohol-induced behaviour. This
contrasts with the greater control and cool serenity of E:

E was wearing an English suit with a loosely bunched
handkerchief in his top pocket and was smoking an
American cigarette ... [...] others who had been more
ambitious than he, had fallen victim to the struggle to be
at the forefront: each had thus become his own
henchman. E, the specialist, had survived every purge
(p. 18).[294]

---

[293] "*Von den fehlenden Mitgliedern traten die beiden Marschälle ein, der
Verteidigungsminister H und der Staatspräsident K, beide aufgeschwemmt,
beide käsig, beide steif, beide mit Orden bekleistert, beide alt und schweißig ...
zwei mit Fett, Fleisch, Harn und Furcht prall gestopfte Säcke ... A, auf das
Lieblingsgetränk der beiden anspielend, nannte sie die 'Gin-gis-Khane'...
Marschall H, ein militärischer Nichtskönner, der sich ... durchgemausert hatte,
indem er einen seiner Vorgänger nach dem andern ... ans Messer lieferte,
raffte sich noch einmal auf, bevor er vor sich hinglotzte, schrie: 'Nieder mit
den Feinden im Schoße der Partei!' ... Man war es gewohnt, die Furcht preßte
Phrasen aus ihm. In jeder Zusammenkunft des Politischen Sekretariats sah er
seinen Sturz kommen, erging er sich in Selbstklagen und griff wild jemanden
an, ohne zu präzisieren, wen er damit meinte.*"
[294] "*Er trug einen englischen Anzug mit locker gebüscheltem Kavalierstuch
und rauchte eine amerikanische Zigarette ... [...] andere, die ehrgeiziger
gewesen waren als er, waren dem Ringen um die vordersten Plätze und somit
sich selber zum Opfer gefallen, und so überstand E als Fachmann jede
Säuberung ...*"

The characterizations of M and B show parallel vocabulary configurations, but the use of similar verbs and modifiers draw together the purely physical traits of M with the the entirely spiritual dimensions of B. Described solely in terms of externals, that is, the shape of her body and the style of clothing she wears to meetings, M is treated by A as an instrument of Dionysian impulse. In an attempt to introduce some comic relief to a tense situation, A asks the following question of D and M: "'So, you two, are you actually sleeping together?'" (p. 45).[295] The only information given about this character, beyond the fact that she holds the education portfolio, is that she appears only in plain, colourless attire, the reason for this being a remark made by A at a point in the past that her breasts, flattered by an elegant dress, would be D's downfall:

> Once, at a meeting of this body, A made a prophecy about M's breasts to the effect that it would one day be from these soaring pinnacles that D would plunge to his death. At the time M had been appearing in particularly elegant attire ... but after this remark came to the meetings of the Politburo in a plain grey two-piece suit (p. 22).[296]

The simplicity of M's spartan apparel and lack of jewelry (p. 22) represent her attempt to de-emphasize the Dionysian effect which she now has on F as well as D:

> "... my God, that's what you call a dress, ... wasn't this why they had carried out the revolution, to introduce beauty," he shouted and then threw his arms around the minister of education, kissing her as if she were a farm girl: "Dior to the workers" (pp. 22-23).[297]

---

[295] "'Nun,' ihr zwei, 'schlaft ihr eigentlich miteinander?'"
[296] "Von ihren Brüsten weissagte einmal A während einer Sitzung des Gremiums, sie seien das Hochgebirge, von dessen Gipfeln der Parteichef zu Tode stürzen werde. Die Parteimuse erschien damals in besonders eleganter Aufmachung ... Seitdem kam M zur Sitzung des Sekretariats nur noch in einem schlichten, grauen Jackettkleide."
[297] "'... Donnerwetter, das sei ein Kleid, ... weshalb man eigentlich die Revolution durchgeführt ... Um die Schönheit einzuführen', schrie er und umarmte und küßte die Erziehungsministerin, als wäre sie eine Bauerndirne: 'Dior den Arbeitern'..."

This contrasts with the Apollonian description of B's spartan lifestyle: "He drank moderately and ate moderately, at banquets a glass of champagne, and that was it" (p. 24).[298] B is also the most erudite and scholarly member of the group:

His German, his English, his French, his Russian and his Italian were perfect, and his study on Mazarin and his depiction of early Indian large states had been translated into many languages ... (p. 24).[299]

B's impressive stature in the scholarly realm is matched by M's impressive physical stature: "The minister of education was blonde and buxom." (*"Die Ministerin für Erziehung war blond und stattlich"*) (p. 22). The infinitive *stürzen* (to fall / to plunge) and its cognate *Umsturz* (a putsch) are used in conjunction with M and B respectively; as cited above, the education minister's physical attributes are mentioned by A as a potential cause of D's downfall. B, in addition to his literary ability, has written a treatise on the nature of waging revolutions: "... his most renowned work was the 'Theory of the Coup d'État,' which was why he was called the Clausewitz of the Revolution" (p. 24).[300] As has been observed of the second pair of ministers, I and F, introduced before the juncture of summation of the conditions of interaction of the first six figures (pp. 18-19), B and M, who are the second grouping after this juncture, display the same chiastic form in terms of the balancing of personal and intellectual characteristics with the characters' governmental responsibilities; I, the attorney and F, the unsophisticated farmer must assume the responsibilities of agriculture and industry respectively: B, the erudite and unmaterialistic scholar and the voluptuous M, described solely in terms of externals, assume the ministries of external affairs and education respectively. The motif of fear of liquidation accompanies the introduction of this pair as well. In the case of M, it is rendered less overtly through her avoidance of clothing which would attract attention and her lack of reaction to F's offensive and abusive treatment. B's cool

---

[298] *"Er aß mäßig und trank mäßig, bei Banketten ein Glas Sekt, das war alles."*
[299] *"Sein Deutsch, sein Englisch, sein Französisch, sein Russisch, sein Italienisch waren perfekt, seine Studie über Mazarin und seine Darstellung der frühindischen Großstaaten in viele Sprachen übersetzt ..."*
[300] *"Am berühmtesten war jedoch seine 'Umsturzlehre', weshalb man ihn den Clausewitz der Revolution nannte."*

them and said nothing further. N felt the fear in the room
(pp. 24-25).[301]

The motif of speculation and alternative interpretations is
incorporated through M's unexpected appearance in a figure-flattering
dress. This is at odds with the sober attire she has favoured since A's
threatening jest of perilous pinnacles:

That she now appeared in a black, low-cut cocktail dress
was confusuing to N, more so because of the jewelry she
wore. There must have been a special reason for this.
She too must also have known of O's arrest. It was only
a question of whether the party muse wanted to distance
herself from D through her dress, a sign of her lack of
concern, or, buoyed up by a desperate courage, it
signalled her intention to flaunt herself as his lover (p.
22).[302]

In addition to this ambiguity N also must consider F's
demonstrative reaction to M's attire, which he interprets as either gallows-
humour or self-assuredness:

... the minister for heavy industry was acting on a
macabre sense of humour ... and apparently expected that
O's disappearance took aim at the chief ideologue and
therefore also at him, [the two alignments are D., B, M, L
against G, I, K, F (p. 16)] although it was also possible
that F's high spirits were genuine, because he may have

---

[301] "'Meine Damen, meine Herren, es mag vielleicht interessieren, der
Atomminister O ist nicht erschienen.' Schweigen. B entnahm der Aktentasche
einige Papiere, begann sie durchzulesen und sagte nichts mehr. N spürte, wie
sich alle fürchteten."
[302] "Daß sie jetzt in einem tief ausgeschnittenen, schwarzen Cocktailkleid
auftrat, verwirrte N, um so mehr, als sie auch Schmuck trug. Der Anlaß dazu
mußte ein besonderer sein. Auch sie mußte von O's Verhaftung wissen. Die
Frage war nur, ob die Parteimuse sich durch ihr Kleid von D. distanzieren
wollte, indem sie sich unbekümmert gab, oder ob sie damit beabsichtigte, sich
mit dem Mute der Verzweiflung demonstrativ als dessen Geliebte zu
benennen."

... the minister for heavy industry was acting on a macabre sense of humour ... and apparently expected that O's disappearance took aim at the chief ideologue and therefore also at him, [the two alignments are D., B, M, L against G, I, K, F (p. 16)] although it was also possible that F's high spirits were genuine, because he may have received solid information that one could expect the overthrow of the party secretary (p. 23).[303]

The measure of contrast for the introduction of the last pair of A and C repeats the Apollonian/Dionysian pattern. The former is described as being housed in unadorned, austere living quarters and having a penchant for young girls being seated next to him as he watches American films. Once he dozes off, the girls are permitted to leave. His sponsorship of the periodic blood-letting is always concealed through his manipulation of the party apparatus. His ability to adopt an arm's-length, virtual observer-status when accusations of corruption and immorality reach his colleagues is suggested through his depiction as an observer of aesthetic representations of scenes of violence and orgiastic drunkeness:

> For years he had lived in a plain, bunker-like building that was hidden away in a forest outside the capital ... [...] Sometimes he would have girls brought in from the city. He would nod at them, and all they had to do was sit next to him for hours at a time watching American films. Then he would fall asleep in his easy-chair, and the girls could go ... [...] He stood with reverence in front of gigantic historical hack paintings from the late bourgeois period, canvasses of battles ... or of hussars in drunken orgies (pp. 26-27).[304]

---

[303] *"... der Minister für die Schwerindustrie [handelte] aus Galgenhumor ... und [rechnete] offenbar damit ... O's Verschwinden gelte dem Chefideologen und so auch ihm, wenn es auch möglich war, daß F's Übermut nicht gespielt war, weil er sichere Nachricht besaß, es sei mit dem Sturze des Parteisekretärs zu rechnen."*

[304] *"Er lebte seit Jahren in einem bunkerartigen, schlichten Gebäude, das in einem Wald außerhalb der Hauptstadt versteckt war ... [...] Manchmal ließ er Mädchen aus der Stadt kommen, denen er zunickte und die nichts zu tun hatten, als neben ihm zu sitzen und stundenlang amerikanische Filme anzuschauen. Dann schlief er in seinem Lehnstuhl ein, und die Mädchen konnten gehen .... [...] Er stand andächtig vor spätbürgerlichen, historischen*

Juxtaposed with A's image of controlled, sterile and static being
is the minister C, whose unconventional affairs, original training as a
concert musician and direct involvement with violence as chief of the
secret police places him solidly within the Dionysian sphere:

As always, C wore a rumpled blue suit. A was in
uniform ... [...] It was an established fact that he was
embroiled in homosexual affairs. [...] Originally he had
been a musician and had a concert diploma. If B was the
grand nobleman, C was the bohemian of the assembly.
[...] His methods were infamous for their cruelty, his
spreading of terror was blatant (p. 26).[305]

With the introduction of the characters complete, the narrative
moves towards the first immediately causal plot-component leading to the
story's main, central event: the overthrow of A. He has convened this
assembly in order to announce that the time has come for a
democratization of the political institutions of the state:

He spoke of the party as a hierarchy whose upper levels
determined its structure, and this was appropriate to the
time of struggle in which the party had found itself; this
struggle was now over, the party had been victorious, all
power belonged to the party, and the next step was one of
democratization within the party itself, thus introducing
the first step in democratizing a new state. But the Party
could only be democratized if the Politburo were
abolished, devolving power to an expanded parliament
(pp. 30-31).[306]

---

*Riesenschinken, vor Schlachtengemälden ... vor Orgien betrunkener Husaren
..."*
[305] *"C trug, wie immer, einen nachläßigen, blauen Anzug. A war in Uniform
... [...] Daß er jetzt in homosexuelle Affären verstrickt war, stand fest.[...]
Ursprünglich war er Musiker gewesen und besaß das Konzertdiplom. War B
der Grandseigneur, war C der Bohemien des Gremiums [...] Die Grausamkeit
seiner Methoden war berüchtigt, der Terror, den er verbreitete,
offensichtlich."*
[306] *"Jetzt sei die Struktur der Partei noch hierarchisch und von oben gelenkt,
was der Kampfzeit entspreche, in der sich die Partei befunden habe; die
Kampfzeit sei jedoch vorüber, die Partei habe gesiegt, die Macht befinde sich*

A's speech generates the motif of reflecting on alternative subtexts attendant to the literal level of discourse. There is in N's mind no doubt that A is seeking to consolidate his power through elimination of the Politburo: ("A wanted to disempower the party by democratizing it, a process which dealt him the chance to install himself as an absolute ruler") (p. 30).[307] The authorial omniscience of *Der Sturz* does not, as mentioned above, encompass the internal musings and motivations of all of its characters in every situation, and there is no corroboration for N's assumption in this respect. There are two questions implicitly posed by the text at this point: is this A's strategy to acquire an even greater measure of power, as N surmises, or is he truly interested in a process of democratization, and given that he has proposed the dissolution of the Politburo, does this imply the automatic liquidation of its members? The text answers the latter question with a qualified "no," that is, A claims that the names compiled for the liquidation-list which includes only the powerful and brutal D, G and F, as well as M, closely associated with D. through their amorous liason and K, the president, (pp. 59-60) was meant to be used only if resistance were encountered: "... the list had been made up for the eventuality that the Politburo resisted self-dissolution" (p. 60).[308] *Der Sturz* is configured in such a way that evidence may be garnered from other portions of the text which may be employed either to support or impugn the authenticity or veracity of this claim. D, G, F, and K are indeed depicted as among the most powerful, influential and ruthless functionaries and it is therefore plausible that these would be the most likely source of resistance to democratization. That the liquidation-list is entirely provisional is clearly undermined by the characterization of A within the context of I's vulnerability: "... because A had never missed a chance to eliminate someone, he was written off as terminal" (p. 14).[309] Even though it must be conceded that his explanation is made as he is

---

bei ihr, der nächste Schritt sei die Demokratisierung der Partei, der damit eine Demokratisierung des neuen Staats einleite; demokratisiert werden könne die Partei jedoch nur, indem man das Politische Sekretariat abschaffe und seine Macht einem erweiterten Parteiparlament delegiere ..."
[307] "A wollte die Partei entmachten, indem er sie demokratisierte, ein Vorgang, der ihm die Möglichkeit zuspielte ... seine Alleinherrschaft endgültig zu installieren."
[308] "... die Liste sei aufgestellt worden für den Fall, daß sich das Politische Sekretariat seiner Selbstauflösung widersetze."
[309] "... weil A noch nie eine Chance ausgelassen hatte, jemanden zu erledigen, gab man ihm keine Chance mehr."

completely vulnerable to the now mutinous assembly and has therefore
nothing to conceal, he is portrayed as a consummate tactician and skilled
manipulator: to suddenly accept his utterances at face value is as
manifestly difficult for the reader as it is for those who have been his
potential prey:

> He was an instinctive connoisseur of human nature who
> recognized and exploited the weaknesses of every rival.
> He knew how to ensnare and hunt down human beings
> and he was better at it than anyone else in the Politburo,
> but he was not one to fight openly one-on-one, he needed
> to do battle with stealth, to attack without warning. He
> set his traps in the jungle that was the Party (p. 36).[310]

On the other hand, L, who is not on the provisional list, is urged
by A to attend to his wife when the meeting is interrupted in an
unprecedented manner by the announcement that she is breathing her last,
but L fears a ruse. In spite of A's apparently uncontrived and empathetic
response, it is impossible to verify its authenticity, and the text does not
contain any reference to the fact that L's wife has in fact been taken
mortally ill.

> "Go, L!" said A, "the thing with the mistresses was a
> crude joke, I take it back. I know your wife was
> important to you. Go to her, the meeting is over
> anyway." As humane as A's words sounded, the minister
> of transportation didn't believe them, so great was his
> fear (p. 34).[311]

Yet in spite of his masterful cunning and horrendous deeds, the
text differentiates at one point between being and doing, inasmuch as the

---

[310] *"Er war ein instinktiver Menschenkenner, der die Schwäche eines jeden
Rivalen kannte and ausnützte, er verstand sich auf den Menschenfang und die
Menschenjagd wie kein anderer im Politischen Sekretariat, aber er war nicht
der Mann des offenen Zweikampfes, er brauchte den Kampf im Versteckten,
den Angriff aus dem Unvermuteten. Seine Fallen legte er im Dschungel der
Partei ..."*
[311] *"'Geh, L!' sagte A, 'das mit den Mätressen ist ein grober Scherz gewesen,
ich nehme ihn zurück. Ich weiß, deine Frau war für dich wichtig. Geh zu ihr,
die Sitzung ist ohnehin beendet.' So menschlich A's Worte klangen, die Furcht
des Transportministers war zu groß, er glaubte ihnen nicht."*

nature of these actions is shown not to be a necessary indication of the nature of the person who has performed them:

> Neither internal struggle nor power had deformed A. He was the way he was, a piece of nature, an expression of his own inherent laws; others had not shaped him, he had shaped himself (p. 38).[312]

The information provided in the depiction of this figure may be called individual symptoms, fragments through which the derivation of a cogently unitary whole does not easily obtain. These in part consist of the solitary and "reverent" ("*andächtig*") (p. 27) wanderings through the exhibits of representational, pre-modernist and "late-bourgeois" paintings, whose subjects might be used metaphorically to infer a variety of common disfunctions - from not having successfully emerged from the Oedipus conflict with a resulting father-complex, to a persecution complex, to nothing more than an atavistic sense of the aesthetic:

> He stood with reverence in front of gigantic historical hack-paintings from the late bourgeois period, canvasses of battles, of sinister looking emperors who condemned their sons to death, of hussars in drunken orgies, of horse-drawn sleighs sweeping over the steppes pursued by wolves (p. 27).[313]

Given this image of A as a figure of unsullied greatness together with the very possible inference of his psychic condition through his solitary nature and appreciation of very particular artefacts, there would seem to emerge the profile of a "highly uncommon man":

> It is, in fact, rather probable that a highly uncommon man experiences filial conflicts with such inescapable intensity because he senses in himself already early in childhood some kind of originality that seems to point beyond the

---

[312] "*A war nicht deformiert, weder durch den Kampf, noch durch die Macht. A war wie er war, ein Stück Natur, ein Ausdruck seiner mächtigen Gesetzmäßigkeit, durch sich selbst geformt und nicht durch andere.*"
[313] "*Er stand andächtig vor spätbürgerlichen, historischen Riesenschinken, vor Schlachtengemälden, vor finsteren Kaisern, die ihre Söhne zum Tode verurteilten, vor Orgien betrunkener Husaren und vor von Pferden gezogener Schlitten, die von Wölfen verfolgt über die Steppen fegten.*"

personal competition with the personal father. [...] Thus
he grows up almost with an obligation (beset with guilt)
to surpass and to originate at all cost. In adolescence this
may prolong his identity confusion because he must find
the way in which he (and he alone) can reenact the past
and create a new future in the right medium at the right
moment on a sufficiently large scale. His prolonged
identity crisis, in turn, may invoke a premature
generativity crisis that makes him accept as his concern a
whole communal body, or mankind itself, and embrace as
his dependents those weak in power, poor in possesions,
and seemingly simple in heart. Such a deflection in life
plan, however, can crowd out his chances for the
enjoyment of intimacy, sexual and otherwise, wherefore
the "great" are often mateless, friendless and childless in
the midst of veneration ... in the years following their
ascendance ... the new momentum which they gave to
their time may now roll over them ... What was once
united by the power of charisma cannot fall apart without
exploding into destructive furor in the leader or in the
masses or in both.[314]

The main event of *Der Sturz* is indeed A's overthrow, yet the text
does not show any real progression from "the power of charisma" to the
explosion of this momentum in a "furor of destruction." The narrated
time of the text is a matter of one or two hours; within this time-frame, A
is described as both uncorrupted by power "Neither struggle nor power
had deformed A." ("*A war nicht deformiert, weder durch den Kampf,
noch durch die Macht*" (p. 38) and as an agent of its complete misuse:
"He used his power senselessly, he gave orders that could not but insult,
his wishes were grotesque and barbaric" (p. 57).[315] This contradiction is
reinforced by the description of A in the scene in which his colleagues
finally gain the upper hand:

A had no weapons left. He was helpless. For the first
time, he was no longer a mystery to N, no longer a genius

---

[314] Erik Erikson, "On the Nature of Psychohistorical Evidence," *Explorations
in Psychohistory* (New York: Simon and Schuster, 1974) pp. 73-75.
[315] "*Er setzte seine Macht sinnlos ein, er erteilte Befehle, die beleidigen
mußten, seine Wünsche waren grotesk und barbarisch ...*"

nor super-human, rather he was a dictator who was nothing more than the product of his political environment (p. 53).[316]

There is also only the most indirect indication to suggest that A is in any way interested in democratic government. His preoccupation with American film, particulary since it is enjoyed under pseudo-erotic circumstances, is as likely to be interpreted as an extension of libidinal impulse to be held in check for the sake of the social(ist) good, as it is to be interpreted as a legitimate and guiltless appreciation of the culture of democratic capitalism, yet the seed of doubt is sown without any resolution to the quandary.

The ultimate level of interpretive abstraction possible in *Der Sturz*, is, appropriately enough, the Freudian mythology of instincts. (cf. chapter one of this study) ("Instincts are mythical entities, magnificent in their indefiniteness. ... we are never sure that we are seeing them clearly.") In his work *Totem and Taboo*, Freud relates the Oedipus Complex to primordial totemic systems, describing a ritual whereby a totem meal is consumed as a substitute for the killing of the father, both a festive occasion and one of mourning, whose occurrence necessitates the participation of all of the members of the group:

> The clan is celebrating the ceremonial occasion by the cruel slaughter of its totem animal ...[...] Each man is conscious that he is performing an act forbidden to the individual and justifiable only through the participation of the whole clan ... When the deed is done, the slaughtered animal is lamented and bewailed.[317]

Freud hypothesizes the most primitive, original social dynamic to be that of the patriarchal horde:

> United, they had the courage to do and succeeded in doing what would have been impossible for them individually. [...] The violent primal father had doubtless been the

---

[316] "*A hatte keine Waffen mehr. Er war hilflos. Zum ersten Male war er für N kein Geheimnis, kein Genie und kein Übermensch mehr, sondern ein Machthaber, der nichts als das Produkt seiner politischen Umgebung war.*"

[317] Sigmund Freud, *Totem and Taboo*, trans. James Strachey, (London: Routledge and Kegan Paul, 1961) p. 140.

feared and envied model of each one of the company of
brothers: and in the act of devouring him they
accomplished their identification with him ... The totem
meal ... would thus be a repetition and a commemoration
of this memorial and criminal deed, which was the
beginning of so many things - of social organization, of
moral restrictions and of religion. [...] What had up to
then been prevented by his actual existence was
thenceforth prohibited by the sons themselves ... (Freud,
p. 143).

The motifs of *Der Sturz* bear a considerable resemblance to this
scheme.   Each meeting of the Politburo begins with a meal whose
components indicate the celebration of a festive occasion: "stuffed eggs,
ham, toast, caviar, schnapps and champagne" ("...*gefüllte(n) Eier(n),
Schinken, Toast, Kaviar, Schnaps und Champagner* ...") (p. 11). At this
meeting of the Secretariat, its members rebel against what they perceive to
be an unacceptable restriction of their power and ability to survive. A is
indeed described as a patriarch and a totem figure: "... this power-product
hid behind his image as the patriarchal ... colossus ... [...] a symbol of the
independence and greatness of the fatherland" (p. 53).[318] The decision to
eliminate A, a task which is delegated to L, is a collective one: ("The
monument stood up. 'You expect me to murder the fellow,' he said") (p.
61).[319] As A is about to be murdered, the motif of mourning is included
through the associations of a previous funeral sparked in N's mind by this
spectacle:

With the exception of the party muse, the Politburo
shouldered the coffin draped with the Party flag through
the state cemetery ... [...] As they began to lower the
coffin into a grave, a completely frozen military band
played the party anthem and "the monument" whispered:
"Hell, I'm going to be next" (p. 62).[320]

---

[318] "*Dieses Machtprodukt verbarg sich hinter dem Bilde des väterlichen ...
Kolosses .... [...] ein Sinnbild für die Unabhängigkeit und die Größe des
Vaterlandes.*"
[319] "*Das Denkmal erhob sich. 'Ihr erwartet, daß ich den Kerl umbringe,'
sagte er.*"
[320] "*Das Politische Sekretariat, ausgenommen die Parteimuse, trug den Sarg,
bedeckt mit der Parteifahne, auf den Schultern durch den Staatsfriedhof ...
[...] Als man den Sarg zu den Klängen einer durchgefrorenen Militärkapelle,*

Not only does this scene incorporate the operation much favoured by this author whereby the course of events turns out to be the precise inverse of the assumptions made of it, it shows how the totem is perpetuated, since A, "a symbol for ... the greatness of the Fatherland" ("*ein Sinnbild für ... die Größe des Landes*") is eliminated by L, "the monument" ("*das Denkmal*") also a symbol for the identity of this particular national and political group. L's insistence on executing A with his bare hands using the president's belt highlights A's undoing as a proletarian act; he thus falls victim to what had become in his eyes the mere artifice of an institutionalized hegemonous proletariat. ("'I'm not an executioner like the rest of you,' answered the monument, 'I'm an honest blacksmith and I'll do it my own way'") (p. 61).[321] In addition, the figure to become the greatest beneficiary of A's usurpation through his succession to the leadership position is the power-hungry D "D wanted to assert his power with every means ..." ("*D wollte die Macht mit allen Mitteln behaupten ...*") (p. 16). The major point of contention and the source of A's threats with respect to D, as previously observed, derive from D's relationship with M: "'So, you two, are you actually sleeping together?'" (p. 44) and "Once, at a meeting of this body, A made a prophecy about M's breasts to the effect that it would one day be from these soaring pinnacles that D would plunge to his death" (p. 22).[322] This is the archetypal conflict hypothesized by Freud, who observes that "They [the primal horde as well as neurotic patients] hated their father, who presented such a formidable obstacle to their craving for power and their sexual desires ..." (p. 143).

Although it is well embedded within the fictional reality of the narrative, the text contains a reference to the term *Wendepunkt* to refer to a turning point in the plot. This juncture is set by L's straightforward admission of fear in naming the suspicion that O's non-attendance has sinister implications. He is the first to speak the unspeakable. Transformed by both alcohol (another instance of the leitmotif of narcotization) and what he perceives to be a desperate, no-win situation, he casts all caution aside to reassert long-held convictions, including the

---

welche die Parteihymne spielte, ins Grab hinunterließ, flüstere das Denkmal: 'Teufel, ich werde der nächste sein.'"
[321] "'Ich bin kein Henker wie ihr', antwortete das Denkmal, 'ich bin ein ehrlicher Schmied und erledige das auf meine Weise.'"
[322] "'Nun, ihr zwei ... schlaft ihr eigentlich miteinander?'" and "Von ihren Brüsten weissagte einmal A ... sie seien das Hochgebirge, von dessen Gipfeln der Parteichef zu Tode stürzen werde."

belief that his political acts have been performed in good conscience and that his impending downfall is due to having been corrupted by the power he had at one time sought to transform and revolutionize:

> ... his despair and his rage had a certain magnificence; although boozed-up and worn-out, he seemed to have once again become the eminent revolutionary he once was ... He said he had fought against a hypocritical and corrupt social order and had devoted his life to the truth ... [...] "Power has seduced me, comrades," he exclaimed ... [...] Suddenly pale, exausted and in a low voice, he continued on: O had been arrested ... and he would not leave the room, because the report that his wife was dying was a lie meant to lure him out of the assembly. [...] It was not yet clear to N, to what extent L's protest could threaten A, yet he felt ... that a turning point had been reached, only he didn't know what kind of turning point it was (pp. 34ff.).[323]

L's declamations initiate a set of parallel situations which demonstrate structural parallelism through the repetition of all of the motifs described in the introductory segment of this text. L's tirade is sparked by a chance occurrence, the impending death of his wife, the necessity to leave the room and the entirely plausible assumption that this is a trap. The motifs at the foundation of this scene are therefore the unforeseeable vicissitudes of chance, the fear of vulnerability and the transparency of discourse (L does not accept A's empathetic urgings at face value). The transition from this first break in the feigned indifference and passively accepted intimidation of one of the major players to the next change in course are punctuated by the motif of jargon (of which the

---

[323] *"... seine Verzweiflung und seine Wut hatten etwas Großartiges; obgleich versoffen und heruntergekommen, schien er jetzt wieder der alte, berühmte Revolutionär geworden zu sein ... Er habe gegen eine verlogene und korrupte Ordnung gekämpft und für die Wahrheit sein Leben eingesetzt ... [...] 'Die Macht hat mich verführt, Genossen,' rief er aus ... [...] O sei verhaftet worden, fuhr er fort, plötzlich bleich, erschöpft und leise ... und er verlasse nicht den Raum, weil das angebliche Sterben seiner Frau nur eine Lüge sei, um ihn aus dem Sitzungszimmer zu locken. [...] N war sich zwar noch nicht darüber im klaren, inwieweit L's Protest A bedrohen konnte, doch fühlte er ... daß man vor einem Wendepunkt stehe, nur wußte N nicht, vor welchem Wendepunkt."*

exclamation "Down with the enemies in the bosom of the party" occurs four times: p. 19; p. 25; p. 36; p. 62) and N's ongoing conditional sentences:

> As L's monstrous sentences burst forth, Marshall H, driven by a terrible fear that the monument's downfall would also pull him into the abyss, shouted repeatedly "Down with the enemies in the bosom of the party"... [...] The question was whether A could be made to lose his composure, lose his perspective, act rashly. Would he admit to the arrests or continue to deny them, -these were all questions to which N had no answer ... (pp. 34-37).[324]

The configuration of F's discourse, which almost immediately follows L's, repeats the pattern described above. F is motivated by extreme fear: "...completely seized with fear and panic, he was so utterly beside himself that he even cut off A in mid-sentence ..." ("*...so mächtig hatte ihn die panische Angst befallen, daß er sogar, besinnungslos vor Furcht, A das Wort abgeschnitten hatte ...*") (p. 38). He adopts an aggressive posture in attacking L and in his panic forgets that L's influence is diminished and that he is no longer aligned with D., against whom he also makes accusations of treason. F's trademark, as seen above, is the use of agrestic maxims with an elusive relationship to the context in which they are uttered:

> The shoe-shine-boy shouted: when the peasants starve, the vicar stuffs himself; when the nobleman's feet get cold, he burns the village down. He claimed, D was betraying the revolution ... After he was done with D, he attacked his allies, ridiculed the minister of education, saying: one went into the house of a horse trader a virgin and came out a whore; ... and to the foreign minister went

---

[324] "*... zwischen den ungeheuerlichen Sätzen, die L ausstieß, [schrie] Marschall H aus jämmerlicher Furcht, in den Untergang des Denkmals hineingerissen zu werden, immer wieder 'Nieder mit den Feinden im Schoße der Partei' ... [...] Die Frage war, ob A sich aus der Fassung bringen ließ, ob er die Übersicht verlieren, ob er voreilig handeln, ob er die Verhaftungen zugeben oder weiterhin leugnen würde, alles Fragen, die N nicht zu beantworten vermochte ...*"

the volley: whoever befriends a mangy wolf, himself
becomes a mangy wolf ...(p. 40).[325]

Yet another chance occurrence effected through the reappearance
of the colonel with a message, this time for F to contact his ministry, puts
an end to F's oratory. The content of this message is not revealed (beyond
a reference to difficulties at his ministry), but the text ascribes F's sudden
change in demeanour to the imposing effect of the colonel's appearance
and the fact that such interruptions are entirely out of the ordinary and are
therefore conceivable as part of a plan to lure certain members away from
the security of the room:

> F, surprised by the interruption and intimidated by the
> military spectacle, became unsure ... glanced through the
> note, crumpled it up ... mumbled, he hadn't meant it the
> way it sounded. [...] The renewed appearance of the
> colonel had been too out of the ordinary. It seemed to
> have been staged. This occurrence was a threat (p.
> 41).[326]

Moreover, F is reproved by the head of the secret service, C, for
having wasted the time of the assembly with his diatribe - an unexpected
turn of events for F, since the reason for jumping to his feet had originally
been the assumption that L's impending purge and that of his one-time
allies of D, B and M was to be carried out by C himself: "The chief of the
secret police ... asked coolly, if F was finished with his nonsense ..." (p.
41).[327] The narrative at this point focuses attention on M's decision to

---

[325] *"Der Schuhputzer schrie, wenn die Bauern hungerten, mäste sich der
Pfarrer, schrie, wenn der Junker kalte Füße habe, brenne er ein Dorf nieder,
behauptete, D verrate die Revolution ... Er griff nach D auch dessen
Verbündete an, machte sich über die Erziehungsministerin lustig, als Jungfrau
gehe man ins Haus eines Pferdehändlers und als Hure komme man wieder
heraus ... und für den Außenminister B gelte, wer sich mit einem räudigen Wolf
befreunde, werde selber ein räudiger Wolf ..."*
[326] *"F, überrascht durch den Unterbruch und eingeschüchtert durch das
militärische Schauspiel, wurde unsicher ... überflog den Zettel, knüllte ihn
zusammen ... murmelte, er habe es nicht so gemeint. [...] Das erneute
Erscheinen des Obersts war zu ungewöhnlich gewesen. Es schien inszeniert zu
sein. Der Zwischenfall war bedrohlich."*
[327] *"Der Chef der Geheimpolizei ... fragte kühl, ob F mit dem Unsinn zu Ende
sei ..."*

powder her nose and a seemingly coincidental glance exchanged between B and C. The reader is thus drawn into the process of speculation which is so characteristic of the text's primary vehicle for its narrative point of view, achieved through N's internal deliberations: M is uncommonly relaxed and unusually attired for this meeting ("She opened her purse and powdered her nose, something she had never dared in a meeting before this") (p. 41);[328] D, with whom M has had or is having a liason ("D went over to her, offered her a light with his gold lighter, stood behind her.") (p. 44)[329] has already exchanged greetings with G, the leader of the opposing faction, with whom he has not been on speaking terms, smiles at the terrified F before taking up position next to A and serving himself some cognac, as the latter has just done ("D grinned at the minister for heavy industry, walked over to A and also poured himself a cognac.") (p. 43);[330] B, who is in D's camp, exchanges a glance as if coincidentally ("*wie zufällig*") with the chief of police (p. 41), thus suggesting that D's camp has a possible understanding with the secret police: N speculates on this possibility, as he considers the common ground between B and C. "They were considered enemies, yet they had much in common: their education, their superiority, their origins in well-known, established families ... some also thought he was a homosexual as was C") (pp. 41-41).[331] Aside from H and F (the most unscrupulously ruthless ministers), the names on the liquidation list are G, D, and M, hence a common denominator between somewhat smug behaviour that sets itself apart from the general tenor of insecurity, perhaps an indication of collusion to sabotage the democratization/purge, but also the possibility that A has discovered the plan and therefore draws up his "hit-list" to include those who are his greatest threat. The reverse could also be true, that is, the list was drawn up by A for C, and C communicated its contents through B to D and M. The text does not provide any more information towards a solution to this fictional riddle than what is available through N's point of view.

L's and F's performances are halted by the "chance occurrences" of urgent messages delivered by a colonel (who is not the one usually on

---

[328] "*Sie öffnete ihre Handtasche und puderte sich, was sie sonst im Verlaufe einer Sitzung noch nie gewagt hatte.*"

[329] "*D ging zu ihr, hielt ihr sein goldenes Feuerzeug hin, blieb hinter ihr stehen.*"

[330] "*D grinste den Minister für die Schwerindustrie an, trat zu A und goß sich ebenfalls Cognak ein.*"

[331] "*Sie galten als Feinde, doch hatten sie vieles gemeinsam: Die Bildung, die Überlegenheit, ihre Abstammung von bekannten Familien des Landes ... auch hielten ihn einige wie C für homosexuell.*"

duty). This heightens the anxiety in these characters to the extent that F, who has not yet lost his fighting form as L has, breaks with the tone of pretense to admit and express what he and his colleagues truly feel: unmitigated fear. "'That's right,' F answered, 'I'm shit scared, I'm afraid.' Everyone stared at F in silence. It was the most extraordinary act, to admit to one's fear") (p. 45).[332] Parallel to L's description as having regained his aura through an expression of the "truth," F, the most despised and disreputable member of the group, also adopts a measured tone and acquires an air of quiet dignity that is admired:

> He sat upright in his armchair, his hands on the table, and he had shed his ugliness. F was a fool, said A ... "A fool," F answered, "really? Are you that sure?" He spoke softly, something he had otherwise never done. Other than L, he said, there were no more old revolutionaries left in the Politburo. What had become of them? [...] Of course, it was a provocation to name the names of the old revolutionaries, but through his admission of fear he had become an opponent A ought to have taken seriously. Instead of this, he let himself be provoked into threatening F, rather than pacifying him. A friendly word, a joke would have restored F to reason, but A had contempt for F, and because of his contempt, he saw no danger and became careless. F, on the other hand, could not retreat. In his desperation he had taken the ultimate risk, and to everyone's surprise, showed character (pp. 45-46).[333]

---

[332] "'Stimmt,' antwortete F, 'ich habe Schiß, ich fürchte mich.' Alle starrten F schweigend an, es war ungeheuerlich, seine Furcht zuzugeben."

[333] "Er saß aufrecht in seinem Sessel, die Hände auf den Tisch gelegt, und alles Häßliche war von ihm gewichen. F sei ein Narr, sagte A .... 'Ein Narr,' antwortete F, 'wirklich? bist du so sicher?' Er sprach leise, was er sonst nie tat. Außer L befänden sich keine alten Revolutionäre mehr im Politischen Sekretariat, sagte er, wo sie geblieben seien? [...] Natürlich war es eine Provokation gewesen, die Namen der alten Revolutionäre zu nennen, doch F war durch das Eingeständnis seiner Furcht ein Gegner geworden, den A hätte ernst nehmen sollen. Stattdessen ließ sich A hinreißen, ihn zu bedrohen, statt zu beruhigen. Ein freundliches Wort, ein Scherz hätte F zur Vernunft gebracht, doch A verachtete F, und weil er ihn verachtete, sah er keine Gefahr und wurde leichtsinnig. F dagegen konnte nicht mehr zurück. In seiner Verzweiflung hatte er alles aufs Spiel gesetzt und zeigte zur Überraschung aller Charakter."

This crisis situation sees the dissolution of the dyadic Apollonian/Dionysian antinomy inasmuch as the Dionysian F expresses his anxiety but does so in a measured, deliberate manner whereas the Apollonian A loses control, permitting the tension of repressed sexuality to be released in an invective of scorn and derision which has no basis in the context of the situation:

> And incidentally, he jeered, this discussion didn't make sense, the filthy pornography he distributed amongst his colleagues had gone to his head, since he obviously thought the party was a whorehouse, and, A added, he also had to ask F's friend, the chief ideologue G, to consider what kind of company he was keeping. With this impulsive and unnecessary threat made to the teetotaller, possibly out of anger at the teetotaller's also having refused to leave the room, A resumed his place (p. 47).[334]

G's ensuing analysis, entirely a product of his Apollonian demeanour, continues the pattern of fanning the flames of his colleagues' anxiety through "reverse-psychology." G sharpens the focus of A's suggestion that the Politburo has become a political anachronism into the notion that any real revolutionary eventually must eliminate himself:

> The teetotaller took immediate revenge. Perhaps because he believed that he had fallen along with F into ill-favour, perhaps only because A's careless rebuke had insulted him. As with many critics, he could not stand to be criticized. [...] "A genuine revolutionary liquidates himself," were the closing words of his speech. The very fear of a purge that had come over some members of the Politburo was the proof that such a liquidation was

---

[334] *"Im übrigen, höhnte er, sei es sinnlos zu diskutieren, dem Schuhputzer seien offenbar die schweinischen Schriften in den Kopf gestiegen, die er unter seinen Kollegen verteile, indem er offensichtlich die Partei für ein Bordell halte, und A müsse F's Freund, den Chefideologen G, doch sehr bitten, sich zu überlegen, mit wem er verkehre. Mit dieser impulsiven und unnötigen Drohung dem Teeheiligen gegenüber - möglicherweise aus Ärger, daß es der Chefideologe auch nicht gewagt hatte, den Raum zu verlassen - nahm A wieder seinen Platz ein."*

necessary, and that the Politburo had outlived its
usefullness (pp. 47ff.).[335]

The motivation for this third stepping stone in the direction of A's
overthrow repeats the ambiguity attendant to the causality of F's and L's
performances: in the case of the latter, chance occurrence that may be
intrigue, in C's case the alternative motivational possibilities of either
revenge for a petty insult or a strategy of fear-induction to further
destabilize or neutralize the very source of the fear. The next step in the
progression of incidents which cumulatively lead to a reversal of the roles
of subject and object of aggression sees the pendulum swing back again
from G's Apollonian performance to the Dionysian sphere of happenings,
even before A has a chance to respond to G's strategy: "A recognized the
trap into which G had lured him.   Yet before A could take action,
something unexpected happened" (p. 51).[336] Marshal K also refuses to
leave the security of the room as have L, F and G. The only motivating
factor in his case is the very unambiguous need to urinate; this both
heightens A's perception of the group's desperation and offends his
sensibilities with respect to self-control and the repression of basic needs:

> The minister for education, M ... jumped up, screaming
> Marshall K was a swine. [...] The bloated *Gin*-ghis
> Khan became aggressive, roaring, what was it to her, the
> prudish cow, and went on roaring, did they think he was
> so idiotic as to go out to have a piss, no, he didn't want to
> be arrested ... his son-in-law and all his old friends had
> been betrayed by A, although they had been honest and
> dedicated revolutionaries, as was he, and therefore he
> would pee when and where he felt like it (p. 51).[337]

---

[335] *"Der Teeheilige rächte sich unverzüglich. Vielleicht weil er glaubte, mit F
zusammen in Ungnade gefallen zu sein, vielleicht auch nur, weil ihn die
unvorsichtige Rüge A's beleidigte. Wie viele Kritiker, vertrug er keine Kritik.
[...] Ein echter Revolutionär liquidiere sich selbst, schloß er seine Rede.
Auch liege gerade in der Furcht vor einer Säuberung, die einige Mitglieder des
Politischen Sekretariats befallen habe, der Beweis, daß eine solche
Liquidierung notwendig sei und daß sich das Politische Sekretariat überlebt
habe."*
[336] *"A erkannte die Falle, in die ihn G gelockt hatte.   Doch bevor A
einzuschreiten vermochte, ereignete sich ein Zwischenfall."*
[337] *"Die Ministerin für Erziehung M ... sprang auf, schrie, Marschall K sei ein
Schwein. [..] Der aufgedunsene Gin-gis-Khan wurde aggressiv, brüllte, was*

A's reaction to this spectacle repeats the motif of unreasoned response and the abandonment of a position of detached, deliberate control and manipulation seen in his response to F's unexpected integrity under fire; A succumbs to the effect of the rumour that O has been arrested, thereby establishing for the first-time reader of the text - and reinforcing the impression engendered by his remark about the colonel who repeatedly interrupts the proceedings ("who was this ass of a colonel ...") ("... *wer denn dieser Esel von einem Oberst sei* ...") (p. 42) - that he is not necessarily behind this apparent elimination. N is surprised both by the target and the intensity of A's volley:

> A's impetuous reaction to this embarrassing and grotesque incident was surprising to N, less so because of the intensity with which the head of state intervened, more because he perceived A's attack to be panic-driven. [...] His furious attacks were aimed, incomprehensibly, not at F, G, or K, but rather at C, whom he owed the most ... Nevertheless he now accused C of having arrested O without A's knowledge and ordered him to rehabilitate O, if that were still possible. [...] A didn't stop at that. He required that the head of the secret police resign. An investigation of his deviant disposition ought to have been untertaken long ago. "I'm placing you under immediate arrest," he raged on and called for the colonel through the intercom (pp. 51-52).[338]

---

denn daran sei, nannte M eine prüde Ziege, brüllte, ob man ihn denn für so idiotisch halte, hinauszugehen, um zu pissen, er wolle nicht verhaftet werden ... sein Schwiegersohn und alle seine alten Freunde seien von A verraten worden, obgleich sie, wie er, ehrliche und überzeugte Revolutionäre gewesen seien, und daher lasse er sein Wasser wann und wo er wolle."

[338] *"Die ungestüme Reaktion A's, die nun auf diesen peinlichen und grotesken Vorfall folgte, überraschte N weniger durch die Leidenschaft, womit der Staatschef eingriff, sondern mehr, weil er A's Angriff als geradezu kopflos empfand; [...] Seine wütenden Angriffe richteten sich nämlich unverständlicherweise nicht gegen F, G oder K, sondern gegen C, dem er doch das meiste verdankte ... Dennoch warf er ihm nun einmal vor, C hätte ohne Wissen A's O verhaftet, und befahl ihm, den Atomminister zu rehabilitieren, wenn das noch möglich sei. [...] A ging noch weiter. Er forderte den Chef der Geheimpolizei auf, zurückzutreten. Eine Untersuchung gegen ihn, seiner*

As with L ("... was one of his mistresses in labour ...") ("... *ob irgendeine seiner Mätressen niedergekommen sei ...*") (p. 33) and F ("... the pornography had obviously gone to the shoe-shine boy's head") ("... *dem Schuhputzer seien offenbar die schweinischen Schriften in den Kopf gestiegen ...*"), A's attack on C zeroes in on the sexual sphere in which any indulgence represents a violation of a primary taboo in A's scheme of things. As A has already ordered the colonel not to interrupt the proceedings again, whatever the circumstance, he is not able to effect the implementation of his command. All representatives of the Dionysian pole, L, F, H and C, along with G, whose discourse is sparked by A's relinquishing of his Apollonian posture, contribute, together with the vicissitudes of chance, to a situation in which the underpinnings of his hegemony are whittled away, step by step. The final instance of A's contempt for libidinous impulse is rendered through the technique of flashback through N's agency. It involves the powerful D as well as C and M, and illustrates how the tactical blunders A has made within the actual meeting are the proverbial insult compounding past injury. If A's voyeuristic and passive sessions with young girls and American film and K's waste-elimination are only mildly grotesque, the scene which demonstrates "the unresolved clash of incompatibles in work and response," (cf. note 259 of this study) is that of the "naked concert:"

> The incident was comical and eerie. The wild sow had at that time received the baffling assignment of rounding up a female band that was to play Schubert's octet "in the raw" for A.

> Seething with rage at the idiotic order, and too much of a coward to refuse it, D had to turn to the minister of education and culture, who in her turn, also incensed and a coward, sought help in the conservatories and music schools; the girls had not only to be musically trained, but well-built too. [...] One of the most talented cellists commited suicide, others scrambled for a spot but were too ugly ... only a bassoonist was not to be found. The wild sow and the party muse sought the advice of the state aunt. Within no time at all, C had a very attractive prostitute with a stately bottom dragged from a prison to

---

abwegigen Veranlagung wegen, sei schon längst fällig 'Ich verhafte dich auf der Stelle,' tobte A und schrie durch die Sprechanlage nach dem Oberst."

bewilderment and with longing as the naked females
played their fiddles and blew their horns in desperation
(pp. 58-59).[339]

A has devised a situation in which two of the body's most
important senses, the visual and the acoustic, are played off against each
other in a way which denies an experience of the Dionysian as an
expression of the aesthetic.[340]   True to the traditional dictates of
functionality and economy of the shorter prose form, even the choice of
composer for this scene is integrated to the immediate textual environment
as well as to thematic considerations: Schubert died at an early age, victim

---

[339] *"Die Affäre war skurril und gespenstisch. Die Wildsau erhielt damals von
A den verblüffenden Auftrag, eine Damenkapelle aufzutreiben, die vor A nackt
Schuberts Oktett spielen sollte.   D mußte sich wutschnaubend über den
idiotischen Befehl und zu feige, ihn abzulehnen, an die Ministerin für
Erziehung und Kultur wenden, die Parteimuse wandte sich ebenso empört und
feige wie D an die Konservatorien und Musikhochschulen; die Mädchen
mußten ja nicht nur musikalisch ausgebildet, sondern auch gut gewachsen sein.
[...] Eine der begabtesten Cellistinnen beging Selbstmord, wieder andere
rissen sich darum, aber waren zu häßlich ... nur eine Fagottistin war nicht
aufzutreiben. Die Wildsau und die Parteimuse zogen die Staatstante zu Rate.
C ließ kurzerhand eine bildschöne Dirne mit stattlichem Hintern aus einem
Korrektionshause ins Stattliche Konservatorium schleppen, das Pracht-stück
war musikalisch völlig unbegabt, aber in einem unmenschlichen Dressurakt
wurde ihm das zum Oktett benötigte Fagottspiel beigebracht ... [...] In der
ersten Parkettreihe saßen in Pelzmänteln und mit steinernen Gesichtern D und
M und warteten auf A, doch der kam nicht. Stattdessen füllte sich der
Barockraum mit Hunderten von Taubstummen, welche die verzweifelt
geigenden und blasenden nackten Mädchen verständnislos und gierig
anglotzten."*
[340]   In her monograph *Nietzsche: Disciple of Dionysus* (Lewisburg: Bucknell
University Press, 1972), Rose Pfeffer discusses the concept of music as one
which transcends the Apollonian/Dionysian antinomy: "To both Schopenhauer
and Nietzsche, music is based on aesthetic principles and criteria of beauty that
are unlike those of painting, sculpture and epic poetry. While the latter arts
represent an Apollonian individuating act, music transports us into a state in
which the boundaries between individuals and the limits of space and time are
broken down, and a sense of mystical unity with the universe is experienced.
Music reveals a world that is unknown and unknowable to reason with its
fragmentizing, isolating activity, but is grasped intuitively by feelings and
instincts" (p. 52).

functionality and economy of the shorter prose form, even the choice of composer for this scene is integrated to the immediate textual environment as well as to thematic considerations: Schubert died at an early age, victim to a sexually transmitted disease, and his was the minority sexual orientation attributed to C. What little "descriptive residue" there is in *Der Sturz*, occuring almost exclusively at the beginning and at the end of the text, can be seen to effect the phenomenon of textual circularity mentioned in the introduction of this study. The opening scene of the text includes a description of the room in which the plot of *Der Sturz* unfolds:

> The meeting room was long and not much wider than the conference table. The bottom half of the walls had brown panelling. The unpanelled part of the walls and the ceiling were white. The seating order was arranged according to the hierarchy of the system. A sat at the head with the Party flag hanging over the white part of the wall. The other end of the table opposite him was unoccupied, and behind that was the meeting room's only window. The window was high and arch-shaped ... [...] L was undermined by a fear of prosecution. He knew that his downfall would happen in time (pp. 11-12).[341]

The funeral procession at the end of the text repeats many of these austere visual effects as well as the description of the hierarchy of power with A and L as its highest and lowest gradations:

> The Politburo shouldered the coffin draped with the Party flag ... The twelve most powerful men of the party and of the country trudged through the snow. [...] A at the

---

broken down, and a sense of mystical unity with the universe is experienced. Music reveals a world that is unknown and unknowable to reason with its fragmentizing, isolating activity, but is grasped intuitively by feelings and instincts" (p. 52).

[341]   *"Das Sitzungszimmer war lang und nicht viel breiter als der Versammlungstisch.   Die Wände waren halbhoch braun getäfelt.   Der ungetäfelte Teil der Wände und die Decke waren weiß.   Die Sitzordnung war nach der Hierarchie des Systems geregelt.   A saß oben. über ihm, am weißen Teil der Wand, hing die Parteifahne.   Ihm gegenüber blieb das andere Tischende leer, und dahinter war das einzige Fenster des Sitzungszimmers. Das Fenster war hoch, oben gewölbt ... [...] Die Furcht vor einer Anklage unterhöhlte L. Er wußte, daß sein Sturz einmal kommen mußte."*

head, shouldering the bier ... Large flakes of snow fell
from a white sky. The functionaries were crowded
together between the graves and around one that had been
freshly dug out ... As they began to lower the coffin into a
grave ... the monument whispered: "Hell, I'm going to be
next" (p. 62).[342]

The only colours in both scenes are brown in the lower portions
(the earth of the readied grave and the shade of the panelling) and white
for both the upper portions of wall and ceiling, graveyard and sky. The
shape of the room is very narrow and oblong, headed by a window rising
up to form an arch - the same shape as a grave with a rounded gravestone.
In both scenes, the highest and lowest positions are represented by A and
L respectively, with the other figures cramped into the narrow space.
Such parallel imagery reflects the nature of the conflict in *Der Sturz*, an
allegory of the disintegrative effect of any fixed ideology or narrow
conformity which denies the basic proclivities of human nature.

In both of Dürrenmatt's texts, thematic complexity encompassing
a most extensive range of human experience from the individual to the
political to the mythical, from psychological to ideological, microcosmic
to macrocosmic proportions, is accomplished through a restricted number
of interrelated motifs, presented in parallel, repetitive clusters. Narrated
time in both instances demonstrates abbreviated proportions: several days
in *The Assignment* and hours in *Der Sturz*. The use of symbol and the
technique of circularity, whereby the expositional strategy presents a
proleptic allegory of the method of closure, in evidence in both texts,
contributes to the allegorical potential of a prose technique which,
although utilizing a realist mode, does so by creating a metonymic axis, as
minimally contiguous and referential as it can be without interrupting the
continuity and comprehensibilty of the discourse. Reduced referentiality
is accompanied by an accretion of levels on the paradigmatic or
metaphoric axis through the device of repetitive language and motifs,
emphasizing similarity and "allembracingness" (Lodge, p. 139). Brevity,
fragmentariness and reduced proportions, "a weakening of metonymic or

---

[342] *"Das Politische Sekretariat ... trug den Sarg, bedeckt mit der Parteifahne
... Die zwölf mächtigsten Männer der Partei und des Staates stapften durch
den Schnee. [...] Vorne hatte A ... die Bahre geschultert ... Der Schnee fiel in
großen Flocken aus einem weißen Himmel. Zwischen den Gräbern und um das
ausgehobene Grab scharten sich dicht gedrängt die Funktionäre ... Als man
den Sarg ... ins Grab hinunterließ, flüstere das Denkmal: 'Teufel, ich werde
der nächste sein."*

syntagmatic relationships - i.e. the relationships of contiguity in time and space, and of cause and effect" (Lodge, p. 104) are especially accommodating to a valorization of the axis of similarity, although this axiom is by no means exclusive to the shorter prose form, nor does this imply that a short text may not valorize the metonymic axis as in the "slice of life" phenomenon. The texts discussed thus far do demonstrate the high profile of the metaphoric axis, even though they do not bear the same generic designations. The last texts to be discussed in this study, Martin Walser's novella *Runaway Horse* and his novel *Jenseits der Liebe* provide the opportunity to measure the proportions of metaphoric and metonymic modes in works which are not only at the more expansive end of the scale of quantity, as are the Dürrenmatt texts, but which seem to provide a more linear and contiguous metonymic axis.

Chapter Five

Martin Walser's Runaway Horse

A major component of this text's thematic constellation and concomitant motif structure is that of the fragility of human perception and its internal motor, more specifically, the dysfunction of the psychic apparatus described clinically as "major affective disorder" (major and manic depression). This essential feature has been overlooked by most critics, whose line of argument, whether in praising or denouncing *Runaway Horse* has been an assessment of its impact as social commentary. Reinhard Baumgart describes Walser's accomplishment with this work as the "squaring of a circle," by which he means the projection of a tenor of social and political criticism from a vehicle which remains entirely within the domain of the private and the personal:

> Whereas he enters seemingly into the most private of spheres, looking at two obvious escape routes out of society, there emerges something which is entirely political: a social system which no longer renders life meaningful. The production of surface appearances define Halm's experience of the system, and in Buch's experience it is a universal fraud. There is not one sentence of the story devoted to the national state of affairs. Nevertheless, it does, as a whole, embody our situation. As the story of two victims who realize too late that that is what they are. Perhaps it is solidarity that Walser's art produces and provokes.[343]

---

[343] *"Indem er sich auf das scheinbar Allerprivateste einläßt, auf zwei ihm gleich naheliegende Fluchtmöglichkeiten aus dieser Gesellschaft, kommt etwas ganz und gar Politisches zum Vorschein: ein soziales System, das keinen Lebenssinn mehr hergibt, das Halm nur noch als eine Produktion von Schein, das Buch als ein Universum des Schwindels erlebt. Mit keinem Satz redet die Geschichte zur Lage der Nation. Und doch enthällt sie als Ganzes unsere Lage. Als Geschichte zweier Opfer, die sich zu spät als solche erkennen. Solidarität also könnte das sein, was Walser's Kunststück provoziert,*

Sigrid Herzog criticizes Baumgart for his "one-track-mindedness," ("Wherever this Baumgart looks, he never sees anything but 'society'") (*"Wo der Baumgart auch hinblickt, immer sieht er nichts als 'die Gesellschaft'"*), goes on to take up a position in contra-distinction to Baumgart, inasmuch as she sees Walser's characters as banal, individual examples of the midlife crisis which has nothing to do with the social environment. Herzog observes that the human crisis at the center of Walser's text is not a viable theme, either of itself or in the form to which Walser has shaped it - her formulation does not render a clear distinction:

> And how can Baumgart expect society to produce a meaningful existence? A "social system" never provides a meaning to life.[!] This is something the individual must discover and determine for himself. [...] However which way biographies take shape, -whether it is an agile vim-and-vigour show-off or a ruminating intellectual - in

---

produziert." Reinhard Baumgart, "Überlebensspiel mit zwei Opfern," *Der Spiegel*, 27 Feb. 1978: 9, pp. 198-199. Similarly, Herbert Knorr in his article "Gezahmter Löwe - fliehendes Pferd: Zu Novellen von Goethe und Martin Walser," *Literatur für Leser 1979:2* describes the thematic impact of Walser's text as primarily social in nature: "Society is the local framework or plot locus projected by an apparently idyllic holiday situation. The novella thematizes the way people must organize the way they think, feel and act within the socio-historical situation of a modern, dichotomous society of illusion, if they are to experience any sense of identity or happiness. If one abstracts from the two central characters, one arrives at the fate of individuals of a society that co-determines individual behaviour and consciousness, consequently eliminating the possibility to communicate about the problem at hand." (*"Sie [die gesellschaftliche Wirklichkeit] ist ein lokaler Rahmen oder Spielort, der im Kontext einer scheinbar idyllischen Urlaubssituation aufgehoben ist. Wie in einer von der Gegenwart bestimmten geschichtlich-gesellschaftlichen Lage - die gekennzeichnet wurde als moderne zerrissene Scheingesellschaft - Menschen ihr Denken, Fühlen und Handeln organisieren bzw. organisieren müssen, um überhaupt noch Identität und Glück zu erfahren, ist in der Novelle thematisiert. [...] Abstrahiert man von beiden [Hauptfiguren], so bedeutet dies das "Schicksal" der Individuen einer Gesellschaft, die in dieser keine Möglichkeit mehr besitzen, aufgrund der von ihr mitproduzierten Verhaltens- und Bewußtseinslagen über die dargestellte Problematik zu kommunizieren."*) (pp. 150-155).

the middle of life comes the down-in-the dumps crisis, where everyone thinks he's a failure and wants to break away like a runaway horse, and then forgets about it. [...] In any case, there is no universal general knowledge to be gained from the whole affair. There is not even a trace of the broader human dimension, not even the slightest attempt to gain a sense of the possibility of transcending given thought patterns or keeping them open-ended. [...] Nothing is left to question, everything is resolved and consistently explained to its conclusion. [...] All done up with a ribbon. *No lose* [sic] *ends.*[344]

Joachim Kaiser also makes the point that the main protagonist lacks viability as a specific example of human nature which transcends its specificity to become generally significant and the possible subject of a literary work of art.[345] Albrecht Weber, although he mentions the element

---

[344] *"Und wieso erwartet Baumgart die Bereitstellung von Lebenssinn durch die Gesellschaft? Ein "soziales System" gibt nie einen Lebenssinn her . [!] Den muß das Individuum schon selber finden und für sich bestimmen. [...] Wie man seine Biographie auch gestaltet, als agiler Vitalitätsprotz oder sinnierender Intellektueller - in der Mitte des Lebens kommt die katzenjammervolle Krise, wo jeder sich für gescheitert hält, ausbrechen möchte wie das fliehende Pferd, und es bleiben läßt. [...] Verallgemeinerungsfähige Erkenntnisse lassen sich aus der ganzen Sache jedenfalls nicht gewinnen. Es fehlt jegliche allgemeinere menschliche Dimension, auch der geringste versuch einer Gewinnung von Transzendenz ... u.a. für die Möglichkeit, Gedankengänge nach vorne offenzuhalten. [...] Nichts bleibt fraglich, alles geht auf und wird konsequent zu Ende erklärt. [...] Fix und fertig. No lose* [sic] *ends." Sigrid Herzog,* "Über den grünen Klee gelobt," *Neue Rundschau,* 1978: 89, pp. 494-95.
[345] "But a secondary school teacher as the main character who determines the perspective of the novella, a civil servant who is irascibly articulate, someone who neurotically protects his independence, who can apparently describe the profile of his illness, but won't - such a character is a synthetic, artificial figure painted over in mystery colours. He keeps himself hidden behind ever new and witty paraphrasings of 'I am the way I am and don't have to prove it.' Walser denies his hero an inner life which comes to fruition, or one that is suspenseful, or contradictory, or alive. The witty attitudes make much of themselves, but they go nowhere and achieve nothing." *("Aber ein Studienrat als Perspektiven-Hauptfigur einer Novelle, ein Beamter von schrullig-wortgewandtem Wesen, jemand, der seine Unabhängigkeit neurotisch verteidigt, der sein Krankenbild zwar angeblich beschreiben kann, aber nicht will, das ist eine synthetische, eine mit Geheimnis-Farbe übermalte Kunstfigur. Der hält sich verborgen*

of psychic disfunction in his discussion of Walser's text, interprets this component as implicit criticism of contemporary society's preoccupation with sexual matters.[346] Although Weber also extrapolates a tenor of social commentary from the vehicle, his observations offer a more cogent description of a central aspect of the text's motif complex; he sees the general within the specific, describing Halm's debilitation as manic depressive (p. 285). (A closer look at the clinical symptoms of manic depression will prove this to be more accurate for Klaus Buch, whereas Halm exhibits the symptoms associated with the other type of major affective disorder: major depression). Weber's observations provide a good starting place from which it is possible to sharpen the focus on the disorder underlying Helmut Halm's persona, not only with respect to human sexual proclivities, but also from the perspective of the subject not at one with itself, perpetually searching for both intellectual and physical integration:

A kind of "hopeless craving,"(p. 1) not only for the suntanned skin on the boardwalk, but in a more general sense, - this is the situation of those who are isolated and hidden away... [...] The dichotomous, inwardly collapsed and insecure figure of Helmut Halm makes visible the ambivalent position of the intellectual, specifically that of the teacher or more generally of the teaching profession; it is therefore also the situation of those who reflect and theorize in a modern, "total" society, that is, one which pervades and dominates every area of life.[347]

---

immer hinter neuen, witzigen Umschreibungen seines 'Ich bin wie ich bin und brauch's nicht zu beweisen' [...] Walser verweigert seinem Helden einen erfüllten, einen spannungsvollen oder widersprüchlichen, einen lebendigen Innenraum. Witzige Haltungen prätendieren, was sie nicht leisten.") Joachim Kaiser, "Martin Walsers blindes Glanzstück : Funktion und Funktionieren der Novelle *'Ein fliehendes Pferd,'" Merkur 1978*, pp. 834-35.

[346] Albrecht Weber, "Martin Walser: Ein fliehendes Pferd," *Deutsche Novellen von Goethe bis Walser: Interpretationen für den Literaturunterricht* vol. 2, ed. Jakob Lehmann (Königstein/Ts: Scriptor, 1980) p. 287.

[347] *"Eine 'Art hoffnungslosen Hungers' (9), nicht nur nach dem Braungebrannten auf der Uferpromenade, sondern generell, ist die Situation des Abgekapselten und Eingeigelten ... [...] Die zwiespältige, in sich gebrochene und durchaus unsichere Gestalt des Helmut Halm macht die ambivalente Stellung des Intellektuellen, besonders des Lehrers oder allgemeiner: des Lehrenden, also des reflektierend-theoretischen Menschen in*

Tilmann Moser's monograph *Romane als Krankengeschichten* (novels as case histories) presents "clinical readings" of several modern texts, including Martin Walser's *Letter to Lord Liszt (Brief an Lord Liszt)*, that is, the author uses an instrumentarium of psychiatric and psychoanalytical disorder-concepts to better grasp fictional figures who display the symptoms of a mental-health dysfunction. In the case of *Runaway Horse*, the main protagonist, Helmut Halm, and his antagonist, Klaus Buch, display attributes which are so idiosyncratic, acute and sustained that the clinical approach suggested by Moser offers insight into what can otherwise only superficially be described as alienation and isolation caused by a materialistic and superficial society. As Moser observes and as will be shown in the following discussion, such an approach does not simply provide fuller access to a text's thematic constellation, it may also provide insight into the principles of the text's formal organization: "Deciphering the neurosis produces a logic which brings with it a first understanding of a chosen art form and creates a point of access to the richness of composition, to the logic of structure and the varying language patterns, all of which would otherwise remain undisclosed."[348] When seen from this clinical perspective - focusing inward *and then* outward - it is possible to ascertain the emergence of a complex of interrelated thematic possibilities from the text's foreground structure; the same hypothesis enables a description of the plot and character configurations and of mimetic detail of *Runaway Horse* in terms of reduced proportions, limited focus and the functionality of all of the text's narrative components. Abbreviated proportions are already in evidence with the number of *dramatis personae* restricted to four players: Helmut Halm, his wife Sabine, Klaus Buch and his wife Helene. This also holds true for narrated time - four days - as it does for the sole location of the action: the resort area of Lake Constance (Überlingen - Nußdorf).

A cursory reading of the text yields the following resume: Helmut Halm, a middle-aged, intellectual, introverted, pre-college teacher plans to spend an uneventful vacation with his wife. Activities will be restricted to

---

der modernen und totalen, d.h. alle Lebensbereiche durchdringenden und beherrschenden, Gesellschaft sichtbar." (pp. 286-287)
[348] *"Die Logik der entschlüsselten Neurose führt oft erst zum Verständnis der gewählten Kunstform und schafft einen Zugang zum sonst eher im Dunkeln bleibenden Reichtum der Komposition, zur inneren Logik des Aufbaus wie den Schwankungen der Sprachgestalt"* Tilmann Moser, *Romane als Krankengeschichten* (Frankfurt: Suhrkamp, 1985) p. 151.

reading Kierkegaard, eating, drinking, smoking and savouring the trauma of an existential crisis in the isolation afforded by beautiful natural surroundings; Klaus Buch, a former university acquaintance, of the same age as Halm but looking remarkably younger, appears on the scene with a wife who really is a generation younger. Buch represents what the common parlance refers to as a "fitness freak." He overwhelms the Halms with his boundless, frenetic energy and a preoccupation / obsession with physical performance. His adolescent attitude in sexual matters, a neurotic insecurity in his relationship with his wife and a pronounced hyperactivity produce a strong sense of revulsion in Halm, but he is not able to extricate himself from the situation because of the charismatic effect of Helene and Klaus on himself and his wife respectively. The conflict is brought to a resolution when Klaus risks his own and Helmut's life by insisting on pitting himself against the forces of a severe storm while boating on the lake: Helmut must wrench himself from his role of ironic acquiescence to push the tiller from Buch's hands, thereby saving himself from imminent death, but thereby inadvertantly pushing Buch overboard. The novella concludes with Helene's revelation of her own and her husband's anguished existence deriving from his perception of contexts as either ideal (Helmut is his most recent idealized object) or disastrous, hence an obsessive compulsion to excel and dominate everyone and everything in his life. Having successfully swum to shore, Buch reappears, exits with his wife as does Halm with his own. Both women's unimpaired ability for empathic response has been portrayed throughout the novella as the saving grace in their husbands' life; Halm now proceeds to relate his thoughts and observations of the last four days to Sabine, beginning his account with the same words with which the novella had begun, thus interposing himself as the fictional narrator of what the reader has assumed to be a third person narration.

None of the commentaries on Walser's text cited in this study addresses in any depth the question of the form of the text as an expression of the genre of the novella. Weber mentions some of the traditionally accepted criteria, including a suggestion that the novella as a "closed form" is therefore the appropriate vehicle for apodictic ideologies:

> The novella structure has been mastered, including the requisite symbol - the "falcon" required by Heyse ... In view of these findings, one shouldn't ask *if*, but rather *why* novellas are still or once more possible. If the closed form of the novella requires and represents a closed society, a closed world picture and/or closed personality structures, this is certainly the case in the literature of the Catholic renewal (LeFort, Bergengruen, Andres etc), but

also in the Marxist sphere of influence (Seghers, Wolf etc). Martin Walser's Marxist sympathies would justify the form, his critical stance and his attempt, *ex negativo*, to postulate the interconnection of society, world-view and personality through its negation.[349]

Both Kaiser and Herzog are more directly critical in their discussion of the genre as an appropriate vehicle for the reality of the late twentieth century. As with Weber, the opinions are based on the standard canon of criteria and the premise that literary form and social structure are homologous equivalents:

> Remarkable how the story is divided up in economic fashion into nine little chapters, in each of which there is an acceleration of the dynamics (Philologists should note that seven chapters begin with an indication of the time). The individual narrative components are nicely rounded off to an integral whole. [...] The classical requirement of a "turning point" has been neatly adhered to. [...] To be specific, it is the novella's classicism that disturbs me. It is not relevant to the times, too simple and really not permissible. If we are to be honest, we can no longer afford closed systems, even as art forms.[350]

---

[349] "*Die Novellenstruktur ist gemeistert einschließlich des Symbols, des von Heyse geforderten 'Falkens.'.. Angesichts des Befunds sollte man nicht fragen, ob, sondern warum heute noch oder wieder Novellen möglich sind. Wenn die geschlossene Form der Novelle geschlossene Gesellschaft, geschlossenes Weltbild und/oder geschlossene Persönlichkeitsstrukturen voraussetzte und repräsentierte, so ist dies durchaus in der Literatur der katholischen Erneuerung (LeFort, Bergengruen, Andres u.a.), aber auch im Marxismus (Seghers, Wolf u.a.) nach wie vor gegeben. Martin Walsers Näherung zum Marxismus würde die Form rechtfertigen, seine kritische Position, den Versuch, ex negativo, durch Verneinung die ideale Folie von Gesellschaft, Weltbild und Persönlichkeit als Ganzheiten zu postulieren*" (p. 294).

[350] "*Beachtlich wie die Geschichte sparsam auf neun Kapitelchen verteilt wird, deren jedes einen Zuwachs an Dynamik einbringt (Philologen sollten darauf achten, daß sieben Kapitel mit einer Zeitangabe beginnen). Die einzelnen Erzählungselemente sind schön zum Ganzen gerundet. [...] Die klassische Forderung nach einem 'Wendepunkt' wurde genau erfüllt. [...] Genaugenommen stört mich an der Novelle ihre Klassizität, die mir unzeitgemäß, zu einfach und eigentlich unerlaubt vorkommt. Geschlossene*

Kaiser, although just as caustic in his criticism of Walser as an epigone, is a little shaky in his theory, otherwise he would not postulate the dramatic stamp of this particular manifestation of the genre and the genre itself as a contradiction in terms (cf. Theodor Storm):

> Although it is a novella, the proceedings read like a piece of theater. One would think he is introducing theater characters. The theater analogy suggests itself not only because we are dealing with a configuration of characters typical to the comedy, but also because the unity of place has been almost pedantically adhered to. Either the characters meet for every possible kind of conversation in restaurants (at least three times), or under the open sky while taking part in some holiday sport (hiking, sailing). And that's it. Only the *finale* takes place in the hero's holiday cottage. Indeed, we can call this the placing of dramatic concentration on character, also typical of Kleist's novellas. [...] Now that Walser has construed and constructed things so well and Germany's readers have given him their applause, we find ourselves horrified at so much clever classicism.[351]

The critics cited here are unanimous in their view of the novella as the closed, most ideal structure attainable in prose or indeed as the structure most amenable to projecting fixed ideals. Walser has in fact drawn on a tradition whose critical reflection has been characterized by normative definitions and apodictic pronouncements, most of which have

---

Systeme können wir uns, wenn wir ehrlich sind, heute nicht mehr mal als Kunststücke leisten" (p. 495).
[351] *"Obwohl Novelle, liest sich der Vorgang wie ein Theaterstück. Er tut, als führe er Figuren vor. Die Theater-Analogie drängt sich nicht bloß deshalb auf, weil es um eine typische Lustspiel-Anordnung geht, sondern auch, weil die Einheit des Raumes fast pedantisch eingehalten sind. Entweder trifft man sich zu allen möglichen Gesprächen im Restaurant, (mindestens dreimal) oder unter freiem Himmel beim Urlaubssport (Wandern, Segelfahrt). Sonst nichts. Nur das Finale findet in der Ferienwohnung des Helden statt. So etwas nennt man doch: dramatische Konzentration auf die Figuren, wie sie auch für Kleistsche Novellen typisch ist. [...] Jetzt, da Walser so gut konstruiert und Lese-Deutschland ihm zugeklatscht hat, erschrecken wir vor so viel cleverer Klassizität" (p. 832).*

been contradicted or shown to be based on faulty premises. In effect, these critics' misrecognition of the relationship of form and content mirrors the antagonist's preoccupation with externals, his acceptance of arbitrary norms and his inability to extrapolate a broader, more abstract framework from the manifest contents of a given context. The analysis proposed in the following paragraphs, since it proposes a model of hermeneutic ambiguity for the text's tenor, is affiliated with the fictional Helmut Halm's "position behind the position," that is, the recognition that no discourse on truth disseminates univocal meaning. As Barbara Johnson has noted,

> To be fooled by a text implies that the text is not constative but performative, and that the reader is in fact one of its effects. The text's "truth" puts the status of the reader in question, "performs" him as its "address." Thus "truth" is not what the fiction reveals as a nudity behind a veil. [352]

Sabine says of her husband's reading: "Mind you, he did change as a result of his reading. After reading a page he wasn't the same man as the one who had turned it" (p. 67). (*"Er verändere sich durch sein Lesen, das schon. Er komme von keiner gelesenen Seite als der zurück, der die Seite aufschlug"*) (p. 95). This statement is of course denied by Halm, whose identity, obscured by a perpetual series of masks and facades, analogous to the artistic ambiguity of a text, has become lost in the shuffle; in one instance he claims that being a petit bourgeois is the hidden "position behind the position," yet goes on paradoxically to project a bourgeois attitude as the external foil: "If I'm anything at all, I'm a bourgeois. [...] He decided that as a bourgeois the best thing for him to do at this moment was to smile and drink a toast to Klaus Buch, ..." (p. 68). (*"Wenn ich überhaupt etwas bin, dann ein Kleinbürger. [...] Er fand, daß er als Kleinbürger in diesem Augenblick am besten lächle und Klaus Buch zuproste ..."*) (p. 96). Through its two main characters, *Runaway Horse* juxtaposes a position of critical observation (shown in the text to be lethal if not subjected to passage through "the other") with one of unreflected submission to arbitrary norms and "established" standards and ideals, hence a prolepsis of the literary debate provoked by this text and only one of the levels of the tenor projected from its vehicle.

---

[352] Barbara Johnson, *The Critical Difference* (Baltimore and London: The Johns Hopkins University Press, 1980) pp.143-144.

Halm's crisis of entrapment within the confines of his own isolated, narcissistic subjectivity is mitigated by his propensity for irony and humour. This ability to step back from oneself, to laugh at one's own folly, to take up position with another subject in order to become a vulnerable object of scrutiny represents an aspect of Halm's character which may be interpreted as a part of the text's parametafictional aspect. That is, what Helmut Halm is able to do is what a writer accomplishes in breaking away from content that is too personal or self-focused to have general relevance or resonance. Heinz Kohut describes the phenomenon of the attainment of broader focus as cosmic narcissism:

> Yet, if a man is capable of responding with humor to the recognition of those unalterable realities which oppose the assertions of the narcissistic self, and if he can truly attain that quiet, superior stance which enables him to contemplate his own end philosophically, we will assume that a transformation of his narcissism has taken place (a withdrawal of the physical accent from the "ego," as Freud put it) and we will respect the person who has achieved it.

> A genuine decathexis [de-focusing of psychic energy] of the self can only be achieved slowly by an intact, well-functioning ego; and it is accomplished by sadness as the cathexis is transferred from the cherished self upon the supra-individual ideals and upon the world with which one identifies. The profoundest forms of humor and cosmic narcissism therefore do not present a picture of grandiosity and elation but that of a quiet inner triumph with an admixture of undenied melancholy.[353]

In addition to this indication of a parametafictional aspect to the figure of Helmut Halm, his inner turmoil with respect to creating a cohesive nexus from disparate memories and perceptions provides further evidence for the assumption that his crisis is in part an allegory of the dilemma of fiction: all fiction, as discourse, is a construct of sometimes tenuous human perception:

---

[353] Heinz Kohut, *Self Psychology and the Humanities: Reflections on a New Psychoanalytic Approach* (New York and London: W. W. Norton and Company, 1985) p. 121.

Helmut was disgusted when he found himself gluing together scraps of memory, coloring them, breathing onto them, inventing texts for them. He was too old for this puppet show. Surely to breath life into the past meant resurrecting an event in a pseudo-vividness that simply denied the pastness of the past (p. 15-16).[354]

By contrast, Buch believes in the reconstruction of reality through the exact duplication of the sequence of words which once constituted it: "As soon as you get the word in the right place, '*Open Sesame!*'" (p. 41-42).[355] Both Hochhuth and Dürrenmatt have already been seen, in the texts analysed in this study, to provide a high profile to the theme of the "constructedness" of fiction, with Hochhuth offering the most readily perceived example of metafiction. Finally, the closural strategy of ending the text with the same lines with which it began makes Helmut Halm into the teller of this story:

"I'm sorry," he said, "but it's just possible that I'll be telling you all about this fellow Helmut, this woman Sabina."

"Go ahead," she said. "I don't believe I'll believe all you say."

"That would be the solution," he said. "So, here goes," he said. "It was like this: Suddenly Sabina pushed her way out of the tide of tourists surging along the promenade and headed for a little table that was still unoccupied" (p. 108-109).[356]

---

[354] "*Helmut hatte sich geekelt, als er sich erlebte, wie er die Gedächtnisfetzen zusammenleimte, wie er sie anmalte, behauchte, Texte erfand für sie. Für dieses Puppentheater war er zu alt. Etwas von früher lebendig zu machen, hieß doch, es auf eine Weise komplettieren, daß das Vergangene in jeder Pseudoanschaulichkeit auferstand, die den Vergangenheitsgrad des Vergangenen einfach verleugnete*" (p. 29)

[355] "*Sobald du das Wort an die richtige Stelle kriegst, SESAM ÖFFNE DICH ...*" (p. 63)

[356] "'*Es tut mit leid,*' *sagte er,* '*aber es kann sein, ich erzähle dir alles von diesem Helmut, dieser Sabine.*'"
'*Nur zu,*' *sagte sie,* '*ich glaube nicht, daß ich dir alles glaube.*'
'*Das wäre die Lösung,*' *sagte er.* '*Also bitte,*' *sagte er.* '*Es war so ...*' (p. 151)
"*Plötzlich drängte Sabine aus dem Strom der Promenierenden hinaus und ging auf ein Tischchen zu, an dem niemand noch saß*" (p. 9 and p. 151).

Halm's deconstructive stance of the "position behind the position" is counterpoised with Buch's phenomenological approach; commenting upon his insistence on mastery of his environment, but his poor negotiation of the maze of human discourse, his wife observes: "[...] Someone who surmounts every obstacle. As long as it's caused by Nature. In the face of Nature he was always courageous, ingenious, invincible. Only with people..." (p. 99).[357] Some of Walser's critics' misrecognition of the multifaceted tenor of the text evokes Klaus Buch's inability to penetrate the surface of contexts and phenomena: "All done up with a ribbon. [...] *No lose* [sic] *ends."* This echoes Buch's predicament of calling for constant challenge and failing to meet it when it arises: "Hella is a challenge for me. She's too much for me. I can't cope with her" (p. 77). (*"Hel ist für mich ein challenge. Sie ist zuviel für mich. Ich schaffe sie nicht"*) (p. 108). Although he does not stumble with the use of trendy foreign expressions, the challenge of the slipping and sliding text of life overtaxes Buch's abilities. Klaus Buch's criticism of a particular historical theory concerning structures on Lake Constance centers on the theory's lack of subtlety as its reason for popular success:

> "The fraud," said Klaus, "is that there never were any lake dwellings there..." [...] "That's exactly what that swindler would like to hear! The man who invented it all, and as a result was made a professor forty years ago, could hug himself because his clumsy and hence successful inventions must have long since made him a millionaire. [...] If I felt the urge to achieve something, it would be a fraud with a solid foundation, a real live proposition" (p. 27-28).[358]

This statement repeats the motif of the tenuous relationship of all discourse to truth, first manifested in Helmut Halm's description of his

---

[357] *"Jemand, der mit allen Schwierigkeiten fertig wird. Wenn sie aus der Natur kommen. Der Natur gegenüber war er immer mutig, einfallsreich, unbesiegbar. Nur Leute ..."* (p. 138).

[358] *"'Der Schwindel ist ... daß dort überhaupt nie Pfahlbauten standen...genauso möchte es der Schwindler, der das alles erfunden hat, und dafür schon vor vierzig Jahren zum Professor ernannt worden ist und sich dann ins Fäustchen lachte, weil er nämlich durch seine plumpen und deshalb erfolgreichen Erfindungen sicher längst Millionär war. [...] Wenn ich zu etwas Lust hätte, dann wäre es ein Schwindel, der Hand und Fuß hat, der es gewissermaßen zu wirklichem Leben bringt'"* (pp. 45-46).

attempt to write his father's biography, ("...resurrecting an event in a pseudo-vividness that simply denied the pastness of the past") (*"den Vergangenheitsgrad des Vergangenen einfach verleugne[n]"*), thus pointing to a plausible connection of the stratum of motifs used to portray Klaus Buch with the parametafictional aspect of the text's tenor. Kaiser also uses water imagery to formulate similar criticism: "One would like to think that the initial premonitions one has are the tip of the iceberg, the danger being that one discovers nothing there other than more water." (*"Man möchte, was man da zu ahnen bekommt, für die Spitze eines Eisbergs halten - auf die Gefahr hin freilich, daß darunter doch nur Wasser fließt"* (p. 836). Both Buch's and Kaiser's statements address the problem of the tenuous relationship between signifier and signified, of the postulation of any context as an expression of subjectivity, with respect to both logical and fictional discourse. Especially Kaiser demonstrates a pronounced animosity towards the scholarly analysis of language: "These constant cameraman-narrator narrow panning shots don't need to be affixed with the technical terms used by Germanists." (*"Diese ständigen, begrenzten Kamera-Erzähler Schwenks brauchen hier nicht mit germanistischen Fachausdrücken beklebt zu werden"*) (Kaiser, p. 831). Kaiser rather espouses a journalistic concept of literature according to which a text is primarily an object of mass consumption with no restriction to its access; he is especially concerned that the narrative focus of Walser's text risk confounding the reader: "And what if this behaviour is misunderstood? Or what if the reader consistently misunderstands this behaviour because of an ironic narrative environment?" (*"Und wenn dieses Verhalten mißverständlich wäre? Oder wenn es in einem ironischen Erzählklima so referiert würde, daß der Leser es immer in eine bestimmte Richtung (miß-) versteht?"*) (p. 832). Klaus Buch's publications are certainly as concrete and accessible as things can get: "And Klaus has published quite a number. On food in general. Well, well. And there are seventy-five thousand people eating according to his theories" (p. 27).[359] The most regrettable aspect of this parallel, however, is the way Kaiser compounds his contempt of scholarly pursuit with a misogynist bent to his criticism: "We are not female students of German literature of the year 2078 who are writing their Ph.D. on the [very] late Romantic Martin Walser." (*"Wir sind keine Germanistik-Studentinnen des Jahres 2078, die über den (Sehr-) Spätromantiker Martin Walser promovieren möchten..."*) (p. 831). Helene Buch

---

[359] *"Und Klaus hat sogar schon mehreres veröffentlicht. Über das Essen allgemein. Aha. Und fünfundsiebzig tausend Leute gibt es, die nach seinen Schriften essen"* (p. 44).

observes the following of her husband's treatment of her: "We'd known
each other for less than three months when he decreed that I would never
make it as a real musician - give it up, you'll only make yourself
miserable. Basta" (p. 101).[360] Walser, himself a Germanist who wrote
his dissertation on Kafka, undoubtedly realized that the choice of *Novelle*
as a generic text marker would be extremely controversial; with *Runaway
Horse* he has achieved the integration of opposing positions of
hermeneutic ambiguity and phenomenological, positivist label-pinning on
the plane of literary analysis to opposing positions (at least on the surface)
manifested by fictional characters; Helmut Halm's resigned acceptance
that ultimate meaning is beyond reach and Klaus Buch's inability to delve
beyond even the manifest surface of reality are affiliated with the
difference between the readerly and the writerly text. As Barbara Johnson
observes:

> Here, then, is the major polarity that Barthes sets up as a
> tool for evaluating texts: the readerly and the writerly.
> The readerly is defined as a product consumed by the
> reader; the writerly is a process of production in which
> the reader becomes a producer: it is "ourselves writing."
> The readerly is constrained by considerations of
> representation: it is irreversible, "natural," decidable,
> continuous, totalizable, and unified into a coherent whole
> based on the signified. The writerly is infinitely plural
> and open to the free play of signifiers and of difference,
> unconstrained by representative considerations, and
> transgressive of any desire for decidable, unified,
> totalized meaning (pp. 5-6).

Walser's text deconstructs the opposition between Klaus Buch
and Helmut Halm, inasmuch as it demonstrates through the use of the
same motif of the constructedness of human discourse and thinking that
they are hampered by the same problem, albeit that Halm has developed a
cynical expertise in dealing with meaning constantly deferred, whereas
Buch is still a novice in the discipline. The shorter prose form as
represented by the novella/short-story possesses the potential, through the
reduction of its metonymic aspect, and axiomatically, a potential increase
in its "writerly" dimension, to be the *"Problemdichtung"* it has often been

---

[360] *"Wir kennen uns noch kein Vierteljahr, da dekretiert er, zur wirklichen
Musikerin reicht es bei dir nicht, laß das sein, du machst dich nur unglücklich
dadurch. Basta" (p. 141).*

described to be, "to open ... perspectives and mirror ... issues concerning human existence that go far beyond the particular context of the story and trigger off reflection and speculation in the mind of the reader."[361] As discussed in the section of this study devoted to the theory of the novella and the short-story, the former is characterized through its "hermeneutic challenge," and the latter through its ability to portray existence as "only an impression, and, perhaps, only an illusion." As a part of the main thrust of contemporary literary theory, it would behove would-be critics of potentially writerly texts to be aware of the meaning of the term and the existence of the literary phenomenon to which it refers, and certainly not to scorn those who attempt to produce a well-informed and reflected line of argument rather than a "readerly," journalistic "pot shot" that misses its target by a wide margin.

Klaus Buch and Helmut Halm both suffer from the social requirement of conformity which imposes a system in which each member becomes a competitor, a potential adversary in a struggle to be better, to achieve more, to acquire more, to outdo the competition. This motif runs through the narrative in various guises. An example of this is the mechanical hammering sound of a couple involved in intimacies experienced by the Halms while in the resort of Grado, leading to Helmut's feelings of inadequacy with respect to his own performance:

> They both lay there, just listening to what a man is capable of. Helmut wouldn't have believed it possible. [...] He was dreadfully embarrased. [...] The fellow next door was in tune with the times. That's how a man must have felt in the old days of the pillory. Anyone falling short of the sexual demands of this age and of society was, so to speak, permanently pilloried. [...] Now to escape. Where to? (p. 44).[362]

Thus the hiatus between the private self and the public self is shown to be, above and beyond the personal and professional sphere,

---

[361] Denys Dyer, *The Stories of Kleist: A Critical Study* (New York: Holmes and Meier, 1977) p. 10.

[362] "*Beide lagen und hörten noch, was ein Mann leisten kann. Helmut hätte das nicht für möglich gehalten [...] Er schämte sich entsetzlich. [...] Der drüben war im Einvernehmen der Epoche. So muß man sich früher am Pranger gefühlt haben. Wer den Sexualitätsgeboten dieser Zeit und Gesellschaft nicht genügte, war praktisch ununterbrochen am Pranger. [...] Jetzt flieh. Wohin?*" (p. 66).

which is the major focus of the text, a broader, a more universal
phenomenon, relating the cause for dysfunction and disintegration to the
pervasive requirements of a collectivity as well as to the ambivalent,
complementary and contradictory drives within the psyche. Helmut's
discomfort with his sexuality therefore has, in addition to inner
dysfunction, the element of external interference: "As a teacher he felt
justified in condemning sexual indifference, which is how society wanted
it, whereas at home he felt justified in trying to condemn sexual pleasure,
which is how he wanted it" (p. 46).[363] Klaus Buch also admits that his
sexual prowess does not always correspond to his true desire: "My dear
Helmut, that's when I have to go indoors ... and although I'm in the mood
to shout and stamp, ... no, I snuggle up to her and caress her awake ..."
(p. 81).[364] Both characters therefore keep up the appearance of fulfilling
the performance requisites consonant with prevailing social views and
objectives. Helmut states: "Only by agreeing can you escape.
Theoretically you know that" (p. 60). ("*Nur durch Zustimmung kommst
du weg. Theoretisch ist das klar*") (p. 87). In accordance with his
introverted focus, Halm grapples with the dishonesty of the appearance
concealing a very different reality on a personal and psychological level:
"Surely to breathe life into the past meant resurrecting an event in a
pseudo-vividness that simply denied the pastness of the past" (p. 15-
16).[365] The extroverted Buch is more willing to participate in the
dishonesty of appearances, but is consequently led to the brink of
disintegration more radically than Halm. Thus he speaks of the wish to
take part in dishonest or fraudulent schemes: "If I felt the urge to achieve
something, it would be a fraud with a solid foundation ..."(p. 28).[366] "He
simply couldn't see a crooked deal without being tormented by the desire
to participate in it" (p. 59).[367] "He was absolutely convinced that he was

---

[363] "*Er glaubte berechtigt zu sein, die Ächtung der Unlust zu betreiben, wie es
die Gesellschaft wollte, zu Hause aber die Ächtung der Lust zu versuchen, wie
er es wollte.*" (p. 69).
[364] "*Mein lieber Helmut, da muß ich hinein... und obwohl mir ganz anders
zumute ist ... ich schmeichele mich hin zu ihr und zärtle sie wach...*" (p. 114).
[365] "*... Etwas von früher lebendig zu machen, hieß doch... den
Vergangenheitsgrad des Vergangenen einfach verleugn(en)*" (p. 29).
[366] "*Wenn ich zu etwas Lust hätte, dann wäre es ein Schwindel, der Hand und
Fuß hat...*" (p. 46).
[367] "*Er könne einfach keinen Schwindel sehen, ohne von dem Wunsch gefoltert
zu werden, an diesem Schwindel zu partizipieren*" (p. 85).

a crook" (p. 98).[368] Thus beyond the contrast of the introverted voyeur and the extroverted exhibitionist there is evidence of an underlying similarity which further deconstructs the oppositional nature of Buch's and Halm's relationship as antagonist and protagonist. More evidence of this similarity is forthcoming in several scenes. The episode of the hiking adventure contains one in which the couples are described feeding pigs contained within an electrified enclosure, a trope for the proclivities of the individual constrained by societal contingencies; especially the use of the modifiers "*zierlich*" and "*jung*" to describe both Klaus Buch ("Suddenly a slight, trim young man was standing at their table") (p. 8). ("*Plötzlich stand ein zierlicher junger Mann vor ihrem Tisch*") (p. 19). and the pigs makes this exegetic operation an easy one:

A herd of young pigs came running up across the patch they had finished grazing. Otto was convulsed with rage. The hikers, prompted by Helmut's example, pulled up some grass outside the fence to feed the slim little pigs. The pigs crowded against the electric fencing because the hikers were not pulling up enough grass and couldn't toss it far enough over the fence. This meant that the ones in front always got electric shocks on the pink bulges of their little snouts (p. 60).[369]

The episode of the fleeing horse tropes Halm's dilemma in its unsuccessful attempt to escape its enclosure, and it is fitting that Buch, who tries so desperately to conform, returns the horse to its captivity: "The closer he came to the horse, the slower he walked, approaching it in a wide arc directly from the side. Finally he was seen to grab the mane, and the next moment he was sitting astride it" (p. 61).[370] The central event of the near-disaster on Lake Constance shows Halm wresting

---

[368] "*Und dann immer das Gefühl, daß alles, was er tue, Schwindel sei. [...] Er war zutiefst davon überzeugt, daß er ein Verbrecher sei*" (p. 137).

[369] "*Eine Herde junger Schweine rannte über ihr Abgeweidetes her. Otto wütete. Sie fütterten die zierlichen Schweine mit Gras, das sie außerhalb des Zauns abrissen. [...] Die Schweine drängten einander gegen die geladene Umzäunung, weil die Wanderer nicht genug Gras rupften und das Gras nicht weit genug über den Zaun hineinwerfen konnten. Dabei kriegten immer die vordersten die elektrische Ladung auf die rosigen Wülste ihrer kleinen Mäuler*" (p. 87).

[370] "*Zuletzt bog er weit aus und näherte dem Pferde genau von der Seite. Ganz zuletzt sah man ihn nach der Mähne greifen und schon saß er droben.*"

control of the boat from Buch, thwarting the latter's attempt at self-
realization, as extreme as it may be. After subduing the horse, Buch
refers to a similar incident in Merano: "You see? If I hadn't stopped that
horse in Merano, I would have been scared of this one" (p. 62).[371] In the
closing pages of the novella, Halm decides to leave Lake Constance for a
new destination - he designates Merano, a symbol for Buch's singular
drive to achieve and overcome, as the new destination - without consulting
his wife, thus paralleling Buch's patriarchal behaviour. However, the
similarity ends here, since he defers to his wife's choice of Montpellier,
"'Just a moment,' said Helmut to the clerk, 'my wife doesn't agree.' [...]
'To ... to Montpellier,' Sabina said, exhausted" (p. 107),[372] the place
where Helene Buch had led a fullfilled existence:

> "Six years ago I spent a semester studying at Montpellier ... With
> thick, thick walls all around." Helmut could not help thinking of
> the thin walls of the hotel at Grado. [...] "Montpellier," said
> Helene, "was the most beautiful time in my life" (p. 97).[373]

The thick walls evoke the emotional endurance, security and
fortitude which both female characters bring to their respective marriages.
Halm's decision to defer to his wife in the choice of the destination
associated with Helene Buch signals the possibility of a change from the
vulnerable position of maintaining an external image to one which is that
of interacting subjects, interacting solitudes, away from and not caring
about the glare of the social eye; Halm defines Montpellier as the place
where shadows can be sewn together, if the sun is too hot: "'What will
we do if it's too hot down there?' 'Oh,' said Helmut with a shrug, 'sew
shadows together'") (p. 108). ("*Was tun wir, wenn es da drunten zu heiß
ist. Ach, sagte Helmut leichthin, Schatten zusammennähen*" (p. 150).
    A common thematic element of *The Assignment* and *Runaway
Horse* is that of the static, isolated, alienated, observing subject unable to
enter into the "dialectic of otherness" of intersubjective experience. This
holds true for both of Walser's male characters, although Helmut Halm's

---

[371] "*Siehst du, wenn ich den in Meran nicht gepackt hätte, hätte ich vor dem
hier Angst gehabt*" (p. 91).
[372] "'*Halt, Moment,' sagte Helmut zu dem Beamten, 'meine Frau ist nicht
einverstanden*' ... '*Nach Montpellier', sagte Sabine ...*" (p. 149).
[373] "*Vor sechs Jahren habe ich ein Semester in Montpellier studiert...
Zwischen ganz dicken Mauern. Helmut dachte unwillkürlich an die dünnen
Wände in Grado. [...] 'Montpellier,' sagte Helene, 'war die schönste Zeit
meines Lebens'*" (p. 135).

stasis is that of the voyeur who does not wish to be seen, and Klaus Buch represents the exhibitionist pole as a figure who defines himself entirely as an object of other observing subjects. Similarly, the women in Walser's novella, although they play supportive rather than the lead roles assigned to Dürrenmatt's female *dramatis personae*, are nevertheless vehicles of interaction which, at least in the case of Sabine Halm, would suggest a solution to the impasse: whether or not Helmut Halm recovers from his crisis through its revelation to his wife is, however, an open question, a "loose end" and as such, one of the aspects of the text's interpretive challenge: the profile of Halm's dysfunction, to be considered later in this discussion, will show that complete dependency on a spouse is a major liability. Helene Buch's role is a close parallel to Sabine Halm's, inasmuch as she sooths her husband each time he utters the phrase "You don't care for me anymore, do you?" (*"Du magst mich nicht mehr, gell?"*). (Hochhuth also describes the stabilizing role of women). Another example of parallel structure is thus to be perceived in the manner in which both men's wives attempt to mediate their husband's crises. Sabine Halm's spontaneity, intuition and ongoing empathic response to her husband's existential aporia is rendered through the technique of leitmotif. The first example of this occurs with her admonition that Helmut always refers to Klaus disapprovingly as "this Klaus Buch" (*"dieser Klaus"*), softening her criticism through playful body contact: "From now on you'll say 'Klaus,' she said. 'Yes,' he said. 'From now on I'll say 'Klaus.' Sabine punched him lightly. She evidently believed they were now agreed. That was fine with him" (p. 20).[374] To atone for rushing his wife out of their apartment in order to avoid its "desecration" by the Buchs, expected to stop by on the way to a common outing, Helmut initiates body contact with his wife; even though uncomfortable in his own body. ("When he wasn't wearing a jacket, the most noticeable thing about him was probably his stomach") (p. 1)[375](cf. also the repeated discomfort of frozen feet), Helmut is able to appreciate his wife's healthy expression of sensuality:

> To apologize for his seemingly endless haste, he quickly ran his thumb along the hollow of her neck. Her head

---

[374] *"'Von jetzt an sagst du Klaus,' sagte sie. "Ja,' sagte er, 'von jetzt an sage ich Klaus.'" Sabine boxte ihn ein wenig. Sie glaubte offenbar, jetzt seien sie sich einig. Das war ihm recht'"* (pp. 35-36).
[375] *"Wenn er keine Jacke anhatte, sah man von ihm wahrscheinlich nichts als seinen Bauch"* (p. 9).

drooped toward her responsive shoulders, her eyebrows rose, her body relaxed into an S (p. 38).[376]

While hiking through what Helmut considers to be breathtaking forests and meadows, he muses on how pleasant it would be to experience these surroundings without Klaus Buch's droning on about the major swindle perpetrated by farmers through crop insurance:

> My God, how marvelous it could be now, alone with Sabina. They spoke very little when they went on a hike. [...] And just when he was wondering whether the weather would hold, she would say: "I don't think we'll have any rain." And then it didn't matter one bit what one of them said or had said or ever would say. Usually he would speak up at that point and say: "Oh my love. My one and only. Sabina" (p. 60).[377]

Although Helmut does not share his inner reaction to the phenomenon of the Buchs with his wife fully until the plot reaches its climax, the line of communication is shown to be solidly in place, and the couple focuses sharply on the reason for a sustained problematic relationship with people who are certainly excellent physical specimens, but whose healthy glow is tarnished rather severely by a sustained display of acutely neurotic behaviour. This would be one of the most improbable things about Walser's text - the fact that a couple such as the Halms, capable of a discourse of introspection, would subject themselves to the unmellowed freneticism of a middle-aged man fixated on the sexual prowess and physical peak of post-adolescence, trying to cheat death by remaining forever young, were the attachment not made plausible by the ever-present basic drive of *Eros*, even among the wise, and the debilitating effect libidinal impulse can cause upon reasoned insight. This thematic

---

[376] "*Um sich für sein anscheinend sinnloses Hetzen zu entschuldigen, schürfte er schnell mit dem Daumen durch ihre Nackenmulde. Ihr Kopf sank auf ihre entgegenkommenden Schultern, die Augenbrauen hoben sich, ihr Körper wurde ein wohliges S.*" (p. 58).

[377] "*Mein Gott, wie schön wäre es jetzt, mit Sabine allein. Sie sprachen selten, wenn sie wanderten. [...] Und wenn er gerade dachte, ob sich das Wetter hält, sagte sie: Ich glaube nicht, das es zum Regnen kommt. Und es war dann völlig egal, ob es zum Regnen kam oder nicht, weil es auch völlig egal war, was einer sagte oder gesagt hatte oder je sagen würde. Meistens hob er dann seine Stimme an und sagte: Ach du. Einziger Mensch. Sabine*" (p. 87).

component is a seminal theme in literature, one which, contrary to Kaiser's opinion, does transcend the specifics of character and situation. On the eve of the singular event of the near-drowning on Lake Constance, both Helmut and Sabine single out libidinal impulse as the reason for the inability to extricate themselves from the both alluring and alienating company of the Buchs. The text can be seen to move, to use Greimas' terminology (cf. chapter one of this study), from a negative contract ("...surely it was the sweetest of all feelings to find that even your own wife was totally in the dark about you") (p. 26),[378] to a positive one ("I'll tell you all about it when we're on the train. [...] "Oh, Sabina. My one and only. Sabina") (p. 107)[379] through the agency of Halm's wife. Nevertheless, Sabine Halm's role as the instrument of resonance through which her husband begins to overcome his isolation falls far short of achieving the "classical proportions" of balance for which Walser has been rapped on the knuckles; she is never once in the text described as a person in her own right, but solely as an extension and a complement to her husband's life and career. Walser certainly shows sensitivity in this area through the subjugated figure of Helene Buch: the gap in Sabine Halm's description is implicit criticism achieved through explicit ellipsis:

> "What a blessing they can't ruin more than our vacation," said Helmut. "Starnberg is too far away." Sabina took Helmut's arm and said: "Don't be so negative." "But I like being negative," said Helmut. "Are we going to have another thunderstorm tonight, Mr. Negative?" she asked pointedly. "Ask Klaus Buch, Mrs. Positive," he said. "Wicked man," she said. "I'm asking you, from now on I'll ask only you, I'll talk only to you, I'll forget every other language in the world except yours, now there!" [...]

> He put his arm around Sabine and squeezed her until she squeaked a little. That made him think of Helene Buch. [...]

> He complained once more about the way she had got out of sailing tomorrow. [...] She was, she said with a nasty

---

[378] "... *das süßeste aller Gefühle sei es doch zu erleben, daß auch die eigene Frau keine Ahnung hat von einem*" (p. 45).

[379] "*Im Zug erzähle ich dir alles [...] Ach du. Einziger Mensch. Sabine*" (pp. 148-149).

little giggle, afraid of falling in love with Klaus.... [...]
"We've both been a little seduced at the moment," he
said. "We'd better watch out. After all, we're farther
along than they are," he said. "Maybe you are," she said.
"Bina," he said, "I know, you aren't. Nor am I. Bina.
You must resist this seduction by the Buch family, my
girl. [...] If they were to come together tonight, she
would be thinking of Klaus and he of Helene, and the
very idea of that was enough to unman him. "Idiot," she
said. "Yes," he said. "Spoilsport," she said. "Yes," he
said. "Moron," she said. "Yes," he said. "Asshole,"
she said. "That'll do," he said and, bending down to her,
kissed her carefully and said: "Oh my love. My one and
only. Sabina" (pp. 72-74).[380]

Although the text does not portray any dialogue between Buch
and his wife when the other couple is not present - a feature consistent
with its point of view deriving exclusively from Halm's observer role - the
significance of Helene Buch's supportive role runs parallel to that of
Sabine Halm. Helmut intones the phrase "Oh my love. My one and only.

---

[380] *"Zum Glück können sie uns mehr als den Urlaub nicht verderben, sagte
Helmut. Starnberg ist zu weit. Sabine hängte sich bei Helmut ein und sagte: Sei
nicht so negativ. Ich bin's doch gern, sagte Helmut. Kommt heute Nacht wieder
ein Gewitter, Herr Negativ, fragte sie anzüglich. Frag Klaus Buch, Frau
Positiv, sagte er. Böser, sagte sie, ich frag dich, ich frag überhaupt nur noch
dich, ich red' nur noch mit dir, ich verlerne alle anderen Sprachen der Welt
außer der deinen, so! [...]*
*Er legte seinen Arm um Sabine, quetschte sie, bis sie ein bißchen quiekste. Da
fiel ihm Helene Buch ein. [...]*
*Er beschwerte sich noch einmal darüber, daß sie sich morgen vorm Segeln
drücke. [...] Sie habe Angst, sich in Klaus ... zu verlieben, sagte sie und
kicherte unschön. [...] Wir sind beide ein bißchen verführt momentan, sagte er,
laß uns aufpassen. Wir sind doch schon weiter als die, sagte er. Du vielleicht,
sagte sie. Bine, sagte er, ich weiß, du nicht. Ich auch nicht. Bine. Wehr dich
doch gegen diese Verführung durch die Familie Buch, Mensch. [...] Wenn sie
einander heute nahekämen, dann dächte sie an Klaus und er an Helene, und
das sei für ihn eine Vorstellung, die ihn abrüste. Idiot, sagte sie. Ja, sagte er.
Alleskaputtmacher, sagte sie. Ja, sagte er. Blöder Hund, sagte sie. Ja, sagte er.
Arschloch, sagte sie. Nicht provozieren, sagte er und beugte sich über sie,
küßte sie vorsichtig und sagte: Ach du. Einziger Mensch. Sabine." (pp. 102-
104)*

Sabina." "*Ach du. Einziger Mensch. Sabine.*" almost with the same obvious frequency as Klaus Buch's rhetorical question "You don't care for me anymore, do you?" ("*Du magst mich nicht mehr, gell?*"). The parallel, subsidiary, supporting and supportive roles played by the women in the text both intensifies and extends the thematic component of alienation to include those who are most disadvantaged in the hierarchy and consequently are most exploited to maintain it.

In order to show what possibilities exist for the reconstruction of the full round of Helmut Halm's character, of which only a part of the circumference is visible, or to use Kaiser's metaphor, to project the dimensions of the iceberg of whose shape only the tip can be observed, this analysis will advance on the premise that the figure of Halm is drawn according to the phenomenon decribed as the "helpless helper." In his study on this topic, Wolfgang Schmidbauer describes a syndrome common in the medical, teaching and social service professions, for which solid evidence may be culled from the motifs carrying the figure of Helmut Halm to cast him as such an example:

> The helper syndrome, defined as a personality structure characterized by the inability to express one's own feelings and needs, in conjunction with a seemingly omnipotent, invulnerable façade, is a very wide-spread phenomenon among care-givers and providers of social services. Several statistical surveys indicate that the mental health of those who belong to the helping professions is in less than satisfactory condition. Among these, the best documented is the situation of the most prestigious professional group, namely physicians. One may readily assume that nurses, social workers, teachers and psychologists would present a similar profile.[381]

---

[381] "*Das Helfer-Syndrom, die zur Persönlichkeitsstruktur gewordene Unfähigkeit, eigene Gefühle und Bedürfnisse zu äußern, verbunden mit einer scheinbar omnipotenten, unangreifbaren Fassade im Bereich der sozialen Dienstleistungen, ist sehr weit verbreitet. [...] Daß es um die seelische Gesundheit bei den Angehörigen der helfenden Berufe nicht sonderlich gut bestellt ist, erweisen einige statistische Studien. Am besten dokumentiert ist die Situation bei dem prestigeträchtigsten Helfer-Beruf, dem Arzt. Doch dürften Krankenschwestern, Sozialarbeiter, Lehrer(innen) oder Psychologen sich in diesem Punkte kaum von den Ärzten unterscheiden.*" Wolfgang Schmidbauer, *Die Hilflosen Helfer* (Reinbek bei Hamburg: Rowohlt, 1980) pp. 12-13.

Along with the facade of invincibility and the inability to give expression to needs and feelings, Schmidbauer also describes the "oral personality," that is, one who is predisposed to become addicted to narcotizing substances, to be in a relationship with a spouse in which that person represents the nurturing, supportive parent who was missing or not present long enough or abusive in the debilitated helper's childhood.[382] The development of a major, debilitating hiatus between the inner self and the public self is described as the result of an early culling process inflicted by parents whereby only those characteristics deemed by them to be desirable or ideal are encouraged. Such ideals are incorporated into the child's super ego, much to her or his detriment if the selection process ignores the fulfilment of basic needs.[383] In a particular case study of this

---

[382] "Addiction is a frequent result when the helper's wife perceives that she is being exploited and ceases to provide a supportive role. (In this respect the essential characteristics of the helper syndrome and those of patriarchal society overlap, both of which rely on exploiting the emotional support a woman provides for a man's work.) Indeed, the woman as wife becomes the sole source for fulfilling the need for human relationships. [...] Due to the early and very pronounced split between the façade and the child, the oral needs for care, recognition and emotional 'feeding' remain at a primitive level. Hence the addictive substance satisfies a need which came into being at an elemental point of development. It allows the addict to withdraw from day- to-day living, which he perceives as an aggregate of strains and burdens with no possibility to ease the tension." ("*Die Sucht bricht nicht selten dann aus, wenn die Ehefrau diese Stützfunktion nicht mehr ausübt, weil sie selbst sich ausgebeutet fühlt. (In diesem Punkt überschneiden sich das Helfer-Syndrom und Grundmerkmale der patriarchalischen Gesellschaft, die auf Ausbeutung der emotionalen Stützfunktion der Frau für die Arbeit des Mannes ausgerichtet sind.) Doch steht die Ehefrau hier für die Befriedigungsmöglichkeiten aus mitmenschlichen Beziehungen schlechthin. [...] Wegen der frühen, stark ausgeprägten Spaltung zwischen der Fassade und dem Kind müssen die oralen Bedürfnisse nach Zuwendung, Bestätigung, emotionalem 'Gefüttertwerden' auf einer primitiven Stufe bleiben. Das Suchtmittel bietet hier eine Befriedigungsmöglichkeit, die auf eben dieser urtümlichen Stufe ansetzt. Es erlaubt dem Süchtigen, aus einer Alltagswelt zu fliehen, die ihm voller Belastungen und ohne Möglichkeit der Entspannung scheint.*") (p. 17).
[383] "By this is meant the parents' ego of ideals to which the child is expected to conform in the most perfect fashion. [...] The sorting-out process brings about a split; the child learns that it may develop its 'good' characteristics, whereas it must split off the 'bad' ones and repress them. Yet it is often the 'bad' characteristics, bad, that is, in the eyes of the parents, that are most essential. They cannot remain split off and repressed without damage being done, for

phenomenon, Schmidbauer desribes a subject with a valorized super-ego and no emotional connection to his pre-adult past.[384] The fictional figure of Helmut Halm presents a profile which corresponds point for point with these observations. The first item to be considered is of course the fact that Halm is a member of the teaching profession, and indeed one who strives to present an inscrutable image, fearing the revelation of his inner self at odds with the ideals of the super ego:

---

they are what make important types of behaviour at all possible, i.e. self-assertion, tenderness, sexual potency, intense emotion. [...] The child learns to set only the highest of expectations for herself or himself and yet acquires almost none of the concrete tools to accomplish anything." ("*Gemeint ist das Ideal-Ich der Eltern, das mit dem Anspruch der perfekten Erfüllung an ein Kind herangetragen wird. [...] Auslese bringt dann eine Spaltung mit sich; das Kind erfährt, das es seine 'guten' Eigenschaften entwickeln darf, seine 'schlechten' hingegen abspalten und verdrängen muß. Oft sind aber gerade diese in den Augen der Eltern 'schlechten' Eigenschaften sehr wesentlich. Sie können nicht ohne Schaden abgespalten und unentwickelt gelassen werden, da sie wichtige Verhaltensweisen [(z.B. Durchsetzung, Zärtlichkeit, sexuelle Potenz, Gefühlsintensität] erst ermöglichen. [...] Man lernt nicht als den höchsten Anspruch an sich zu stellen, und kriegt kaum konkrete Mittel in die Hand, um auch etwas zu erreichen...") (pp. 11-13).*

[384] "He now had no more access to his feelings at that time. The emotional access to his childhood ... had been extinguished. [...] [Patient's name] makes a very solid impression, he speaks with a quiet, strong voice, very evenly and steadily. He contends with difficulties in a quiet, circumspect manner, observing all the rules of ethics and reason. This invulnerability is a sure indication that the individual identifies with his super-ego. Thus can one anticipate all of the objections he will make to emotionally driven, spontaneous, and therefore possibly 'wrong' behaviour and phantasizing. Of course this happens with an attendant loss of spontaneity, creativity and breadth of experience.' ("*Zu seinen Gefühlen von damals hat er keinen Zugang mehr. Der emotionale Zugang zur Kindheit ist ... ausgelöscht. [...] [Name des Patienten] wirkt sehr gefestigt, er spricht mit ruhiger, kräftiger Stimme, sehr gleichmäßig und wohlgesetzt. Alle Schwierigkeiten werden mit Ruhe, Umsicht, nach den Regeln von Ethik und Vernunft angegangen. Diese Unangreifbarkeit ist ein sicheres Kennzeichen der Identifizierung mit dem Über-Ich. Alle möglichen Einwände gegen emotional gesteuertes, spontanes, darum möglicherweise 'falsches' Verhalten und Phantasieren sind bereits vorweggenommen. Freilich geschieht das auf Kosten der Spontaneität, Kreativität und Erlebnisvielfalt*") (pp. 74-77).

Helmut did not like people around them to have ideas
about himself and Sabina that were accurate. [...] To
succeed in promoting mistaken conclusions always made
him feel good. Incognito: that was his dearest image.
[...] Whenever, in school or in his neighborhood, he saw
evidence of being recognized for what he was, of
familiarity with attributes to which he had never
admitted, he wanted to escape. [...] They made use of a
knowledge about him whose accuracy he had not
conceded. Made use of it to deal with him. To
subordinate him. To make him perform. {They knew
how to manipulate him} And the more they knew how to
manipulate him, the greater became his longing to be once
again unrecognized. As long as someone knew nothing
about him, all things were possible (p. 3-4).[385]

This facade motif reoccurs throughout the text as an anchoring
component in its repetitive structure. The first reference made to the
physical environment of the *dramatis personae* is accomplished through
the filter of this motif:

He had not invented the vacation role that Mrs. Zürn
expected of him. All he had done was adjust his
behaviour to accord with his notion of what Mrs. Zürn
liked best. The result had agreeably little to do with him.
[...] He and this Dr. Zürn continued to pass each other
as two mysteries of equal status. [...] In the slightly
exaggerated courtesy with which they were treated by the

---

[385] *"Helmut mochte es nicht, wenn die Umwelt sich über Sabine und ihn
Gedanken machen konnte, die zutrafen. [...] Sobald es ihm gelang,
Fehlschlüsse zu befördern, fühlte er sich wohl. Inkognito war seine
Lieblingsvorstellung. [...] Jedesmal, wenn ihm das Erkannt- und
Durchschautsein in Schule oder Nachbarschaft demonstriert wurde, die
Vertrautheit mit Eigenschaften, die er nie zugegeben hatte, dann wollte er
fliehen. [...] Die benützten Kenntnisse über ihn, deren Richtigkeit er nicht
bestätigt hatte. Sie benützten sie zu seiner Behandlung. Zu seiner
Unterwerfung. Zu seiner Dressur . [...] Und je mehr die ihn zu nehmen
wußten, desto größer wurde seine Sehnsucht, wieder unerkannt zu sein. Wenn
jemand von ihm noch nichts wußte, war alles noch möglich" (pp. 12-14).*

Zürns, Helmut perceived the degree of reserve that was most agreeable to him (pp. 5-6). [386]

In accordance with the clinical profile presented above, the immunity this figure has developed to emotive interaction has, in addition to its buffering function in the reality of the present, the attendant effect of supressing the past origins of the emergence of this dichotomy of inner and outer self:

> Behind him there was practically nothing. If he tried to remember, he saw motionless images of streets, squares, rooms. No action. His memory-images were pervaded by a lifelessness as if in the wake of a disaster. As if the people did not yet dare to move. In any case, they stood silently against the walls. The center of the images usually remained empty. [...] The names and faces he evoked would appear. But for the condition in which they appeared to him, *dead* was much too mild. Probably his memory was no worse than other people's. And, like most people, he was fascinated by his youth and childhood. But then the silent, odorless, colorless scenes would mean nothing to him (p. 15). [387]

---

[386] "*Er hatte die Urlaubsrolle, die Frau Zürn von ihm erwartete, nicht erfunden. Er hatte lediglich sein Benehmen so eingerichtet, wie es, nach seinem Gefühl, Frau Zürn am liebsten hatte. Was dabei zustande kam, hatte mit ihm angenehm wenig zu tun. [...] Er und dieser Dr. Zürn gingen als zwei ebenbürtige Geheimnisse aneinander vorbei. [...] Helmut spürte in der ein bißchen zu höflichen Zuvorkommenheit, mit der man von Zürns behandelt wurde, die ihm angenehmste Form von Distanz*" (pp. 15-16).

[387] "*Hinter ihm war so ziemlich nichts. Wenn er sich erinnern wollte, sah er reglose Bilder von den Straßen, Plätzen, Zimmern. Keine Handlungen. In seinen Erinnerungsbildern herrschte eine Leblosigkeit wie nach einer Katastrophe. Als wagten die Leute noch nicht, sich zu bewegen. Auf jeden Fall standen sie stumm an den Wänden. Die Mitte der Bilder blieb meistens leer. [...] Die Namen und Gestalten, die er aufrief, erschienen. Aber für den Zustand, in dem sie ihm erschienen, war tot ein viel zu gelindes Wort. Er hatte wahrscheinlich kein schlechteres Gedächtnis als andere. Auch zogen ihn Jugend und Kindheit in der bekannten Weise an. Aber dann konnte er nichts anfangen mit den stummen, geruchlosen, farblosen Szenen*" (pp. 28-29).

The ambiguity and fragmentary nature of experience, especially
of that which is long past, and the consequent subjective nature of
constructing an opinion, with respect to context and significance, is also
shown through the letter Halm painfully remembers having written in a
humourous vein to the student newspaper in his school: "The deeper the
teacher fades into the past, the more exalted will the students' reverence
become" (p. 5). [388] Also within the rubric of this motif of the antinomy of
coherent exterior and ambiguous, ambivalent interior are Kierkegaard's
diaries, which Halm looks forward to reading in the hope that personal
revelation, implied by the term "diary," will turn out to be discourse of an
impersonal nature:

> He had planned to read Kierkegaard's diaries and had
> brought along all five volumes. [...] He hadn't the
> faintest idea what Kierkegaard had entered in his diaries.
> Unimaginable that Kierkegaard could have jotted down
> anything private.   He yearned to get closer to
> Kierkegaard. Perhaps he was only yearning so that he
> could be disappointed. [...] A diary devoid of anything
> private: what could be more fascinating? (pp. 2-3). [389]

One need only call to mind the Kierkegaard epigraph to
Dürrenmatt's *The Assignment*, cited from *Either/Or* to establish the
relevancy of this example of intertextuality: "When a spider plunges from
a fixed point to its consequences, it always sees before it an empty space
where it can never set foot, (no matter how it wriggles)." [390] An excerpt
from this same work serves as this novella's epigraph:

> "From time to time one comes across novellas in which
> certain persons expound opposing philosophies.   A
> preferred ending is for one of those persons to convince

---

[388] *"Je tiefer der Lehrer in der Vergangenheit versinkt, desto höher wird in den
Schülern die Andacht steigen" (p. 14).*
[389] *"Er hatte sich vorgenommen, Kierkegaards Tagebücher zu lesen. [...] Er
wußte überhaupt nicht, was Kierkegaard in seinen Tagebüchern notiert hatte.
Unvorstellbar, das Kierkegaard etwas Privates notiert haben konnte.   Er
sehnte sich danach, Kierkegaard näher zu kommen. Vielleicht sehnte er sich
nur, um enttäuscht werden zu können. [...] Ein Tagebuch ohne alles Private,
etwas Anziehenderes konnte es gar nicht geben" (p. 11).*
[390] *"Wenn eine Spinne von einem festen Punkt sich in ihre Konsequenzen
hinabstürzt, so sieht sie stets einen leeren Raum vor sich ..."*

the other.   Thus, instead of the philosophy having to
speak for itself, the reader is favored with the historical
result that the other person has been convinced.   I regard
it as a blessing that in this respect these papers offer no
enlightenment."[391]

      Sören Kierkegaard,   *Either/Or*

The imagery of the castle of Neuschwanstein, a structure whose
interior was, for the most part, never completed, is an apt expression of
the facade motif with its attendant evocation of insularity and difficult
access:

> To be inaccessible, that became his dream.   And he found
> it difficult not to allow the slender, pointed, steep-sided
> rocky fortress to become a permanent image.   A kind of
> super-Neuschwanstein seemed to be burning itself into his
> imagination (p. 4).[392]

The letter Halm writes to Buch but never sends also is an
expression of the motif an inscrutable exterior masking inner
incompletion, of a fortification established to ward off intruders:

> My ideal is to be able to look on silently when I am being
> misunderstood.   To agree with the misunderstanding is
> something I would like to learn.   [...] And I want you to
> know that I am not interested in finding out something
> about myself, let alone saying something about myself.
> [...] My heart's desire is to maintain privacy. This is a
> wish I share with the majority of all living people. We
> consort like battleships.   [...]   The more someone else

---

[391]   *"Man trifft zuweilen auf Novellen, in denen bestimmte Personen
entgegengesetzte Lebensanschauungen vortragen.   Das endet dann gerne
damit, daß der eine den anderen überzeugt. Anstatt daß also die Anschauung
für sich sprechen muß, wird der Leser mit dem historischen Ergebnis
bereichert, daß der andere überzeugt worden ist. Ich sehe es für ein Glück an,
daß in solcher Hinsicht diese Papiere eine Aufklärung nicht gewähren."*
[392]   *"Unerreichbar zu sein, das wurde sein Traum.   Und er hatte Mühe, die
schlanke, spitze, nach allen Seiten vollkommen steil abfallende Felsenburg
nicht zu einem andauernden Bewußtseinsbild werden zu lassen.   Ein
Überneuschwanstein wollte sich einbrennen in seine Vorstellungen"* (p. 13).

knows about me, the greater would be his power over me
... (p. 21).[393]

The statement that all human interaction is predominantly of a
hostile character is one of the signals in the text which likely triggered its
interpretation as social commentary. Although it is false to reject the
aspect of social commentary as less than germane to the text's
interpretative possibilities, it is an over-simplification to regard it as its
primary objective. All of the texts discussed in this study (*Atlantik-
Novelle, Die Berliner Antigone, The Assignment, Der Sturz, Jenseits der
Liebe*) do indeed describe human interaction in the context of the
exchange of hostilities, yet in each case the social implications constitute a
subsidiary stratum of the tenor, whose major thrust is to define the more
fundamental paradoxes within the individuals who make up the
collectivity and construct of society. In Walser's scheme of things,
drawing an analogy between human interaction and naval battle
formations says at least as much about the mental condition of the subject
who makes the statement as it does about the reality he seeks to define.

The facade motif is, in a number of instances, expressed through
utterances of an ironic stamp, and as such make the inference of
dysfunction associated with its occurrence a more tenuous interpretation,
since irony may imply, as discussed above, the ability to distance oneself
from the immediacy or seriousness of a given situation. Hence yet another
"loose end." Thus Klaus Buch speaks of Halm's early ability to
undermine the face value of discourse:

> At school, Helmut had always written in the most soulful
> mood-prose. But his cleverest trick had been to read
> aloud the most outlandish phrases in a totally
> dispassionate voice (p. 25).[394]

---

[393] *"Mein Ideal ist es, zusehen zu können, wenn man falsch verstanden wird.
Dem Mißverständnis zustimmen, das möchte ich lernen. [...] Ich bin nicht
interessiert, etwas über mich zu erfahren, geschweige denn, etwas über mich zu
sagen. [...] Mein Herzenswunsch ist zu verheimlichen. Diesen Wunsch habe
ich mit der Mehrzahl aller heute lebenden Menschen gemeinsam. Wir
verkehren miteinander wie Panzerschiffe [...] Je mehr ein anderer über mich
wüßte, desto mächtiger wäre er über mich, also ..." (pp. 36-37).*
[394] *"Helmut habe in der Schule immer die schmelzendsten Stimmungs-bilder
geschrieben. Aber sein großer Trick sei dann gewesen, die ausschweifendsten
Wortgebilde mit einer gänzlich interessenlosen Stimme vorzulesen" (p. 41).*

Similarly, when asked by the Buchs what it is they read during the evening instead of watching television, the response is: "'De Sade ... And Masoch,' Sabina chimed in ..." (p. 26) (*"De Sade.... Masoch auch, maulte Sabine nach"*) (p. 43). Sabine's use of mythological imagery to describe the oceanic effect of sailing meets with a similar rejoinder:

> Never before had she been so aware of her skin. She felt
> as if she had been on Mount Olympus for a massage and
> was now returning to earth, growing heavier by the
> minute. "Regards from Apollo the masseur," said
> Helmut (p. 35).[395]

As the couples are together on the eve of the sailing incident, Helene Buch speaks of her seventy-one-year-old mother as a person who still possesses considerable vigor. When she inquires about Helmut's parents, the reaction is "Helmut turned his thumb straight down" (p. 70). (*"Helmut senkte den Daumen steil nach unten"*) (p. 99). After going through endless photographs of her equally healthy family members, Helmut takes his leave, saying: "he was more grateful to the Buchs for this evening than anything else. No-one, as long as he could remember, had so fortified him. So uplifted him. So richly rewarded him" (p. 71).[396] After a difficult trek in the rain through heavy underbrush and fields with no paths, Helmut must exercise special control in accepting Klaus Buch's reminder that he had claimed to know where he was taking them:

> ... If he had even the slightest inkling of my hatred, he
> would run away. At the same time he gave Klaus Buch a
> friendly pat on the shoulder ... "If the Israelites had had
> to rely on me, they would still be in Egypt. Thank God,
> he had himself under control again. [...] There was
> nothing he loathed more than this state of being exposed
> to another person. In fact, something approaching zest
> for life could really only develop in him when he
> experienced the difference between the internal and the

---

[395] *"So habe sie ihre Haut noch nie gespürt. Sie habe das Gefühl, sie sei im Olymp zu einer Massage gewesen, und kehre jetzt, schwerer und schwerer werdend, zur Erde zurück. Masseur Apoll läßt grüßen, sagte Helmut"* (p. 55).
[396] *"... er danke den Buchs für diesen Abend mehr als für alles andere. So gestärkt habe ihn, soweit er sich erinnern könne, noch niemand. So aufgerichtet. So beschenkt"* (p. 101).

external. The greater the discrepancy between his true feelings and his facial expression, the greater his enjoyment. Only when he appeared to be someone else, and was someone else, did he really live. Only when he lived a double life did he really live. [...] When he gave way to an outburst - whether of anger or joy -- he was usually immediately overcome by an almost uncontrollable depression. He felt at the end of his tether. Then anyone could do what they liked with him (pp. 54-55). [397]

More derision from Buch is the result when the latter inquires how much farther it is to the highest point in their hike and is told by Helmut that they are already there; once again, Helmut is hard put to maintain his air of equanimity:

When Klaus Buch was about to laugh again, Hella cried: "Klaus, please, it makes Helmut quite sad when you laugh like that."

He tried to send her a look which she would find impossible to decipher. He wished to look mysterious. And tough. And inscrutable (p. 57). [398]

---

[397] "... wenn der jetzt nur einen Hauch meines Hasses spürt, rennt der weg. Dabei klopfte er Klaus Buch freundlich auf die Schulter ... Wenn das Volk Israel auf mich angewiesen gewesen wäre, säße es heute noch in Ägypten.Gott sei Dank, er hatte sich wieder unter Kontrolle. [...] Es gab überhaupt nichts Ekelhafteres für ihn als dieses Offendaliegen vor einem anderen. So etwas wie Lebensfreude entwickelte sich bei ihm wirklich nur aus dem Erlebnis des Unterschiedes zwischen innen und außen. Je größer der Unterschied zwischen seinem Empfinden und seinem Gesichtsausdruck, desto größer sein Spaß. Nur wenn er ein anderer schien und ein anderer war, lebte er. Erst wenn er doppelt lebte, lebte er. [...] Ließ er sich zu einem Ausbruch hinreißen - egal ob des Ärgers oder der Freude -, überfiel ihn danach meistens eine geradezu panische Schwermut. Er glaubte sich verloren. Jeder konnte jetzt machen mit ihm, was er wollte" (p. 80).
[398] "Als Klaus Buch wieder lachen wollte, rief Hel: Klaus bitte, Helmut wird ganz traurig, wenn du so lachst.
Er versuchte, einen Blick hinzukriegen, den sie überhaupt nicht verstehen konnte. Er wollte rätselhaft aussehen. Und hart. Und undurchdringlich" (p. 83).

For someone as dysfunctional and/or non-introspective as Klaus Buch, it comes as no surprise that the exterior created by Helmut, whom the latter can best describe as "Our HH" (*"unser Ha Ha"*) is accepted at face value. In portraying her husband's admiration for Helmut, Helene creates an ideal image which runs a close parallel with the quiet, strong, solid, even temperament described in the case study above:

> 'It's like finding buried treasure,' he said. You - he felt that - you with your quiet determined manner could have made him whole again. That's what he lacked, your common sense, your sense of proportion, your inner calm (pp. 102-103).[399]

The construct of the character of Helmut Halm also leaves no doubt about the tendency in "helpless helpers" to aspire to above average achievements, to set goals beyond the ken of the average individual. An example of this is the school where Helmut is employed:

> "What school are you at anyway?"
>
> "Eberhard Ludwig," Helmut said, doing his best not to sound proud.
>
> "Oh," said Klaus Buch, "congratulations - oh well, you were always tops, of course" (p. 78).[400]

Helmut is also described as having read Nietzsche in French at an early age: "My old HH, forever gnawing away at problems, reading Zarathustra in his swim trunks ..." (p. 78)[401] and "That was something he had done as a boy of fifteen. He had read Zarathustra while lying on his stomach. Snob that he was, he had read the French translation. *Ainsi*

---

[399] *"Es ist, wie wenn ich einen Schatz gefunden hätte, hat er gesagt. An dir, das hat er gespürt, an deiner ruhigen, festen Art, hätte er gesund werden können. Das hat ihm gefehlt, deine Vernunft, deine Ausgeglichenheit, die innere Ruhe" (p. 143).*

[400] *"'An welcher Schule bist du eigentlich?' 'Am Ebe-Lu,' sagte Helmut so unstolz als möglich. 'Oh,' sagte Klaus Buch, 'gratuliere, naja, du warst eben immer Spitze, klar'" (p. 111).*

[401] *"Mein alter Ha-Ha, die große Problemschraube, Zarathustra in der Badehose gelesen ..." (p. 109).*

parlait Zarathustra" (p. 3)."[402] The other occurrences of the Zarathustra motif also establish its significance as the valorization of the spiritual at the expense of the body's requirements: "He had read Zarathustra at fourteen. Way ahead of all of them. Puberty with a crown of thorns" (p. 11).[403] Finally, this motif of Nietzschian self-overcoming, of a helpless and fearful *"Übermensch,"* is expressed through a composite daydream image:

> ... he had been obsessed with the notion that clutching his right hand was a person of the size of a seven-year-old child, and that this person was Friedrich Nietzsche, aged forty but reduced to the dimensions of a seven-year-old. And his terrible fear of Otto made him cling to Helmut's hand (p. 89).[404]

Another interlocking motif within this complex is that of the repression of libidinous drive. The first example of this describes how Halm, in his interaction with students, has come by the nickname of "Kiwi" (the original German is *"Bodenspecht"*):

> While they were talking he would keep his eyes fixed on the toes of their shoes or their feet. Just as he did in school. Hence the nickname "Kiwi." It must have been the girls who had induced this posture of head and body in him. With their pitiless blouses and pants (p. 8-9).[405]

Similarly, Halm demonstrates restraint in the company of Helene Buch: "Helmut found it hard not to look only at Hella. He had to look

---

[402] *"Das hatte er als Fünfzehnjähriger getan. Zarathustra hatte er auf dem Bauch liegend gelesen. Snob, der er war, hatte er die französische Übersetzung gelesen. Ainsi parlait Zarathustra"* (p. 11).
[403] *"Schon mit vierzehn Zarathustra gelesen. Ihnen allen voraus. Pubertät mit Dornenkrone"* (p. 23).
[404] *"... er führe an seiner rechten Hand einen Menschen von der Größe eines siebenjährigen Kindes und dieser Mensch sei Friedrich Nietzsche, aber in seinem 40. Lebensjahr, aber reduziert auf die Maße eines Siebenjährigen. Und der hatte entsetzliche Angst vor Otto [Halm's dog] gehabt"* (p. 124).
[405] *"Er sah den Herrschaften, während sie redeten, auf die Schuh- beziehungsweise Zehenspitzen. Das tat er ja auch in der Schule. Darum Bodenspecht. Es dürften die Mädchen gewesen sein, die diese Kopf- und Körperhaltung bei ihm bewirkt hatten. Mit ihren rücksichtslosen Blusen und Hosen"* (p. 20).

carefully past her because the others might have noticed how insatiable his eyes were" (p.29).[406] When Helene Buch pulls off her upper clothing during the first sailboat excursion, Halm once again demonstrates the unobtrusive powers of observation afforded by peripheral vision: "Suddenly Hella removed her top, tucked it away... and lay down on the bow. Resorting to his professional glance, Helmut observed her breasts as he looked past them" (p. 30).[407] Halms's sexual relationship with his wife is described as a desire whose satisfaction is perceived as something alien and strange rather than natural and fulfilling: "Nothing would then seem as unbearably comical as any activity determined by or directed toward sexuality. [...] To desire it, yes. To do it, no" (p. 45).[408] The same motif, including a topless Helene Buch and the discretion of Helmut Halm's peripheral vision, occurs in the episode of the hiking excursion: "Since Hella wasn't wearing a bra, she was naked to the waist after taking off her jacket and blouse. [...] Again Helmut looked at them by looking past them" (p. 54).[409]

The majority of the manifestations of the facade motif leave little doubt about the true nature of "the position behind the position" in this figure as one of entrapment and stasis more than of retreat and distance:

> ... martyred inertia. It was his favorite mood. [...] That heaviness, sweating a bit. With approval. Heavy and sweating and pale. [...] Himself a heavy, sweating corpse, that was his favorite mood, martyred inertia. [...] He had nothing to worry about: he had his revulsion. His position behind the position (p. 47).[410]

---

[406] "*Helmut hätte am liebsten nur noch Hel angeschaut. Er mußte vorsichtig an ihr vorbeischauen, weil die anderen sonst gesehen hätten, wie wenig er sich an diesem Mädchen sattsehen konnte*" (p. 47).

[407] "*Plötzlich zog Hel ihr Oberteil weg, verstaute es, ... und legte sich auf das Vorschiff. Mit Hilfe seines professionellen Blicks sah Helmut ihre Brüste im Vorbeischauen an*" (p. 49).

[408] "*Nichts kam ihm dann so unerträglich komisch vor wie alle vom Geschlechtlichen bestimmten oder auf es gerichteten Handlungen. [...] Wollen, ja. Tun, nein*" (p. 68).

[409] "*Da Hel keinen Büstenhalter trug, hatte sie, als sie Jacke und Bluse ausgezogen hatte, einen nackten Oberkörper. [...] Helmut schaute wieder nur im Vorbeischauen hin*" (p. 79).

[410] "*...blutige Trägheit, das war seine Lieblingsstimmung. [ ] Er, eine schwere, schwitzende Leiche, das war seine Lieblingsstimmung, blutige Trägheit. [ ] Er hatte seinen Ekel. Seine Position hinter der Position. Er*

Several instances of this motif, as the one cited above, characterize the relationship between exterior and interior in terms of the ultimate paradox that the direction and ultimate goal of life is death. Thus the dichotomy is shown to be, above and beyond a state of salvific numbness and the buffering distance of irony, one in which the predominance of *Thanatos*, the drive to self-destruct, emerges:

> For many years he had done little but prepare himself to live with what had been destroyed. Nothing attracted him so much as things that had been destroyed. Some day or other he would do nothing from morning to night but surround himself with what had been destroyed. His aim was to transform his own present into a condition resembling as closely as possible the destroyed nature of the past. Already he wanted to belong to the past. That was his objective. Within him, around him, before him, he wanted everything to be as fragmentary as in the past. After all, a person is dead far longer than he is alive (p. 16).[411]

Similarly, the death-dream which Halm experiences describes the condition for existence as the ability to negate, to deny that existence:

> He dreamed he was turning over in his coffin and that, in spite of the complete darkness, he sensed that one side of the coffin was missing. [...] But where the side was missing his hand kept groping apprehensively. [...] Involuntarily he rolled down on the other side of the step and lay where he landed. [...] He knew he would emerge into daylight, among people. And he knew there was only

---

hatte seine Freude am Mißverstandenwerden. Täuschung, war das nicht die Essenz alles Gebotenen? Das Ziel der Scheinproduktion" (p. 70).
[411] "Im Grunde tat er seit Jahr und Tag nichts, als sich vorzubereiten auf den Umgang mit dem Vernichteten. Ihn zog nichts so an wie dieses Vernichtete. Irgendwann einmal würde er von morgens bis in die Nacht nur dieses Vernichtete um sich versammeln. Sein Ziel war es, schon die eigene Gegenwart in einen Zustand zu überführen, der der Vernichtetheit des Vergangenen so ähnlich als möglich war. Schon jetzt wollte er vergangen sein. Das war seine Richtung. Es sollte in ihm, um ihn, vor ihm so fetzenhaft sein wie im Vergangenen. Man ist ja viel länger tot als lebendig" (p. 30).

one condition: if even a single person recognizes you, it's all over, forever. He woke up in terror and thought: the new life (pp.49-50).[412]

The culminating point for this leitmotif of affirmation through negation, of the paradoxical ambivalence of *Eros* and *Thanatos*, occurs in the scene in which Helmut, clinging to the sailboat, emits shrieks of fear in the face of death, the very same sounds he had produced at the point of orgasm and engenderment of life:

> Had he ever felt so utterly shattered? He gave a great wail. During those last few months, when he had still been having sex with Sabina, he had experienced exactly the same sensation, that of being destroyed. [...] Each time he had wailed like that. A long-drawn-out, steadily rising wail (p. 87).[413]

This scene is entirely consonant with the development of this motif as the description of an individual who permits, if not seeks out, the ongoing obscuration of the boundaries of identity, for which the ultimate allegories are both sexual union and death. Both Hochhuth and Dürrenmatt also describe extreme life and death situations, the proximity of the resolution of the greatest of antinomies as the cause of a heightened resonance of this paradox already contained, but until now, more or less muted, unobserved within the psyche.

Halm's behaviour pattern is also indicative of a depressive syndrome, which along with manic depression, constitutes the two most prevalent forms of affective disorder. Some of the symptoms observed in

---

[412] "Er träumte, er drehe sich in seinem Sarg um und habe trotz der vollkommenen Dunkelheit den Eindruck, daß eine Sargwand fehle. [...] Aber da, wo die Wand fehlte, mußte die Hand ängstlich hinaustasten. [...] Er rollte, ohne es zu wollen, auf der anderen Seite der Stufe abwärts und blieb liegen. [...] Er wußte, daß er zurückkommen würde ans Tageslicht, zu den Leuten. Und er wußte, es gab nur eine Bedingung: wenn dich ein einziger erkennt, ist es aus, für immer. Er erwachte vor Angst und dachte: das neue Leben" (pp. 73-74).

[413] "War er je so zerschlagen gewesen. Er heulte auf. In den letzten Monaten, in denen er noch geschlechtlich mit Sabine verkehrt hatte, hatte er genau dieses Gefühl erlebt, das Gefühl, vernichtet zu sein. [...] Jedes Mal hatte er so geheult. Ein lang gezogenes, immer höhere Töne erreichendes Heulen" (p. 122).

Halm are a dysphoric mood (feeling ill at ease, hopeless), self-reproach and excessive guilt, disinterest in sexual activity and thoughts of death (Scully, p. 52).

To this facade motif at the nucleus of the novella's restricted motif complex are subsumed even the few sparse elements of the text's subsidiary detail: the Halms' dog, Otto, turns out to be female, (p. 91 / p. 126) and the fabric of Halm's socks is artificial (p. 48 / p. 71). From this repetitive presentation of a stable, coherent exterior masking fragmentation, fragility and destabilization, there emerges a fourfold interlocking thematic projection: the identity crisis experienced for the most part in middle age, described psychoanalytically as generativity versus stagnation;[414] the crisis of the helpless helper and his depressive syndrome; that of the universal and ultimately ambivalent basic drives and antithetic complements of *Eros* and *Thanatos* within the psyche; and that of the destabilized, deconstructed text.

The narcotization motif, a prominent feature in each work analysed in this study (with the exception of Hochhuth's *Die Berliner Antigone*) is once again in strong evidence; it touches every character in *Runaway Horse*, whose profile of symptoms of the helpless helper would be incomplete without this ingredient. In the first example, which occurs as the couples eat dinner together, the consumption of alcohol provides relief from the dredging up of details of late adolescence by Klaus Buch, thus bringing together the motifs of narcotization and suppression of the past:

> Helmut and Sabina were drinking the heaviest, most
> expensive Pinot Noir, of which Helmut had five large

---

[414] "Generativity is primarily the interest in establishing and guiding the next generation, although there are people who, from misfortune or because of special and genuine gifts in other directions, do not apply this drive to offspring but to other forms of altruistic concern and of creativity, which may absorb their kind of parental responsibilty. The principal thing is to realize that this is a stage of growth of the healthy personality and that where such enrichment fails altogether, regression from generativity to an obsessive need for pseudo-intimacy takes place, often with a pervading sense of stagnation and interpersonal impoverishment. [Cf. Helmut Halm] Individuals who do not develop generativity often begin to indulge themselves as if they were their own one and only child." (Cf. Klaus Buch) Erik H, Erikson, *Identity and the Life Cycle* (New York: International Universities Press, 1968) p. 97.

glasses and Sabina two. Helmut felt himself lapsing into
a delicious, somber state of languor (p. 17).[415]

The evening is brought to a close with the same motif: "Helmut
would have liked another glass or two of that wine. But Klaus was
already on his feet ..."(p. 18).[416] When the couples come together on the
next day at the appointed time, the scene is introduced with the same
motif: "Before very long, Helmut managed to steer the stroll along the
promenade into a wine tavern. He confessed that he had never had
anything else in mind: the idea of having to spend an evening without
wine simply paralyzed him" (p. 39).[417] After the fleeing horse episode,
the same pattern is adhered to, only the motif appears in conjunction with
that of the suppression of libidinous drive: "What a beautiful void,
Helmut thought. Now to drink and sink to the bottom" (p. 67).[418] "He
drank quickly. He wanted to get drunk as quickly as possible. Should he
admit to himself that he was in love with this girl Hella?" (p. 69).[419] The
evening finishes on the same note: "He pretended to be embarrassed and
quickly left the room. As a matter of fact, he was ready to burst into
tears. He was drunk" (p. 71).[420] The ensuing exchange that takes place
between Helmut and Sabina about the influence the Buchs are having on
their relationship, since it takes place after a certain level of intoxication
has been attained, mitigates to a certain degree the resolve that might be
attributed to Halm in this unprecedented expression of feeling and
perception: "Helmut and Sabina, heavy with wine, traipsed homeward.
[...] 'I'm drunk,' he said. 'We are,' she said. ' I am,' he said. 'We

---

[415] *"Helmut und Sabine tranken den schwersten, teuersten Spätburgunder.
Helmut trank fünf Viertel davon. Sabine zwei. Er spürte, wie er in einer
schönen düsteren Schwere versank. Weit weg von ihm turnte Klaus Buch die
Erinnerungen nach ..." (p. 31).*
[416] *"Helmut hätte gern noch ein oder zwei Viertel von diesem Waldulmer
getrunken. Aber Klaus Buch stand schon"(p. 33).*
[417] *"Es gelang Helmut, den Promenadenbummel schon bald in eine Weinstube
zu lenken. [...] Der Gedanke, einen Abend ohne Wein verbringen zu müssen,
lähme ihn" (p. 59).*
[418] *"Welch eine wunderbare Leere. Jetzt trinken und versinken" (p. 95).*
[419] *"Er trank rasch. Er wollte möglichst rasch betrunken sein. Sollte er sich
eingestehen, daß er diese Hel liebe?" (p. 98).*
[420] *"Er trat rasch hinaus. Tatsächlich war ihm zum Heulen zumute. Er war
betrunken" (p. 101).*

are,' she said. 'Who cares?' he said..." (pp. 72-73).[421] The scene in which Helene Buch reveals the true nature of her husband, presumed to be deceased, would also not be possible without the disinhibiting effect of alcohol: "'We could also offer you a twelve-year-old Calvados,' Sabina said" (p. 96).[422] Filling and refilling the glasses punctuates this scene in its entirety:

> Helene drank the Calvados that Helmut had refused. Sabina filled all three glasses again. Helene was the first to reach for the refilled glass. [...] Helene said "God, this Calvados is good." [...] She finished her drink. Sabina poured her another. "Now I'm the only one drinking," she said. "Cheers," said Sabina and drank too. [...] She finished her glass. Sabina filled it. [...] She drank up her Calvados and held out her glass for Sabina to fill. "Cheers," she said. Sabina drank too (pp. 97-98). [423]

Helene's admission of her husband's and her own tortured existence is followed by yet another infusion: "She finished her drink, held out her glass, had it filled, said 'Cheers,' and drank. [...] She jumped up. Walked up and down. Holding the glass. Having it filled. Drinking" (p.100).[424] Her husband's unexpected appearance, the fact that he is alive, does not alter the frequency of this motif: "She looked at Klaus and, keeping her eyes on him, poured herself a Calvados and said

---

[421] *"Helmut und Sabine, schwer vom Wein, trotteten heimzu. [...] 'Ich bin betrunken,' sagte er. 'Wir,' sagte sie, 'sind.' 'Ich,' sagte er. 'Wir,' sagte sie." (pp. 102-103).*
[422] *"'Wir könnten dir auch einen zwölf Jahre Calvados anbieten,' sagte Sabine" (p. 133).*
[423] *"Helene trank den Calvados, den Helmut abgelehnt hatte. Sabine schenkte alle drei Gläser wieder voll. Helene war die erste, die nach dem frisch gefüllten Glas griff. [...] Helene sagte, 'mein Gott ist dieser Calvados gut.' [...] Sie trank aus. Sabine schenkte ihr wieder ein. Jetzt bin ich die einzige, die trinkt, sagte sie. 'Zum Wohl,' sagte Sabine und trank mit ihr. [...] Sie trank ihr Glas leer. Sabine schenkte ein. [...] Sie trank ihren Calvados leer und hielt Sabine das Glas zum Füllen hin. Sie sagte: 'Prost.' Sabine trank mit ihr" (pp. 134-136).*
[424] *"Sie trank aus, hielt das Glas hin, kriegte es gefüllt, sagte 'Prost,' und trank. Sabine trank mit ihr." (pp. 139-141).*

'Cheers,' then drank it down and looked at Klaus again" (p. 104).[425]
Once Helene and Klaus have made an exit and this scene has drawn to a close, its final punctuation is not unexpected: "Helmut sat down, lit a cigar, poured himself a Calvados, and said: 'Cheers.' And drank" (p.105-106).[426]

   The last example of this motif of narcotization is an allusion both to the illusion of reality through drug-induced perception and through the subjectivity of fiction, calling to mind Hochhuth's juxtaposition of dreamed and/or drug-induced experience depicted in *Atlantik-Novelle*. The following citation is not only significant in grasping the construct of the character of Klaus Buch, it has allegorical implications for the text in its entirety. The intertextual inference is based on four words uttered by Klaus Buch as he battles the forces of nature on Lake Constance with a frenzied passion not usually ascribed to ordinary mortals: "Lucy in the sky" (p. 120). The source of this interjection and its apparent significance constitute an interpretational possibility possessing the flavour of the unheard of event in its own right: The Beatles' song *Lucy in the Sky with Diamonds* from the album *Sgt. Pepper's Lonely Hearts Club Band*. The full text, to be qouted in its entirety because of the many parallels between it and *Runaway Horse*, is as follows:

> Picture yourself in a boat on a river,
> With tangerine trees and marmalade skies
> Somebody calls you, you answer quite slowly,
> A girl with kaleidoscope eyes.
> Cellophane flowers of yellow and green,
> Towering over your head.
> Look for the girl with the sun in her eyes,
> And she's gone.
> Lucy in the sky with diamonds,
> Follow her down to a bridge by a fountain
> Where rocking horse people eat marshmallow pies,
> Everyone smiles as you drift past the flowers,
> That grow so incredibly high.
> Newspaper taxis appear on the shore,
> Waiting to take you away.
> Climb in the back with your head in the clouds,

---

[425] "Sie sah Klaus an, ihn ansehend, füllte sich einen Clavados ein, sagte 'Prost,' trank das Glas leer und sah wieder Klaus an" (p. 145).
[426] "Helmut setzte sich, zündete sich eine Zigarre an und schenkte sich Calvados ein und sagte: 'Prost.' Und trank." (p. 147).

> And you're gone.
> Lucy in the sky with diamonds,
> Picture yourself on a train in a station,
> With Plasticine porters with looking glass ties,
> Suddenly someone is there at the turnstile,
> The girl with the kaleidoscope eyes.[427]

The title of this song is considered to be, through the initial consonants of its nouns (LSD), a description of the generating moment of a "trip" whose characteristics are then described. The symptoms of LSD use, not unlike those of manic depression in some users, will be shown at a later point in the discussion to be displayed in the figure of Klaus Buch. The most unexpected result from a comparison of *Lucy in the Sky with Diamonds* and *Runaway Horse*, however, are the number of motifs and images in common to both texts. The first line of these lyrics of course describes the scene of a boat on a body of water, the *"Mittelpunktsereignis"* of the novella. The line of the lyric at the very centre of the text (rocking horse people, line 11 out of a total 22), evoking the image of a child on a rocking horse, is the central symbol of the novella (a childish Klaus Buch, referred to by the owner of the horse as *"der Bub,"* subduing a horse that has bolted). Lines 19 and 21, ("Picture yourself on a train in a station" and "Suddenly someone is there at the turnstile") as well as other items of vocabulary (taxis, marmalade skies, looking glass, the girl with the sun in her eyes) present many similarities with the scene at the end of the novella:

> I'll tell you all about it when we're on the train. [...] "A taxi, in fifteen minutes." [...] "You're looking right through me as if I were an empty jam jar. [...] "The Rhine," she said. [...] She was sitting in the evening sun. "Suffused in light, my Sabina," he said ... [...] Looking out from the years as from a bower of roses... [...] Suddenly Sabina pushed her way out of the tide of tourists ...(p. 107).[428]

---

[427] The Beatles, *"Lucy in the Sky with Diamonds," Sgt. Pepper's Lonely Hearts Club Band.* Capitol Records, *1967.*

[428] *"Im Zug erzähle ich dir alles. [...] Ein Taxi in einer Viertelstunde. [...] Du siehst durch mich hindurch wie durch ein leeres Marmeladeglas. [...] Sie saß in der Abendsonne. [...] 'Du Angeschienene, du,' sagte er. [...] Plötzlich drängte Sabine aus dem Strom ..." (pp. 148-151).*

The image of a bridge by a fountain, of eating and drifting past
flowers, has a parallel in one of Klaus Buch's reminiscences: he recalls
having bathed in the fountain, surrounded by flowers, in the market square
of the university town of Tübingen. This portion of the city is bordered on
the one side by the Neckar river and by a small tributary on the other,
over which bridges have been built to connect this central area with the
area on the other side of the tributary. The segment of text referred to is
as follows: "... there had been boxes of geraniums around the edge of that
fountain and before Klaus Buch had been able to take the dip ordered by
Helmut they had removed two of them" (p.14).[429] The motif of the
kaleidoscope with its evocation of a moving spectrum of colour also has a
parallel in *Runaway Horse*. One instance of this is the flood of colour,
provided by the flowers at the Halm's vacation apartment, with special
emphasis on the taller variety:

> ... Helmut and Sabina were standing on the porch
> contemplating Mrs. Zürn's riotous medley of a flower
> garden ... Mrs. Zürn had once told Helmut that she was
> embarrassed about the bars over the apartment windows,
> which was why she had planted phlox, foxglove, rose
> campion and, especially, those tall hollyhocks. Helmut
> had replied that once you became used to the bars you
> didn't see them anymore, whereas the glorious show of
> flowers was a daily miracle (p. 66).[430]

The description of colour as the storm gathers on Lake Constance
repeats this motif of a kaleidoscope effect:

> In the sky, inky patches of every shade of blue had flowed
> together. In the course of the afternoon everything had
> grown more definite. At some places in the inky streams
> there were now even distinct silvery borders. [...] The

---

[429] "*Auf dem Rand des Marktplatzbrunnens hätten Geranienkisten gestanden,
von denen sie, bevor Klaus Buch das von Helmut befohlene Bad habe nehmen
können, zwei Kistchen heruntergenommen hätten*" (p. 28).
[430] "*... Helmut und Sabine ... betrachteten Frau Zürns wild gemischten
Blumengarten ... Frau Zürn hatte einmal zu Helmut gesagt, sie geniere sich
dafür, daß die Ferienwohnung Gitter vor den Fenstern habe, deshalb habe sie
Phloxe, Fingerhüte, Königskerzen und vor allem die hohen Malven gesetzt.
Helmut hatte gesagt, wenn man die Gitterstäbe einmal gewöhnt sei, sähe man
sie nicht mehr, die Blumenpracht dagegen sei täglich ein Wunder*" (p. 94).

water had absorbed all these colours and concentrated
them in a dense blend. In the water one could see all the
blues, the silver, the pink; together they produced a blue
of increasing steeliness flooded by a violet gold. And it
was into this that the thundery squalls ripped their black
scars (p.82).[431]

Motion and colour are also a part of the closing scene of the text:

The train was arriving. Helmut said to the locomotive,
which was brown with a white stripe [the original
German is *"Helmut sagte zu der farbigen Lokomotive
..."*] and reminded him of a father confessor: *Qui tollis
peccata mundi"* (p. 108).[432]

The heightened sensory perception of "cellophane flowers of
yellow and green, / towering over your head and "...flowers, / that grow so
incredibly high" corresponds to the description of the heightened
synaesthetic perception of transcendence afforded by towering trees and
transluscent foliage in the novella; Klaus Buch describes the gigantic trees
in his garden and the surreal birdsong that he experiences at dawn:

I have some huge trees in my garden, that's where the
birds start up even before the sun has properly risen. [...]
Like a giant echo chamber resounding, reverberating,
with birds' voices. It's as if the whole world were reduced
to the nave of a church. And the fantastic part is that the
chamber itself, the nave, just imagine, doesn't stay in one

---

[431] *"Im Himmel waren Tinten jeden Blaus langsam zusammengeflossen. Im
Lauf des Nachmittags hatte alles an Bestimmtheit zugenommen. An einigen
Stellen waren in den Tintenflüssen sogar entschiedene silberne Borten
entstanden. [...] Das Wasser hatte alle diese Farben aufgenommen und sie zu
einer dichten Mischung konzentriert. Man sah im Wasser alle Blaus, das
Silber, das Rosa: zusammen ergab sich ein immer stahlflüssigeres Blau, in
dem ein violettes Gold flutete" (p. 115).*
[432] *"Der Zug fuhr ein. Helmut sagte zu der farbigen Lokomotive, die ihm
vorkam wie ein Ordensgeistlicher: Qui tollis peccata mundi" [who takes away
the sins of the world]" (p. 150).*

place, it rises, you can hear it, it rises up into the air (p. 81).[433]

The motif of an oceanic feeling evoked by the overwhelming proportions experienced in nature is also associated with the character of Helmut Halm. Thus he looks forward to an experience which transcends the boundaries of perception:

> He promised them a hike through magnificent, silent forests. Then a view ranging from the Vorarlberg to Bern. He could feel his voice verging on the rhapsodic. Walking in the forest would be like walking in a cathedral. Only that the light would be more vivid and the air better. The most importatnt thing about these forests was that they could still evoke that old feeling of infinity (p. 52).[434]

The first expression of this motif occurs in conjunction with the metaphoric image of *Neuschwanstein*, evoking both stasis and upward motion as a spatial description of the act of contemplating the infinite from the position of mortality to which every human being is consigned:

> A kind of super-Neuschwanstein seemed to be burning itself into his imagination. And forests. Always he saw forests. Saw himself trotting through forests. Without moving he would trot along, penetrating farther and farther into the forest, which, fortunately, never ended. Forests without end, that must be perfection (p. 4).[435]

---

[433] *"Ich habe in meinem Garten ein paar gewaltige Bäume ... [...] Ein Riesenhallraum schwingt da, überschwingt von Vogelstimmen. Es ist, als wäre die ganze Welt nur noch ein Kirchenschiff. Und das Phantastische, der Raum selbst, das Kirchenschiff, stell dir das vor, bleibt nicht an Ort und Stelle, es hebt sich, du hörst es, es hebt sich in die Luft"* (p. 113).

[434] *"Er versprach eine Wanderung durch schöne, stille Hochwälder. Dann einen Rundblick von Vorarlberg bis nach Bern. Dann spürte er, wie sein Ton sich heben wollte. In den Wäldern werde es sich gehen wie in lauten Domen. Blos das Licht werde lebendiger und die Luft besser sein. Das Wichtigste an diesen Wäldern sei, daß sie noch das alte Gefühl der Endlosigkeit erzeugten"* (p. 76).

[435] *"Ein Überneuschwanstein wollte sich einbrennen in seine Vorstellungen. Und Wälder. Immer sah er Wälder. Sah sich durch Wälder traben. Ohne sich*

This motif, as does that of falsified contexts, renders the
oppositional boundaries between Halm and Buch less distinct. The
linkage of this motif to two such dysfunctional, self destructive individuals
contradicts any claim that Walser is a "(very) late Romantic"; Walser's
treatment of these figures is in fact the same subversion of a romantic
"Weltanschauung" accomplished by Thomas Mann in *Death in Venice*.
As Helmut Jendreiek observes: "What Aschenbach experiences in the
fictional reality of the novella as a Romantic-Wagnerian fulfillment is
shown through Thomas Mann's critical stance towards Wagner to be a
phenomenon of decay and ruin."[436] It is not a coincidence that Halm's
choice of image in characterizing his inner life is the castle of
Neuschwanstein, an empty monument built at the behest of an unstable
ruler primarily for the enjoyment in solitary of Wagner's music.
Similarly, the intertextual component *Lucy in the Sky with Diamonds*, as
an expression of the narcotization motif, is not - as this artifact of popular
culture has been conceived to be - an endorsement of drug-induced
aesthetic perception, but rather an indictment of this idealization.
Scanning back over the points of comparison between the novella and the
lyrics reveals a pattern of negation and de-idealization of the latter's
"enhanced" perception. Halm's idealization and dependence on his wife,
although a possible way out of the existential dilemma, can also be seen as
a liability, and certainly is at her expense. The motif of the fountain in
Runaway Horse describes Klaus Buch acquiescing at an early age to the
demands of an idealized figure, in this instance Halm. The kaleidoscope
motif also reveals negative connotations: the flowers hide anti-theft bars
on the window, the colours on the lake are the prelude to the near death of
both Halm and Buch, and the locomotive represents an escape to that
which "lies beyond" hence the reference to vestments and liturgy; it also
repeats the motif of escape first introduced in conjunction with a
disillusioned Klaus Buch: "The income from one more apartment
building and they would put out to sea. Set their course for the Bahamas"
(p. 30);[437] "The one thing he was looking forward to was the Bahamas

---

zu bewegen, trabte er und kam immer tiefer hinein in Wälder, die, zum Glück,
kein Ende hatten. Wälder, die kein Ende haben, das ist überhaupt das
Vollkommene" (p. 13).

[436] Helmut Jendreiek, *Thomas Mann: Der demokratische Roman* (Düsseldorf:
August Bagel Verlag, 1977), p. 228.

[437] "Noch ein Mietshaus mehr, dann stächen sie in See. Kurs Bahamas" (p.
48).

with their steady trade wind" (p. 77);[438] "He was a fantasist. Right away he started about the Bahamas again. Off to the Bahamas with Helmut. That was his latest idea" (p. 100).[439]

The figure of Klaus Buch is perhaps the most enigmatic of the four players, with a behaviour pattern that does not correspond to the usual profile of human functionality and disability: the fluctuations from anxiety, depression and insecurity to the experience of elation, heightened sensory perception, an obsessive sex drive and feelings of omnipotence accumulate to form a picture of an individual to whose fictional construct justice cannot be done by merely re-stating the disapproval and alienation which characterize his reception by his counter-player within the text: "We are somewhat disgusted. And do so with express approval, for Helmut also squirms with embarrassment" (Kaiser, p. 837).[440] Kaiser also is of the opinion that the revelation made by Helene Buch about her husband's disability, coming as it does at the end of the novella, represents a radical change of focus, in other words, the provision of an insight into this character who could not have been seen in this light until this point has been reached: "Only at the very end, when all of the effects have been exhausted, is the remaining truth revealed. [...] Walser makes a complete fool out of the character Klaus Buch" (pp. 836-837).[441] In fact, from the point in the text when this character is introduced, a mode of behaviour and reactions that is so markedly beyond the conventional parameters of variation expected within these (in other words, beyond the merely unusual or obnoxious), is established, causing the reader to take special note of the extraordinary phenomenon which is the fictional figure of Klaus Buch. His rapid-fire speech and hyperactivity, an exaggerated optimism bordering on euphoria alternating with despondence and pronounced irritability, the terror and shrieking each time his hand is licked by the Halms' dog, the countless number of times he asks his wife if she still likes him, falling asleep on her shoulder as might a four-year-old in the presence of the Halms and insisting that Helmut reproduce verbatim (à la bedtime story) one of their former teacher's maxims, and clinging to his neck once he has done so - all of these motifs accumulate to present a

---

[438] *"Er freut sich nur noch auf die Bahamas mit ihrem ständigen Passat"* (p. 107).
[439] *"Er war ein Phantast. Sofort hat er wieder von den Bahamas angefangen. Mit Helmut auf die Bahamas. Das war sein neuester Einfall"* (p. 139).
[440] *"Wir ekeln uns ein wenig. Und tun es mit ausdrücklicher Genehmigung, denn Helmut windet sich dabei auch vor Verlegenheit."*
[441] *"... ganz zuletzt, wenn alle Effekte abgeschöpft sind, wird die andere Wahrheit nachgeliefert. [...] Walser macht diesen Klaus zum Total-Narren."*

profile of mental illness which suggest the symptoms of the affective
disorder called manic depression.[442]   Klaus Buch's hyperactivity and
involvement in many activities is clearly one of this character's traits:
"'Good God, almost eleven!' he said. [...] At six thirty A.M. he and
Hella would go for a run, at seven play tennis, then go for a sail ..." (p.
18-19).[443]   As Klaus falls asleep on his wife's shoulder, she explains the
reason for his fatigue, describing a scene in which hyperactivity is coupled
with a false sense of expertise and ability, common in manic depression:
"Hella explained that every morning for the past few days Klaus had run
five times around the track at the marina, she being the timekeeper, his
best time was 5:11, which meant Klaus must have considered himself a

---

[442] "The essential feature of a manic episode is a distinct period when the
predominant mood is elated, irritable, or expansive. [...] The elevated or
intensified mood in a manic episode has various manifestations. Some patients
are euphoric, extremely cheerful or happy. [...] Other patients are expansive:
they involve themselves in a large number of activities and may have an
insatiable craving for social interactions. They are not selective in their
involvement and are propelled by seemingly boundless enthusiasm. [...] ...
irritability may progress to hostility, belligerence, and assaultiveness. [...]
Hyperactivity is a common symptom of the manic syndrome. [...] Under the
pressure of an increased desire to be sociable, indiscriminate contacts with
distant acquaintances occur. [...] Expansiveness, grandiosity, impaired
judgement, and boundless enthusiasm frequently lead to reckless driving ... and
intense, exaggerated sexual activity. [...] Some manic individuals accost
strangers and attempt to engage them in ... unrealistic schemes. Speech is
commonly rapid or pressured. [...] Telling jokes, making puns or plays on
words, and a preoccupation with unimportant but amusing details are common.
Dramatic or exaggerated forms of expression such as singing or gesturing may
occur. The sound of words may enchant the patient, leading to clanging, a
phenomenon characterized by word selection based on sounds rather than
meanings. The irritable individual is prone to hostile tirades when frustrated.
[...] It is not uncommon for the manic to believe that he or she is an expert on
a topic of which he or she is not. [...] Rapid shifts in mood (lability) is
commonly associated with manic syndrome. This phenomenon is characterized
by an abrupt change from exuberance and elation to anger or depression." Jon
A. Bell, "Affective Disorder," *Psychiatry* Ed. H. Scully (Media, Pennsylvania:
Harwal Publishing Company, 1985) pp. 51-52.
[443] "'*Mein Gott, bald elf,' sagte er. [...] Morgens um halb sieben laufen sie,
um sieben spielen sie Tennis, vormittags segeln sie ...*" (p. 33).

superchampion runner ..."(p. 41).[444] While on the ill-fated hike through the rain, Helene happens upon a piano in the inn where the couples are to have lunch; playing this instrument causes a dramatic show of despondence in Buch: he will later be shown to have decreed his wife's talent to be mediocre in a bid to establish complete dominance - an indicator of the manic depressive's narcissitic vulnerability:

> They saw Klaus Buch dashing wildly off. Clear across
> the meadows. Suddenly he stopped, changed direction,
> ran toward a tree, leaned against the trunk, put his hands
> in his pockets, and stared straight ahead (p. 56).[445]

Buch's notion of a worthwhile hike sets its minimum duration at six hours ("For herself and Klaus, a hike was something not to be accomplished in less than six hours") (p. 57)[446] and his driving habits are also in accordance with the frenetic profile of this illness: "He stepped on the gas, then immediately had to brake, they were already there" (p. 75).[447] Another repetitive element in the characterization of Klaus Buch is that of elated mood, boundless enthusiasm, rapid speech coupled with an abrupt change from elation and exuberance to despondency. After a hiatus of twenty-three years, the enthusiasm with which Klaus Buch is gripped at this chance meeting with someone who was more of a tormentor than a friend ("Just because his parents had had a big house on the hill, ... Helmut had ... tried, sometimes successfully, to incite the other kids not to walk home with Klaus Buch") (p. 31),[448] illustrates the "indiscriminate contacts" associated with the disorder:

---

[444]   "*Hel erklärte, daß Klaus seit einigen Tagen jeden Morgen auf den Sportplatz ... fünf Runden gelaufen sei; ... beste Zeit, 5:11; ... also habe Klaus sich für ein läuferisches Genie halten müssen*" (p. 62).

[445]   "*Sie sahen Klaus Buch in einem geradezu wilden Tempo fortrennen. Quer über die Wiesen. Plötzlich stoppte er, änderte seine Richtung, rannte weiter, auf einen Baum zu, lehnte sich an den Stamm, steckte die Hände in die Tasche und sah vor sich hin*" (p. 81).

[446]   "*Für sie und Klaus sei Wanderung etwas, was nicht unter sechs Stunden zu erledigen sei*" (p. 82).

[447]   "*Er drückte aufs Gas, mußte gleich wieder bremsen, man war schon da*" (p. 105).

[448]   "*... Helmut ... habe sogar Mitschüler, zeitweise erfolgreich, aufgehetzt, nicht mit Klaus Buch heimzugehen*") (p. 50).

Well, if that isn't a joke, Helmut! Say, Helmut, what do
you say to that? [...] This Klaus Buch couldn't stop
enthusing about his boyhood friend Helmut. [...] A sort
of   ingrown   single-mindedness   [inzüchtige
Zielsüchtigkeit].   Saint Frantic in person [die heilige
Hektik in Person]   Simply inflamed.   Barefoot and
inflamed, that's the only way he knew his Helmut (pp.
10-11).[449]

The "clanging," not rendered in the English translation of this
passage, and the expansiveness described above is also in evidence at the
next encounter in the narrative sequence: "Klaus Buch evidently preferred
to recount the past in drastic terms.   [...]   Klaus Buch was simply
churning with sounds, smells, noises; the past heaved and steamed as if it
were more alive than the present" (p. 16),[450] yet Buch's mood is
immediately altered by the unwanted affection of the Halms' dog:

...this time, since they were sitting in one of the Hecht's
old, low-ceilinged rooms, the sound was so dreadful that
even Helmut leaped up, that even people at other tables,
even in the other rooms, leaped up. [...]

On his return, Klaus Buch failed to find the thread to lead
him back into his orgy of memories. For a while he and
Hella looked on silently ... (pp. 17-18).[451]

Similarly, Buch's mood on the first sailing expedition changes
from one of unbounded enthusiasm with respect to his attachment to the
Lake Constance area, to irritation at the "millions" some academic is said

[449] "Also, wenn das nicht lustig ist, Helmut. Mensch Helmut, wie findest du
das? [...] Dieser Klaus Buch konnte nicht aufhören, von seinem Jugendfreund
Helmut zu schwärmen.   [...]   So eine inzüchtige Zielsüchtigkeit.   [...] Die
heilige Hektik in Person" (p. 23).
[450] "Klaus Buch erzählte das Vergangene am liebsten drastisch.   [...]   Bei
Klaus Buch rollte es nur so von Tönen, Gerüchen, Geräuschen: das
Vergangene wogte und dampfte ..." (p. 30).
[451] " ... diesmal war der Schrei, weil sie in einer der alten niederen Hecht-
Stuben saßen, so furchtbar, das auch Helmut aufsprang, daß auch Leute an
anderen Tischen, in Nebenstuben sogar aufsprangen. [...]
Als Klaus zurückkam, fand er nicht mehr in die Erinnerungsfeier hinein. Er
und Hel schauten eine Zeit lang stumm zu ..." (p. 32).

to have made with a bogus theory, to one of horror at his wife's ironic remark that his book on nutrition is precisely the type of swindle he wishes he could undertake:

> Meanwhile Klaus had become so enamored of the area that he was planning a big book about Lake Constance, to be called: *Let Europe Drink Thy Waters.*

> Klaus Buch said it was time to put an end to that fraud over there. He pointed to the prehistoric lake dwellings of Unteruhldingen that they happened to be passing. [...] "If I felt the urge to achieve something, it would be a fraud with a solid foundation, a real live proposition." "But haven't you achieved that?" laughed Hella. "The seventy-five thousand people who eat according to your books are pretty real, aren't they?" For a moment he looked at Hella aghast - his tongue was working against the inside of his upper lip, bulging it out as if the tongue were imprisoned there - then he laughed, louder than Hella had laughed. [...] Then he turned to Hella, and said in a deadly serious, utterly hopeless, tone: "You don't care for me anymore, do you?" (pp. 28-29).[452]

Clanging, expansiveness, ebullient good humour and sudden irritability also mark the scene in the inn on the couples' hiking adventure, following on the heels of the crisis provoked by Helene's impromptu piano performance:

---

[452] *"Klaus sei inzwischen so in die Gegend vernarrt, daß er ein großes Bodenseebuch plane. Titel: Laß Europa aus dir trinken. [...] Klaus Buch sagte, mit dem Schwindel da drüben sollte man auch einmal aufräumen. Er zeigte auf die Unteruhldinger Pfahlbauten ... Wenn ich zu etwas Lust hätte, dann wäre es ein Schwindel, der Hand und Fuß hat... Das hast du doch geschafft, sagte, lachend, Hel. Die fünfundsiebzig tausend Leute, die nach deinen Büchern essen, sind doch ziemlich real. Er schaute Hel einen Augenblick lang entsetzt an - seine Zunge arbeitete von innen gegen die Oberlippe und wulstete die Oberlippe, als halte die sie gefangen -, dann lachte er lauter als Hel gelacht hatte. [...] Dann sagte er in einem furchtbar ernsten, geradezu hoffnungslosen Ton zu Hel: Du magst mich nicht mehr, gell?" (pp. 45-46).*

Helmut told him they were already there. This made
Klaus Buch laugh so uproariously that he had to stand
up. "The Höchste" he kept shouting. "The Höchste,
Hella would you believe it, we're on the Höchste - 'the
Highest' -by God, I'd call this the *All*-highest!" [...]

Klaus Buch swore at the food. To begin with, his
schnitzel was too thickly breaded; secondly, it was pork
instead of veal; thirdly, the salad was a limp mess. He
did not spare the waitress. (pp. 56-57).[453]

Lability (mood swing), clanging, hyperactivity and exaggerated
forms of expression are also in evidence in the sequence leading up to the
storm:

Helmut had to help hoist the sails. Klaus Buch would
insist on merrily calling out each instruction two to four
times, as if Helmut were an idiot. Even so, Klaus Buch
frequently had to come skipping across to show Helmut
where to put his hand. [...] Klaus Buch cursed Lake
Constance. That it was an impotent old bag, could only
do it once a day ... Just look around: a landscape of
muggy, floppy rags, just look, those houses over there,
and those hills, just look, the sky, everything hanging,
hanging, hanging ... What a shit of a lake. [...] We are
in the realm of the dead. Dreary isn't the word for it
[*Farbloses farblos im Farblosen*]. So all we can do is
chew the rag. Let's chew the rag then.
He said this with incredible ferocity, his loose lips and
unruly tongue moving in an obscene parody of speech
(pp. 75-76).[454]

---

[453] "*Helmut sagte, man sei schon droben. Da kriegte Klaus Buch einen
Lachanfall, daß er aufstehen mußte. 'Der Höchste,' rief er immer wieder, 'der
Höchste, Hel, was sagst du dazu, wir sind auf dem Höchsten, also diesen Berg
würde ich einfach den Allerhöchsten taufen.' [...] Klaus Buch fluchte auf das
Essen. Erstens war ihm die Panierung zu dick, zweitens war das
Schweinefleisch, drittens war der Salat ein Matsch. Er tat nichts, um die
Bedienung zu schonen" (pp. 82-83).*

[454] "*Helmut mußte helfen, die Segel zu setzen. Klaus Buch hörte nicht auf, ihm
im fröhlichsten Ton alle Anweisungen zwei- bis viermal zuzurufen. [...]
Trotzdem mußte Klaus Buch des öfteren herantanzen und Helmut auch noch*

Klaus Buch's obsession with sexual matters, his intense activity and his preoccupation with and revelation of intimate details relating to this area also figure prominently in the text. The first example of public intimacy occurs after one of the many times Klaus is reassured by his wife that she still likes him: "He quickly turned his head so that her kiss landed on his mouth. Then he ran his tongue all around his lips so as not to lose one particle of Hella's kiss" (p. 29).[455] Another statement which fits within this rubric is made by Buch with respect to the intimacies Halm enjoys with his wife as well as to the Buchs' own variation on this theme:

> He was sure that Helmut, who, even as a boy, had been past master of the bizarre, had developed a gorgeously, heavily ritualized art of screwing. It was a good thing that nowadays everyone could screw to his own taste. Hella and he, for instance, were into bouncing. That had literally nauseated his first wife (p. 30).[456]

The most objectionable manifestation of Buch's bizarre preoccupation with the "nitty-gritty" of sexual matters also occurs at this point in the text. Its recognition as a symptom, were there no broader basis of evidence, would be a tenuous abstraction, since this motif could be explained at the level of the text's vehicle - as a form of revenge for having been ostracized by Halm due to his wealthy background, or indeed as proof that Buch was able to "measure up" after all:

---

die Hand führen. [...] Klaus Buch fluchte auf den Bodensee. Ein impotenter Sack sei das, der könne nur einmal am Tag ... Jetzt schaue sich das einer an: eine Landschaft aus schwülen Lappen, schau, die Häuser da und dort, die Hügel, schau, der Himmel, alles hängt, hängt, hängt ... Das ist schon ein Scheißsee. [...] Wir sind im Totenreich. Farbloses farblos im Farblosen. [...] Jetzt müssen wir halt quatschen. [...] Er sagte das märchenhaft wild und machte dabei mit seinen unbefestigten Lippen und der ungebärdigen Zunge unflätige, das Sprechen parodierende Bewegungen" (pp. 105-107).
[455] *"Er hatte rasch seinen Kopf so gedreht, daß ihr Kuß seinen Mund traf. Danach leckte er seine Lippen um die Lippen herum, damit auch gar nichts von Hels Kuß verlorengehe" (p. 47).*
[456] *"Er sei sicher, daß Helmut, der schon in seiner Jugend ein Meister der Bizarrerie gewesen sei, eine schön düstere und reich ritualisierte Bumskultur entwickelt habe. Zum Glück sei man so weit, daß heute jeder nach seiner Façon bumsen könne. Hel und er, zum Beispiel, stünden unheimlich aufs Federn. Seiner ersten Frau sei es dabei echt schlecht gewesen" (p. 48).*

If during their group masturbation he hadn't been able to
prove that his penis was the equal of any other, he would
really have been desperate. [...] But the one who got the
biggest laugh had been Helmut, Klaus Buch cried
ecstatically. [...] For in those days Helmut had had -
something he surely no longer was bothered with - a
knotty problem with his foreskin. A real little cauliflower
of a foreskin at the orifice, that's what Helmut had had.
Needless to say, that had interfered with a fine, long-
range jet. [...] Pulling it back was unfeasible. Much too
painful. So what does our Helmut do? Takes his thumb
and forefinger and pinches the skin in front firmly
together. Lets his water come. Holds on tight. The skin
balloon fills and fills. And when it's about to burst, our
HH fires away. [...] Sheer ambition has made our HH
aim steeper than steep and he squirts the whole lot into
his own face (pp. 31-32).[457]

This anecdote is followed by yet another which matches the
previous one in terms of Buch's elated mood in playing the role of an
exhibitionist-narrator:

The rest were all rubbing away nicely, it was dark, of
course, we couldn't turn on the light, or talk, so we
thought we all had the delicious agony of our lust well
under way when suddenly we heard Helmut's voice
saying very, very softly: "Now I've got to the real thing."

---

[457] *"Wenn er nicht bei der Gruppenonanie hätte beweisen können, daß sein
Geschlechtsteil es mit jedem anderen aufnehmen konnte, wäre er wirklich
verzweifelt damals. [...] Aber den größten Lacherfolg schaffte doch Helmut,
rief Klaus Buch voller Freude. [...] Helmut habe nämlich damals, was er
inzwischen ja sicher längst nicht mehr habe, knifflige Vorhautprobleme gehabt.
So einen richtigen Blumenkohlsträußel von Vorhaut habe Helmut vor der
Mündung gehabt. Da sei natürlich kein schlanker, weithin reichender Strahl
möglich gewesen. [...] Zurückziehen ging nicht. Tat viel zu weh. Was also tut
unser Helmut? Klemmt vorne die Haut mit Daumen und Zeigefinger ganz
zusammen. Läßt Wasser kommen. Hält fest zu. [...] Und als er zum Platzen
voll ist, spritzt unser Ha-Ha los. [...] Vor lauter Ehrgeiz hat unser Ha-Ha
steiler als steil gezielt und spritzt sich die ganze Ladung selber ins Gesicht"* (p.
51).

[...] Klaus repeated the words Helmut was supposed to
have said and explained that everyone in that cellar had
immediately grasped that for the first time our HH had
managed to pull back his foreskin over the glans (p.
33).[458]

The final example of this motif of a compulsive libidinal focus,
exuberance, expansiveness and clanging in the form of alliteration and
repetition and the tendency to propose unrealistic schemes, occurs in the
scene preceding the storm, in which Buch declares himself in effect to be a
master in the art of living and an expert in solving existential (read sexual)
crises and proposes the scheme of a retreat to the Bahamas:

When a raindrop splashes onto my skin, I could scream
with delight. When I look up into a tree, I could shriek
for love of chlorophyll. [...] I'd like to stay brilliant, you
know? Bright. Outstanding. And noble. Noble through
and through. Like untearable silk, that's what I'd like to
be. Raw silk, of course.
[...] ... Helmut, if you come along to the Bahamas, it'll
be the salvation of both of us. [...] ... Helmut would be
... welcome to consult him if in need of reassurance as to
the length of his penis; [...] If each of them remained
alone, each would have to wangle his own miserable way
through life, seizing loot, securing loot, consuming loot,
seizing more loot, and so on.
Helmut, man, let's aim for the top. [...] Remain great.
Become greater. The greatest. We two are the greatest, I
swear it. Life is calling us. I'll get you out of your
doldrums, kiddo. I'll fix you up again. [...] I'll turn you
on, man. I'll put such an appetite into your belly, you'll
go straight up in the air, want to bet? First of all, you'll
come to us in Starnberg. [...] Helmut, man, in
Starnberg, you know, I often sit naked on the terrace
from four to seven in the morning, listening to the birds.

---

[458] "*Wir anderen waren schon alle ganz schön am Reiben, ... da hörten wir
plötzlich Helmuts Stimme ganz leise sagen: Jetzt bin ich ans Pure gekommen.
[...] Klaus wiederholte den Satz, den Helmut gesagt haben sollte, und erklärte,
jeder in diesem Keller habe sofort verstanden, daß es unserem Ha-Ha jetzt zum
ersten Mal gelungen sei, seine Vorhaut über die Eichel zurückzuziehen*" (p.
52).

[...] My dear Helmut, that's when I have to go indoors ...
and although I'm in the mood to shout and stamp, to leap
in the air, dive onto her, no, I snuggle up to her and
caress her awake, but even before she is quite awake I
have the seduction already in place so that, when she
opens her eyes, when her lips part, she already desires me
(pp. 78-82).[459]

In her monograph on depression, Edith Jacobsen observes that
"Manic-depressives show a special kind of infantile narcissistic
dependency on their love object. They require a constant supply of love
and moral support from a highly valued love object."[460]
This is rendered in the text through Klaus Buch's repeated
rhetorical question "You don't care for me anymore, do you?" The
interpretation of the character of Klaus Buch as a manic depressive is only
one of the two plausible hypotheses to be derived from the hermetic motif
complex which constitutes his depiction. The other, as indicated above, is
that many items in his behaviour are indicative of substance abuse,
specifically one of the hallucinogens, LSD, as alluded to by Buch's wild
exclamation "Lucy in the sky." The most significant point in enabling the
premise of this interpretive duality is the fact that in many individuals,

---

[459] *"Wenn mir ein Regentropfen auf der Haut zerplatzt, könnte ich schreien vor
Begeisterung. Wenn ich in einen Baum schaue, könnte ich aufschreien vor
Liebe zum Chlorophyll. [...] Ich möchte brilliant bleiben, verstehst du.
Glänzend. Großartig. Und fein. Durchdringend fein. Unzerreißbare Seide
möchte ich sein. Wildseide, versteht sich. [...] Helmut, wenn du mitkommst
auf die Bahamas, sind wir beide gerettet. [...] Helmut könne zu Klaus Buch
kommen ... wenn er sich lediglich hinsichtlich der Länge seines Glieds
beruhigen wolle; [...] Wir zwei sind die größten, ich schwöre dir. [...] Dich
turn ich an, Mensch. Dir mache ich einen Appetit in den Leib, daß du
senkrecht in die Luft gehst, wetten? Du kommst zuerst einmal zu uns nach
Starnberg. [...] Mensch, Helmut, in Starnberg, verstehst du, in Starnberg sitze
ich morgens oft von vier bis sieben nackt auf der Terasse und höre den Vögeln
zu. [...] ...da muß ich hinein ... und ... obwohl ich lieber brüllen würde,
stampfen, hochspringen, mich auf sie hechten, nein ... ich ... zärtle sie wach,
aber schon bevor sie ganz wach ist, placier ich die Verführung, daß sie, wenn
sie die Augen aufschlägt, wenn die Lippen sich lösen, mich schon will." (pp.
108-114).*
[460] Edith Jacobsen, *Depression. Comparative Studies of Normal, Neurotic and
Psychotic Conditions* (New York: International Universities Press, Inc., 1971)
pp. 231-232.

both during the immediate hallucinogenic state and well after the peak of the drug's impact, symptoms are observed which are the same as the affective disorder of manic depression:

> The acute paranoid state develops when the tripper becomes exceedingly suspicious or grandiose ... Suspiciousness can result in mindless running from, or assaulting, the object of one's suspicions. Grandiosity, more common, can culminate in megalomaniac ideas of omniscience and indestructibility. [...] Almost every variant of emotional disorder has been seen in the period following the LSD experience. Perhaps the most common is the chronic anxiety state. [...] A few persons have ... phobias or strange body symptoms. [...] Manic states and psychotic depressions also are observed. These mimic their naturally occurring counterparts.[461]

Buch's reaction to the feeling of the Halms' dog's tongue on his hand represents the most visible manifestation of anxiety and paranoia, and occurs as a repeated motif; the first example of Buch's dog-phobia is presented right after this character is introduced: "Suddenly Klaus Buch jumped up with a shriek and waved one hand about as if it had been burned and pierced by a bullet" (p. 10).[462] The next occurrence is in the "*Hecht-Stube*," as cited above. The scene is repeated in the next wine bar visited by the couples:

> Suddenly Klaus Buch yelled: "No!" Sabina said: "Now it's happened" Helmut shouted: "Otto, down." Klaus Buch stood holding up one hand with the other as if it were seriously injured. [...] Klaus, still clutching his hand, said: "He's got such a cold wet tongue, Christ you've no idea. And always me, why always me? Can you explain that? (pp. 39-40).[463]

---

[461] Sidney Cohen, *The Drug Dilemma* (New York: McGraw-Hill Book Company, 1969), pp. 30-32.

[462] "*Plötzlich fuhr Klaus Buch mit einem hellen Schrei hoch und schüttelte eine Hand durch die Luft, als sei ihm gerade verbrannt oder durchschossen worden*" (p. 22).

[463] "*Plötzlich schrie Klaus Buch: Nein. [...] Klaus Buch stand, hielt mit der einen Hand die andere, als sei die schwer verletzt. [...] Klaus, weiterhin seine Hand haltend, sagte: Er hat eine so kalte, nasse Zunge, Mensch, du hast doch*

Similarly, when the Buchs fetch the Halms for their exploration of the countryside, Buch is not able to drive for fear of being licked: "But Klaus wouldn't reach for the gear shift for fear that Otto would take the opportunity to lick his hand" (p. 51).[464]   All of the motifs cited in conjunction with the interpretation of the manic state can be seen as psychoactive effects of hallucinogens.   The euphoria alternating with despondency, the importance attached to one's own thoughts, the ability to recall details from the past and increased aesthetic perception are all ascribed to the action of the drug:

> ... self-boundaries seem to disintegrate; and the user soon comes to feel a sense of oneness with the universe. There may also be a sense of unusual clarity, and one's thoughts may begin to assume extraordinary importance. Moods may change radically, from gaiety to depression, from elation to fear, or vice versa. [...] Some regard the use of LSD as a form of psychotherapy, since they believe it increases one's self-knowledge and self-awareness, largely through the recall of old and hitherto buried memories.[465]

Also the motifs of increased libidinal impulse and the wish to drop out (Buch's repeated wish to go the Bahamas) are a part of the syndrome.[466]   Buch displays this aspect with his remark to the effect that

---

überhaupt keine Ahnung. Und immer bloß mich, warum denn immer bloß mich" (p. 60).

[464] *"Aber Klaus konnte die Hand nicht an den Schaltknüppel legen, weil er Angst hatte, Otto werde das ausnützen und seine Hand ablecken"* (p. 76.)

[465] Patricia M. Wald and Peter Barton Hutt, *Dealing with Drug Abuse : A Report to the Ford Foundation* (New York, Washington, London: Praeger Publishers, 1972) p. 92.

[466] "After taking acid I suddenly realized that what was important in the world and beautiful were the flowers and the sun and the sky and the grass and I recognized that all the games we play every day, all that materialistic crap, is just a lot of bullshit. I knew I didn't want to play those games anymore and I decided to drop out, live my life in contemplation and appreciation of the beauty around me. [...] There is no question that LSD is the most powerful aphrodisiac ever discovered by man. The three inevitable goals of the LSD session are to discover and make love with God, to discover and make love with yourself, and to discover and make love with a woman." Timothy Leary, as

life is too short to neglect love-making for work: "Klaus Buch said life was too short to waste it on work. ... 'Only people who are sexually inadequate need work'" (p. 68).[467] Although there is no scientific evidence to support the claim that LSD is a physical aphrodisiac (Louria, p. 146), it is said to cause mental eroticism: "The images one sees, the figures, the fantasies ... may be viewed in the delusional experiences in overwhelmingly erotic fashion" (p. 146). It would seem rather spurious to claim that the information provided to the Halms by Helene Buch on her husband's true character comes as a surprise. Among other items, she mentions that he considered all of life's undertakings to be fraudulent (p. 98 / p. 136), that he often would awaken in a cold sweat (p. 98 / p. 137), that he had become belligerent and assaultive (p.100 / p. 139), that he did not know how to deal with people (p. 99 / p. 138), that in his work he pushed himself beyond the limits of his abilities (p. 98 / p. 136). These are the very traits whose revelation is prepared through the motif strands discussed above: paranoia, profound insecurity and anxiety, hyperactivity and aggression. Finally, if one calls to mind the definition of the grotesque as "the unresolved clash of incompatibles," (cf. chapter four) causing both bemusement and aversion, hence disorientation, the manic extremes through which this character is concretized may be readily described as an example of the grotesque. Thus the figure of Klaus Buch goes far beyond representing the fool, as Kaiser would have it. He in fact presents the reader with an instance of interpretive difficulty, of disorientation, as does Helmut Halm with the open question of his disability and rehabilitation; in this sense, the characterizations of these *dramatis personae* are entirely up to the standard of the other writerly texts dicussed in this study.

The last element of Walser's *Runaway Horse* to be considered is the symbol contained within the title and described in the scene in which Buch subdues a runaway horse. In his discussion of Walser's novella, Albrecht Weber has observed that the image of a horse that has bolted and is recaptured symbolizes both Halm's and Buch's attempts to remove themselves from the scrutiny imposed on every person in a social and cultural context: "Breaking away from society leads back into the same society; escape is impossible, since neither the individual nor the social

---

cited in Donald B. Louria, *The Drug Scene* (New York, Toronto, London, Sydney: McGraw-Hill Book Company, 1968) pp. 144-145.
[467] "*Klaus Buch sagte, das Leben sei zu kurz, als das man es mit Arbeit vergeuden dürfe [...] Nur Leute, die erotisch nicht völlig da sind, brauchen Arbeit.*" (p. 97)

determinants can be changed" (pp. 292-293).[468] Weber's exegesis of this symbol includes the specific relevancy of the fleeing horse as a trope for Helmut Halm's encounter with Klaus Buch:

> The symbol of the fleeing horse would then be tailored specifically to fit Klaus Buch. [...] In nature Klaus Buch could "identify with ... a runaway horse" (62). He knows "You should never stand in the path of Runaway Horse," but in dealing with a human being he blindly blocks Helmut off from the front, does not afford him the chance to avoid confrontation, ... but rather exacerbates his aggression to the point of eruption (p. 293).[469]

Exception must be taken with the assertion that Halm's act is one of blind aggression: it is an act of the will to survive with the unintended consequence of Buch's brush with death.[470] More correct is Weber's recognition of the possibility of a connotation of Eros through the symbol of the horse: "Halm called himself ironically 'a horseman from way back.' Indirectly he is evoking the totemic bond between horse and human, the erotic symbolism of the stallion" (293).[471] Through the concept developed by Lacan of the concomitant deferment of meaning and

---

[468] *"Ausbruch aus der Gesellschaft endet in der Gesellschaft, aus der keine Flucht möglich ist, weil weder die individuellen noch die sozialen ... Bedingungen geändert werden (können)."*

[469] *"Das Symbol des fliehenden Pferdes wäre also eindeutig auf Helmut Halm zugeschnitten. [...] Klaus Buch konnte sich zwar in der Natur "in ein fliehendes Pferd hineindenken" und wußte, daß man "nicht von vorne auf das Pferd zugehen darf' (90), im Umgang mit Menschen aber geht er blind und frontal Helmut Halm an, läßt ihn nicht ausweichen ... sondern steigert dessen Aggressionen bis zum blinden Ausbruch."*

[470] "When Helmut saw that the waves washing aboard were about to pour into the cockpit, he kicked the tiller out of Klaus Buch's hand. Then everything happened at once. The boat shot back into the wind. Klaus Buch toppled backward into the water ... The boat righted itself" (p. 86). (*"Als Helmut sah, daß die über Bord laufenden Wellen jetzt gleich ins Cockpit schlagen würden, stieß er mit einem Fuß Klaus Buch die Pinne aus der Hand. Jetzt passierte alles gleichzeitig. Das Boot schoß wieder in den Wind. Klaus Buch stürzte rückwärts ins Wasser. Das Boot richtete sich auf"*) (p. 120).

[471] *"Halm nannte sich ironisch einen 'alten Ritter' (91). Indirekt sprach er damit die totemartige Verbundenheit des Menschen mit dem Pferd an, die erotische Symbolik des Hengstes ..."* (p. 293).

the deferment of desire, described by Brooks as the elusive achievement of "proper integration in the course of life and death," ("*Symbolization and Fictionmaking*," p. 219) as well through consideration of a mythological level to the symbolism of the horse, it is possible to expand Weber's suggestion to a more complete hypothesis. A mythological interpretation is in part indicated as a plausible path for the exegesis of the confrontation with the forces of nature (both horse and water) through the language of the fictional figure who nearly succumbs to its power:

> Christ, how they used to sail in the Aegean. They had to tie each other to the boat or they would have been washed overboard. [...] Once they sailed from Thasos to Rhodes more under and through the waves than over the top of them (pp. 76-77).[472]

Klaus Buch's subduing the horse yet nearly perishing in a watery cataclysm evokes the mythological figures of Pegasus, his creator, the god Poseidon, god of the sea ("Pegasus can be related partly to the original horse nature of Poseidon as a sky and earth god") and the hero Bellerophon.[473] Bellerophon is the mythical figure who was assisted in conquering the Chimera by the winged horse Pegasus. "But Bellerophon's success went to his head ... when he tried to force his way into the company of the gods on Olympus by trying to ascend to the celestial city on Pegasus, the winged horse threw him ..." (Reinhold, p. 321). Reinhold notes that Pegasus, in addition to the Roman transformation of this symbol into one of immortality, also represents creativity, "flights of the imagination," and is said to have created Mt. Helicon, the seat of the Muses, with the stamp of his hoof. (p. 156). Both Klaus Buch and Helmut Halm are shown in the text to be in a struggle with deferred integration, both in the abstract sense of the mind as well as the concrete sense of the body, leading to the final stopping place of death. Buch's initial struggle with nature is successful in his subduing of the horse, a trope for aspiring to a deferment of mortality, but also a deferment of the acceptance of the fact that rationality cannot provide an answer to the paradox that existence leads only to non-existence; Halm's experience has been not to attempt to overcome but to ignore or de-

---

[472] "*Mein Gott, wie sind sie in der Ägäis gesegelt. Anbinden mußten sie einander, sonst wären sie über Bord gespült worden. [...] Einmal sind sie von Thassos nach Rhodos mehr unter den Wellen durch als über sie hin*" (p. 107).
[473] Meyer Reinhold, *Past and Present: The Continuity of Classical Myths* (Toronto: Hakkert, 1972) p. 424.

emphasize the physical aspect of his being - he would not have been capable of such a physical feat and in a symbolic sense this lack permits the valorization of *Thanatos* over *Eros*, the lethargy and ease of decay into nothingness over the will to live to the fullest capacity in defiance of death, in contradistinction to Buch's position, which is the obverse of this emphasis. The second encounter with nature shows, however, that only a balance of both forces is possible; whichever is repressed will eventually force its way into recognition: Buch nearly destroys himself and Halm clings to life ("... you actually lived in that instant, you went out of yourself, HH, for an instant you failed to maintain your pretense, this is the instant you are stuck with ...") (p. 93).[474] On a metafictional plane, this outcome of events indicates the greater viability of the "position behind the position," of the poetic, iconoclastic discourse of deferred meaning, the admission of ambivalence and the power of flights of the imagination, tempered by the needs and constraints of physical, mortal existence, over the hollow discourse of, and acquiescence to the majority view.

The intertextuality of the novella's citations of the works of Kierkegaard is of particular significance in describing the way in which the motif complex and the various strata emanating from this nexus cohere. Aside from the epigraph, which connotes the inability of the logical, referential discourse of metonymy to render the "truth" of ultimate meaning, to reconcile the insular discourse of interacting subjects, the text's protagonist expresses the desire to acquaint himself with Kierkegaard's diaries, from which the following excerpt is provided on two occasions as examples of his act of reading:

> *During my sojourn here in Gilleleie I visited Esrom, Fredensborg, Frederickvaerk and Tidsvilde. The latter is known chiefly for Saint Helen's Spring, to which the entire local population makes a pilgrimage on Midsummer Day* (pp. 92 & 106).[475]

---

[474] "... *du hast eben gelebt in diesem Augenblick, du bist aus dir herausgegangen, Ha-Ha, eine Sekunde lang hast du den Schein nicht geschafft, an dieser Sekunde klebst du jetzt ...*" (p. 129).

[475] "*Während meines Aufenthaltes hier in Gilleleie habe ich Esrom besucht, Fredensborg, Frederickvaerk und Tidsvilde. Der letzte Ort ist vornehmlich durch die Helenenquelle bekannt, wohin die ganze Umgegend zur Zeit des Johannistages wallfahrtet*" (pp. 128 & 147).

Of the four Danish localities referred to here, two are of subsidiary significance for the novella: Fredensborg is the seat of Danish royalty, hence a repetition of the motif of Neuschwanstein, and Frederickvaerk is a coastal area, thus topographically similar to the locale of Überlingen/Nußdorf. More importantly, reference is made to the feast of Saint John the Baptist, a possible reference to a rebirth which Halm has experienced during his immersion in the waters of Lake Constance. This feast also coincides with the summer solstice, marking the beginning of the high point of the natural seasonal cycle of growth and blossoming. Linked with this reference to the cycle of monumental time, a structural motif employed by Dürrenmatt in his treatment of the theme of women's individuation, is the mention of a pilgrimage to a spring, a source of renewed vitality, which carries the name Helene. The Halms' destination of Montpellier has already been described as a type of homage to Helene Buch, a corrective step over the original destination of Meran, associated with the insular, disintegrating "self-conquerer," Klaus Buch. The change in destination is underlined through the repetition of the vocabulary item "pilgrimage" ("*Wallfahrt*"), used first to describe the initial attraction to this figure:

> By whistling, stopping to look at trees, and commenting on Birnau church lying up there so loftily ... Helmut tried to prevent their walk to the hotel Seehalde from looking like a pilgrimage to Klaus Buch (p. 23).[476]

A closer investigation of the significance of Kierkegaard as the source of this intertextuality also permits an understanding of the linkage between the two types of integration which are deferred: the ironic epistemic quest along a chain of signifiers who, through their presence, both constitute and of necessity indicate the absence of that which they signify, and the erotic quest for the non-differentiation of the womb. In his monograph on Kierkegaard, John Vignaux Smyth observes of this analogy:

> ... the structure of the ironic relation here is that of *abrogated or interrupted erotic desire*, a movement of desire ... toward a moment of "possession" that never occurs. [...] The ... unironical subject "constantly seeks

---

[476] "*Durch Pfeifen, Bäumebetrachten und einen Kommentar über die hoch erhaben daliegende Kirche Birnau ... versuchte Helmut zu verhindern, daß der Gang zum Hotel Seehalde als eine Wallfahrt zu Klaus Buch erscheine*" (p. 39).

to penetrate the object, and his misfortune consists in the
fact that the object constantly eludes him" (p. 274). The
ironic subject, however, believes full well that objects like
the soul and the Ideas are inevitably "recalcitrant" and
"impenetrable" (p. 106) and that intellectual possession is
fictional in this sense *to the same extent* as erotic
possession. He is thus "always seeking to get outside the
object, and this he attains by becoming conscious that the
object has no reality" (p. 274). On the other hand, we
may see that irony also achieves a certain very real kind
of power, potency, or mastery, through playing on the
very fiction of possession that it exceeds and strives to
demystify.[477]

The end of the fiction of *Runaway Horse* shows the beginning of
a journey to a place which symbolizes the sharing of the elusive quest to
be integral; the recognition is reached that reality is a construct reached
through a bringing together of the sometimes poorly illuminated
perception of individuals, (sewing shadows together / *"Schatten
zusammennähen"*) and the text underlines this through the relativization
and de-idealization of its own content by turning back on itself, explicitly
underlining its own fictional character.

---

[477] John Vignaux Smyth, *A Question of Eros: Irony in Sterne, Kierkegaard,
and Barthes* (Tallahassee: Florida State University Press), pp. 218-222.
Citations from Sören Kierkegaard, *The Concept of Irony: With Constant
Reference to Socrates* Translated by David Swenson and Lillian Swenson.
Revised by Howard A. Johnson. (Princeton: Princeton University Press, 1959).

Martin Walser's *Jenseits der Liebe*

Walser's novel, so designated on the title page, comprises a theme complex which overlaps to some extent with that of *Runaway Horse*. The title of the text bears a close resemblance to Freud's *Beyond the Pleasure Principle (Jenseits des Lustprinzips)*, a seminal work in its proposal of the observation of a death drive within the psychic apparatus. The novel's leading character, Franz Horn very clearly demonstrates this degenerative impulse as part of a major affective disorder, culminating in an attempt to commit suicide. The novel describes the final days of decline leading to this event. Horn undertakes a last trip as a sales representative for a company manufacturing dentures, a firm which he has helped to build but in which he has become redundant and subordinate to a younger, more highly trained and educated colleague. The downward turn in his career has caused domestic strife - the technique of flashback is used to describe the abuse to which he had begun to subject his wife and children; flashback also is employed to show the strained relationship in the work environment and his decline in an exploitative situation. Horn is shown returning home after failing in this venture, finally succumbing to his acute despondency in a suicide attempt. Among the symptoms of the illness which manifest themselves repeatedly throughout the text are a pronounced dysphoric mood, lethargy and motionlessness (patients are clinically described as "psychomotorically retarded"), self reproach and excessive guilt, fatigue and disruption of normal sleep patterns, and a change in appetite, in Horn's case, a craving for food. (Cf. Bell, p. 52). Here too, the narcotization motif is an element with a high repetition frequency. The problem of elusive and deferred meaning is also touched upon, that of the "dramaturgy of the subject," although it is not clearly treated as a necessary or inescapable "given" of every interaction between subjects, but rather as a symptom of Horn's illness: in other words, this motif does not open up possibilities of interpretation on the metaphoric axis, but rather is anchored in the metonymy of its fictional referentiality, perhaps reflecting Horn's inability to stand above the dilemma and immediacy of an overwhelming web of obstructions:

> One and the same person suddenly appeared to him one way and then to be completely different. Could that possibly be related to his own changing needs? Was that why he sometimes saw Thiele a certain way and at other times quite differently? He had finally concluded that

Thiele simply was as he thought he was, but that he was
also completely different (p. 79).[478]

In spite of the text's focus on this depressed, despondent condition
and a structural backbone of recurring motifs, imagery and symbolism, to
be discussed in the following analysis, there are many narrative elements
in the form of descriptive residue which serve the text's mimetic function,
but do not fit the pattern of integration, functionality, linkage and
restricted proportions observed in the other texts under discussion in this
study. For this reason, the analysis of this text will be restricted to noting
some rudimentary examples of cohesiveness and unity of effect in terms of
parallel and repetitive structure as well as of those components which fill
in the gaps and thus alter the proportions of a usually more abbreviated
and truncated metonymic axis.   An analysis which goes beyond
demonstrating this essential difference would expand the framework of
this discussion to a text type which is not the object of investigation.

A central motif in *Jenseits der Liebe* which projects an
unambiguous theme complex of exploitation, depression and the death
drive is the teeth motif. Horn has fallen from grace as a representative of
a firm which manufactures dentures; awakening in the morning, he must
always contend with fiercely clenched teeth, a physical manifestation of
tension; Horn's way of grinning renders a grotesque image, evoking the
image of a grimacing skeletal head. The text opens with the lines: "When
Franz Horn woke up, his teeth were clenched. He felt his upper and lower
jaw as though they were a colossal mass" (p. 7).[479] Horn's wife's choice
of terms to describe his mood after a day at work is noted as entirely
appropriate:

> She had said that his grim, clenched-jaw look was
> becoming more and more prominent. When she had said
> that, he had noticed that his teeth really had clenched
> together. With massive force. As if it were a competition

---

[478] *"Ein und dieselbe Person erschien ihm plötzlich so und gleich darauf völlig
anders. Ob das von seinen wechselnden Bedürfnissen abhing? Ob er deswegen
Thiele manchmal so und manchmal ganz anders sah? Er hatte sich schließlich
gesagt, Thiele ist eben so und auch ganz anders" (p. 79).*
[479] *"Als Franz Horn aufwachte, waren seine Zähne aufeinandergebissen. Ober-
und Unterkiefer spürte er als gewaltige Blöcke."*

to see which was the stronger, the upper jaw or the lower jaw (p. 32).[480]

The failure to negotiate a new contract in London is followed by the same tension:

The truth is, even before this, he could not ease the biting down of his upper teeth into his lower lip and beyond. And nevertheless, the previous biting down of the upper teeth had been easier to bear than this pressure of the lower against the upper teeth. He could not but think that in this way he might bite himself to death. When the lower teeth had bitten all the way through and up, they would finally sink into the brain (p. 77).[481]

This physical symptom repeats itself also as Horn returns to his apartment: "The pressure exerted by the lower molars increased" (p. 107).[482] A passenger on the train who happens to have the same grim facial features sparks the following inner discourse:

Should I strike at your chin from the side, so that the pressure from your lower jaw is relieved for a second ... you see, I know about it too, look, I have the same clenched jaws, above and below (p. 110).[483]

The scene leading up to the suicide attempt also draws on this motif in the final and most vivid rendition of its significance as a portend

---

[480] "Sie hatte gesagt, er werde immer verbissener. Als sie das gesagt hatte, hatte er bemerkt, daß seine Zähne tatsächlich zusammengebissen waren. Und zwar mit äußerster Kraft. Als finde da ein Wettkampf statt, ob der Ober- oder Unterkiefer stärker sei."

[481] "Wahr ist, daß er den Biß der Oberzähne in die Unterlippe und darüber hinaus schon damals nicht einfach lösen konnte. Und trotzdem, der Biß der oberen Zähne früher war viel leichter zu ertragen als dann der Druck der unteren Zähne gegen die oberen. Er mußte daran denken, daß er sich auf diese Weise zu Tode beißen könnte. Wenn die unteren Zähne sich nach oben durchgebissen haben würden, versänken sie am Ende im Gehirn."

[482] "Der Druck der unteren Backenzähne nahm wieder zu."

[483] "Soll ich Ihnen von der Seite gegen das Kinn schlagen, daß Sie diesen Druck des Unterkiefers eine Sekunde lang los sind ... ich kenne das nämlich, schauen Sie, bei mir genau dieselbe Verbissenheit von unten nach oben."

of the novel's culmination (hence it must be noted that here too, circularity is a compositional principle); in this instance, Horn observes his image in a mirror:

> If anything could make this sight more repulsive, it was the way this greasy, puffy, whining face now began to grin. As if it were a conditioned response, his face could produce the most horrifying grin. [...] His jaws were already in motion. As never before. At completely irregular intervals the upper or lower jaw would suddenly click open, snap away from its counterpart like lightning and then immediately slam back shut. And press down. The other jaw would brace itself against the pressure, twitch away, then slam back, adding even more force to the pressure. Then it was the other's turn again. The corners of his mouth drew apart to reveal his teeth. Drew back. Drew apart (p. 143).[484]

The use of the technique of leitmotif is also evident in the treatment of the symptom of lethargy and heaviness: "Seated among the people, Horn felt heavy. He had the feeling that he was the heaviest of them all. No-one sank so far into his seat as did he" (p. 38).[485] This stasis is also described in the London hotel room: "The longer he lay there, the heavier he became. Therefore he had only to lie there. Therefore lie there he did" (p. 63);[486] "He felt himself to be so heavy, that whenever he didn't concentrate intensely, he fell back onto the bed. His

---

[484] *"Wenn die Widerlichkeit dieses Anblicks noch durch etwas gesteigert werden könnte, dann dadurch, daß dieses fettige, verquollene, wehleidige Gesicht noch zu grinsen anfinge. Und wie auf Befehl, produzierte sein Gesicht sofort das scheußlichste Grinsen. [...] Seine Kiefer fingen schon an. Wie noch nie. In ganz unregelmäßigen Abständen klappte plötzlich der Unter- oder Oberkiefer weg, holte blitzschnell aus und schlug sofort wieder zu. Und preßte. Der andere stemmte dagegen, zuckte plötzlich weg, schlug sofort wieder zu und schickte noch mehr Kraft in den Druck. Dann wieder der Andere. Die Mundwinkel fletschten weg von den Zähnen. Wieder her. Wieder weg."*
[485] *"Horn saß schwer zwischen den Leuten. Er hatte das Gefühl, er sei der schwerste von allen. Keiner sank so tief auf seinem Sitz wie er."*
[486] *"Je länger er lag, desto schwerer wurde er. Er mußte also nur liegen bleiben. Also blieb er liegen."*

body parts were so heavy they hurt" (p. 44).[487] Similarly, the final scene in Horn's apartment includes the description of this sensation: "He had the feeling that his face was flowing downwards. In any case, it was heavy again. It hung down. He felt how his hanging, fluid face was becoming heavier and heavier" (p. 141).[488] The forest scene in Coventry also incorporates this motif: "For the time being, even when he hopped on grassy areas that seemed solid, he sank in up to his ankles. The brown water splashed up into his pants beyond his knees" (p. 60).[489]

The narcotization motif is also many times repeated: "Horn hurried to his room and poured himself a glass of cognac" (p. 8);[490] "Just as Horn had fetched another two bottles of rosé, he had bumped up against Mrs. Liszt in the narrow hallway. She was returning from the toilet" (p. 28);.[491] "He went to the cupboard to get himself three bottles of beer" (p. 31);[492] "Three to six cans or bottles in an evening" (p. 32);[493] "Hilda came with the cognac. And after three glasses he was able to move his upper and lower jaw at will" (p. 32). [494]Another motif is that of confinement or crampedness, the expression of the feeling of obstructive, confining proportions, projected onto various contexts and objects from Horn's perception of being overwhelmed and his ever diminishing sense of self-worth. Thus the city he visits on his business trip is characterized as a claustrophobia-inducing environment: "None of the housing units was more than three meters wide. Yes indeed, another suburb began here, an epoch which could afford four-meter-wide façades" (p. 48).[495] Another image which would otherwise seem residual is that of the Indian bus

---

[487] "*Er fühlte sich so schwer, daß er, wenn er sich nicht scharf konzentrierte, sofort wieder aufs Bett fiel ... [...] Seine Glieder schmerzten vor Schwere.*"

[488] " *Er hatte das Gefühl, sein Gesicht fließe abwärts. Es war auf jeden Fall wieder schwer. Es hing. Er spürte, wie sein hängendes fließendes Gesicht immer noch schwerer wurde.*"

[489] "*Vorerst sank er, auch wenn er auf scheinbar solide Wasenstücke hüpfte, bei jeder Landung knöcheltief ein. Das braune Wasser klatschte innen in seinen Hosen an den Beinen hoch bis über die Knie.*"

[490] "*Horn eilte in sein Zimmer und schenkte sich ein halbes Glas Cognac ein.*"

[491] "*Als nämlich Horn gerade wieder 2 Flaschen von dem Weißherbst geholt hatte ... war er im engen Gang auf Frau Dr. Liszt gestoßen, die gerade vom Abort zurückkam.*"

[492] "*Er ging zum Schrank und holte sich drei Flaschen Bier.*"

[493] "*3 bis 6 Dosen oder Flaschen pro Abend.*"

[494] Other examples are on pp. 34, 43, 53, 56, 87, 108, 123, 127, 139, 141.

[495] "*Breiter als 3 m war keine der Hauseinheiten ... Jawohl, da begann eine zweite Vorstadt, eine Epoche, die sich 4m breite Hausfronten leisten konnte.*"

driver: "The bus driver was an Indian whose hands seemed too small for everything he had to use them for. ... that he could even bring this double-deck-bus through the bumper-to-bumper traffic" (p. 52).[496] The scene in the forest on the outskirts of Coventry describes the encroachment of the city on the natural environment, troping Horn's own dilemma of obstructions and abuse:

> It was only a worn-out plot of forest at the city limits.
> [...] Between the hedges and the field there remained but
> a narrow strip of grass. He knew that he had to come to
> a stream. Suddenly a pheasant ran past his feet. But
> instead of running through one of the furrows into the
> open field, it ran as if crazed into the dense, impenetrable
> hedge. [..] When he was looking for a way to cross the
> stream, a few times he came up to spots where the stream
> had been piled over with construction rubble and old
> tires. [...] Barbed wire prevented access to the stream
> (p. 59).[497]

The small-mindedness and exploitative nature of Horn's colleague von Liszt and his wife who have managed to displace him into his position of diminished significance within the firm is reflected by the description of her artwork:

> She did paint. Quite tiny pictures. No bigger than a
> postcard. With the tiniest brushes. But there were an
> uncanny number of things to see in them and everything
> was rendered with cutting precision. An old four-sided
> tower beyond a piercingly yellow grain field that had been
> mown, and on the front edge of the cornfield a dead raven

---

[496] "Der Omnibusfahrer war ein Inder, dessen Hände für alles, was er hier bediente, zu klein zu sein schienen ... Daß der diesen zweistöckigen Bus durch den stoßstangendichten Verkehr brachte."

[497] "Es war nur ein zertappter Stadtrandwald. [...] Dort blieb zwischen Hecke und Acker nur noch ein schmaler Grasstreifen. Er wußte, daß er zu einem Bach kommen mußte. Plötzlich rannte ein Fasan vor seinen Füßen. Aber anstatt durch eine der Furchen übers freie Feld zu fliehen, rannte der wie wahnsinnig in die undurchdringliche harte Hecke. [...] Als er eine Möglichkeit suchte, den Bach zu überqueren, kam er ein paar Male an Stellen, an denen der Bach mit Bauschutt und alten Reifen zugeschüttet war. [...] Der Zugang zu diesem Bach war mit Stacheldraht verwehrt."

being attacked by insects. Every part of the stubble of
the harvested Liszt-blond grain field had been painted.
And leaning ... at the foot of the tower was a small girl
looking across at the raven. She had raised up one knee
and pressed with both hands flat against the wall of the
tower. [...] "Mrs. von Liszt will soon be earning more
than I do with her miniature paintings," said Dr. Liszt.
"And when living space becomes smaller," said Dr. Liszt,
"Mrs. Liszt's art will be in great fashion" (p. 99).[498]

The description of this canvas contains elements which link it to
another series of motifs: these create the image of a church spire or tower,
a symbol for the promise of transcendence as traditionally guaranteed by
submission to an oppressive, exploitative hierarchy, set in the midst of a
natural environment which has been plundered, or "harvested" until such
pervasive control has rendered it lifeless. The imagery is contrastive also
in terms of light and dark, blossoming and decay; the bright or upward-
leading end of the polarity is also rendered through both the glow of
candles, evoking hope and solemnity, as well as the light colour of
growing vegetation, but has its positive signification undermined by its
juxtaposition with death and darkness. The skyline of Coventry as
described in the novel is one example of this motif: "The cathedral was
visible between the polytechnical institute and the factory buildings. [...]
The April sun shone down, highlighting the industrial proletariat of middle
England. Alleluia" (p. 47).[499] The neighbouring area is given the same
treatment: "The stream called Sowe is nothing more than an oil-drainage
ditch, one greasy black rainbow after another. [...] He always got off the

---

[498] *"Sie malte ja. Ganz kleine Bilder. Nur Postkartengröße. Mit winzigsten
Pinseln. Aber auf diesen Bildern war unheimlich viel zu sehen und alles war
schneidend genau deutlich. Ein alter viereckiger Turm jenseits eines
abgemähten, durchdringend blonden Kornfeldes, und am vorderen Rand des
Kornfeldes ein toter Rabe, über den sich Käfer hergemacht hatten. Jede
einzelne Stoppel des abgeernteten lisztblonden Kornfeldes war gemalt. Und
am Fuß des Turms ... lehnte sich ein kleines Mädchen, das herübersah zu dem
Raben. Es hatte ein Knie angezogen und beide Hände flach gegen die Wand
des Turms gepreßt. [...] Frau von Liszt verdient mit ihren Kleinformaten bald
mehr als ich, sagte Dr. Liszt. Und wenn die Wohnungen noch kleiner werden,
sagte er, wird Frau von Liszt die große Mode."*
[499] *"Zwischen Fabrikgebäuden und Polytechnikum tauchte die Kathedrale auf.
[...] Das Industrieproletariat Mittelenglands in der alles hervorhebenden
Aprilsonne. Halleluja."*

taxi at the ancient church of the Virgin Mary" (p. 49).[500] One of Horn's
fantasies draws together the trappings of Christianity's celebration of the
birth of Christ with the imagined murder of his own children:

> What would happen now? Maybe Hilda? If possible, with
> the children, that's it, isn't it?! And each of them with a
> Christmas tree decorated with burning candles in their
> hand, right?! [...] He could not prevent himself from
> imagining that he would then pull out two small knives
> from his breast pocket and stab both children in the heart,
> causing them to sink down onto him in so heartfelt a way
> as they had never before done ...(p. 25).[501]

The scene in which Horn strikes his daughter after she has
accidentally burned a hole in a valuable rug uses similar imagery:

> As keen as always to make peace and to reconcile, she
> now lit a candle. [...] The burning sulphur tip flew onto
> the rug. [...] And now there was a burn mark as large as
> a finger-nail, impossible to remove, in a light-coloured,
> patternless area of the rug. [...] Horn raised himself up
> and smashed Amanda directly in the face. (pp. 85-
> 86).[502]

The description of the driveway leading up to the residence of
Keith Heath, the owner of London Dentures with whom Horn is not able

---

[500] "*Der Bach Sowe ist also der reine Ölabflußgraben, ein schwarzschmieriges
Regenbogenfeld am anderen. [...] An der uralten Jungfrau-Maria-Kirche war
er immer aus dem Taxi gestiegen.*"
[501] "*Was sollte denn kommen. Hilde vielleicht?! Womöglich mit den Kindern,
ja?! Und jedes einen mit brennenden Kerzen besteckten Weihnachtsbaum in
der Hand, ja?! [...] Er konnte sich nicht gegen die Vorstellung wehren, daß er
dann zwei kleine Messer aus seiner Brusttasche zöge und sie den zwei Kindern
ins Herz stieße, daß die dann so innig wie noch nie an ihm zusammensänken
...*"
[502] "*Immer auf Versöhnung und Friedensstiftung erpicht wie sie war, zündete
sie jetzt eine Kerze an. [...] Der brennende Schwefelkopf flog auf den
Teppich. [...] Und jetzt mitten in einer hell musterlosen Stelle ein
fingernagelgroßer, absolut unentfernbarer Brandfleck. [...] Horn richtete sich
auf und schlug Amanda mitten ins Gesicht.*"

to negotiate a new contract and therefore the personification of Horn's final failure, uses the same contrast of dark and light:

> He left the car standing there. Went through the gate. Through the avenue of black-crowned yew trees that was as straight as an arrow. [...] The sun was now shining, causing the decaying house to radiate an entirely bright, honey-green light. Over the lower west wing of the house, a giant, half-dead elm tree stretched out a handfull of bizarre branches, bizarre because they were leafless (p. 69).[503]

This motif extends to narrative elements which otherwise could only be described as descriptive residue; Horn observes two figures descending from the train on his journey home, one associated with the transcendent aspirations inherent in religious belief and the other with oppression and subjugation: "Aside from Horn only a nun and an African left the train in Ravensburg" (p. 13).[504] The conversation which Horn dreams of having with Heath contains a description of the latter's illness. Heath uses the image of the spring flower cowslip, which possesses a long stem and a flame-shaped yellow blossom, to describe his deterioration:

> But in his imagination he can only reach the house through a tube. The inside of the tube is illuminated by candles shedding a friendly, yellow glow. [...] Oh yes, go ahead and have another look at this beautiful cowslip blossom. A more beautiful depiction of a festering urethra isn't possible. So spring-like (pp. 74-77).[505]

---

[503] "*Er ließ das Auto stehen. Ging durchs Tor. Durch die kerzengerade hinaufführende Allee schwarzkroniger Eibenbäume. [...] Die Sonne schien jetzt und brachte das helle Honiggrün des brüchigen Hauses förmlich zum Leuchten. Eine riesige, schon halb abgestorbene Ulme reckte eine Handvoll bizarrer, weil laubloser Äste über den niederen westlichen Teil des Hauses.*"
[504] "*In Ravensburg stiegen außer Horn nur eine Nonne und ein Neger aus.*"
[505] "*Aber in seiner Vorstellung kann er das Haus nur durch eine Röhre erreichen. Die Röhre ist innen von Kerzen freudlich gelb erleuchtet. [...] Ach ja, werfen Sie ruhig noch einen Blick auf diese schöne Schlüsselblume. Schöner kann man die Harnröhrenvereiterung nicht darstellen. So frühlingshaft.*"

The novel uses this motif to describe Horn's final dream in the unconscious state precipitated by an overdose of sleeping pills. The tongue of fire which in biblical tradition appeared over the head of each of the Apostles at Pentecost is described as accompanying the image of his wife at his bedside, but as the image becomes more discernable it proves to be that of the wife of the major agent of Horn's exploitation, his employer Thiele: "Hilda came up closer. The name hovered over her like a flame. 'Epiphany,' Horn thought, and now the 'everything's going to be all right' feeling came over him. [...] It wasn't Hilda, it was Mrs. Thiele" (p. 155).[506]

In spite of the functionality and higher degree of integration achieved by these leitmotifs, among whose number only those which are more significant have been mentioned, the novel has many components which do not adhere to the principles of limited focus and functional proportions, of which only two out of many examples will be noted here. The conversation Horn has with an Irish gentleman, whom he has mistaken for Heath's chauffeur, touches on the subject of literature - with no purpose other than to demonstrate this figure's loquaciousness. This figure is one of several used to demonstrate Horn's onerous sense of guilt generated by self-assertion and the compulsion to create a favourable impression (other examples of this motif are the barber, p. 45, the imagined encounter with a stranger, p. 90, Frau von Liszt, p. 99, the doorman, p. 101).:

> He was from Belfast. But his mother was from a village
> near Dublin. He has five children. He had come over in
> 1934. When he had come home at five today, he first of
> all had finished reading his novel before going to bed.
> Had Horn ever read a book by Maurice Walsh? Or by
> G.E. Bates? Here Horn would definitely have to catch up
> on his reading. The greatest of them all is Yeats, of
> course. Right, right, right. Even abroad, there is no
> longer any debate that Yeats was the greatest, the best
> and the most profound poet who had ever lived. His
> grandfather had known Yeats personally. He was ready
> to swear a solemn oath to that, as he realized that this
> might be difficult to accept in such a place as the

---

[506] *"Hilde kam näher. Der Name schwebte über ihr als eine Flamme. Pfingsten, dachte Horn und kriegte das Jetzt-wird-alles-gut-Gefühl. [...] Es war nicht Hilde. Es war Frau Thiele."*

Working Men's Club in Coventry-Cheylesmore at high
noon (p. 53).[507]

Another example of expanded proportions is the conversation
Horn overhears on his train journey home. It presents a situation which is
a loose parallel to Horn's, inasmuch as a senior executive, accompanied
by two subordinate colleages, the older of which is over zealous in not
losing ground to his younger associate, is rebuked for his efforts. Every
minor detail of the conversation is rendered:

> Apparently the boss had rented a large industrial space to
> manufacture certain items, and the one who had rented
> the space to him was now claiming that the rent was so
> low because it had been agreed that the boss would buy
> the building after two years. Now the two years had past,
> and the boss must have indeed made a contractually
> binding offer. Lawyers were now supposed to clear all of
> this up. The young lawyer started to read *der Spiegel*.
> The magazine for the exhausted. [...] The one who was
> fifty-five, even while eating his sandwiches, went on
> making more and more suggestions as to how to avoid the
> obligation to purchase. The boss was beginning to have
> enough of this and said several times that what had today
> been discussed and resolved was all that could be
> discussed and resolved today. The older lawyer chewed
> on in silence. Then it suddenly occurred to him that one
> couldn't even see this as conditions of a reverse
> transaction, therefore one must not accept responsibility

---

[507] "*Er sei aus Belfast. Aber seine Mutter sei aus einem Dorf bei Dublin. Er
hat fünf Kinder. 1934 kam er herüber. Als er heute morgen um fünf
heimgekommen sei, habe er noch zuerst seinen Roman fertiggelesen, bevor er
ins Bett gegangen sei: Ob Horn je ein Buch von Maurice Walsh gelesen habe.
Oder von G.E. Bates. Also das müsse er unbedingt nachholen. Der größte ist
natürlich Yeats. Klar, klar, klar. Das werde ja heute auch im Ausland
nirgends mehr bestritten, daß Yeats der größte, beste, tiefste Dichter sei, der je
gelebt habe. Sein Großvater habe Yeats persönlich gekannt. Das schwöre er
feierlich, weil er einsehe, daß man sowas einem am hellen Mittag in einem
Working Men's Club in Coventry-Cheylesmore nicht ohne weiteres abnehme.*"

for the obligation to disclose. He called the opponent's legal brief a greatly overblown legal opinion (p. 111).[508]

These examples should suffice to illustrate the hypothesis that the text, while aiming for the integration of many of its narrative components, displays a more prominent metonymic axis. It demonstrates the fuller proportions of a work more commited to the mimetic function of depicting, above and beyond the essentials necessary for comprehension, a "slice of life," a record of lived experience, including those details which elude the attempt to shape meaning out of disparity and dispertion, hence a structural reflection of a part of the work's thematic trajectory. Because of these expanded and more diffuse proportions of a compositional principle that is more additive and photographic rather than concise, minimal, hermetic, yet resonant, *Jenseits der Liebe* does not conform to the pattern observed of the other texts under discussion in this study.

---

[508] *"Offenbar hatte der Chef dort eine große Halle für irgendeine Fabrikation gemietet, und der, der sie ihm vermietet hatte, hatte jetzt behauptet, er hätte sie ihm zu diesem billigen Preis gemietet, weil ausgemacht worden sei, der Chef kaufe die Halle nach zwei Jahren. Die zwei Jahre waren jetzt um, irgendwie mußte sich der Chef tatsächlich vertraglich gebunden haben, jetzt sollten die Juristen alles wieder ins reine bringen. Der junge Jurist fing an, den Spiegel zu lesen. Die Zeitung für Erschöpfte. [...] Der 55jährige machte, auch während er seine belegten Brote aß, ununterbrochen neue Vorschläge, wie man den Kaufzwang abwehren könne. [...] Allmählich wurde das auch dem Chef zuviel. Er sagte des öfteren, daß man mehr als man heute erreicht und besprochen habe, heute nicht erreichen und besprechen könne. Dann kaute der Altjurist ein paar Minuten stumm. Dann fiel ihm plötzlich ein, daß von einem Rückabwicklungsverhältnis gar keine Rede sein könne, also dürfe man sich auch keine Auskunftspflicht anlasten lassen. Den Schriftsatz der Gegenseite nannte er ein reichlich überdimensioniertes Rechtsgutachten."*

Conclusion

One of the most significant findings to emerge from an examination of the tradition of the German-language novella is that it is not merely a historical artifact, but a viable category of the artistic prose form, known in the American tradition as the short story. Central to its definition is the concept of the hermetic plurality of a tenor, projected from a vehicle which, although cast in the discourse of referentiality, may reach the very boundaries of comprehension; it extirpates any component which does not contribute to an interlocking motif complex and compact thematic constellation. This is described structurally as a reduction or truncation of the metonymic axis of narrative with the attendant possibility of a more prominent figuration of its metaphoric potential.

The only text of the corpus which does not demonstrate this configuration bears the generic designation "novel." It has been shown that this text projects as its tenor the single thematic stratum of psychic dysfunction within an exploitative environment; it uses a vehicle which leaves fewer gaps in the metonymic axis of referentiality and contiguity. The other texts of the corpus have in common the attribute of a tenor whose thematic statement is hermetic and multidimensional, emanating from a vehicle that is elliptic and at times cryptic.

These texts share common thematic coordinates. Reality is rendered as a construct of perception of the individual, isolated subject, seeking integration and individuation, yet denied any verifiable realization; to transcend the irony of signification and self-actualization is to do so on a fictional and a mythical level. The ultimate paradox is that of the both complementary and contradictory drives of *Eros* and *Thanatos*; the Dionysian/Apollonian dialectic represents the historical equivalents of the Freudian concepts of super-ego (the Lacanian Symbolic) and id (the Lacanian Imaginary), with the more specific polarity of *Eros* and *Thanatos* attributed to the id. The tenuous nature of awareness and perception are linked to this aporia through the Lacanian concepts of the Imaginary and the Symbolic. This "myth" of our instincts, as Freud calls it, is a prominent feature in each of these texts. The dreamwork of the psyche, psychic numbing, the theme of narcotization and the indictment of ideology are all elements drawn upon in the texts under mention to portray a contemporary reality which challenges the human capability to make sense of its context. Elusive and illusive meaning also finds expression in the many examples of metafiction which underlines the tenuous relationship of any proposed scheme of reality with its true referent. The frequent instances of intertextuality reaching the outermost boundary of historical and psychological perception in references to mythology also indicate the intention to show the diachronic as well as the synchronic character, the cornerstones of a tradition of ways of establishing sense and meaning.

Another significant observation to be made of the texts forming the corpus of this analysis is their iconoclastic nature. As Bakhtin postulates, the goal of all artistic prose is to undermine the conventions of established meaning and to propose new contexts and concepts for making sense out of chaos. Hochhuth, Dürrenmatt and Walser all ascribe special significance and promise to the emerging role of women as a new opportunity for resonance and synthesis in a human environment which has always stressed difference over similarity. Perhaps the most illuminating observation to be made of the novella's potential for valorization of the metaphoric over the metonymic axis, of similarity and integration over difference and contiguity, is the commitment to draw on the best creative and imaginative insights of the past with a view to synthesizing the disparities and incongruities of the present, creating the spark of resonance and balance, if only in a hypothetical, consciously fictional manner, to deconstruct the oppositional, binary mode which is such a hallmark of human perception.

List of Works Cited

Primary Sources

Brecht, Bertolt. *Werke.* Berlin and Weimar: Aufbau Verlag, 1988.

Büchner, Georg. *Sämtliche Werke und Briefe: Leonce und Lena.* Vol. 1. Hamburg: Christian Wegner Verlag, 1971.

Dürrenmatt, Friedrich. *Werkausgabe in Dreißig Bänden: Abu Chanifa und Anan ben David.* Vol. 23. Zürich: Diogenes, 1985.

------------------------ *Der Auftrag oder Vom Beobachten des Beobachters der Beobachter: Novelle in vierundzwanzig Sätzen.* Zürich: Diogenes, 1986.

------------------------ *The Assignment Or On the Observing of the Observer of the Observers.* Trans. Joel Agee. New York: Random House, 1988.

------------------------ *Der Sturz.* Zürich: Diogenes, 1985.

------------------------ *Die Physiker.* Zürich: Diogenes, 1985.

Freud, Sigmund. *Beyond the Pleasure Principle.* Tr. and ed. by James Strachey. New York: Liveright, 1961.

------------------------ *Totem and Taboo.* Trans. James Strachey. London: Routledge and Kegan Paul, 1961.

Goethe, Johann Wolfgang von. *Faust I. Sämtliche Werke.* Vol. 6.1. München: Carl Hanser Verlag, 1986.

------------------------ *Faust.* Trans. Barker Fairley. Toronto and Buffalo: University of Toronto Press, 1970.

------------------------ *West-Östlicher Diva: Noten und Abhandlungen.* Berlin: Akademie Verlag, 1952.

------------------------ Letter of 29 Jan. 1827 in *Johann Peter Eckerman: Gespräche mit Goethe.* Vol. 19 of *Sämtliche Werke.* München: Karl Hanser Verlag, 1986.

Hochhuth, Rolf. *Atlantik-Novelle.* Reinbek bei Hamburg: Rowohlt, 1985.

Jung, C.G. *The Collected Works of C. G. Jung: The Archetypes and the Collective Unconscious.* Vol. 9 Part 1 .Trans. R. F. C. Hull. London: Routledge and Kegan Paul, 1959.

------------------------ *The Collected Works of C. G. Jung: The Spirit in Man, Art, and Literature.* Vol. 15. Trans. R.F.C. Hull. London: Routledge and Kegan Paul, 1966.

Musil, Robert. *The Man without Qualities.* Vol. 2. London: Secker and Warburg, 1954.

Pausch, Birgit. *Die Schiffschaukel.* Reinbek bei Hamburg: Rowohlt, 1984.

Rilke, Rainer Maria von. *Der Panther. Auslese.* Eds. Garland C. Richmond and George H. Kirby. New York: McGraw-Hill Book Company, 1968.

Saint Joseph Edition of the Holy Bible. New York: Catholic Book Publishing Company, 1963.

Shakespeare, William. *Hamlet. The Complete Works of William Shakespeare,* Ed. William George Clark and William Aldis Wright. New York: Grosset and Dunlap, 1911.

The Beatles. "Lucy in the Sky with Diamonds." *Sgt. Pepper's Lonely Hearts Club Band.* Capitol Records, 1967.

The Odyssey. Trans. W. H. D. Rouse. Winnipeg: The New American Library of Canada Mentor Classics, 1966.

Tieck, Ludwig. *Schriften.* Vorbericht zum 11. Band. Berlin: G. Reimer, 1829.

Walser, Martin. *Ein fliehendes Pferd.* Frankfurt: Suhrkamp, 1978.

------------------------ *Runaway Horse.* Trans. Leila Vennewitz. New York: Holt Rinehart and Winston, 1980.

------------------------ *Jenseits der Liebe.* Frankfurt: Suhrkamp, 1979.

Secondary Sources

Adams, Hazard and Searle, Leroy, eds. "Charles Sanders Pierce." *Critical Theory Since 1965.* Tallahassee: Florida State University Press, 1986. 637-644.

Amacher, Richard, and Lange, Victor, eds. *New Perspectives in German Literary Criticism.* Princeton: Princeton University Press, 1979.

Bakhtin, M. M. *The Dialogic Imagination.* Austin: University of Texas Press, 1981.

Bal, Mieke. *Narratology: Introduction to the Theory of Narrative.* Toronto: University of Toronto Press, 1985.

Baldeshwiler, Eileen. "The Lyric Short Story: The Sketch of a History." *Short Story Theories.* Ed. Charles E. May. Np.: Ohio University Press, 1976. 202-213.

Barthes, Roland. *S/Z.* Paris: Seuil, 1970.

Baumgart, Reinhard. "Überlebensspiel mit zwei Opfern," *Der Spiegel,* 27 9 Feb. 1978: 198-199.

Bell, Jon. A. "Affective Disorders." *Psychiatry.* Ed. James H. Scully. Media, Pennsylvania: Harwal Publishing Company, 1985. 49-56.

Bennett, E. K. *A History of the German Novelle.* 2nd ed. Cambridge: Cambridge University Press, 1965.

Booth, Wayne. *The Rhetoric of Fiction.* Chicago and London: University of Chicago Press, 1961.

Braak, Ivo. *Poetik in Stichworten.* Würzburg: Universitätsdruckerei H. Stürtz, 1974.

Brooks, Peter. "Freud's Masterplot." *Literature and Psychoanalysis.* Ed. Shoshana Felman. Baltimore and London: The Johns Hopkins University Press, 1985. 280-300.

------------------------ "Symbolization and Fiction-Making." *Explorations in Psychohistory,* Ed. Robert Jay Lifton. New York: Simon and Schuster, 1974. 214-230.

------------------------ "The Idea of Psychoanalytic Criticism." *Discourse in Psychoanalysis and Literature.* Ed. Shlomith Rimmon-Kenan (London and New York: Methuen, 1987. 1-18.

Campbell, Joseph. *The Power of Myth.* New York: Doubleday, 1988.

Carroll, David. *The Subject in Question.* Chicago and London: The University of Chicago Press, 1982.

Chase, Richard. *Quest for Myth.* Baton Rouge: N.p., 1949.

Chatman, Seymour. *Story and Discourse.* Ithaca and London: Cornell University Press, 1978.

Chodorow, Nancy. *The Reproduction of Meaning.* Berkeley: University of California Press, 1978.

Cohen, Sidney. *The Drug Dilemma.* New York: McGraw-Hill Book Company, 1969.

Collins Dictionary of the English Language. Ed. Patrick Hanks. London & Glasgow: Collins, 1979.

Cuddon, J.A. *A Dictionary of Literary Terms.* Middlesex: Viking Penguin, 1985.

Culler, Jonathan. *Structuralist Poetics.* London: Routledge and Kegan Paul, 1975.

Daiches, David. Rev. of *Anatomy of Criticism* by Northrop Frye. *Modern Philology* 56 (1958): 69-72.

de Man, Paul. *Allegories of Reading.* New Haven and London: Yale University Press, 1979.

de Vries, Ad. *A Dictionary of Symbols and Imagery.* New York and Amsterdam: North Holland Publishing Company, 1974.

Doderer, Klaus. *Die Kurzgeschichte in Deutschland.* Darmstadt: Wissenschaftliche Buchgesellschaft, 1972.

Durand, Régis. "On Aphanisis: A Note on the Dramaturgy of the Subject in Narrative Analysis." *Lacan and Narration. The Psychoanalytic Difference in Narrative Theory.* Ed. Robert Con Davis. Baltimore and London: Johns Hopkins University Press, 1983. 860-870.

Durzak, Manfred. *Die deutsche Kurzgeschichte der Gegenwart: Autorenportraits, Werkstattgespräche, Interpretationen.* Stuttgart: P. Reclam, 1980.

Dyer, Denys. *The Stories of Kleist.* New York: Holmes and Meier, 1977.

Eagleton, Terry. *Literary Theory. An Introduction.* Oxford: Basil Blackwell, 1983.

Erikson, Erik H. *Identity and the Life Cycle.* New York: International Universities Press, 1968.

------------------------ "On the Nature of Psychohistorical Evidence." *Explorations in Psychohistory.* New York: Simon and Schuster, 1974. 42-77.

Felman, Shoshana. "Beyond Oedipus: The Specimen Story of Psychoanalysis." *Lacan and Narration.* Ed. Robert Con Davis. Baltimore and London: The Johns Hopkins University Press, 1983. 1021-1053.

Felperin, Howard. *Beyond Deconstruction. The Uses and Abuses of Literary Theory.* Oxford: Clarendon, 1985.

Flieger, Jerry Aline. "The Purloined Punchline: Joke as Textual Paradigm." *Lacan and Narration.* Ed. Robert Con Davis. Baltimore and London: The Johns Hopkins University Press, 1985. 941-967.

Friedman, Norman. *Form and Meaning in Fiction.* Athens: The University of Georgia Press, 1975.

Frye, Northrop. *Anatomy of Criticism.* Princeton: Princeton University Press, 1957.

Gilbert, Sandra M. "Literary Paternity." *Critical Theory Since 1965.* Eds. Hazard Adams and Leroy Searle. Tallahassee: Florida State University Press, 1986. 486-496.

Gordimer, Nadine. "'The Flash of Fireflies.'" *Short Story Theories.* Ed. Charles E. May. N.p.: Ohio University Press, 1976. 178-181.

Gregg, Richard B. *Symbolic Inducement and Knowing.* Columbia: University of South Carolina Press, 1984.

Hauff, Jürgen and Heller, Albrecht, eds. *Methodendiskussion.* Frankfurt: Athenäum Fischer, 1972.

Helbling, Robert E. "Dürrenmatt Criticism: Exit the Grotesque?" *Play Dürrenmatt*, Ed. Moshe Lazar. Malibu: Undena Publications, 1983. 175-188.

Hempfer, Klaus W. *Gattungstheorie*. München: Wilhelm Fink, 1973.

Henel, Heinrich. "Anfänge der deutschen Novelle." *Monatshefte*. 77.4 (Winter 1985): 433-448.

Hernadi, Paul. "Recent Genre Theory." *Theories of literary Genre*. Ed. Joseph P. Strelka. University Park and London: Pennsylvania State University Press, 1978. 192-208.

Herzog, Sigrid. "Über den grünen Klee gelobt." *Neue Rundschau* 89 (1978): 492-495.

Hocking, Charles. *Dictionary of Disasters at Sea during the Age of Steam* Vol. 1. Sussex: Lloyd's Register of Shipping, 1969.

Jacobsen, Edith. *Depression Comparative Studies of Normal, Neurotic and Psychotic Conditions*. New York: International Universities Press Inc., 1971.

Jakobson, Roman. "Linguistics and Poetics." *Style in Language*. Ed. T. Sebeok. Cambridge: Massachusetts Institute of Technology Press, 1960. 350-377.

------------------------ "Vers une science de l'art poétique." *Théorie de la littérature. Textes des Formalistes russes*. Ed. and trans. Tsvetan Todorov. Paris: Seuil, 1965. 9-13.

Jardine, Alice. "Pre-Texts for the Transatlantic Feminist." *Yale French Studies* 62 (1981): 220-236.

Jendreiek, Helmut. *Thomas Mann: Der demokratische Roman*. Düsseldorf: August Bagel Verlag, 1977.

Johnson, Barbara. *The Critical Difference*. Baltimore and London: The Johns Hopkins University Press, 1980.

Jurgensen, Manfred. *Deutsche Literaturtheorie der Gegenwart*. München: Franke, 1973.

Kaiser, Joachim. "Martin Walsers blindes Glanzstück Funktion und Funktionieren der Novelle 'Ein fliehendes Pferd.'" *Merkur* (1978): 828-838.

Kayser, Wolfgang. *Das sprachliche Kunstwerk*. Francke: Bern und München, 1971.

------------------------ *The Grotesque in Art and Literature*. Trans. Ulrich Weisstein. Bloomington: Indiana University Press, 1963.

Kermode, Frank. *The Sense of an Ending: Studies in the Theory of Fiction*. New York: Oxford University Press, 1967.

Kierkegaard, Sören. *The Concept of Irony: With Constant Reference to Socrates*. Translated by David Swenson and Lillian Swenson. Revised by Howard A. Johnson. Princeton: Princeton University Press, 1959.

Revised by Howard A. Johnson. Princeton: Princeton University Press, 1959.

Kilchenmann, Ruth. *Die Kurzgeschichte*. Stuttgart: Kohlhammer, 1971.

Knorr, Herbert. "Gezahmter Löwe - fliehendes Pferd Zu Novellen von Goethe und Martin Walser." *Literatur für Leser* 2 (1979): 139-157.

Kohut, Heinz. *Self Psychology and the Humanities: Reflections on a New Psychoanalytic Approach*. New York and London: W. W. Norton and Company, 1985.

Kostelanetz, Richard. "Notes on the American Short Story Today." *Short Story Theories*. Ed. Charles E. May. Ohio University Press, 1976. 214-225.

Kristeva, Julia. "Women's Time." *Critical Theory Since 1965*. Eds. Hazard Adams and Leroy Searle. Tallahassee: Florida State University Press, 1986. 471-483.

Kritsch Neuse, Erna. *Die deutsche Kurzgeschichte*. Bonn: Bouvier, 1980.

Lacan, Jacques. "The Mirror Stage as Formative of the Function of the I as Revealed in Psychoanalytic Experience." *Critical Theory Since 1965*. Eds. Hazard Adams and Leroy Searle. Tallahassee: Florida State University Press, 1986. 734-738.

Laufhütte, Hartmut. "Gattungsbegriff und Gattungsgeschichte. Die deutsche Kunstballade." Lecture. Germanistentag in Hamburg. Hamburg, 2 April 1979.

Leibowitz, Judith. *Narrative Purpose in the Novella*. The Hague, Paris: Mouton, 1974.

Lifton, Robert Jay. *Explorations in Psychohistory*. New York: Simon and Schuster, 1974.

Lodge, David. *The Modes of Modern Writing: Metaphor, Metonymy, and the Typology of Modern Literature*. Ithaca: Cornell University Press, 1977.

Louria, Donald B. *The Drug Scene*. New York, Toronto, London Sydney: McGraw-Hill Book Company, 1968.

Malmede, Hans Hermann. *Wege zur Novelle*. Stuttgart, Berlin, Köln, Mainz: Kohlhammer, 1966.

May, Charles E. ed. *Short Story Theories*. Ohio University Press, 1976.

McCartny, Robert J. "East Germany Paralysed by Honecker's Illness." *The Montreal Gazette* 14 Sept. 1989: A8.

Meyers Großes Universal Lexikon. Vol. 6. 11.

Miller, H. Hillis. "Ariadne's Thread: Repetition and the Narrative Line." *Critical Inquiry* 3 (1976): pp. 57-77

Neuschäfer, Hans-Jörg. *Boccaccio und der Beginn der Novelle.* München: Wilhelm Fink, 1969.

Nöth, Winfried. "The Semiotic Framework of Text-linguistics." *Current Trends in Textlinguistics.* Ed. Wolfgang U. Dressler. Berlin: Walter de Gruyter, 1978. 21-34.

Paulin, Roger. *The Brief Compass.* Oxford: Clarendon Press, 1985.

Pfeffer, Rose. *Nietzsche: Disciple of Dionysus.* Lewisburg: Bucknell University Press, 1972.

Piscator, Erwin. Preface to *Der Stellvertreter.* Hamburg: Rowohlt, 1963.

Reichert, John. "More than Kin and Less than Kind: The Limits of Genre Theory." *Theories of Literary Genre.* Ed. Joseph P. Strelka. University Park and London: The Pennsylvania State University Press, 1978. 57-79.

Reinhold, Meyer. *Past and Present: The Continuity of Classical Myths.* Toronto: Hakkert, 1972.

Ricoeur, Paul "The Metaphorical Process as Cognition, Imagination, and Feeling." *On Metaphor.* Ed. Sheldon Sacks. Chicago and London: The University of Chicago Press, 1979. 141-157.

------------------------ *The Rule of Metaphor.* Transl. Robert Czerny. Toronto and Buffalo: University of Toronto Press, 1975.

Rohner, Ludwig. *Theorie der Kurzgeschichte.* Frankfurt: Athenäum, 1973.

Ruegg, Maria. "Metaphor and Metonymy." *Glyph 6.* Eds. Rodolphe Gasché, Carol Jacobs, Henry Sussman. Baltimore and London: The Johns Hopkins University Press, 1979. 141-157.

Saldivar, Ramon. *Figural Language in the Novel.* Princeton: Princeton University Press, 1984.

Schaeffer, Jean-Marie. "Du texte au genre." *Théorie des genres.* Ed. Gérard Genette and Tsvetan Todorov. Paris: Édition du Seuil, 1986.

Scharfman, Ronnie. "Mirroring and Mothering in Simone Schwarz-Bart's *Pluie et vent sur Tëlumée Miracle* and Jean Rhys' *Wide Sargasso Sea.*" *Yale French Studies.* 62 (1981): 88-106.

Schleifer, Ronald. "The Space and Dialogue of Desire: Lacan, Greimas, and Narrative Temporality." *Lacan and Narration.* Ed. Robert Con Davis. Baltimore and London: The Johns Hopkins University Press, 1985. 871-890.

Schmidbauer, Wolfgang. *Die Hilflosen Helfer.* Reinbek bei Hamburg: Rowohlt, 1980.

Schönhaar, Rainer. *Novelle und Kriminalschema.* Bad Homburg v.d.H., Berlin, Zürich: Verlag Dr. Max Gehlen, 1969.

Schönhaar, Rainer. *Novelle und Kriminalschema*. Bad Homburg v.d.H., Berlin, Zürich: Verlag Dr. Max Gehlen, 1969.

Schröder, Rolf. *Novelle und Novellentheorie in der frühen Biedermeierzeit*. Tübingen: Niemeyer, 1970.

Seigneuret, Jean Charles, ed. *Dictionary of Literary Themes and Motifs* New York: Greenwood Press, 1988.

Shaw, Valerie. *The Short Story*. London and New York: Longman, 1983.

Silz, Walter. *Realism and Reality*. Chapel Hill: University of North Carolina Press, 1954.

Simon, Bennett. "Tragic drama and the family: the killing of children and the killing of story-telling." *Discourse in Psychoanalysis and Literature*. Ed. Shlomith Rimmon-Kenan. London & New York: Methuen, 1987. 152-175.

Singer, Alan. *A Metaphorics of Fiction*. Tallahassee Fla.: Florida State University Press, 1983.

Smyth, John Vignaux. *A Question of Eros Irony in Sterne, Kierkegaard, and Barthes*. Tallahassee: Florida State University Press.

Spycher, Peter. *Friedrich Dürrenmatt. Das erzählerische Werk*. Frauenfeld und Stuttgart: Verlag Huber, 1972.

Staiger, Emil. *Grundbegriffe der Poetik*. 8th ed. Zürich: Atlantis, 1968.

Steinberg, Meir. *Expositional Modes and Temporal Ordering in Fiction*. Baltimore: Johns Hopkins University Press, 1978.

Steiner, George. *Antigones*. New York and Oxford: Oxford University Press, 1984.

Steinhauer, Harry. "Towards a Definition of the Novella." *Seminar*. vol. VI, No. 2 (June 1970): 154-174.

Swales, Martin. *The German Novelle*. Princeton: Princeton University Press, 1977.

Thomson, Philip. *The Grotesque*. London: Methuen & Co. Ltd., 1972.

Todorov, Tsvetan. *Introduction à la littérature fantastique*. Paris: Edition de Seuil, 1970.

Torgovnick, Marianna. *Closure in the Novel*. Princeton: Princeton University Press, 1981.

Trousson, Raymond. *Un Problème de littérature comparée: Les études de thèmes. Essai de méthodologie*. Paris: Les Lettres Modernes, 1965.

Uspenskij, B. A. et al. "Theses on the Semiotic Study of Cultures." *Structure of Texts and Semiotics of Culture*. Ed. Jan Van der Eng and Grygar Moymir. The Hague: Mouton, 1973). 1-28.

Wapnewski, Peter. "Gedichte sind genaue Form." *Die Zeit,* 28 Jan. 1977: 25.

Waugh, Patricia. *Metafiction: The Theory and Practice of Self-Conscious Fiction.* London and New York: Methuen, 1984.

Weber, Albrecht. "Martin Walser: Ein fliehendes Pferd." *Deutsche Novellen von Goethe bis Walser: Interpretationen für den Literaturunterricht.* Vol. 2. Ed. Jakob Lehmann. (Königstein/Ts: Scriptor, 1980. 281-299.

Weissenberger, Klaus. "A Morphological Genre Theory." *Theories of Literary Genre.* Ed. Joseph P. Strelka. University Park and London: The Pennsylvania State University Press, 1978. 229-253.

Weisstein, Ulrich. *Comparative Literature and Literary Theory: Survey and Introduction.* Transl. William Riggan. Bloomington and London: Indiana University Press, 1973.

White, John H. *Mythology in the Modern Novel.* Princeton: Princeton University Press, 1971.

von Wiese, Benno. *Die deutsche Novelle von Goethe bis Kafka.* Vols. I & II. Düsseldorf: A. Bagel, 1962.

------------------------ *Novelle.* 2nd ed. Stuttgart: J. B. Metzler, 1969.

Willems, Gottfried. *Das Konzept der literarischen Gattung.* Tübingen: Niemeyer, 1981.

Winner, Thomas G. "Structural and Semiotic Genre Theory." *Theories of Literary Genre.* Ed. Joseph P. Strelka. University Park and London: The Pennsylvania State University Press, 1978. 254-268.

Wirick, Gregory. Rev. of *Memories* by Andrei Gromyko. *The Montreal Gazette* 12 Aug. 1989: K4.

Wright, Elizabeth. *Psychoanalytic Criticism.* London: Methuen, 1984.

Index